Meddling in the Ballot Box

T0369656

Meddling in the Ballot Box

The Causes and Effects of Partisan Electoral Interventions

DOV H. LEVIN

OXFORD
UNIVERSITY PRESS

OXFORD
UNIVERSITY PRESS

Oxford University Press is a department of the University of Oxford. It furthers
the University's objective of excellence in research, scholarship, and education
by publishing worldwide. Oxford is a registered trade mark of Oxford University
Press in the UK and certain other countries.

Published in the United States of America by Oxford University Press
198 Madison Avenue, New York, NY 10016, United States of America.

Library of Congress Cataloging-in-Publication Data
Names: Levin, Dov H., author.
Title: Meddling in the ballot box : the causes and effects of partisan electoral interventions / Dov H. Levin.
Description: New York, NY : Oxford University Press, [2020] |
Includes bibliographical references and index.
Identifiers: LCCN 2020014309 (print) | LCCN 2020014310 (ebook) |
ISBN 9780197519882 (hardback) | ISBN 9780197519899 (paperback) | ISBN 9780197519929 (online) |
ISBN 9780197519905 (updf) | ISBN 9780197519912 (epub)
Subjects: LCSH: Elections—Corrupt practices.
Classification: LCC JF1083 .L48 2020 (print) | LCC JF1083 (ebook) | DDC 324.9/045—dc23
LC record available at https://lccn.loc.gov/2020014309
LC ebook record available at https://lccn.loc.gov/2020014310

3 5 7 9 8 6 4 2

Paperback printed by LSC Communications, United States of America
Hardback printed by Bridgeport National Bindery, Inc., United States of America

Contents

Figures

Tables

Acknowledgments

When I look back at the intellectual debts, as well as the debts of gratitude, accumulated during the long process of writing this study I become very thankful that such debts aren't monetary in nature. Had that been the case, I would need at least a few additional lifetimes to pay them all back.

My largest intellectual debts are to the three scholars at UCLA who generously lent their talents and time to this manuscript. First and foremost, they are to Arthur Stein. Without Art's highly discerning and perceptive feedback and suggestions on the draft versions of my arguments and various early draft chapters, the quality of the arguments made here in general, and of the manuscript in particular, would have been far poorer. Every time I left a meeting with him over one or another aspect, I came out feeling that I better understood what needed correction, how to correct it, and what I needed to do next—even when his comments called, as they sometimes did, for the heavy revision or even abandonment of much of what we had just discussed.

Barbara Geddes's feedback on the earliest versions of my arguments in her research design course saved me months of aimless wandering down blind methodological alleys. Her subsequent methodological and other feedback also helped to construct this work into a solid empirical house rather than a flimsy sand castle. Likewise, Robert Trager's trenchant comments and very helpful suggestions, both at the early stages of this manuscript and in its more recent near-final draft, were invaluable in improving its quality in all of its aspects and helping it reach its current form. I was truly very fortunate to have all three of these people in my committee.

Other scholars were also kind enough to carefully read and provide very useful feedback and comments on various early parts of this manuscript. Especially notable in this regard were Giacomo Chiozza, Deborah Larson, Benjamin Miller, Etel Solingen, Michael Thies, and Mark Trachtenberg. Special thanks in this regard is due to the late Mark Kleiman, who gave very valuable feedback and helped resolve a last-moment yet critical administrative problem. Likewise, Jeffrey Lewis, Christopher Tausanovich, and the staff at ATS provided important methodological help at multiple important points. These acts of intellectual kindness and charity are greatly appreciated.

While at UCLA I was also fortunate to meet an outstanding group of friends and colleagues who provided crucial early feedback on this project. Especially notable in this regard were Matthew Gottfried, Ron Gurantz, Or Honig, Chad

Nelson, Jeff Paris, and Javier Rodriguez. Thank you all for your perceptive feedback.

Special thanks are due to Richard Hu and Uwe Steinhoff. As this manuscript was nearing completion I greatly benefited from a second round of feedback. At the University of Hong Kong I had an opportunity to conduct a book workshop with four of my colleagues—Wilfred Chow, Courtney Fung, Enze Han, and Kai Quek—who read the manuscript and provided highly valuable feedback throughout. Other academic colleagues elsewhere were also kind enough to give very useful feedback on various parts of the near-final manuscript; these include Steve Chan, Andrew Enterline, Daniel Silverman, and Melissa Willard-Foster. Additional thanks are also due to Hovannes Abramyan. The manuscript is much improved thanks to their feedback.

Many thanks to Dave McBride and Holly Mitchell at Oxford University Press for their skillful guidance during the publishing process. I also thank the two anonymous reviewers of this manuscript. Thanks also to the project manager Anitha Jasmine and the copyeditor Debra Ruel for their professional production and copyediting of this manuscript. The manuscript has greatly benefited from their essential inpute.

In addition to the people mentioned, I am also indebted to a number of organizations and foundations for their generous financial support. A pre-doctoral fellowship from the Institute on Global Conflict and Cooperation helped speed up the completion of my PhD. A postdoctoral fellowship at the Institute for Politics and Strategy (IPS) at Carnegie Mellon University enabled me to start the lengthy process of expanding and revising this manuscript. Likewise, research funding from the Moody/LBJ Library Grant-in-Aid Award, the George C. Marshall/Baruch Fellowship, the General Research Fund (Early Career Scheme) by the Research Grants Council (grant number 27611719), and additional special assistance from IPS gave me much of the funds necessary for the multiple archival research trips that the data collection process for the PEIG dataset and the case studies that this book required.

I was fortunate to have encountered highly professional staff in all three of the political science departments I have been in. Special thanks in this regard go, at UCLA, to Joseph Brown; to faculty and staff at CMU; and at HKU to Sharon To, May Yim, and Daniel Tsang. An especially emphatic thanks for support throughout is to RSO. I also wish to sincerely thank the librarians and archivists in the various archives and libraries I went to for this manuscript (see Bibliography) for their patient assistance, the names of whom are too numerous to list here.

Earlier versions of some limited portions of this manuscript have been published before in "When the Great Power Gets a Vote: The Effects of Great Power Electoral Interventions on Election Results," *International Studies*

Quarterly 60, no. 2 (2016): 189–202, and "Partisan Electoral Interventions by the Great Powers: Introducing the PEIG Dataset," *Conflict Management and Peace Science* 36, no. 1 (2019): 88–106. I would like to deeply thank Daniel Nexon, Caroline Hartzell, and the anonymous reviewers of both pieces for accepting articles on what was, at the time, a virtually unknown topic among most International Relations scholars and many publics.

I must also add a note of thanks to some of key inanimate objects whose hard work, without serious breakdowns, enabled me to complete this study: The two laptops on which much of this manuscript was written, Dell Vostro 1000 s/n 80043-432-043-035 and Acer Aspire E15 s/n NXMS8AA00142919AE23400, and the GE A950 camera s/n A140013989 with which I have taken pictures of most of the archival documents used here. To borrow a phrase from Marie Kondo, they have indeed brought me joy.

Finally, I would like to thank my parents, Florence and Joseph Levin, to whom this book is dedicated. Their encouragement in the course of writing this book, in far, far more ways than can be listed in this short acknowledgment, is deeply appreciated. It is said that one of the most important things in life is to be born to good parents. I couldn't agree more.

1

Introduction

Hiding in Plain Sight

> [George] Washington must go. . . . [A] friend of France must succeed him in that eminent office. . . . I propose . . . to send orders and instructions to our minister plenipotentiary at Philadelphia to use all the means in his power in the United States to bring about . . . Washington's replacement.
> —French Foreign Minister Charles Delacroix, January 16, 1796[1]

In early 2013, a few days before the presidential elections in Kenya, the U.S. Assistant Secretary of State for African affairs, Johnny Carson, publicly warned during a press conference that a victory by Uhuru Kenyatta, then under ICC indictment, would lead to serious "consequences" to Kenyans.[2] A year later Russia was discovered to be covertly funding a major political party in the 2014 Moldovan election.[3] Two years later, in 2016, hackers working on behalf of Russia's intelligence agencies secretly hacked into the computers of the U.S. Democratic National Committee and the email accounts of some senior members of the Hillary Clinton election campaign and stole tens of thousands of emails and other sensitive documents from these sources. Some of these documents were leaked directly through specially created websites. Other messages were covertly supplied to WikiLeaks which then made them public during the run-up to the election.[4] In this same time period the Russian government, via various intermediaries, secretly spent millions of dollars on producing and then disseminating ads and other messages via various social media tools attacking Hillary Clinton and promoting Donald Trump's candidacy.[5]

---

[1] In Bemis 1934:258–259.

[2] Simon Tisdall, "Kenyatta Victory Promises Trouble for Kenya," *The Guardian*, March 8, 2013.

[3] "Moldova: Pro-Russia Party Banned from Elections after OCCRP Exposé," *Organized Crime and Corruption Reporting Project*, November 28, 2014.

[4] "Report on the Investigation into Russian Interference in the 2016 Presidential Elections," Volume 1, March 2019 (hence, the Mueller report).

[5] Indictment, *United States v. Internet Research Agency and others*, February 16, 2018.

Meddling in the Ballot Box. Dov H. Levin, Oxford University Press (2020). © Oxford University Press.
DOI: 10.1093/oso/9780197519882.001.0001.

These three interventions are recent examples of a method of foreign intervention, partisan electoral intervention, in which a foreign power intentionally intervenes in an election in another country to help or hinder one of the candidates or parties, using various costly covert and overt methods. These methods range from, for example, providing funding for their preferred side's campaign, to public threats and/or promises made by an official of the great power prior to the elections, to "dirty tricks," to various pre-election "punishments" or concessions by the intervener to the target, and to the creation of campaigning materials or the provision of campaigning expertise to the preferred side.[6] Although the latter example, the Russian intervention in the 2016 U.S. elections, has frequently been described in the public discourse utilizing various synonyms to the word "unprecedented," that is far from being the case.

Pre-modern elections, which featured small electorates of various elites, already attracted the attention of major powers from time to time. For example, the elaborate method by which popes have been chosen since the 13th century, the locking up of cardinals in a single building with limited access to the outside world (i.e., the Papal Conclave), was instituted by Pope Gregory X in part in order to prevent the foreign powers of the day from continuing to interfere in papal elections (Rollo-Koster 2015:245–246). This reform, and further attempts over the following centuries to protect the secrecy of the election proceedings from such meddling, failed to prevent frequent and multiple interventions by the European powers of the day. In one of the most consequential cases of such meddling, the intervention by Charles V, the Holy Roman emperor, in his favor led to the election of Cardinal Giulio de' Medici (Clement VII) to the papal throne in 1523. Clement VII's policies led the Protestant Reformation to become an irreversible development and to the sacking of Rome for the first time in the second millennium (Baumgartner 2003:98–102).[7]

Likewise, the handful of European monarchies in which the king was chosen by an assembly of the local nobility were common targets of foreign machinations. In those elected monarchies the first evidence of the sovereign's upcoming timely or untimely demise frequently unleashed preparatory covert campaign visits by prospective royal contenders in hospitable foreign courts and elaborate preparations for the royal elections within the chancelleries of the interested foreign powers. For example, Polish royal elections in the 17th and 18th centuries became notorious throughout Europe for repeatedly turning into the loci of open meddling by many of the continental great powers, with Russia, Austria, and France being the most common offenders. In one such case, the

---

[6] For a more detailed definition see Chapter 2.

[7] Indeed, by the early modern era some major powers earned a de facto right to veto some papal candidates not to their liking (Hunt 2016:224).

June 1697 royal elections, the Russian czar Peter the Great sent a public note to the Polish nobility on the eve of the elections threatening a collapse of an Anti-Turkish alliance and a Russian declaration of war on Poland if the "wrong" candidate, the Prince de Conti, were selected. Then, in a secret nighttime meeting with their preferred candidate, Augustus of Saxony, as well as representatives of Austria and Prussia among others, they agreed to pool their financial resources in order to bribe most of the Polish noble electorate which had gathered in Wola to select the new monarch. These measures helped lead to the victory of Augustus in this election and his accession to the Polish throne. Some historians see the success of this Russian intervention as the beginning of the end of Polish independence (Lewitter 1956).[8]

When modern executive elections featuring mass electorates began to occur in the late 18th century, they frequently attracted the attention of almost every major power. France, for example, openly intervened in the 1796 U.S. elections in order to prevent the reelection of George Washington and then (after Washington decided to retire on his own volition), the election of John Adams. For example, the French government published a decree in late October 1796 permitting the French navy to board and search any American merchant ship they detected on the high seas and confiscate the goods on it without compensation—a major restriction on U.S. trade with Europe (DeConde 1958). In 1797, the British government secretly intervened in a French general election (the Election of year V) through covert funding to a conservative coalition, in an (eventually unsuccessful) attempt to bring an early end to the French Revolution and eventually restore the Bourbons to power. It nevertheless received, in the immediate aftermath of this intervention, thank-you notes from many of the successful deputies for the "liberal supplies" they received from the British government (Fryer 1965:196).

Imperial Germany, for example, intervened in the 1877 French elections due to its worries, in Bismarck's words, that "a clerical France is altogether incapable of maintaining durable peaceful relations with Germany" as well as a secret request for electoral assistance by the then-leader of the Republicans, Gambetta. Bismarck accordingly created a full-fledged military crisis with France in the run-up to these elections, complete with significant German troop increases on the German-French border areas and an embargo on the export of a key war materiel (horses)—a 19th-century equivalent of a DEFCON 2 alert (Stone 2012; Mitchell 1979:chap. 6). The victory of the republican side in this election, despite

---

[8] These measures led to a split in the electorate in favor of Augustus (what was called in this era a double election), after an earlier voting round in which Conti, with the assistance of French bribes in his favor, almost won, enabling Augustus, closer to the scene of the election, to get himself crowned as King (Lewitter 1956).

serious electoral shenanigans by the conservative president Patrice MacMahon, led to the collapse of the Monarchists strength and the consolidation of the Third French republic. Like their Czarist predecessors, the Soviet Union covertly intervened in the 1923 British elections for Labor, funding its election campaign to the tune of £10,000 (US$749,000 in 2016 dollars) (Carley 2014:85). Labor's victory in this election enabled it, for the first time in its political history, to win executive power and name a new Prime Minister.[9]

During the Cold War, electoral interventions became a common feature of great-power politics. Indeed, according to a new dataset constructed by the author (see Chapter 5), the U.S. and the USSR/Russia intervened in this manner 117 times between 1946 and 2000—that is in about *one of every nine* competitive national-level executive elections during this period.

The American founding fathers were quite cognizant of recent European history and of the potential opportunity that competitive elections created for foreign meddling. Accordingly, preventing partisan electoral interventions in the elections of the fledging American republic was an important concern of the 1787 Constitutional Convention. For example, from the little that we know about the creation of the Electoral College, one key reason for its establishment as a method for selecting presidents was in order to prevent foreign meddling in American presidential elections. As Alexander Hamilton described in his justification of the Electoral College in Federalist 68, "[the] most deadly adversaries of republican government . . . [come] chiefly from the desire in foreign powers to gain an improper ascendance in our councils . . . by raising a creature of their own to the chief magistracy of the Union. But the convention have guarded against all danger of this sort, with the most provident and judicious attention."

This attempt to meddle-proof the American Republic failed. Prior to 2016 there were at least five electoral interventions in American presidential elections using a variety of covert and overt methods by Nazi Germany, Revolutionary France, Great Britain, and the Soviet Union, some using quite similar methods. For example, one of the main methods used by Nazi Germany in their attempt to prevent Franklin Delano Roosevelt's election to a third term in the 1940 U.S. elections was the covert leak (via a bribed U.S. newspaper) of a captured Polish government document four days before the election that supposedly showed Roosevelt to be a "hypocrite" and a "warmonger" (Farago 1972).

Likewise, if it had been up to some unscrupulous American politicians this number would have been even higher. For example, senior members of the Federalist Party seem to have secretly tried to persuade the British government

---

[9] Ironically, the exposé of a supposed Soviet electoral intervention a few days before the 1924 British elections, the (in)famous Zinoviev letter, was almost certainly a forgery, probably created by Russian exiles (Andrew 2009:148–152).

to intervene in their favor in some manner in the run-up to the 1812 election. As the British Ambassador to the U.S. described it, the Federalists were "despairing of overthrowing the [Madison] Administration in any other way." The British government, however, spurned this offer, choosing instead to try to offer the Madison Administration a concession on the issues in dispute between the two countries.[10]

1.1 The Key Questions and My Arguments

As the preceding examples illustrate, when we refer to partisan electoral interventions we are discussing a common form of intervention in the modern world, a tool of great power politics used by both democratic and non-democratic great powers in various kinds of targets. It involves a violation of sovereignty, a major building block of the modern international system, in a pivotal domestic institution—the national-level elections and the process by which the executive is peacefully replaced or retained. Through its possible effects on the target's leadership, and in such overt interventions the target's public, electoral interventions can have significant intentional and unintentional effects on the target's welfare on various important dimensions. Indeed, recent research has found such interventions in certain circumstances to increase the amounts of domestic terrorism in the target as well as the chances of democratic breakdown (Levin 2019b, 2020) and affect the attitudes or preferred policies toward the intervener in the target (Shulman and Bloom 2012; Corstange and Marinov 2012; Bush and Prather 2017b; Tomz and Weeks 2020). In a world in which competitive elections are a significant feature of domestic politics in more than half of all states (Freedom House 2019), from full democracies to "competitive authoritarian" to partially democratic regimes, this form of intervention can nowadays be used in and potentially affect a very wide swath of states. However, until very recently, scant systemic research has been conducted about this phenomenon and we still know relatively little about its causes and effects.

This study is the first book-length study of partisan electoral interventions as a discrete, stand-alone phenomenon. By examining electoral interventions in this manner, I am able to construct and test a new, better explanation for their occurrence than existing research which discusses such interventions—if at all—together with other unrelated forms of meddling to which far more attention

---

[10] See, for example, Foster, Letter to Foreign Office, November 29, 1811 UK National Archives. I thank Robert Trager for directing me to this example. The spurned Federalists felt that their political position was so weak that they eventually decided not to even field a presidential candidate of their own in 1812, choosing instead to support a malcontent member of the Democratic-Republican Party named Dewitt Clinton.

is given. This increases our ability to predict when and where such meddling will occur. I am also able, as a result, to provide a first-of-its-kind theory and analysis of a key aspect of electoral interventions—what their effects usually are on the target's election results. I find such interference to have a significant impact in the desired direction in most situations, frequently in a magnitude sufficient to determine the identity of the winner. I use a multi-method framework in order to answer these two questions, including case studies drawn from in-depth archival research, the statistical analysis of a new, original dataset of electoral interventions, and the analysis of election surveys from specific cases of intervention.

As for the causes of partisan electoral interventions, I argue that they occur when two concurrent conditions exist. The first condition is that the great power perceives its interests as being greatly endangered by a significant candidate or party within the target. That candidate or party has inflexible preferences on important issues that diverge from that of the great power. These inflexible preferences are due to that candidate or party being either greatly constrained by its political base on these issues and/or ideologically committed to particular positions. That, in turn, makes many of the conventional policy responses (various forms of carrots and sticks aimed at resolving disagreements) appear potentially ineffective or too costly to the great power.

The second, more important condition is that another significant domestic actor within that country wants or is willing to be aided by the great power in this risky manner (i.e., "collude" with it in this intervention). Partisan electoral interventions, unlike other types of interventions, are usually "inside jobs." This is due to the fact that an electoral intervention is essentially an attempt to strengthen (or create) a domestic election campaign for a particular party and/ or candidate in the target. Accordingly, the would-be intervener needs the information (or "local knowledge") local actors have (and use in order to campaign) about the electorate's preferences and the best ways to intervene in its favor.

When one (or both) of these conditions is missing, partisan electoral interventions will rarely if ever occur. If the first condition is missing, the great power is expected to prefer not to intervene, utilizing instead its wide range of resources in order to secure its interests through low-cost, conventional diplomacy. When the second condition is lacking, that is, when no significant presidential candidate/major party within that country is willing to be aided in this manner, the great power will not intervene in an election *even when* the first condition is present. Without a domestic actor's significant cooperation and the provision of its "local knowledge," the great power's chances of success in such an undertaking become so low that it usually prefers to choose other, more costly but more favorable, options.

Of course, partisan electoral interventions are not the only type of foreign policy activity or type of intervention in which "invitations to intervene" can play a role in the decision-making process. Even a cursory look, for example, into Thucydides' famous history of the Peloponnesian War would note many cases in which the help by a domestic faction, or the expectation of receiving such help, played an important role in Athens' or Sparta's decision to attempt to conquer particular city-states during that war (see Thucydides [1972]:318, 368–369, 388). Likewise, some other kinds of American interventions during the Cold War, from secret coups to full-scale military invasions, seem to have also been sometimes at the "invitation" of significant domestic actors within the target (Karabell 1999:225, 227–228; Grow 2008:193–194).

The big difference, however, between electoral interventions and other kinds of military operations and/or interventions is the centrality of finding such cooperative allies to its operational feasibility and therefore to the decision-making process of the operation. Successful interstate wars, for example, have frequently been prosecuted both in the ancient and in the modern era without the victor getting any cooperation whatsoever from a domestic actor within the rival state. As will be later described in detail, this is rarely if ever the case in electoral interventions, making the role of finding "domestic help" within the target absolutely essential for such an intervention to be worthwhile for the intervener.

As for the second question, the effects of electoral interventions on the intervened election results, I present four main hypotheses. The first three are derived from the model of causes noted earlier. First, I argue that such interventions usually increase the electoral chances of the aided candidate. The intervener and the aided side avoid doing (or agreeing to) electoral interventions when the chances of the assisted side are perceived as quite good or quite bad. In the former case the would-be assisted side prefers to avoid the various possible costs to it from agreeing to such an intervention, such as, for example, harming its electoral position in the longer term by alienating voters who, for a variety of reasons, may resent or fear the influence of the foreign power. In the latter case the great power will prefer not to waste its resources on a "lost cause." Therefore, electoral interventions will usually occur in marginal elections where the resources provided by the intervener are more likely to make a difference.

Second, I claim that *overt* electoral interventions are *more* effective than covert interventions. The great power will not intervene overtly unless informed by the aided side that a domestic backlash will not occur prior to the elections. When backlash is unlikely, overt interventions are expected to be more effective because the great power can outbid the local politicians for the target public's support, and/or the amount of resources that can be provided through such an intervention is larger.

Third, I claim that electoral interventions are much less likely to effectively help an aided party/candidate competing in a founding election[11] than in a non-founding/later election and will, in actuality, oftentimes harm it. In such situations the aided side's inexperience with elections leads its "local knowledge" to be of very low quality—which, in turn, will cause requests for useless or even harmful forms of assistance from the great power. I also examine the effects of such interventions when a challenger is aided versus when an incumbent is helped. Predictions derived from two different literatures have opposing expectations in this regard—one, from the literature on the "incumbency advantage" in comparative politics, would expect such interventions to be of more benefit to the challenger while a prediction derived from the literature of intelligence studies, which expects cooperation to be easier with an incumbent government, would predict the opposite.

Some readers may wonder as to the reason for the focus of this study only on electoral interventions done by a great power. Partisan electoral interventions can indeed be done and have been done by states which don't belong to this category. Iran, for example, probably intervened in the 2010 Iraqi elections.[12] Libya under Muammar Kaddafi may have intervened, among other cases, in the 2009 French elections with covert funding to Nicolas Sarkozy's campaign.[13] Likewise, Hugo Chavez, the former leader of Venezuela, intervened in some elections conducted in nearby Latin American countries such as in Peru (2006) and Nicaragua (2006, 2011) (Vanderhill 2013:105–106, 118–120). Nevertheless, the present study will not discuss electoral interventions by non-great powers.[14] This is for three methodological and theoretical reasons.

First, due to the unusual nature of great powers, the dynamics that lead a great power to intervene in other countries' elections may differ from those operating in non-great powers. Great powers, for example, tend to usually have a surplus of resources and a variety of available policy tools to deal with a would-be target besides meddling in its elections. Likewise, one of the basic components of being a great power is the limited ability of other countries to "punish" it for its various activities (Bull 1984:1). The decision-making calculus leading (or not leading) to

---

[11] The first competitive election ever to occur in a particular country, or following a significant authoritarian interregnum. See Chapter 2 for further details.

[12] David Ignatius, "Tehran's Vote-Buying in Iraq," *Washington Post*, February 25, 2010.

[13] Peter Allen, "French Television Broadcast Interview in which Gaddafi Says He Funded Former President Sarkozy's Election Campaign," *Daily Mail*, January 29, 2014. This case is currently under a criminal investigation by the French government.

[14] Likewise, interventions by non-state actors (transnational terrorist groups, NGOs, IOs, global media conglomerates, etc.) are excluded unless they are directly controlled by an intervening great power (via funding, etc.) or clear evidence exists that their intervention was done at the request of, or due to pressure from, such an intervening state.

an electoral intervention by smaller powers, who do not usually enjoy either benefit, may as a result be quite different.

Furthermore, minor powers are far more open to coercion than great powers are—so if a minor power intervention in question is in, say, a stronger state, its activities may be the result of outright coercion by a politician in the major power rather than any desire on the side of the minor power to meddle in the elections of that country.[15] Separating the bona fide minor power interventions from what are effectively acts of compliance by the minor power with a successful attempt of compellence by a stronger state's leadership creates additional significant empirical and theoretical challenges for studying such activities when done by minor powers.[16]

Second, while constructing PEIG,[17] I discovered that the majority of electoral interventions are covert in nature. In order to be reasonably certain that all interventions of these countries have indeed been located, the standard technique for gathering cross-national event data for the post–World War II era—various newspaper indexes and databases—would not suffice. Access to and research in dozens of state archives around the world would be required as well—a task not possible at present due to the inaccessibility of many of these archives to foreign scholars as well as obvious time, language, and funding limits.

Third, the available data indicates that a vast majority of partisan electoral interventions, like most other forms of intervention (Bull 1984:1–2), are indeed being done by the great powers.[18] Accordingly, the analysis in the subsequent chapters is applicable to most electoral interventions done overall around the world. Other aspects of the methodology, definitions, and theoretical assumptions will receive more elaboration in Chapter 2.

1.2 Existing Research on Electoral Interventions

In spite of the ubiquity and possible importance of electoral interventions, they receive very little attention from political scientists. This stands in contrast to extensive investigation over the past three decades within political science into

[15] The recent Ukrainegate scandal, which led to the 2019–2020 impeachment trial of President Trump, is one example of this dynamic.
[16] In other words, a separate theoretical framework is needed for when such coercion is utilized by politicians in the stronger power toward weaker ones for their own domestic electoral purposes, and other, similar situations.
[17] Acronym for Partisan Electoral Interventions by the Great powers.
[18] For example, if the number of public accusations that a foreign power conducted a partisan electoral intervention in a particular election are in any way correlated with actual interventions, minor powers are far less likely than world powers to carry them out. In their sample, Bubeck and Marinov have similar findings (Bubeck and Marinov 2019:119–120).

the causes and effects of other types of interventions. Some scholars, for example, have focused on covert interventions (mostly covert coups) (Forsyth 1992; Downes and Lilley 2010; Berger et al. 2013; Poznansky 2015; Carson 2018). Others have focused on overt military interventions either in general (Levite, Jentleson, and Berman 1992; Kegley and Hermann 1995; Vertzberger 1998; Finnemore 2003; Koch and Sullivan 2010; Saunders 2012; Kreps 2011) or for certain goals or in certain violent phenomena. For example, some of these scholars have focused on military interventions for the purpose of regime change in general or democratization in particular (i.e., foreign-imposed regime changes, or FIRCs) (Meernik 1996; Peceney 1999; Owen 2003; Enterline and Grieg 2005; Pickering and Pencey 2006; B. Bueno de Mesquita and Downs 2006; Peic and Reiter 2011; Downes and Monten 2013; Lutmar 2015; Willard-Foster 2019). Others have focused on humanitarian interventions and peacekeeping (Page-Fortna 2008; Seybolt 2008; Kuperman 2008; Weiss 2012; Kydd and Straus 2013; Choi 2013; Hultman, Kathman, and Shannon 2013), while a third group has focused on interventions in civil wars (Balch-Lindsay and Enterline 2000; Regan 2002; Findley and Teo 2006; Gent 2008; Kathman 2011; Salehyan, Gleditsch, and Cunningham 2011; Aydin 2012; San-Akca 2016). Another group of international relations (IR) scholars has focused on the use of sanctions for various interventionist goals (Marinov 2005; Allen 2008; Von Soest and Wahman 2015).

Nevertheless, prior to 2016 only two articles had been published on partisan electoral interventions in IR (Shulman and Bloom 2012; Corstange and Marinov 2012), neither of which had as its main focus the causes of such interventions. Aside from these two pioneering exceptions, when electoral interventions were mentioned, if at all, in the academic IR literature (see, e.g., Drezner 1999:2–3; Gaubatz 1999:112–113; Downes and Lilley 2010:285–286), it was usually as a short prelude to the discussion of other phenomena.

Similarly, in comparative politics a large and thriving literature has developed over the past few decades on foreign election assistance, democratization, and democracy promotion (Geddes 1999; Finkel, Pérez-Liñán, and Seligson 2007; Scott and Steele 2007; Kelley 2009; Hyde 2011; Simpser and Donno 2012; Ichino and Schundeln 2012; Bush 2015; Bush and Prather 2017a; Asunka et al. 2019). Parts of this literature has, at times, briefly noted partisan electoral interventions, especially those conducted in the last few decades (see, e.g., Lowenthal 1991; Reichhardt 2002; Levitsky and Way 2010; Bunce and Wolchik 2011; Donno 2013). However, even when partisan interventions are noted in this literature, they are usually classified and aggregated with other acts under the general rubric of "external influences on democratization" or "democracy promotion abroad." As a result of this classification, scholars in this literature do little to separate between partisan interventions and neutral interventions, completely non-electoral external influences, or, in some cases, even between actions of state and non-state actors. Lumping all such activities (and actors) together leads this literature to overlook key differences between these activities and electoral interventions in their main motivations, effects, and costs—and has accordingly inadvertently discouraged it from an in-depth analysis of this intervention method or of its causes.

The handful of IR scholars who have begun, very recently, to discuss the causes of electoral interventions do so in theoretical frameworks where such interventions are lumped together with other, unrelated phenomena. That leads, however, to explanations which overlook key qualitative differences between electoral interventions and other kinds of interventions, differences that are critical to understanding when and why electoral interventions occur.

One aggregation of this kind (O'Rourke 2018) lumps partisan electoral interventions with violent covert regime change operations (or covert FIRCs) in order to explain U.S. covert regime change operations during the Cold War. O'Rourke argues that there are three key factors that determine whether or not the United States carried out a covert FIRC during this period, the first two determining whether such an operation is done and the third affecting whether it is done covertly or overtly.[19] The first factor is whether the U.S. government has incompatible policy preferences between itself and the government in question (O'Rourke 2018:45–46). The second factor is whether it has a plausible political alternative to the foreign government in question. According to O'Rourke, the U.S. government will choose to conduct such a FIRC only when the alternative in question has two major characteristics: First, the political alternative is relatively strong compared to the government or rival in question. If it is not, the FIRC is likely to fail. Second, that actor fully shares the U.S. government's policy preferences. That will guarantee that its FIRC will lead it to gain "better" behavior out of the country in question if the FIRC succeeds. If such an actor does not exist, the U.S. can create such an actor from scratch (O'Rourke 2018:46–47).

The third factor is the material and especially the reputational cost for the U.S. According to O'Rourke, covert FIRCs are chosen instead of overt FIRCs in order to reduce the material costs involved in such operations and to avoid creating or projecting a belligerent image as overt regime change activities inevitably do. The U.S. will choose an overt FIRC only in the very rare circumstance in which the

---

[19] O'Rourke also creates a threefold typology of goals that the U.S. pursues through such covert FIRCs during the Cold War: offensive, preventive, and hegemonic. Interestingly, and in contrast to the patterns among the violent FIRC methods (43.4% offensive, 29.6% preventive, 27.8% hegemonic), none of the sixteen electoral intervention cases she locates are coded as offensive; 68.5% are coded as preventive and the remainder (31.5%) are coded as hegemonic (a statistically significant difference)—another major difference between electoral interventions and other types of FIRCs even according to her own typology.

material and reputational costs are low and/or a covert FIRC has little to no plausible chance of success (O'Rourke 2018:60–61).

However, the great power—although it prefers, of course, as strong and as ideologically compatible a partner as it can possibly find—faces far more limitations in regard to potential partners in electoral interventions than it usually has in a covert FIRC. The pool of existing parties able to win executive power through the ballot box in most democratic countries is usually far smaller than the number of, for example, senior military officers or dissident/exile groups with some plausible chance of conducting a successful coup d'état in most authoritarian countries. The existing parties' policy positions usually reflect a significant share of the local political spectrum, and their preexisting "brand names" and voter attachments leave little space for out-of-the-blue political newcomers.[20] While completely new parties composed only of political neophytes do occasionally arise and win a few seats, they usually need a few election cycles until they develop the necessary political experience and voter following to win executive power.[21] A great power interested in the outcome of an upcoming election, and with far less knowledge of local politics in the would-be target than domestic political entrepreneurs, will usually not have either the time or the ability to create additional options ex nihilo for such an intervention. Likewise, as noted, the local actors will frequently have strong incentives not to accept such aid when it might harm their own political interests. These incentives are far more common when the local actor knows that she needs to win strong active support from large numbers of present and future voters from all across the target country— not just the obedience of the common soldiers under her command or the passive acquiescence of the target country's civilian population.

As a result of this far more limited menu of would-be clients in electoral interventions the would-be interveners in electoral interventions, unlike the case in covert FIRCs, will usually be forced to aid clients with significant weaknesses vis-à-vis the undesired side or in general. Likewise, they will frequently have no choice but to accept a client with significant policy incompatibilities so long as it is at least somewhat better than the undesirable government or actor.

---

[20] Even most founding elections are dominated in practice by the main opposition/pro-independence groups and/or the government party with such established brand names and followings derived from the pre-independence era or from the authoritarian past/previous democratic period.

[21] It should be noted that even the rare recent partial exception to this regard, Donald Trump, was only able to become president thanks to his success in capturing one of the two main political parties and "brand names" in American politics during the U.S.'s presidential primaries. In most other countries, the leadership of the main political parties is determined through a vote of only the partys' parliamentary representatives and senior party officials, or the would-be candidates in the party primaries need to get through some kind of formal process of vetting or approval by the former before they are permitted to run.

Secondly, the factors that determine whether a covert or an overt electoral intervention are chosen seem to be quite different from those regarding covert and overt FIRCs. As noted, O'Rourke expects overt FIRCs to be quite rare compared to their covert brethren due to the material and reputational costs. That prediction is indeed borne out in O'Rourke's dataset on American covert operations in regard to non-electoral FIRCs. She finds six overt American FIRCs during the Cold War era—only 7.4% of all FIRCs when the handful of covert electoral interventions that she locates are included, and only 9.2% when they are excluded (see data in O'Rourke 2018:77).

However, O'Rourke doesn't code or count any overt electoral interventions as overt FIRCs. As can be seen in Chapter 5, when such data is collected and coded in my dataset of partisan electoral interventions (PEIG) I find forty-two American and Soviet/Russian overt interventions—or 35.9% of all electoral interventions by both great powers.[22] In other words, overt electoral interventions are not uncommon phenomena—and are more than three times as common compared to covert electoral interventions than overt FIRCs are compared to covert FIRCs; this is a statistically significant difference.[23] Such a significant difference, not predicted by a theoretical framework which aggregates both kinds of interventions, indicates that other factors, such as the preferences of the assisted side, may have far greater importance when it comes to the choice between covert and overt electoral interventions.[24]

A second aggregation of this kind (Bubeck and Marinov 2019) develops a theoretical framework that lumps partisan electoral interventions together with equally ill-fitting neutral interventions.[25] They construct new optimization and formal models which attempt to explain when foreign powers decide to try to affect any characteristic of an upcoming election, either its horserace or its procedural aspects. According to Bubeck and Marinov, a partisan electoral intervention is chosen by the foreign power prior to a relevant election in a would-be target within a policy menu that includes three major options: a partisan

---

[22] Twenty-seven of these overt electoral interventions are by the U.S.

[23] Chi-square test significance at $p < 0.001$, test statistic 15.3.

[24] See also a recent review of O'Rourke's book (Poznansky 2019) for a similar point. The range of potential direct costs from an overt electoral intervention is also narrower than for most overt FIRCs. For example, unlike the case of overt FIRCs, overt electoral interventions do not seem to usually create the key "pottery barn" effect or potential cost (O'Rourke 2018:51). In other words, if a successful overt electoral intervention destabilizes the target in some manner, the intervener is not usually seen as being morally responsible for "fixing" it. Furthermore, electoral interventions, due to the object of the intervention, have a "natural" breakpoint (i.e., election day) that makes the cutoff of any new/further assistance, regardless of whether the intervention was covert or overt, relatively easy to do.

[25] While in the narrow technical-mathematical sense these two options can be potentially delinked, the theoretical framework presented in their writings meshes them closely together, as described here.

electoral intervention, a neutral or process intervention designed to affect the election's overall integrity and fairness, and non-intervention.[26] Both process and partisan interventions are seen by Bubeck and Marinov as able to frequently affect who wins an upcoming election—hence decision-makers in the would-be intervener are believed to perceive either kind of intervention (or some kind of mixture of both) as a feasible alternative option for affecting the results of an upcoming election (Bubeck and Marinov 2019:52–54). When it comes to partisan interventions, the more the target country in question is strategically important to the would-be intervener and the more polarized the main candidates in question are on policy issues of importance to it (and vice versa), the more likely are partisan electoral interventions to be chosen over neutral interventions or "doing nothing" (Bubeck and Marinov 2019:55).[27]

The nature of the would-be intervener can also sometimes matter in this regard. Due to the fact that process interventions are expected to usually make partisan interventions more effective, process interventions encourage liberal powers with a preference for democracy (such as the U.S.), and, accordingly, an overall higher tendency for conducting such interventions, to also conduct more partisan interventions (Bubeck and Marinov 2019:57–58).[28]

However, there is little evidence that neutral and partisan electoral interventions are usually perceived by decision-makers as two possible policy alternatives for getting or keeping the "right" side into power. Accordingly, a theoretical framework that analyzes these two different types of interventions together will suffer from serious flaws in explaining one or both of them. For example, in-depth research into specific cases where the U.S. and other democratic countries pressured incumbents in both the pre- and post-Cold War era to hold competitive (or more competitive) elections has found little to no evidence of any partisan (i.e., anti-incumbent) motives being involved (Brown 2001; Brown 2005; Kim and Biak 2011:chap. 2). Likewise, most research on election

[26] When polarization is very high, and a candidate with the "wrong views" is seen as quite likely to win an election, a fourth option—conducting a coup d'état before the elections (or in anticipation of one)—becomes, according to this argument, a worthwhile option for a foreign power as well (Bubeck and Marinov 2019:195–196).

[27] Bubeck and Marinov also discuss situations where two different powers support two different sides in a particular election, what they call "election wars" (2019:58–65). However, while the entry of a second power affects whether and how much power spends on process interventions, such an entry (or a possible entry) does not seem to have an effect on whether either side enters the fray/does a partisan intervention besides its overall magnitude. Likewise, as will be seen in Chapter 5, those situations (which I call double interventions) tend to be quite rare in practice.

[28] When the process intervention (i.e., improving the quality of elections in the target) inadvertently harms the preferred side, the liberal power as "compensation" is expected to do an electoral intervention in its favor (O'Rourke 2018:56–57).

observation notes the usually neutral goals of the providers of election observation (see, e.g., Hyde 2011).[29]

There is also a major difference in the level of politics involved within the intervener, which makes decision-makers quite unlikely to perceive these two different types of interventions as policy alternatives for achieving the same goal. Neutral interventions, especially in the post–Cold War era, are usually "low politics," decided at relatively low levels of the U.S. government or even done nearly automatically in certain situations.[30] In contrast, the evidence available from cases of such interventions indicates that partisan electoral interventions are "high politics," with decisions of whether to conduct them or not being made at senior U.S. government decision-making levels (secretary of state, president, major decision-making forums such as the 303 Committee,[31] etc.). Some examples of the levels of decision-making in which partisan electoral interventions are determined will be seen in subsequent chapters. While in a handful of cases (such as in the Philippines in 1953 or Slovakia in 1998) the two intervention methods were indeed used together, the neutral part was and is usually seen as a secondary, adjunct component to a far larger and more significant partisan intervention. Not surprisingly, some of Bubeck and Marinov's earlier predictions about the effects of interactions between partisan and neutral interventions didn't pan out.[32]

Secondly, Bubeck and Marinov assume that, both in neutral and in partisan interventions, the acceptance of such electoral assistance by the aided actor is assured or near-automatic. In Bubeck and Marinov's main models the target is a non-strategic actor playing no active role in the decision by the foreign power whether to intervene or not. When, in a secondary separate formal model,

[29] Likewise, the exact ability, if any, of many democracy promotion methods to promote democracy (and presumably benefit the opposition) in practice is still hotly debated within the academic literature on this topic (Knack 2004; Kelley 2008:222–223, 249; Finkel, Perez-Linan, and Seligson 2007; Scott and Steele 2007; Hyde 2011:chap. 4; Bush 2015). See also the examination of the effects of one key neutral method (election observation) in Chapter 6.

[30] For example, some scholars on this topic describe the acceptance or invitation of election observers to observe an election in the last two decades as an outright norm (Hyde 2011).

[31] This was the high-level body (sometimes named instead the 5412/2 Special Group or the 40 Committee) in charge of approving significant covert activities by the U.S. government between the 1950s and the mid-1970s. This committee included senior representatives from the State Department, the Defense Department, the CIA, and the White House—usually the current undersecretary of state, the deputy secretary of defense, the director of the CIA, and the national security advisor. Under Nixon and Ford the current attorney general or the chairmen of the joint chiefs of staff were included as well. Memo, "Membership on the 40 Committee and Predecessor Organizations" 1975, NSC Presidential Records, Intelligence Files/Box 1/DDEL.

[32] For example, in an earlier paper, Bubeck and Marinov, using the same main model as in their 2019 book, expected that the interaction between neutral and partisan forms of intervention would lead the U.S. (as a liberal power) to conduct significantly more partisan interventions after the end of the Cold War (2017:543). In their book and sample, however, they find a small decline (2019:114–115)—indicating that the relationship between these two forms of intervention may be different from what their own model expects.

Bubeck and Marinov do permit the would-be assisted actor independent action in response to a potential partisan intervention, it is only expected to do acts which would further encourage such foreign assistance (Bubeck and Marinov 2019:203–205).

While that may well be the case in regard to some of the less controversial neutral intervention methods (such as election observation), this is unlikely to be the case when it comes to the partisan ones. Partisan foreign assistance, in whichever format it is provided, can also impose various significant costs in both the short and medium term on the would-be assisted actor. That, in turn, will lead the domestic actor, in many cases, to reject such assistance offers in their entirety, preventing a partisan intervention from occurring. As a result, the desires and preferences of the likely assisted sides play a far larger role in determining whether a partisan intervention occurs or not than Bubeck and Marinov acknowledge.

1.2.1   Research on the Effects of Electoral Interventions

As noted in the previous section of this chapter, scant scholarly attention has been paid to the effects of partisan electoral interventions in political science. Some scholars over the last few years, including the author, have begun to examine the effects of partisan electoral interventions on the welfare of the target or on the target public's preferred policies toward the intervener (Corstange and Marinov 2012; Bush and Prather 2017b; Levin 2018b, 2019b; Tomz and Weeks 2020).

However, until very recently, any scholarly interest shown in the effects of electoral interventions on the target's elections has primarily come from qualitative scholars from two very different subfields. The first are diplomatic historians who note such interventions as part of a larger study on a particular era or on interstate relations. The second are scholars in intelligence studies who discuss such interventions as part of a broader qualitative analysis of the effectiveness of various activities conducted by the CIA and other intelligence agencies. Among these scholars, significant controversy exists as to the electoral effects, if any, of such interventions. For example, quite a few historians studying particular cases involving electoral interventions either largely dismiss their effects on the results of the relevant elections or even view them as counterproductive (DeConde 1958:chaps. 13–14; Barnes 1982:663–664; Miller 1983:52–53; Gustafson 2007:49, 73–74).[33]

---

[33]   For a similar qualitative estimate of the effects of Russian electoral interventions since the end of the Cold War see Way and Casey 2018.

In contrast, other scholars, usually from intelligence studies, see electoral interventions as being quite effective and decisive, in electoral outcomes (Daugherty 2004:4–7; Haslam 2005:13–15; Prados 2006:627).[34] Interestingly enough, many of the same scholars who claim that electoral interventions are effective are also, at the same time, very harsh critics of the utility of various other types of interventions (such as covert coups or paramilitary activities).

The handful of quantitative exceptions, surveys, and survey experiments which have tried to estimate the effects on such interventions on voters, have focused thus far on the effects these interventions had on their views of the intervener (Corstange and Marinov 2012; Shulman and Bloom 2012). They do not attempt to ascertain what was the relationship between this public view of the electoral intervention and their voting choices at the time. Each of these studies also focused on one particular case (Ukraine 2004, Lebanon 2009)—with their representativeness of it to such interventions in other times and places remaining unclear.

In one of the studies discussed in the previous section (Bubeck and Marinov 2019:52, 160–163), an argument about the effects of electoral interventions on election results is derived from their model on their causes. They argue in their model that given the incumbency advantage enjoyed by incumbents even in fully democratic countries, an electoral intervention will usually be more effective when it is designed to assist incumbents rather than challengers. They then provide support for this claim with a difference-in-means analysis of a sample of electoral interventions,[35] finding that when the U.S. intervenes for an incumbent, and it is the only intervener, that incumbent is likely to gain votes, but when it supported challengers they usually did not electorally benefit. However, the method of analysis used here—a dichotomous measure recording whether the assisted side saw an increase of any magnitude in its overall vote—is quite crude, being unable to assess whether this increase was of any substantive significance Likewise, a difference-in-means test cannot, of course, account for other factors that can potentially affect the assisted side's vote share.

1.3 Plan of This Book

The remainder of this study develops and further examines the two key questions about partisan electoral interventions noted here. In Chapter 2, I lay out in detail

---

[34] As one of these scholars noted in a concluding chapter in which most covert activities of various types are dismissed as unnecessary and costly failures to boot, "The CIA Political Actions [electoral interventions] were successful within their immediate parameters" (Prados 2006:627).

[35] See Appendix H for a discussion of Bubeck and Marinov's dataset—a sample of neutral and partisan interventions in only 10% of all elections.

my assumptions and theoretical arguments on the causes and effects of partisan electoral interventions. I then conclude by describing the qualitative and quantitative methods that are used to investigate these questions and provide a more detailed definition of the partisan electoral interventions used in this study.

The next two chapters get into the six case studies used to test my argument about the reasons why great powers choose to utilize a partisan electoral intervention. Chapter 3 includes the first set of three detailed case studies of the decision-making process that led the U.S. to decide to intervene in three foreign elections and the choice of the exact methods of intervention utilized: the electoral interventions in the 1953 West German elections, in the 1958 Guatemalan elections, and in the 1946 Argentinean elections. These electoral interventions also provide some "real life" examples of the various methods used for this purpose by interveners: covert funding of the assisted side, dissemination of "scandalous" information on the "undesired" side, pre-election public threats and promises, provision of increased monetary assistance and other benefits to the target in a targeted manner, and so forth. Chapter 4 includes three detailed case studies of the decision-making process that led the U.S. to decide to not intervene in three other elections: the 1967 Greek election, the 1958 Venezuelan election, and the 1965 Philippine election.

Chapter 5 provides an overview of the universe of American and Soviet/Russian interventions from 1946 to 2000 based upon the dataset of such interventions (PEIG) that I have collected describing the initial results and general patterns found as to both countries' interventions.

The following two chapters, Chapters 6 and 7, test my arguments about the effects of electoral interventions on the intervened election results. In Chapter 6, I conduct the large-N statistical test of the four main hypotheses and check for any possible selection bias. I also examine the effectiveness of different electoral intervention tools and the effect of the overall magnitude of the electoral intervention. As noted, the statistical test of the first three hypotheses on the effects is also an indirect statistical test of the causes argument. Chapter 7 continues the analysis of the effects of electoral interventions, utilizing a different method: election surveys. Such an analysis enables also a direct examination of some of my theoretical mechanisms. The analysis accordingly focuses on two intervention cases where such election surveys with the relevant questions exist: the 1992 Israeli elections and the 1953 West German elections. The next chapter, Chapter 8, examines the applicability of my arguments about the causes and effects of electoral interventions to a recent (in)famous case—the Russian electoral intervention in the 2016 U.S. elections. I use here the already available information in both regards in order to examine this "out-of-sample" electoral intervention case which occurred after draft versions of my arguments on both questions were already constructed.[36]

The concluding chapter, Chapter 9, first summarizes the findings from the preceding chapters regarding the causes of partisan electoral interventions and their effects on election results. It then discusses the wider contributions of this study to other subfields in IR and American and comparative politics. It then discusses the dangerous possibility of the return, utilizing cybertools, of a premodern related form of such interventions—direct meddling in the vote tallies. It concludes with future directions for research on this topic.

---

[36] For the analysis of two of the hypotheses about the effects, as well as a brief summary of my argument on the causes, see Levin 2016a (early view publication in March 2016).

2

Why They Meddle in Elections—And What Are the Effects on the Results

In this chapter, after describing my theoretical assumptions, I present in greater detail my arguments as to the causes of partisan electoral interventions as well as their effects on election results. I then briefly describe the methods by which I plan to test these arguments. Both the causes and the effects of electoral interventions are examined here in a theoretical framework in which a great power is in the position to provide costly election resources to a domestic actor who is contesting the elections within another country. The great power and the domestic actor then decide whether to undertake (or agree to) an electoral intervention and how to do it.

A partisan electoral intervention is defined in this book as a situation in which one or more sovereign countries intentionally undertakes specific actions to influence an upcoming election in another sovereign country in an overt or covert manner which they believe will favor or hurt one of the sides contesting that election and which incurs, or may incur, significant costs to the intervener(s) or the intervened country.[1] Election resources are defined here, as in much of the elections literature in comparative and American politics (for two examples: Nimmo 1970:45; Denver and Hands 1997b:77), as any factor which may increase the electoral chances of a given candidate/party regardless of its nature (in the domestic context money, endorsements, volunteers, etc.).

2.1 Key Underlying Ideas and Assumptions

Before beginning the in-depth development of my arguments, certain key ideas or assumptions need to be clarified. These assumptions underlie the logic of the theoretical framework presented here and illustrate why we should not treat such activities as unimportant curiosities, regardless of their targets in certain cases. Also one or more of these assumptions are not necessarily uncontroversial among some scholars of international relations or political science. Accordingly,

---

[1] See the operationalization of this definition in section 2.4.

Meddling in the Ballot Box. Dov H. Levin, Oxford University Press (2020). © Oxford University Press.
DOI: 10.1093/oso/9780197519882.001.0001.

it is best to briefly explain and justify these key ideas rather than assuming, in advance, that the reader agrees with the author in this regard.

The first key idea is that *the preferences of the leaders (or parties) in power can matter*. Accordingly, it may indeed be rational, at least in some situations, for a great power to care which leader or party is in power, or may come to power, in another country—even if the leader (or party) in question does not have some unique negative or positive characteristics.

States, and the decision-makers within them, have multiple plausible options in most situations, and different leaders may choose differently among them. The constraints posed by the international environment or domestic conditions on states, even small ones, are rarely so tight as to preclude more than one policy option to the decision-makers. Indeed, many factors in IR which are seen as constraints on decision-makers' choices (such as the lack of resources) can nevertheless often permit a rather wide range of possible behaviors (Stein 2006:191–192, 194). As Arnold Wolfers has noted, with the rare exception of situations in which the state's immediate survival is at stake (the international equivalent of a house being on fire), "it is hard to conceive of situations which leave no room at all for choice and thus for the expression of differences" among decision-makers (1962:15–16).

Even if leaders are assumed to be rational, that doesn't mean that most, or all, of them will choose the same way when facing the same situation. Perfectly rational actors can differ in their decision criteria—whether, for example, they prefer relative or absolute gains, short-term or long-term gains (i.e., their discount factor), risk acceptance, etc. (Stein 1990:106–107, 109–110, 137–140, 173–174). Rational actors can also differ in their views of the long-term viability of a given or potential cooperative interaction with another player or even about the survival chances of that particular actor in the long term (i.e., the "shadow of the future"). Furthermore, they can differ in the assessments of their country's ability to afford at least one act of defection by the other actor, the latter being a prerequisite for any act of cooperation (Stein 1990:100–102, 108).

For example, a rational leader who believed in the early 1950s that the capitalist system was doomed to failure in the long term and that communism was the "wave of the future" would, all else being equal, probably make a different choice on whether to ally with the U.S. than a similarly rational leader who thought that capitalism had a fighting chance or was economically superior. If the rationality assumption were relaxed somewhat, and it was accepted that qualities such as the particular personalities or other psychological traits of certain leaders may affect their decision-making in certain situations (Etheredge 1978; Greenstein 1992; Renshon 2006; Saunders 2012; Kertzer 2016; Yarhi-Milo 2018; Rathbun 2019), then the scope for "leader effects" could, of course, be even greater.

Indeed, even the favorite realist example for such systemic constraints with the "weak suffering what they must," Thucydides' famous Melian dialogue, has the Melian leadership eventually deciding to fight the Athenians despite heavy odds largely in the hopes of receiving Spartan help due to its alliance with them ([1972]:404–406). This was not an unreasonable decision, unlike the way the Athenians (and realists ever since) had portrayed it in the dialogue, given that the Spartans frequently came to the help of even rather minor allies during the war (see, e.g., Thucydides [1972]:389) and the Melians were able to withstand the subsequent Athenian siege for a few months, eventually surrendering only due to an act of treachery within Melos. Had the weak, in this case, been a bit more fortunate, they may have not needed to suffer whatsoever.

Nor, for that matter, do the exigencies of electoral competition, the constraints that democracies usually place on the executive, and the near-universal desire of incumbents to remain in power, always force all elected democratic leaders or parties, regardless of their own personal preferences, into enacting the preferred policies by the "median voter" in their countries. First, as many scholars have noted (Grossman and Helpman 2001:chap. 2; Osborne 1995:279–281; Kartic and McAfee 2007), the results of the Downsian median voter theorem, which expects the candidate's policy platforms to converge toward the preferences of the median voter, are highly dependent on this model's simplified assumptions. Any relaxation of these assumptions with more realistic ones, such as there being more than two significant candidates or parties (the norm in most democracies) or that the candidates have character and are not merely faceless party functionaries, would lead to results permitting the victorious candidate to promise (and/or implement) different policies from those of the losing candidate.

Second, a leader, once in power, can many times use the "bully pulpit" and the powers of his or her office to shift the median voter (or a majority of the public) toward his or her preferred policies. Indeed, one study estimates that at least one quarter of all significant policy preference changes within the American public between 1935 and 1979 were a result of such efforts (Page and Shapiro 1983, 1992; see also Matsubayashi 2013). Evidence of such effects has been found in other democracies as well (Maravall 1999; Ward 2006).

Third, in some real-life situations the various constraints imposed by democratic institutions and public opinion, even in the most consolidated of democracies, nevertheless leave a certain latitude for the incumbent to shape policies in various issue areas as he or she sees fit (Nordlinger 1981; for examples see Byman and Pollack 2001:141–142).[2] Indeed, as Adam Przeworski (2010:147–148) notes,

---

[2] If the relevant public is largely indifferent to many foreign policy issues in general and/or they have little effect on its vote choice (as may be the case at times) the leader's latitude would, of course, be even wider.

any political system that tries to make an elected government accountable to its public must, in order to provide the elected officials with the necessary incentives to do a good job, also give these officials a certain amount of slack or "agency costs."

Not surprisingly, the recent wave of quantitative research on "leader effects" has been providing increasing amounts of systematic evidence in support of this assumption.[3] Growing systematic evidence now exists for the effects of leader characteristics (or "leader effects") on various aspects of their country's foreign policy such as the perusal of nuclear weapons, threatening of economic sanctions, or the chances of entering, escalating, and winning a militarized dispute. Leader characteristics which have already been found in this research to "matter" include age (Horowitz, McDermott, and Stam 2005; Potter 2007; Bak and Palmer 2010; Bertoli and Trager 2019), leadership style (Keller and Foster 2012), past experience as a rebel or revolutionary leader (Colgan 2013; Fuhrmann and Horowitz 2015), military experience (Horowitz Stam, and Ellis 2016), tenure in office (Chiozza and Choi 2003; Potter 2007; Bak and Palmer 2010; Ausderan 2015), reputations of various kinds (Wolford 2007; Lupton 2018), ideology or hawkish tendencies (Heffington 2018; Bertoli, Dafoe, and Trager 2019), responsibility for a recent conflict (Croco 2015), the executive's education (Barcelo 2018), perceived or actual madness (McManus 2019), and cultural background (Dafoe and Caughey 2016). While some of these "leader effects" do become insignificant in more democratic regimes, some studies find such effects to persist in democracies as well (see, e.g., Horowitz, Stam, and Ellis 2016; Dafoe and Caughey 2016; Heffington 2016; Lupton 2018; Bartoli and Trager 2019). The small band of qualitative scholars and political psychologists who have long made various "leader effects" arguments are now being joined by growing parts of the international relations field.

In other words, contra to Waltz's famous claims about the first image (1959:19–20, 27–30, 64, 231–232), we have theoretical and empirical reasons to believe that different leaders may have both different and generalizable effects as well as systemic evidence that such effects actually exist in some cases. That, in turn, makes it frequently rational for a great power to "care" who rules, or may rule, another country in many situations.

The second key idea is that *decision-makers believe that the preferences and nature of the leaders (or parties) in control of another country that they are dealing with matter*. These beliefs, in turn, frequently affect their behavior toward foreign leaders and countries. Although systematic research related to this assumption

---

[3] For the small but growing systematic research on the effects of political parties or the leaders support coalitions on foreign policy see Palmer, London, and Regan (2004); Arena and Palmer (2009); Clare (2010); Mattes, Leeds, and Carroll (2015).

has been rather limited to date, significant evidence nevertheless exists in its support. As one scholar notes, policy-makers in the U.S. "take it as an article of faith" that the identity and preferences of foreign leaders have a significant effect on their countries' policies (Byman and Pollack 2001:108). Even American statesmen known for their adherence to realist tenants were no different in this regard. Henry Kissinger, for example, one such self-described realist, admitted after his retirement from office that, "As a professor, I tended to think of history as run by impersonal forces. But when you see it in practice, you see the difference personalities make" (Isaacson 1992:13). We now know that Kissinger was indeed personally involved in numerous attempts to get rid of "problematic" foreign leaders in various electoral and non-electoral ways during the Nixon and Ford administrations, such as Salvador Allende (Gustafson 2007; Weiner 2007:294–295).

This is true even for leaders of non-democratic states. Recent historical research on Bismarck, for example, has found that much of his foreign policies in the 1870s toward various European democratic and semi-democratic regimes were based on Bismarck's belief in "the primacy of the domestic politics of other countries" and the need to strengthen the factions/parties within the relevant countries which had domestic and/or foreign policy preferences which happened, directly or indirectly, to be congruent with current German interests (Stone 2010:36, 56–57, 65, 90–92). Likewise, notwithstanding their public propaganda about liberal democracy being merely an elaborate capitalist charade, Soviet leaders seem to have frequently believed that who won power in the U.S. (and other democracies) mattered and would have important effects upon their country's foreign policies (Shevchenko 1985:198, 214–216, 277–278; Jakobsen 1998:67; Fursenko and Naftali 2006:296–297, 338–340, 356, 413, 498).

As a result, many major states' intelligence and diplomatic services invest significant amounts of resources in uncovering various facts about the characteristics of the foreign leaders that they are facing. The CIA, for example, is known to have had since the late 1940s a special unit (The Medical and Psychological Assessment Cell or MPAC) dedicated to identifying the true physical and mental states of world leaders. These facts and resources are frequently utilized in real-life decision-making. For example, U.S. President Jimmy Carter requested and heavily utilized specially created psychological profiles of both Menachem Begin and Anwar Sadat while successfully mediating the 1978 Camp David talks between Israel and Egypt.[4]

This information also plays an important role in policy formulation. For example, one recent study which analyzes the sources from which states derive

---

[4] "Spies Track Physical Illnesses of Foreign Leaders," *Voice of America*, September 19, 2011.

inferences about the intentions of other states based on a special dataset of such inferences finds that one important source of inferences is the characteristics of the leaders in question and that "states are indeed acutely concerned with the internal affairs of other states" (Trager 2017:31, 36, 39).

There is also some systematic evidence, from a few of the previously noted leader effects studies (Potter 2007; Bak and Palmer 2010) that this can sometimes directly affect policy outputs, finding that a leader's age and tenure can affect the chances of other states starting a major military crisis with them. As for political parties in general, Schultz (2001) finds that both democracies and non-democracies, when dealing with a democracy, will take into account the behavior and beliefs of the major political parties within that country's political system, both those within and outside the government. Indeed, they frequently base their decision whether to escalate a crisis on the behavior of both the government and the opposition.[5]

The third key idea is that *elections aren't determined only on economic conditions— and politicians know that that is indeed the case.* Given that situation, foreign powers should have, at least in theory, various ways to effectively intervene in many elections elsewhere. A cursory reading of much of the scholarly research in American and comparative politics may lead a reader at times to reach the conclusion that the aggregate economic performance of the economy, however exactly it is measured by scholars or conceptualized by the voters, is the only really important factor in predicting election results in consolidated democracies (for some examples see Tufte 1978:65, 121–124; Fiorina 1981:26–27; Erikson 1989; Aguilar and Pacek 2000; Lewis-Beck and Stegmaier 2000:183; Lewis-Beck, Nadeau, and Elias 2008). Accordingly, the quality of the election campaigns run by the various candidates, election-year events, and the various issues raised during it should have little to no significant effect on the results. Likewise, barring foreign policy events of the magnitude of a World War II (hereafter WW2), foreign policy is expected to have little effect as well.

The aggregate economic situation in the run-up to the election usually has, of course, an important effect upon election results in many cases. Nevertheless, there is clear evidence from multiple research agendas in political science that it is far from the only important systematic factor. For example, some scholars of the economic vote have increasingly acknowledged that the pre-election political and institutional context in a particular country (or the "clarity of responsibility") may have significant effects on the perceived responsibility of the incumbent for his or her administration's recent performance (Powell and Whitten 1993). As a result, in some elections in some democratic countries the

---

[5] Schultz's model holds even when the opposition parties also have ideological/policy preferences (2001:101–107).

effect of the economic conditions on the vote choice has been found to be overall quite small (Duch and Stevenson 2008:81–85).

Furthermore, as even some proponents of the economic vote have long acknowledged, incumbents are not helpless captives of the business cycle, or of their past economic record, and can in many cases take various actions in the run-up to the election in this regard to improve their reelection chances. Known examples in modern democracies range from trying to "goose" the economy in the run-up to the election (Nordhaus 1975; Tufte 1978; Canes-Wrone and Park 2012) to promising or providing various kinds of "pork" to select groups of voters (for some examples see Mayhew 1974; Denmark 2000; Stokes et al. 2013). In the case of "pork," at least, clear evidence exists that its provision can indeed significantly improve the incumbent's reelection chances (Stein and Bicker 1994; Ames 1995; McCubbins and Rosenbluth 1995; Costa-i-Font et al. 2003; Litschig and Morrison 2010; Huet-Vaughn 2019).

Foreign policy in general and specific foreign policy issues in particular can also have a significant effect in many elections, even when the issue or event in question is not a WW2-style cataclysm. As for Israel, for example, the scholarly consensus is that government performance on foreign and security affairs has been the main factor usually determining vote choice in the past few decades (Arian and Shamir 1999:268). Even outside of this perhaps unusual case, one can frequently find elections, even in Organisation for Economic Co-operation and Development (OECD) countries, in which various foreign policy issues, from the contribution of troops to an ongoing war fought by other countries (Australia 1966), to the accession to a trade agreement (Canada 1993), to relations with the U.S. (Germany 2002), are believed to have played an important role in the voter's choice (Duch and Stevenson 2008: 86–87).[6] Even the U.S., frequently given as the paradigmatic example of how foreign policy issues "don't matter" in national elections, this is far less the case then it may initially seem. For example, some researchers who have included measures of foreign policy performance into models predicting U.S. presidential elections since 1948 have found substantially significant effects for this factor, especially among low information voters (Zaller 2004; see also Nincic 1992; Aldrich et al. 2006).

The question of exactly what effects the main campaign's strategy, tactics, events and messages can have on the election results remains very hotly debated within the American and comparative politics research on this topic, with sharply conflicting research findings in both directions.[7] Nevertheless, there

---

[6] "Vietnam the Issue at Australian Polls," *The Guardian,* November 21, 1966.

[7] A recent paper, for example, on the effects of Hitler's speeches on voting for the National Socialist party (the NSDAP) has found virtually no such campaign effects (Selb and Munzert 2018). For a similar conclusion from a recent set of field experiments in the U.S. see Kalla and Brockman (2018).

is some empirical evidence that effective, well-designed election campaigns, while incapable of performing miracles, are able in many situations to provide some significant electoral benefits to a party or candidate. This is the case even in the usually well-funded and organized U.S. elections. For example, in-depth analyses of the effects of candidates' campaign messages in the 2000 and 2008 U.S. elections found that effective campaign messages and ads were sometimes able to lead to significant shifts in support toward the supported candidate during the campaign, especially in situations where various external events made their messages more salient (Johnston, Hagen, and Jamieson 2004; Kenski, Hardy, and Jamieson 2010).

As for major campaign events, for example, analysis of the effects of the two presidential conventions in the 2004 U.S. elections found that the Democratic convention gave a significant boost to John Kerry (Weinschenk and Panagopoulos 2016). Likewise, an analysis of major events in the 2000 U.S. elections found that they had significant effects on support for the candidates with, for example, the debates benefiting George W. Bush and the convention aiding Al Gore (Hillygus and Jackman 2003). Finally, at the legislative level, U.S. members of Congress who became caught in an alleged scandal of some kind (financial improprieties, sexual, corruption, etc.) in the run-up to an election (usually, where relevant, a major campaign topic) saw a decline of 5% on average in their vote share (Basinger 2013).

Improved campaigning and get-out-the-vote (GOTV) techniques have also been found by some scholars to be able to affect a certain side's vote share. For example, according to one study of the 2008 U.S. elections, the creation by the Obama campaign of a field office in a certain county increased democratic vote share by 0.8%—a modest yet large enough effect to have pushed three states (with fifty-four electoral college votes) in which the election was very close into Obama's column (Masket 2009). Some such voter mobilization techniques (such as door-to-door canvassing) have been found to be effective in mobilizing voters also in some large-scale field experiments both in the U.S. and in Europe (Gerber and Green 2000; Green, Gerber, and Nickerson 2003; Nyman 2017).[8]

As a result, some research on the overall effects of election campaigns estimates that a well-executed campaign can have an effect as large as 6% of the vote—a difference as large as the vote margin between the losing and winning side in many elections (Vavreck 2009:20, 108–109). Likewise, evidence has been found recently from some pre-election surveys (Blais et al. 2004:561) that at least in some elections in some countries the main issues debated during the election

---

[8] Likewise, as will be seen later in this chapter (Hypothesis 7), research from elections around the world has found that an advantage in overall campaign resources (such as money) can be a major benefit to its holder.

affected the vote of at least one of every ten voters—an average effect larger than that of the economy in most of the elections that were investigated.

Not surprisingly, there seems to be a near-universal belief among politicians and their advisors that their (re)election campaigns, their responses to various major domestic issues arising during the election period, and how effective they are in "goosing" the economy and/or "bringing home the bacon" all have important effects on their electoral chances (see examples in Mayhew 1974:57; Tufte 1978:5–8; and Vavreck 2009:9–10). Likewise, politicians seem to be quite aware of the potential effects that their foreign policy performance and/or their stands on various foreign policy–related issues can have, at times, on their electoral chances—although they tend to be quite tight-lipped in publicly acknowledging this (at least as to their own behavior in this regard) (Nincic 1992:chap. 4; Gaubatz 1999:85–86; Grow 2008:xii, 45–49, 155–156, 171–172).

Accordingly, there is little reason to believe that the aggregate economic conditions, important as they may well be in many cases, leave no space for other significant factors to affect national level elections. Foreign powers should therefore have, at least in theory, various ways to effectively aid the preferred candidates/parties in many elections of interest.

2.2 Causes of Electoral Interventions

I argue that partisan electoral interventions occur when two concurrent conditions exist. The first is that a significant domestic actor within the target wants or is willing to be aided by the great power in this risky manner. Without such an actor's consent and cooperation the feasibility of an electoral intervention becomes so low that a great power will rarely if ever try to intervene. The second is that the great power perceives its interests as being endangered by another significant candidate/party within a democratic target. This candidate/party has very different and inflexible preferences on important issues—that is, the actor is either greatly constrained by his or her political base on these issues and/or ideologically committed to particular positions or actions.

As noted, this theory on the causes of partisan electoral interventions assumes that the preferences of leaders matter and that the leaders in other countries are, accordingly, concerned with the preferences of both those who are in power as well as their potential replacements. Nevertheless, a great power will have, at most times and in most countries, very little incentive to invest significant resources (which an electoral intervention requires) in affecting the nature of the leader and/or the ruling coalition of another country. This is true even when a less-than-"perfect" leader or party may come to power or if issues of major importance to the great power are being debated or potentially affected. The ability

of the great power to use its surplus and wide range of resources in order to secure its interests through low-cost conventional diplomacy, the costs of such
interventions, and the danger of turning the unfriendly but still "reasonable" domestic actor into an outright enemy,[9] will all usually prevent an electoral intervention from being seriously considered.

Things are different, however, if in the relevant country there exists an important political actor of a type which has (or is perceived to have or soon
have) very different and inflexible preferences on issues of significant interest
to both it and the great power.[10] Such situations may be the result of two possible conditions. The first is the domestic actor's political base. Many of the voters
who are part of the domestic actor's "core" constituency may themselves hold
these different preferences and be willing to punish the actor if he or she makes
any compromises. In such situations, even if the party leadership privately holds
more "pragmatic" views, the fear of severe political punishment for committing
a major "heresy" will force them to be very inflexible when negotiating with the
great power on this issue.[11] The second is the domestic actor's own preferences
on this issue. Like old dogs, most politicians have been found to rarely change
their various core political values over the course of their political careers

[9] For example, much of the difficult relations between the Obama administration and Hamid
Karzai, which have seriously hampered U.S. policies vis-à-vis Afghanistan, seem to have been due
to Karzai's anger over the (unsuccessful) intervention of the former in the 2009 Afghan presidential elections in an attempt to prevent his reelection (Emma Graham-Harrison, "US 'Tried to Oust
Hamid Karzai by Manipulating Afghan Elections," *The Guardian*, January 10, 2014).

[10] Such issues of sufficiently significant interest to the great power to see an intervention as worthwhile can involve, for example, key foreign policy initiatives by that power, survival of a major alliance, denial of critical strategic resources, stability of an important world region, or increased
influence by an enemy power in a key country/area. The critical factor that generates the major threat
perception in these cases is the combination of the significant disagreement on a key issue or issues
with inflexibility (real or perceived) on it by that actor—not either disagreement on such issues or inflexibility in and of themselves. Bad domestic behavior by local actors, such as domestic corruption,
does not usually seem to lead, on its own, to such threat perceptions by the great powers—barring the
rare cases where it is perceived as directly affecting other issues of key significance to that would-be
intervener.

[11] For a similar logic as to the causes of forcible regime change, see Willard-Foster (2019). As will
be seen later, due to the different political contexts in which electoral interventions usually occur, as
well as the far greater importance of the domestic opposition and its preferences in the process that
leads to an electoral intervention, these dynamics nevertheless usually lead to very different types of
targets of electoral interventions (compared to FIRCs) in practice—threatening leaders and parties
which are domestically politically strong (or are widely perceived as strong) rather than relatively
weak ones. For the political incentives major parties may sometimes have to hold hard-line, "extreme" positions see Eguia and Giovannoi (2019). Likewise, recent research (Lupu 2014) has found
that one of the main reasons for sudden dramatic collapses in public support for major political
parties in democracies is their abandonment of major, long-standing policy positions for short-term
gains. Such policy shifts may lead in some cases to a mass, irreversible desertion by core supporters—
especially if those short-term gains fail to materialize. Accordingly, politicians frequently have good
reason to fear the possible political consequences of a break with their core supporters on such "hot
button" issues—even if these core supporters are, as is usually the case, a minority (or even a small
minority) of the voting population.

(Putnam, Leonardi, and Nanetti 1979; Searing, Jacoby, and Tyner 2019). The party leaders may be of a type which is very committed to those particular different preferences due to their core values (or other personal reasons), unwilling to enact policies which are incongruent with them.

Following the logic of the bargaining model (Fearon 1995; Powell 2006), in order to create a bargaining range on the issue in dispute under either of these two conditions, in other words one in which an "acceptable solution" to the "obstinate" domestic actor now includes a solution of the kind preferred by the great power, the great power will need to use (or credibly promise) very costly policy options (military coercion, very large amounts of foreign aid, etc.).[12] For example, the U.S. would have needed to use extraordinary measures in the early 1950s in order to convince a hypothetical West Germany under the SPD's Karl Schumacher to join the European Defense Community (EDC). Given that the EDC was widely believed to make German reunification impossible until the Cold War ended (Ninkovich 1988:94), for Schumacher to join it would have meant abandoning his deeply held commitment to quick reunification. Indeed, as will be seen in Chapter 3, American decision-makers thought that this goal would be unattainable under an SPD government.

In such situations the great power has an incentive to find an effective yet lower cost option by which to promote its interests in the target (i.e., create a "better" bargaining range). In countries with competitive elections, intervening in an election in order to bring, or to keep, in power a domestic actor which is less domestically constrained[13] and/or of a "friendlier" type can potentially be such a low cost yet effective solution. Competitive elections are usually one of the least costly ways by which unwanted incumbents can be replaced by their electorate (Przeworski 2010:167). Accordingly, when dealing with such obstinate domestic actors, if a great power is able to find a way to effectively harness this domestic institution in the would-be target for its own needs, an electoral intervention could potentially be both the cheapest way to replace the incumbent (or prevent his or her coming to power) as well as cheaper than bargaining with the target when

---

[12] Another alternative, organizing a coup against the leader/party in question, would either be an infeasible or far more costly alternative. In most established democracies, and some newer ones, civil–military relations are such that a military coup, let alone a foreign-induced coup, is in the realm of the inconceivable. Even in democracies or new/semi-democracies where that is a feasible option, the costs are usually at a whole order of magnitude above that of an electoral intervention in an equivalently sized country. For example, the American covert coup d'état in Guatemala in 1954 (when an electoral intervention was infeasible) cost the U.S. at least $6 million with the original cost estimate being half of that, or $3 million ($21.9 million in 2016 dollars) (Prados 2006:121). In contrast, as will be seen in Chapter 3, the cost for the U.S. of intervening in a Guatemalan election four years later was $97,000 ($655,000 in 2016 dollars)—or 3.2% of the original cost estimate of the 1954 FIRC.

[13] In other words, a domestic actor whose political base is largely composed of voters with different and/or more moderate preferences on the issue in dispute who will accordingly be less likely to punish (and may even reward) this actor if he or she compromises with the great power on this issue.

ruled by such actors. In summary, electoral interventions are usually considered in order to prevent (or to change) an undesirable situation rather than somewhat improve an overall preferable or acceptable situation.[14]

However, the existence of this situation is merely a necessary rather than a sufficient condition for an electoral intervention, even in regard to democratic targets. An electoral intervention is usually not the only available option to the great power, and it can choose or substitute (Most and Starr 1989) other options as well. These other costly options range from attempting nonetheless to negotiate with the unfriendly domestic actor to removing it by various violent means (from aiding coups to a military invasion). While, as noted, an electoral intervention is usually cheaper than the other options, its *feasibility* (i.e., chances of success) can greatly vary even between democratic targets. Accordingly, if the feasibility of an electoral intervention is low, the great power will prefer other, more feasible, options. The only very rare exceptions are the *in extremis* cases in which a great power perceives an unusually high level of threat emanating from a certain actor concurrent with a complete lack of any other pre- or post-election options.[15]

I argue that in order for an electoral intervention to be feasible, and therefore be the chosen option, the great power must obtain the cooperation of a significant domestic actor within the target which can, with such aid, win the election. This cooperation provides the intervener with crucial and irreplaceable local knowledge from the domestic actor on the best methods to intervene as well as, when relevant, the most effective way to deliver it (covert/overt, etc.).[16] The

---

[14] The argument made here does not imply that the fact that great powers intervene to prevent a certain undesirable policy outcome means that a successful electoral intervention will lead necessarily to a better policy outcome (in its eyes) to be achieved in practice afterwards. The latter is a separate theoretical and empirical question due to the differences between the pre and post- election situations. For example, the post-election political incentives faced by the assisted victorious side, now firmly in power, may differ from those it faced prior to the election. With that noted, the preliminary evidence elsewhere indicates (Levin 2018b) that some great powers are able sometimes to gain at least some of their policy goals through such successful interventions.

[15] In other words, in those situations, the great power is willing to utilize a policy option that it knows to have a very low chance of success. One such possible "no collusion" exception was the Soviet intervention in the 1984 U.S. elections, caused to a significant degree (according to currently available information) by extreme Soviet fears that President Reagan was planning to conduct a preemptive nuclear strike on the USSR (Andrew and Mithrokhin 1999:243). Another known rare case of non-collusion, the U.S. electoral intervention in Chile in 1970, seems to have been due to a major bureaucratic mishap caused, to a large extent, by the (erroneous) belief of the then-U.S. Ambassador to Chile that Allende, if victorious, would be anyway blocked from coming to power by the incumbent President Frei or the Chilean military—making a truly effective U.S. electoral intervention unnecessary (Gustafson 2007).

[16] As will be seen in further detail in the next section, the domestic actor's information about the expected reaction to an overt electoral intervention in general, or by that foreign actor in particular, plays a key role in whether a covert or an overt intervention is chosen—with an overt intervention usually avoided in situations where a backlash within the target public is expected to occur (which could, in turn, harm the assisted side's electoral chances).

intervener then utilizes this information from the client to craft for it an electoral intervention that both sides believe has good chances of success.

Electoral interventions, unlike other types of interventions, are usually "inside jobs." This is due to the fact that an electoral intervention is essentially an attempt to strengthen (or create) a domestic election campaign for a particular party and/or candidate in the target. Indeed, as one scholar notes, the secret agents in charge of covert electoral interventions many times "resembled nothing less than a group of political campaign consultants" (Johnson, in Daugherty 2004:82). The role of the great power in an overt electoral intervention has also been frequently described by contemporaries in these terms, such as the assisted side's "campaign manager" or "impresario."[17] As a result, in order for an electoral intervention to work, the intervener needs the type of high-quality private information that the top politicians and/or the major parties within that country have and use in order to campaign—such as what the relevant voter groups' preferences are, which messages to use and/or how to package and deliver the messages in order to be productive in that particular context, and where to invest resources in the various campaign activities so as to maximize vote/seat share, etc.[18]

One of the important roles of political parties around the world has been to serve as aggregators of such private political knowledge to the benefit of the candidates running on their behalf. As some researchers on parties and campaigns note, even in the American case (well known for its "skeletal" or "thin" parties), the two political parties have served, among other things, as important sources for various kinds of information on voters and GOTV activities for the candidates which compete in their name at various levels of government (Bohne, Prevost, and Thurber 2009:498, 503).[19] Indeed, it seems that one of the main reasons why campaign consultants in the U.S. tend to work with only one of the two main parties is that in order to do their job, they are provided by the

---

[17] These are two representative quotes from media descriptions of President Clinton's role in the American interventions in the 1996 Israeli and Russian elections (William Safire, "The Biggest Election," New York Times, May 2, 1996; Steven Erlanger, "Just Whose Elections Are They, Anyway?" New York Times, May 26, 1996).

[18] From my examination of who exactly was aided in such intervention in PEIG it is clear that the great powers do not usually have the ability to create significant parties/parties in other independent countries (i.e., create its own "opportunity"). The most that the great powers have been able to usually do in this regard is to convince some preexisting grassroots parties and/or politicians in the target to agree on a single presidential candidate and/or a common candidate slate for a parliamentary election—both acts naturally requiring quite heavy cooperation with the intervener on the side of the relevant local actors.

[19] Likewise, one should note that this need for information is true even for most of the various independent domestic groups which sometimes also aid candidates running in U.S. elections. As one scholar noted, despite changes in campaign finance law banning such coordination "in the 2004 election, [the presidential] campaigns engaged in a surprising amount of communication with purportedly independent 527 organizations" (Johnston 2006:1169, 1178–1179, 1184–1185). See also Rutenberg and Zernike (2004).

party with such sensitive, high-quality information (Bohne et al. 2009:501–502). In the other main subtype, the "thick" "mass" and/or "clientelistic" parties, in which the connections with the voters are far deeper and more frequent, the party performs this role as well (for developing world examples see Chandra (2004:139) and Stokes (2005:316–319).[20]

Such information can be quite important for a successful electoral intervention given that even supposedly minor details may have a significant effect on how a particular message is received by and affects the relevant foreign audiences. For example, even an apparently minor issue such as whether, in a speech to a foreign audience, President Obama noted his name with or without one of its components could lead different foreign audiences to have significantly different reactions to it (Weismel-Manor and Stroud 2010). Likewise, significant differences existed and continue to exist in the nature of election campaigns and their main features between democracies (Plassner 2009; Plassner and Lengauer 2009:266–268). Different electoral systems, to give one example, seem to frequently lead to very distinct types of election campaigns (Fox 2018:1903–1905). As a result, knowing how to campaign in one democracy does not necessarily mean knowing much of, or enough on, how to do so in another democracy. Furthermore, even if the intervention is limited to the covert supply of campaign funds, the intervener still needs to know at the very least how much funds to supply, when and where to give them, and to whom within a particular campaign they should be given in order to achieve the desired results without exposure.[21] This type of information is also not easy to locate.

Given the limited understanding that both American and non-American policy-makers usually have of the domestic politics of other nations (Drezner 2010),[22] the would-be intervener usually wouldn't have, or be able to collect, a sufficient amount of the needed information. As a result, in order to have a

---

[20] For some of the most recent methods by which parties have been performing this role see Sasha Issenberg, "America Exports Democracy, Just Not the Way That You Think," New York Times, March 14, 2014.

[21] As Richard Bissell, a former deputy director of plans (i.e., covert operations) in the CIA, once noted in a closed talk, when the U.S. gave such covert funding the side it supported usually knew about it, but was, of course, unwilling to publically admit that fact (Marchetti and Marks 1983:335–336). The current method of campaign financing in American elections, in which large amounts of campaign funding can openly (and legally) come from private and corporate donors, may at least in theory make it relatively easy for a foreign power to covertly intervene via covert funding by using a domestic American firm/individual who received from it a "padded" contract. However, no evidence was found for the use of such methods (i.e., such interventions in U.S. elections without any contact with the candidate or campaign) in practice, including in the 2016 Russian intervention. Furthermore, the current U.S. campaign finance system is quite unique in a comparative perspective—so such methods of intervention are anyway unavailable to the great powers elsewhere.

[22] On the general ignorance of CIA agents of local conditions or even the language of the countries to which they were posted see Godson (1995:48, 61) and Weiner (2007:471). The KGB had similar problems (Andrew and Mitrokhin 1999:54, 555, 557; Andrew and Gordievsky 1990:536).

significant chance of success, assisting a particular party/candidate without any coordination with them will not suffice and may even harm their chances.[23] Instead, the intervener needs the cooperation of the preferred candidate/party which has this local knowledge.

Not surprisingly, such cooperation between the intervener and the aided candidate/party and its centrality to the intervention process is usually quite evident in cases of electoral interventions on which we have good information. For example, the U.S. intervention in the October 1952 Japanese elections was, to a significant extent, the result of repeated requests by then–Japanese Prime Minister Shigeru Yoshida for an American intervention in his and the Liberal Party's favor. Furthermore, each one of the acts that the U.S. carried out in order to help Yoshida in the run-up to the election was the result of detailed Japanese requests for this purpose, such as a public statement by the U.S. Ambassador to Japan a week before the election promising continued U.S. foreign aid in the near future.[24]

In other words, even in a country in which the great power intervener recently ended a six-year-long occupation, and whose new political institutions and constitution were, to a large extent, unilateral impositions by its former occupation regime,[25] the intervening country still needed the cooperation of and the private political knowledge supplied by the domestic party on whose behalf it was intervening in order to know how to effectively assist it. Other examples of this pattern can be seen in the detailed case studies in Chapters 4 and 5.[26]

Such cooperation, however, is not automatic. Even if such aid could be useful, the domestic actor will often reject such an external offer (or not request it), thus preventing an intervention from occurring. For example, in the 1968 U.S. presidential election, the Democratic presidential candidate, Hubert Humphrey, despite a severe shortfall of campaign funding, flatly rejected a secret Soviet offer to provide covert financial and other aid to his campaign. As a result, the

---

[23] A ham-fisted overt intervention, for example, could lead to a backlash in the target against the assisted side and reduce support for it—a widely known possibility. See the later discussion of this issue.

[24] For details on this U.S. intervention see, for example, Foreign Relations of the United States (hence FRUS) 1952–1954, vol. 14 (2): 1178, 1181–1182, 1186–1189, 1268, 1273, 1275–1276, 1280–1286, 1328–1332.

[25] For example, the 1947 Japanese constitution was originally written in English by American officials in the U.S. Occupation Authority and then translated into Japanese.

[26] Likewise, as one researcher of the U.S. intervention in the 1948 Italian elections notes, the intervention heavily "drew on the unflinching support of Tarchiani [the Italian ambassador to the U.S.] and his expertise in assessing Italian politics" (Karabell 1999:42–43, 47–49). For one Soviet example, from the 1972 West German elections, see Memorandum of Meeting (Moscow) August 1–2, 1972, Pavel Stroilov Archive. For a more recent example, the U.S. intervention in the 1996 Russian election, see Memorandum of telephone conversations, Clinton to Yeltsin, February 21 and May 7, 1996 NSA Archive.

Soviets dropped all further attempts to intervene in that election (Dobrynin 1995:174–176).[27]

Such rejections occur because electoral aid, while potentially useful, also carries significant costs and/or risks for the domestic actor.[28] First, its intentional and/or inadvertent exposure may hurt the actor's standing in future elections. If the intervention is overt, the electorates' knowledge of the intervention may hurt the aided actor in later elections even if it is helpful in the short term. A desire that their candidate or party be accountable only to them, fears of the long-term effects of such foreign influence on their preferences or decision-making, or various nationalist considerations may all lead many otherwise supportive voters to be wary of such actors, reducing their long-term electoral viability and/or domestic legitimacy.

Even if the intervention is covert, the possibility of exposure (partial or full) remains a significant risk for the domestic actor. As could be seen in recent events in the U.S., even when the actual effects of such an exposed covert intervention remain highly contested in the public arena, the unambiguous evidence for its occurrence in favor of the victor can be sufficient in and of itself to significantly reduce the assisted leader's legitimacy in the eyes of much of their public.[29] Likewise, strong suspicions (supported by some circumstantial evidence) within the target of collusion between the assisted side and the foreign power during this intervention can cause,—even without the conduct of, or prior to the conclusion of, an official investigation on this question (or, for that matter, the finding of a "smoking gun")—serious damage to the victor's standing among many voter groups.[30] Similar effects are

[27] This Soviet offer was due to their great fear of Nixon, then seen as extremely anti-Soviet or, as Khrushchev once described him (in private), "a typical product of McCarthyism, a puppet of the most reactionary circles in the United States. *We'll never be able to find a common language with him*" (my emphasis) (Shevchenko 1985:108; Dobrynin 1995:176). For other examples of such rejected offers see Andrew and Gordievsky (1990:496) and Chapter 4 of this book.
[28] These potential costs, when combined with full control by the incumbent of their state's resources (i.e., an effective domestic alternative), seem to be one key reason why incumbents in authoritarian regimes do not seem to usually request such an electoral intervention in order to further "pad" an all-but-certain victory.
[29] See, for example, Joy-Ann Reid, "Trump Could Address These Legitimacy Questions—But He Won't," *Daily Beast,* January 14, 2017; Chuck Todd, Sally Bronson and Matt Rivera, "Rep. John Lewis: 'I Don't See Trump as a Legitimate President,'" *NBC News,* January 14, 2017; Bryan Logan, "James Clapper: US Intelligence Assessment of Russia's Election Interference 'Cast Doubt on the Legitimacy' of Trump's Victory," *Business Insider,* September 23, 2017. The repeated attempts by President Trump to nevertheless deny that this Russian intervention had occurred or that it was designed to help his candidacy indicate quite well even his deep worries in this regard.
[30] For one example from this case see Jennifer Agiesta, "CNN Poll: Trump Approval at New Low as Russia Concerns Grow" *CNN,* November 9, 2017. Some American commentators, including many with center-right leanings, openly declared when Russiagate started that the finding of such a "smoking gun" by the Mueller investigation (or through other venues) would be in their eyes a sufficient justification for the outright impeachment of President Trump. See, for example, Megan McArdle "Let Trump's Election Stand," *Forbes,* December 13, 2016; John Yoo and Saikrishna Prakesh,

seen in other cases where a covert electoral intervention was inadvertently exposed.[31]

Second, by reducing its dependence upon domestic resources to win elections, such aid may also inadvertently reduce that actor's contacts with and feedback from the electorate, damaging its ability to understand the public's desires and therefore its electoral viability in the longer term.[32] Third, such electoral aid often includes a quid pro quo between the intervener and the aided actor as to particular policies once the actor is (re)elected. Such promises impose upon the domestic actor "sovereignty costs," reducing its freedom of action once in power more than it would have otherwise (at least regarding the policies in question). Even if the actor would eventually find ways to evade fulfilling these promises, the potential costs involved in breaking them (i.e., deteriorating relations with the "betrayed" great power) may be significant.[33]

Accordingly, external electoral aid will be accepted or requested only by domestic actors who believe that it will overall work to their advantage.[34] From the various scholarly literatures which discuss when domestic actors decide to use "unconventional" measures in order to ensure their political survival and/or promote policy goals (i.e., from changing the electoral system [Boix 1999], to requesting IMF loans [Vreeland 2003], to attempting to enlist foreign/transnational actors to help stop various domestic human right abuses [Keck and Sikkink 1998]), we would expect two major types of actors to agree to accept or request such electoral aid.

"Don't Prosecute Trump. Impeach Him," *AEI*, December 5, 2017; and Jim Geraghty, "Impeachment Is Not a Mulligan," *National Review*, December 19, 2017. See Chapter 8 of this book for a further discussion of 2016.

[31] For the example of the exposed CIA intervention in the 1984 El Salvadorian election see Edward Cody, "Reports of U.S. Covert Aid Seen Hurting Duarte," *Washington Post*, May 13, 1984.

[32] For related arguments on the potential downsides of assistance for domestic activists from international NGOs see Bob (2005:184–185). A milder version of this problem seems to sometimes exist even in relations between domestic big donors and the parties they donate to. For recent complaints in this regard, even among reformist Republicans, about the detrimental effects of the GOP's dependence on wealthy donors on attempts to renew the GOP's governing agenda see, for example, Ross Douthat, "The Republican Party's "Donorism" Problem," *New York Times*, March 6, 2013; and Reihan Salam, "The Roy Moore Debacle Should Shock the GOP into Changing Its Ways. It won't," *Slate*, December 13, 2017.

[33] For related arguments on the potential downsides of external aid to the recipient in a civil war or non-violent civil disobedience campaign see Salehyan (2010:507) and Chenoweth (2013:54–55, 175–176, 225), respectively.

[34] Aside of a concern with whether the intervention is overt or covert in its nature (see the next section), the exact forms of aid desired by the domestic actor are expected to be derived from highly idiosyncratic domestic conditions such as how good its campaign fundraising efforts from domestic sources has been in the preceding months, the main issues "on the table" between the intervener and the target in the run-up to the elections, the topics which the voters care about the most or which have dominated the political agenda before the start of the election campaign, the main things that the voters or key voter groups dislike the most about the assisted side (party or leader) and/or about their main opponents, and so forth.

The first type is the **fragile victor**. By that type I mean that the relevant party has succeeded in winning power and is currently in control of the state; however, the existing political balance of power or the ongoing structural domestic changes within the state are greatly reducing its ability/chances to win power in future elections.

The second type is the **blocked/weakening loser**. By that type I mean that the relevant party is officially or unofficially blocked from assuming power in the given state regardless of the political support that it musters among the public.[35] The electoral intervention could be one possible way to end its exclusion.[36] Alternatively, the party has repeatedly failed to win an election and/or has been suffering major political defeats which greatly hurt its ability to win power in the near to medium term.

Usually these dynamics, and the nature of the party systems of many democratic and semi-democratic countries, will greatly constrict the number of potential domestic partners the intervener can "work with," forcing it to accept less than optimal partners for this purpose.[37] Nevertheless, in some cases more than

[35] An effective blocking of a challenger candidate or party (in practice or in widespread pre-election perception) could be implemented by the incumbents using a variety of methods. Examples include: an informal agreement (in parliamentary systems) among all other major parties to never include it/be part of a coalition government with that party or (in a two-round presidential election) to never endorse its presidential candidate/support the other candidate if it reaches the second round, preventing it from accessing certain key electoral resources (such as any coverage by major local media organs or bank loans/campaign donations); the creation or maintenance of electoral institutions or regulations intentionally designed to be heavily biased against it; or the heavy use of election fraud against its candidates. Some of these techniques have been used successfully by incumbents even in fully established democracies (such as post-WW2 France and Italy)—so this is not a situation only encountered by some parties/candidates in new democracies or "competitive authoritarian" regimes (see example in next footnote).

[36] In other words, the domestic actor may believe that its exclusion from power would end following certain electoral results. For example, if the excluded/blocked party won a sufficiently large number of seats in parliament, or, in a presidential system, its candidate defeated other candidates, then it would become impossible for the other incumbent political actor(s) to continue excluding it from power without the political system coming to a halt and/or unleashing massive public opposition (demonstrations, etc.) which would force its hand. For example, one of the persistent fears of the U.S. (and many Italians) with regard to Italy during the Cold War was that if the Italian Communist Party became sufficiently strong it would become impossible to form a viable coalition in the Italian parliament without its support. That, in turn, would end its unofficial exclusion from power, forcing the ruling Christian Democrats into, at the minimum, a formal coalition government with the Communist Party if not even stepping down from power and accepting a Communist-led government (see, e.g., Njolstad 2002). Likewise, all else being equal, it would be easier for a military to carry out a coup against an "unwanted" party/candidate who won the election by a "squeaker" than a party/candidate that won it by a clear, convincing majority—if only due to the higher probability of mass civilian protests (and perhaps even disobedience by some of the common soldiers) against the coup in the latter scenario—situations most militaries loathe to face. For evidence from related research in authoritarian politics, finding that opposition parties in non-competitive regimes are far more likely to turn to violence or other non-conventional tactics than their brethren in more competitive regimes see Franklin (2002).

[37] As a result, great powers looking for would-be "partners in crime" will usually be well aware, even from a shallow understanding of the country in question derived from media reports or unsophisticated embassy reporting, of the possible partners worth "checking out" (if not contacted by

Table 2.1 Summary of the Main Predictions—Causes of Partisan Electoral Interventions (Hypotheses 1–3)

		GP Sees Implacable Actor B	
		Yes	No
Actor A Wants Aid	Yes	Electoral Intervention Likely Any requests or offers are usually accepted, close cooperation on intervention	No Electoral Interventions Any requests of assistance are rejected by GP
	No	No Electoral Interventions Any offers of interventions are rejected by would-be partner	No Electoral Interventions

one domestic actor may be in this situation and be willing to ask for (or accept) such foreign electoral assistance. Given the aforementioned intervener's main goal in doing an electoral intervention, it will choose to offer its assistance to the main candidate or party perceived as both having the best chances of winning the election and being willing to accept its assistance.

As a result of these dynamics on both sides, unless a viable domestic actor of either of these two types exists in conjunction with a great power fearful of one of this domestic actor's opponents, an electoral intervention is highly unlikely to occur. The presence of only one of these conditions will rarely suffice to bring about an intervention (see also Table 2.1).

H1: *A great power will not perform an electoral intervention unless it perceives, in a target with competitive elections, a significant actor with very different/inflexible preferences as endangering its interests.*

H2: *Domestic actors which are neither fragile victors nor blocked/weakening losers will not request (or agree to) an electoral intervention on their behalf by a great power.*

H3: *Great power electoral interventions will not usually occur if the domestic actor which is supposed to benefit from this aid refuses to accept it.*

them first). Likewise, given the relatively small number of major powers, domestic actors will usually be well aware which major foreign powers may be "interested" in assisting them.

2.3 The Effects on Election Results

Partisan electoral interventions are not the only factor which can affect the results of a particular election. Nevertheless I argue, based on my explanation for the causes of electoral interventions described in section 2.2, that they can significantly increase the electoral chances of the supported candidate or party. This is the result of the process by which a would-be intervener and a would-be client "choose" each other and agree to an electoral intervention.

Thus, a great power will not likely support a potential client if that client will still likely lose the election. Under these circumstances, a great power will usually judge that other means will better serve its interests.[38] Similarly, a potential client will likely reject an offer of electoral aid by an outside power if they believe that they will win the election in the absence of such assistance. In these circumstances, the greater risk comes from the possible medium- and long-term costs involved in receiving such an intervention in their favor.

As noted in section 2.2, these costs include harming the client's electoral position in the longer term by alienating voters who, for a variety of reasons, may resent or fear the influence of the foreign power. Such electoral aid also often includes a quid pro quo in which the candidate enacts policies favored by the intervener in return for electoral support. Such promises impose upon the client "sovereignty costs." That is, they reduce the client's freedom of action with respect to those, and perhaps other, policies preferred by the foreign power. As a result, we should expect most cases of electoral interventions to occur in marginal elections: those in which the result is highly uncertain or one side lags but remains electorally viable.[39] In such situations, electoral interventions are most likely to have a significant effect on the results of the election. Given that, all else being equal, the more resources that a particular candidate or party has, the more likely they are to win (Sudulich and Wall 2010:1; Benoit and Marsh 2008:874), we can assume that interventions usually increase the electoral chances of the aided party or candidate.[40]

---

[38] Given the costs that electoral interventions impose on the intervener, the great power will prefer to not waste resources on what it perceives as "futile" ones. Likewise, an electoral intervention on behalf of a failed candidate will likely undermine the great powers' position with the victorious candidate or party—which, if it has any hopes of using other (costlier) methods to affect its behavior post-election, would make those methods less likely to succeed.

[39] Naturally the final results of an intervened election may be less close then predicted prior to the intervention- the intervention may have had a larger then average effect, the actors may have misperceived at the time of the intervention how close the election would be, or exogenous factors made the election less close then expected between the intervention request and election day (due to a sudden economic crisis etc.). Accordingly the final results of any particular intervened election do not provide, on its own, a guide to how "close" the election was going to be (or was perceived to be) at the time of the intervention.

[40] In a similar manner to the arguments of scholars of the "economic vote," I don't, of course, argue that a successful partisan electoral intervention would guarantee a victory of its beneficiaries—just

H4: *An electoral intervention for a particular candidate or party will increase its electoral chances.*

Whether a great power chooses covert or overt forms of electoral intervention likely matters a great deal. Conventional wisdom expects that overt electoral interventions, as other kinds of overt interventions, rarely work as intended. It assumes that public intervention produces a backlash against the intervener and thus harms the prospects of the side that it supports.[41] This view implies that a covert intervention, so long as it remains hidden, will be more effective.

However, this ignores the potential benefits of overt interventions. Moreover, great powers that engage in electoral interventions will take steps to minimize the risks of a backlash. In this, they benefit from the information provided by their client about how best to calibrate their electoral intervention in light of local sensibilities, preferences, and politics. Indeed, if overt interventions always failed (as the conventional wisdom expects), then overt electoral interventions would be an inherently irrational act and we would expect such interventions to become very rare over time. This is not what we see in PEIG.[42] And, as noted in Chapter 1, the evidence for blowback effects remains uncertain; Corstange and Marinov (2012:664–669) failed to find evidence of a backlash in their study.[43]

Covert and overt electoral interventions involve different mixes of costs and benefits. Overt electoral interventions allow for more extensive electoral manipulation (and higher chances of success) but carry with them some kind of risk of blowback. Consider the distributional politics model of Dixit and Londregan (1996:1136–1140), in which politicians can win elections by promising the transfer of resources to various "persuadable" voter groups (thus "buying" their votes).[44] In the context of an electoral intervention, this model suggests that great

---

that it might significantly increase its vote share from what it would have been otherwise, all else being equal.

[41] To give one example of this view, Huntington (1999:39) claims that "the more the United States attacks a foreign leader, the more his popularity soars among his countrymen who applaud him for standing tall ... the best way for a dictator of a small country to prolong his tenure in power may be to provoke the United States into denouncing him as the leader of a 'rogue regime' and a threat to global peace."

[42] For example, nineteen of the overt interventions in PEIG had occurred during the 1980s and 1990s.

[43] For similar findings in interventions in two recent referendums (Greece 2015 and the UK 2016) as well as in a fully authoritarian, non-electoral context see Bush and Jamal (2015); Matush (2018); and Walter et al. (2018).

[44] In two closely related domestic analogs, recent research in American politics has found that the ability of Congresspersons to publically claim credit for particular pork (or government spending) is a far more effective method for them to get votes, etc. than merely "bringing home the bacon" and letting the facts "speak for themselves" or, for that matter, conventional campaigning and advertising (Grimmer, Messing, and Westwood 2012). Likewise, scholars have found that when U.S. presidents actively and openly campaign on behalf of their own parties' senatorial candidates in midterm elections, activities strategically targeted so as to favor candidates who are fighting close senate races,

powers, due to their resource advantages, will usually enjoy a superior ability to promise the foreign population the transfer of particular resources—or threaten the loss of existing resources—to that of any local politicians. As a result, direct, overt messages from the great power conveying threats or promises to the target's public can produce a significant shift in the public's voting patterns. However, as decision-makers have long known,[45] overt electoral interventions are risky—if the public in the target country dislikes any facet of the overt intervention it can lead to a backlash against the preferred candidate, hurting rather than helping their chances of being elected.

In contrast, a covert intervention carries far lower chances of a backlash due to the inherent secrecy in the provision of the electoral aid. However, the lower risk comes with reduced effectiveness. This is due to the nature of covert interventions. A covert operation needs to provide enough assistance to the client so they will have a good chance of winning the elections while being, at the same time, greatly limited in the means, or the magnitude of the means, they can use. This limitation is necessary in order to avoid exposure and to enable "plausible deniability" (for this general feature of covert operations see Lowenthal (2003:173–174). As one former senior CIA official noted, maintaining covertness "almost always" imposes a significant "operational penalty" on the relevant operation (Bissell 1996:214–215).[46] The chances that this delicate balancing act will lead to the under-provision of electoral aid to the client, no significant improvement in their prospects, and a subsequent defeat in the elections are far higher than in overt interventions.

The intervener, knowing the benefits and risks of each subtype, will act strategically when choosing the method of intervention, using the information it has on the target public's preferences (as usually provided by the client) in order to maximize the client's electoral prospects. For example, in the American electoral intervention in the 1969 Thai elections the U.S. government chose to intervene in a covert manner largely because the side that it was aiding demanded complete secrecy in the provision of the U.S. electoral aid, claiming that "A leak would destroy them."[47] Likewise, one major reason why the U.S. decided to intervene in

these candidates are significantly more likely to be elected than they would have otherwise (Cohen et al. 1991).

[45] For German and British examples from the early 1940s see Stout (1997). For an American example from the early 1950s see FRUS 1952–1954 6: 499–500; and FRUS 1952–1954 14 (2): 1329. In Dixit and Londregan's (1996: 1135, 1138–1139) terms, this is the situation when the voters have strong ideological preferences vis-à-vis the intervener or the relevant issues which overwhelm any other economic preferences, etc.

[46] As Bissel noted, "the penalty usually takes the form of limiting funds, logistic support, personnel or the level of technology" among other factors (1996:215).

[47] FRUS 1964–1968 27: Document 398. The assisted side may be sometimes aware of the possible limitations of covert aid—but nevertheless prefer it to overt electoral assistance that it expects will

an overt manner in the 1953 West German elections was because of Chancellor Konrad Adenauer's pressure for various overt acts of intervention in his favor. As will be seen in Chapter 3 in greater detail, Adenauer was of the belief throughout the pre-election period that overt acts by the U.S. in his favor would improve his electoral chances. Indeed, Adenauer even needed, in a few instances, to reduce the increasing fears of some American officials in the run-up to the elections of a possible backlash against him as a result.[48]

As a result, when the intervener knows or receives information from the client indicating that an overt electoral intervention is likely to lead to a backlash, it will choose a covert intervention. However, because of the lower effectiveness of covert interventions, the intervener is more likely to fail in such cases. Alternatively, when the intervener knows or receives information indicating that much of the target public is likely to respond positively to an overt intervention, it will choose this option. In such cases, where a backlash is unlikely to occur (or the expected backlash is far smaller in magnitude than the expected wave of increased support), the greater expected effectiveness of an overt intervention will lead the intervener to choose this option, increasing its chances of success. As a result of this strategic behavior, when an overt electoral intervention is used, the intervener is more likely to succeed. In contrast, when the intervener uses a covert intervention, it is more likely to fail.

H5: *Overt electoral interventions are more likely than covert electoral interventions to benefit the aided candidate or party.*

Another factor which affects the effectiveness of electoral interventions is the target's experience with competitive elections. The political information that the client has about voter preferences and the best ways to manipulate an election does not come "out of the blue"; rather, it is usually derived from the client's experience in conducting one or more previous competitive (or relatively competitive) elections in the target.[49] As a result, in situations where a given country has no experience, or no recent experience, with competitive elections, the quality of the information usually available to the client is quite low or insufficient. For example, as one anonymous member of the International Republican Institute (IRI) team sent by the U.S. government to help the Romanian opposition in the first post-Communist elections noted about the opposition's political experience

---

lead to a counterproductive backlash against it or getting "nothing" to assist it in its bad political situation.

[48] See, for example, James Conant Oral History, Conant Papers, Pusey Library, Harvard University.
[49] For the great importance of previous national-level elections in teaching parties how to successfully compete for office see Anderson (2009:772).

and knowledge, "They were like children. They were at the sixth grade level politically" (in Carothers 1996:38).[50] Twenty-one years earlier, the U.S. Ambassador to Thailand had complained in a secret telegram that the Thai government which the U.S. was trying to assist in the 1969 elections "betrayed a woeful lack of understanding" of how democratic politics and elections worked after more than a decade of uninterrupted authoritarianism.[51]

In such situations, even perfectly rational domestic actors may frequently make significant tactical and strategic mistakes when trying to improve their political fortunes. For example, the literature on the adoption of electoral systems has found that, in many new democracies, the quality and quantity of information on voter preferences, etc. available even to the major political actors were so meager or inaccurate that they often, in attempts to manipulate the electoral system in their favor, supported the adoption of, or changes to, an electoral system which severely damaged their political prospects. The rate of mistakes in electoral manipulation was found to greatly decrease once the relevant actors acquired some experience with competitive elections within their polities (Kaminski 2002; Shvetsova 2003).

Likewise, research on the determinants of the number of presidential candidates in presidential systems has found that in founding elections, due to this initial deficit of information about the electorate's preferences, the various political parties are less likely to effectively coordinate on choosing a common candidate or candidates, thus running in many cases a suboptimally large number of presidential candidates given the presidential election formula. In the following election, when more information has become available, this coordination failure is usually rectified by the relevant parties (Jones 2004: 81–83).[52]

When the target has no experience with competitive elections, as is the case in founding elections, the quality of the information that the client can provide to the intervener on how to help it win the election is usually quite low. In such situations, where the intervener has little to no sound "inside information" to guide its intervention, it is more likely that the electoral intervention will be insufficient and/or even counterproductive.[53] That, in turn, reduces the chances of the electoral intervention aiding in practice the preferred candidate/party.

---

[50] See also Thomas Friedman, "East Bloc Trip Buoys Baker Yet Alerts Him to the Odds," *New York Times*, February 12, 1990; and Mark Frankland, "East Adrift as the Masters Abandon Ship," *The Guardian*, December 10, 1989.

[51] FRUS 1964–1968 27: Document 408.

[52] Indeed, it is common practice in many lab experiments, in order to avoid getting misleading results due to such ignorance of the experiment's rules, to have the subjects play a trial round before the "real" experiment begins.

[53] As noted in the previous section, any experience/knowledge that the intervener may have with elections in its own country is of very limited utility on its own given the significant differences even between democratic countries and electorates and the lack of high quality knowledge of this type on other country's within the intervener. Accordingly, such experience cannot serve as a substitute to the lack of experience on the client's side.

H6: *Electoral interventions will be less likely to help an aided party/candidate competing in a founding election than in non-founding/later elections.*

A third factor that may affect the effectiveness of electoral interventions is the political position of the client prior to the election, that is, whether it is the challenger or the incumbent. Two contrasting predictions can be derived depending upon the literature consulted. The first prediction for this factor is derived from a major strand in the literature on the effects of campaign spending. In this strand of literature, both in American (Jacobson 1978; Kenny and McBurnett 1997; Jacobson 2006) and comparative politics (in many democracies) (Johnston and Pattie 1995; Forrest 1997; Palda and Palda 1998; Carty and Eagles 1999; Shin et al. 2005; Benoit and Marsh 2010), challengers usually benefit more than incumbents from an increase in campaign resources. Accordingly, we would expect an external intervention to benefit a challenger client more than an incumbent client.

This challenger advantage would exist for two reasons. First, the incumbent will usually have higher name recognition and be of more well-known quality than the challenger. As a result, the ability of the incumbent to use various resources in order to shift public opinion in their favor is far lower (Jacobson 1978: 469; Jacobson 2006: 205–206). Second, past election victories may make it harder for the incumbent, who usually starts with a higher base of prior support, to utilize available resources effectively, being at a more advanced stage of diminishing returns to campaign resources (Denver and Hands 1997a: 184).

The alternative prediction on this factor is derived from various literatures in IR and in intelligence studies. Extrapolating from these literatures, we would expect that, given the international-domestic dimension of interaction that is involved, efforts by a foreign actor to aid its preferred candidate would suffer from decided difficulties which wouldn't normally exist in interactions between purely domestic actors (i.e., between say local donors and a candidate). These difficulties would lead resources received by an external electoral intervention to differ in their effects from domestically gathered resources, aiding the incumbent client more than a challenger client.

This incumbency advantage would be so for two reasons. First, it is much easier for the external intervener to communicate and coordinate with the incumbent client than with a challenger client. As part of his or her control of the executive branch, the incumbent controls the state's foreign policy apparatus. Furthermore, due to being the legitimate government, secret recurring communication between it and other governments is an expected and legitimate part of the incumbent's duties. As a result, communication and coordination between the incumbent and an intervener in order to influence an upcoming election is relatively easy.

In contrast, the challenger has few established legitimate channels through which he or she can communicate with other governments. While such communication is, of course, achievable it is far more difficult to establish and regularly maintain. For example, in order to arrange a single meeting between himself and the leaders of the Chilean Christian Democratic party (when they were still part of the opposition) so as to determine whether to support it in the 1964 Chilean elections, President Kennedy had to organize a full academic conference on Latin America at George Washington University to which Eduardo Frei and other leaders of the Christian Democrats were invited as speakers. Their ostensible presence in Washington, D.C., for this purpose then created an opportunity for a secret meeting between Frei and the President (McCarthy 1972: 254–255).

As a result, coordination between the intervener and the challenger is harder to maintain for this purpose than between an intervener and an incumbent. Lower levels of coordination, in turn, increase the chances of miscommunications and mistakes by either side during the election campaign, thereby reducing the chances of success.

Second, it is harder for the intervener to provide sufficient aid to a challenger client than to the incumbent client both in covert and overt interventions. As scholars of covert operations have long noted, it is harder for an intelligence service to carry out covert activities in countries, even democratic ones, where the government has cool or hostile relations with their own government (for examples see Godson1995:44; Andrew and Mitrokhin 2005:chap. 17; Prados 2006:46). As a result, when the challenger is covertly aided, the operational environment will make it harder for the intervener to convey the electoral aid and vice versa. As for overt interventions, it is easier to find an effective (or more effective) way to intervene when an incumbent is aided. For example, when the incumbent is aided, positive inducements which can be provided immediately to the target public (foreign aid, conclusion of favorable agreements, etc.) are usually more feasible. Such positive inducements may often be more effective than positive inducements which include components which can only be carried out after an election (promises, etc.), as is usually the case when a challenger is aided in this manner.

H7: *Electoral interventions will differ in their effects between assisted incumbents and assisted challengers.*

2.4 Testing the Arguments

Abstract theorizing is of limited value unless there are ways to examine one's claims empirically. In order to test the arguments given in this chapter with regard to each of these components, this book will use two main methods: statistical analysis and historical case studies. The methods used in each case will depend on the nature of the problem investigated and data availability.

As for the first question—the causes of electoral interventions, given the nature of the argument proposed here—much of the data required in order to code and test this argument directly through statistical methods is very costly to collect and/or unavailable for many cases of Soviet/Russian and/or U.S. interventions. For example, the evidence required for testing a crucial component of this argument, that is, the existence of extensive cooperation between the great power intervention and the aided domestic actor, is usually among the types of data (identifying characteristics/names of the sources of particular information, etc.) which are the last to be declassified when documents on such interventions are released by the U.S. This is in contrast to the relatively more limited data needed for the coding for the other question (who intervened and when, which party was supported, methods of intervention, etc.). Likewise, some components (such as the great powers' threat perception) may be difficult to code cross-nationally in a fully satisfactory manner.

Nevertheless, three methods to test this argument are available and are used here. The first is to measure a proxy of one of the key conditions of this argument (the need for cooperation with a significant local domestic actor)—that is, whether the supported candidate and/or party is a fragile victor or a blocked/weakening loser. For that purpose I utilized a new dataset that I constructed called PEIG (Partisan Electoral Intervention by the Great-powers) of all cases of partisan electoral interventions by either the U.S. or the USSR/Russia between 1946 and 2000 (see further description here and in Chapter 5).[54] Each one of the cases of partisan electoral intervention in PEIG were coded as to the aforementioned proxy based upon available data (from various primary and secondary sources) about the client's political situation prior to the intervention. If this argument (esp. Hypothesis 2) is correct, then we would expect that in most of the cases of electoral intervention the beneficiaries of this intervention will exhibit this proxy condition.

The second method is the in-depth analysis of six case studies in which such interventions were done (or seriously considered) by a great power chosen out of the previously mentioned dataset and auxiliary data.[55] An article by Plümper,

---

[54] PEIG is freely available for download on the author's dataset at www.dovhlevin.com.

[55] In the course of collecting the data for PEIG, I also came across forty or so cases in which a partisan electoral intervention was seriously proposed or considered by the U.S. or the USSR/Russia

Table 2.2 The Case Studies (Possible Targets) by Selection Criteria

		GP Sees Implacable Actor B	
		Yes	No
Actor A Wants Aid	Yes	W. Germany 1953 Guatemala 1958 Argentina 1946	Philippines 1965
	No	Venezuela 1958	Greece 1967

Troeger, and Neumayer (2019) on qualitative case selection in such situations, based upon an in-depth Monte Carlo simulation of various suggested selection criteria in the literature, provides advice on case selection in such situations. It recommends completely ignoring the dependent variable and choosing the case studies based upon the independent variables in which the researcher is most interested. Within those independent variables the researcher should attempt to achieve as much variation as is possible. At the same time, variation on the other independent variables (or controls) should be minimized as much as possible. This case selection method also largely conforms with Seawright and Gerring's (2008: 300–301) description and recommendation of the "diverse" case selection design.

Accordingly, these six case studies were chosen on the two main independent variables of interest to the first part of this study (causes of electoral intervention): whether the great power perceives a particular domestic actor in the target as implacable or not and whether another domestic actor in the target wants or is willing to receive such electoral aid or not. Each one of the six cases represents one of the four possible combinations that these two independent variables can create (see Table 2.2) while keeping other possibly important "control" variables (period, intervener) as identical as possible (e.g., examining only cases in which the U.S. intervened or seriously thought of intervening).

A further benefit of this choice of case studies is that it controls for two of the most potentially important control variables: who the intervener is and the period in which the intervention is occurring (or proposed). As can be seen in

---

but no intervention was eventually done. This auxiliary dataset of non-interventions, unlike that of the cases of interventions, is not comprehensive. As some senior National Security Council (NSC) officials later noted, in direct contrast to approved covert activities, the NSC would frequently destroy (or leave unrecorded) proposals of covert operations, including for electoral interventions, which were eventually not approved (Kibbe 2002:30). Nevertheless, this auxiliary data, in combination with PEIG, could be useful as a locus from which cases for analyzing the causes of electoral interventions are chosen.

Table 2.2, all of these cases occurred during the same period (the first half of the Cold War) and were done (or not done) by the same intervener—the U.S.[56] Furthermore, each of these six countries was considered by American decision-makers during this period to be of major strategic importance for various reasons. All six test cases are analyzed using structured-focused comparison (George and Bennett 2005), checking, via process tracing and congruence, for the same set of observable implications in each process in which a would-be intervener decides whether to intervene or not.

For example, if the argument proposed here is correct, we would expect in cases of intervention to find the intervener perceiving one of the significant domestic actors in a particular country as someone with whom "they can't do business" either in general or on an issue seen as central to the relations between the two countries. We would expect this perception about that actor to be a major reason for the great power to seriously consider intervening against it in an upcoming election. We would expect to find a major effort by the great power to locate a suitable domestic partner for such an intervention and/or an "invitation to intervene" on its behalf by such an actor.

On the side of the domestic actor, we would expect the aided party to have agreed to, if not invited, the great-power intervention. Likewise, we would expect a domestic actor which has invited such an intervention (or agreed to accept one) to have suffered from severe political damage prior to requesting and/or accepting this aid (repeated electoral failures, major party splits, official/unofficial permanent exclusion from power, etc.) and/or, if in control of the executive, to be in a very tenuous political situation (weak/declining domestic support base, inferior organizational capabilities vs. main political rivals, etc.).

Furthermore, after an intervention is decided upon by the intervener, we would expect most of the significant specific acts done as part of the intervention (provision of covert funds, public threats/promises, etc.) to be decided upon and carried out in close cooperation between the intervener and the aided party/leader in the target. Indeed, the initiative for many of these specific acts (and the exact details of many of them) is expected to come from the target rather than the great-power intervener.

Finally, if only one of the just-mentioned conditions were present we wouldn't expect any significant electoral intervention to occur. A great power which sees all of the significant political actors in a given country as "acceptable" is expected to not be interested in intervening nor to allow itself to be pulled into an

---

[56] Choosing cases from this time period (the early Cold War) also assures us that sufficient information on the key aspects of interest, that is, usually secret interactions with local actors, would usually be available/declassified—which, given the high sensitivity of these intervention acts in many of the countries in question, and a desire by the U.S. government (and the CIA) to protect sources, frequently can take, as noted, a long time to come out.

intervention by one of the domestic actors requesting its help in an upcoming election. Likewise, if the great power sees one of the domestic actors as one with whom "they can't do business" but is unable to locate domestic help within the target, it is expected to usually prefer to "sit out" the election, waiting to see the election results before taking any significant actions. As for the domestic actor, it is expected not to accept an offer to intervene on its behalf nor make a request for a significant intervention when it perceives its political situation as relatively good or at least acceptable.

Naturally, this case selection method could lead to potential concerns about the applicability of findings from these six case studies to electoral interventions occurring in later periods and/or by other interveners with authoritarian regime types. In order to address (among other reasons) these concerns, in Chapter 8 I also conduct a preliminary analysis of the process that led to a seventh, more recent intervention case by a different intervener—the 2016 U.S. elections.

In order to collect the necessary data for this purpose I visited the various relevant archives where the required primary archival documents were available such as the U.S. National Archives at College Park, Maryland.[57] Secondary sources are used largely for factors not usually well covered by primary documents at these archives, such as the overall political situation of the relevant domestic actors.

A third, indirect method of testing this argument is through the statistical tests of some of the arguments about the effects of electoral interventions (Chapters 6). As was described in section 2.3, the first three hypotheses on the effects of electoral interventions (Hypotheses 4–6) are directly derived from my argument about the causes of such interventions. Accordingly, if most or all of these three hypotheses are confirmed, that would also indirectly strengthen our certainty in the argument about the causes of such interventions and vice versa.

As for the second question, the effects of such interventions on the election results in the target, I will examine it utilizing two different methods. The first method is a large-N statistical study utilizing a new dataset of all U.S. and Soviet/Russian partisan electoral interventions (see further description later in this chapter). This will be used to examine whether the probabilistic hypotheses posited as to the effects of such interventions are indeed accurate as to the universe of cases (i.e., whether the posited correlations exist).

A plausible model of the factors that affect cross-national voting, of the type frequently used in the economic voting literature, is required in order to investigate these hypotheses. Accordingly, I use the approach recently employed by two major scholars in this subfield, Timothy Hellwig and David Samuels (2007), and then add the relevant electoral intervention variables.

---

[57] See the list of archives visited for this purpose in the bibliography.

In order to investigate the main independent variable, great power electoral interventions, in a large-N framework, I constructed a dataset of all such interventions between January 1, 1946, and December 31, 2000[58] which were done by the U.S. and the USSR/Russia called PEIG. This focus was due to the unique availability of relatively complete data on covert electoral interventions performed by these two countries which was not available for other great powers. The former USSR/Russia is unusual among post-1945 authoritarian powers (i.e., China) in that summaries of the archives of its secret services for most of the 20th century were smuggled to the west by a defector (see later description). As for the U.S., due to a somewhat more relaxed declassification process for many of the relevant archives, the Pike and Church Committees,[59] and greater public/international interest, far more information is available on its post-1945 covert activities than for any other democratic great power (i.e., France or Britain).[60]

A partisan electoral intervention is defined in PEIG as a situation in which one or more sovereign countries intentionally undertakes specific actions to influence an upcoming election in another sovereign country in an overt or covert manner which they believe will favor or hurt one of the sides contesting that election and which incurs, or may incur, significant costs to the intervener(s) or the intervened country. This definition was chosen in order to capture, as closely as possible, the phenomena commonly referred to when partisan electoral interventions are publically discussed, proposed, and/or denounced. For the purpose of constructing the dataset, I operationalized such interventions as follows: in order to be coded as an electoral intervention, the acts done by the intervener[61] required an affirmative answer to two questions: (1)Was the act *intentionally* done in order to help or hurt one of the sides contesting the election for the executive? (2) Did the act clearly carry significant costs which were either (a) immediate (cost of subsidizing the preferred candidate's campaign/a covert intervention) and/or (b) longer-term/potential (loss of prestige/credibility if a public intervention fails and/or long-term damage to the relations once act

---

[58] The dataset stops at the end of 2000 in order to give time for information on great power covert interventions from the most recent past to "come out," thus reducing as much as possible the chances of missing cases of electoral interventions of this kind.

[59] Investigative committees set up by the U.S. House and Senate, respectively, in the mid-1970s in order to investigate the covert activities of the CIA.

[60] Data availability issues for many "smaller" states such as Iran, Saudi Arabia, or North Korea (as well as various restrictions on access to the archives of many democracies) makes the investigation of non-great power interventions of this kind also quite problematic at present—see Chapter 1.

[61] Acts done by private citizens of a great power on their own volition, such as American campaign consultants hired for pay by a candidate/party in another country to give it campaigning advice, are excluded. Activities by organizations largely funded by one great power, such as the NDI (National Democratic Institute) or IRI, are counted as a partisan intervention if the election-related assistance provided in the run-up to an election in a given country is designed so as to exclusively help only one particular side contesting it rather than being available to all interested parties/candidates (as is usually the case with the preceding examples).

Table 2.3 The Main Activities Coded and Used in Partisan Electoral Interventions

Main Activities Coded as Interventions
Provision of campaign funds to the favored side either directly (to candidate/party coffers) or indirectly.
Public and specific threats or promises by an official representative of intervening country
Training locals (of the preferred side only) in advanced campaigning and get-out-the-vote (GOTV) techniques
Dissemination of scandalous exposés/disinformation on rival candidates
Designing (for the preferred side only) of campaigning materials/sending campaigning experts to provide on-the-spot aid
Sudden new provision of foreign aid or a significant increase in existing aid and/or other forms of material assistance
Withdrawal of part or whole of aid, preferred trading conditions, loan guarantees, etc.

is done or exposed)?[62] Each case which is found to fit to these criteria is then coded as to other relevant aspects (covert/overt,[63] intervener, party/candidate supported, etc.).[64] A list of the main kinds of activities which fit this criteria and that are the most commonly used by the intervener for this purpose is presented in Table 2.3. Acts of a great power which do not fit one or more of these criteria are listed in Table 2.4.

An in-depth description of the main patterns found in PEIG is available in Chapter 5. A more detailed description of the way this definition was operationalized, the bibliographic sources consulted, and the data collection methods is provided in Appendix B. A detailed list of all 117 cases of partisan electoral interventions is provided in Appendix A. A further description of the statistical methodology used in order to test this large-N statistical study is available in Chapter 6.

The second method used in order to examine this question will be a single election level examination of the effects of such interventions on election results in select intervention cases. For that purpose, in Chapter 7 I examine survey data from elections in which such overt interventions had occurred and relevant questions were asked by the pollsters immediately before or very shortly after the election. Such data is available from two cases of intervened elections: West

[62] See Appendix B for a further description of how potential costs were defined.
[63] To be coded as a covert intervention, all of the significant acts done in order to help a particular party/candidate must have been either a secret and/or the connection between those acts and the election was not known to the average voter in the target.
[64] One should note that this definition of a partisan electoral intervention does not include in any manner cooperation between the intervener and the assisted side and, accordingly, cases were coded as such an intervention regardless of whether evidence was found or not for the occurrence of collusion (which, for the more recent intervention cases, was anyway highly unlikely to be yet available).

Table 2.4 Examples of Activities Not Coded as Partisan Electoral Interventions

Examples of Excluded Activities
Invitation of preferred candidate to international conferences, IOs, a visit to another country (unless it includes concrete concessions/promises as well)
Photo-ops/meetings of candidate with world leaders/official representatives of the intervener with no concrete results otherwise
Provision of foreign aid of various types in order to enable the holding of free elections and/or improve their quality (without subsequent attempts to affect the results)
Generic/neutral statements of support for the proper conduct of the electoral process (with no endorsements of a particular candidate/side)
Secret/open refusal of leader/officials of the intervener to publicly meet with a candidate or his/her representatives
Positive/negative things said about a candidate/party by the intervener before an election with no concrete threats/promises
Leaks to the press of reports of disagreements between the intervener and the target, etc. "Regular" election monitoring

Germany 1953 and Israel 1992. This single election level analysis will be used in order to examine whether the findings at the large-N level (and the theoretical arguments upon which they are based) are congruent overall with the micro-level patterns found in intervention cases (i.e., that the large-N correlations are not spurious). Chapter 8 will further examine that, to the greatest extent possible at present, in regard to a non-American electoral intervention—the Russian intervention in the 2016 U.S. elections.

The following chapters will implement this research design and test the seven hypotheses proposed here. In Chapters 3 and 4 I will begin to analyze the causes of electoral interventions directly via an in-depth analysis of six cases where an electoral intervention was seriously considered by the great power.

3

Throwing Their Hat into the Ring

When Electoral Interventions Occur

Why would Russia do this?
— Steve LeVine, *Quartz*, December 12, 2016[1]

The above question, asked frequently in the U.S. after the exposure of the Russian intervention in the 2016 U.S. election, is just the most recent inquiry of this kind in many countries in the aftermath of such overt or exposed meddling by various great powers. This chapter will begin to empirically investigate this question. In Chapter 2, I argued that electoral interventions usually occur when two concurrent conditions exist. The first is that a great power perceives its interests as being endangered by a significant candidate/party within a democratic target. This candidate/party has different and inflexible preferences on important issues— that is, the actor is either greatly constrained by his or her political base on these issues and/or is ideologically committed to particular positions. The second is the existence of another significant domestic actor within the target who wants (or is willing) to be aided in this manner. When these two conditions are missing, partisan electoral interventions will rarely, if ever, occur.

As one key component of investigating this argument, six cases were chosen from the PEIG dataset and auxiliary data (see the selection method in Chapter 2). In this chapter the first three cases are investigated (West Germany 1953, Guatemala 1958, and Argentina 1946) where both concurrent conditions are present (see Table 3.1). The next chapter will analyze the other three cases. Some additional notes on related historiographical points are noted in Appendix D.

In the analysis of all of these case studies I keep an eye out to avoid as much as possible, in Henri Bergson's memorable phrase, "the illusion of retrospective determinism," trying to comprehend and understand the range of possible election results and futures as seen by the relevant actors at the time rather than assuming that what eventually transpired in each case was bound to happen and that actors who believed, or planned, otherwise must have been misinformed or wrong.

[1] Steve LeVine, "FAQ: What you need to know about Russia's election hack and why U.S. senators say it 'should alarm every American,'" *Quartz*, December 12, 2016.

Meddling in the Ballot Box. Dov H. Levin, Oxford University Press (2020). © Oxford University Press.
DOI: 10.1093/oso/9780197519882.001.0001.

Table 3.1 The Case Studies (Possible Targets) by Selection Criteria (Investigated Cases in This Chapter Are Shaded)

		GP Sees Implacable Actor B	
		Yes	No
Actor A Wants Aid	Yes	W. Germany 1953 Guatemala 1958 Argentina 1946	Philippines 1965
	No	Venezuela 1958	Greece 1967

These cases are analyzed using structured-focused comparison[2] checking, via process tracing and congruence, for the same set of observable implications in each process in which a would-be intervening country decides whether to intervene in an election.

For example, if the argument proposed here is correct, we would expect in intervention cases to find the intervener perceiving one of the significant domestic actors in a particular country as someone with whom "they can't do business" either in general or on an issue seen as central to the relations between the two countries. We would expect this perception about that actor to be a major reason for the great power to seriously consider intervening against it in an upcoming election. We would expect to find a major effort by the great power to locate a suitable domestic partner for such an intervention and/or an "invitation to intervene" on its behalf by such an actor. Furthermore, if the great power happens to have more than one such potential willing partner, we would expect it to choose the one perceived as having stronger chances of winning.

On the side of the domestic actor, we would expect the aided party to have agreed to, if not invited, the great-power intervention. Likewise, we would expect a domestic actor who has invited such an intervention (or agreed to accept one) to have suffered from severe political damage prior to requesting and/or accepting this aid (repeated electoral failures, major party splits, official/unofficial permanent exclusion from power, etc.) and/or, if in control of the executive, to be in a very tenuous political situation (weak/declining domestic support base, inferior organizational capabilities vs. main political rivals, etc.).

Finally, after a partisan electoral intervention is decided upon, we would expect most of the significant specific acts done as part of the intervention to be decided upon and carried out in close cooperation between the intervener and

---

[2] George and Bennett 2005.

the aided party/leader in the target. Indeed, the initiative for many of these specific acts (and the exact way to conduct them) is expected to come from the target
rather than the great power intervener.

3.1 Saving a European Army: The 1953 West German Election

3.1.1 U.S. Interest in Germany in the Early 1950s

During the early Cold War, the United States had three important goals vis-à-vis
Western Germany (and Western Europe). The first was protecting West Germany
from future Soviet aggression. The second was creating a security framework
which would tie Germany to the West and prevent the inevitable future increase
in German material capabilities from leading it to threaten its neighbors yet
again. The third was to create the conditions which would enable the eventual
withdrawal of American troops from Germany in particular and from Europe in
general, the long-term presence of the latter there being seen by most American
decision-makers of the 1940s and 1950s as neither desirable policy-wise nor politically feasible, in American domestic terms, in the long run.[3]

In this context, the creation of the European Defense Community (hence
EDC) seemed to American decision-makers to be the perfect policy for achieving
all three goals simultaneously. The EDC was to be an EU circa 1990s–style organization differing from it in the focus of integration being on the military
sphere rather than on the economic one. It was to create among its six would-
be founding members (France, West Germany, Italy and the Benelux countries),
among other things, a common European military into which all German military units would be completely integrated and put under the control of a joint general staff. With such a large European military, of which West Germany would
be an inseparable part, the "German question" would be solved and Western
Europe would have the independent military capability for defending itself from
a possible Soviet attack, thus enabling the U.S. to eventually withdraw its military forces from Europe. Not surprisingly, getting West Germany and the other
five would-be members of the EDC to ratify the EDC agreement became the
main policy goal of the late Truman administration specifically vis-à-vis West
Germany.[4]

---

[3] Trachtenberg 1999; McAllister 2002.

[4] McAllister 2002:171–173, 214–215, 224.For details on the EDC see NATO notebook series, "The
European Defense Community," November 1,1953/Records pertaining to the EDC/box 1/U.S. embassy, Paris/Record Group 84 (henceforth RG84), U.S. National Archives in College Park, Maryland
(hence NARA). The reduced-sized divisions (or groupments) contributed by each member were to
be without logistical support (which was to be supplied at the integrated European Corp level), thus

The new Eisenhower administration was, if at all, even more dedicated to this policy. For example, as the new secretary of state, John Foster Dulles, described in the first State Department–JCS meeting in late January 1953, the EDC was so obviously superior to all other available options that the only reason he could see for any further internal discussion of alternatives was in order to create "dummy options" which he could use for bargaining pressure on signatories like West Germany who hadn't yet ratified the treaties.[5]

Likewise, Eisenhower firmly believed in the importance of approving the EDC as a way to achieve the three aforementioned policy goals. Indeed, his decision as the commander of the North Atlantic Treaty Organization (NATO) to endorse the EDC in mid-1951 was probably one major reason why the Truman administration decided to pursue the EDC after some initial skepticism as to its military viability.[6] Not surprisingly, in the early Eisenhower administration's policy document on Germany (the NSC 160/1) the EDC was described as the "most acceptable solution" to the various U.S. goals vis-à-vis Germany.[7] As a result, only after the EDC was eliminated once and for all as a viable option by its rejection in the French parliament in August 1954 was the U.S., despite its strenuous efforts, willing to give it up and accept other policy options for achieving these goals.[8]

3.1.2 The "Shaky Victors": Adenauer and the CDU

The Christian Democratic Union (hence CDU) is seen nowadays as a model of democratic political success, described by some as Germany's "natural party of government."[9] Likewise, its first chairman, Konrad Adenauer, who ruled Germany for a record-breaking fourteen straight years, is seen as one of Germany's greatest leaders. Indeed, some historians nowadays even name this whole period in German history as "the Adenauer Era."[10] Adenauer and the CDU's eventual victory in the 1953 West German elections played an important role in both of these events.

Few observers of West German politics would have expected these developments in the early post-war years.[11] Indeed, this would have been

---

making it virtually impossible for any German ground units provided to the EDC to function independently of the common European army.

[5] Memorandum, January 28, 1953, in Foreign Relations of the United States (hence FRUS) 1952–1954 5:712–713.

[6] McAllister 2002:210–215.

[7] FRUS 1952–1954 7:514.

[8] McAllister 2002:230, 242–243.

[9] Glees 1996:88.

[10] See citations in Irving 2002:xvii–xviii.

[11] Schwarz 1995(1):420, 449; Nicholls 1997:72; Greystone Press 1964:170.

seen as a far more plausible occurrence as to its main competitor—the Social Democratic party (hence SPD) and its first two leaders, Kurt Schumacher and Erik Ollenhauer. The SPD was one of Germany's oldest and best known parties. It had begun gathering a significant following and already contesting elections in the late 19th century. During the Weimar era and until the rise of the Nazis in the early 1930s, the SPD was Germany's largest party and the prototypical example of the mass party. While the SPD, of course, suffered during the Nazi era from persecution, it quickly rebounded after WW2, recreating a strong, effective, and experienced party organization. By 1948, for example, it had nearly 900,000 members—more than any other German party.[12] In an era in which the mass party model still predominated,[13] this was a major competitive advantage. Furthermore, thanks to the efforts of its first postwar leader, Kurt Schumacher, the SPD, in contrast to the Weimar era, was a relatively cohesive party, which suffered from little factionalism.[14] It also benefited from the impeccable anti-Nazi credentials of many of its leaders (a major plus in the post-WW2 era) with Schumacher, for example, widely admired for his staunch resistance to the Nazi regime which culminated in his having spent ten years in a concentration camp.[15]

Unsurprisingly, with much of the German right discredited, destroyed, or illegal and all of the previously mentioned advantages, the SPD was widely believed to be—or to quickly become—Germany's dominant party in the early post-war years. This belief was strengthened by the pre-1949 local election results in many of the occupied regions of West Germany in which the SPD greatly surpassed, by a significant margin, its pre-Nazi strength.[16]

The CDU's, and Adenauer's, situation was far less favorable. The Christian Democratic Party was a first-of-its-kind attempt to create a center-right party which transcended the class and religion (Catholic/Protestant) fault lines which characterized German politics during Weimar and beforehand.[17] In that effort they had had little pre-existing popular following to depend upon. For example, the Weimar-era party which Adenauer and many other CDU leaders had left, the Zentrum (the Catholic party), rarely got more than 10%–14% of the votes during that era.[18] Likewise, despite major efforts in this regard, the CDU still remained in this period a Catholic-dominated party both in membership and in voting patterns.[19] Not surprisingly, the CDU

---

[12] Edinger 1965:104, 139, 142, 194–195.
[13] Duvarger 1954.
[14] Edinger 1965:111.
[15] Ibid.: 65, 104, 190.
[16] Edinger 1965:139, 195, 199; Germany 1964:170.
[17] Irving 2002:60; Schwarz 1995:335–336.
[18] Edinger 1965:196; Nohlen and Strover 2010:776–777.
[19] Nicolls 1997:88.

consistently had far less members then the SPD, a problem which became worse by 1953.[20]

The relatively low membership also reflected lower organizational strength and effectiveness of the CDU. The party organization was quite dysfunctional during the 1949 elections. After the 1949 elections, despite some efforts in this regard, little significant improvement had occurred. As one local CDU party functionary complained, the CDU organization was "a purely Platonic affair. The fact that it is such, constitutes one of our prime weaknesses."[21]

Konrad Adenauer's own personal political position was not much better at this point. Before the rise of Hitler, Adenauer's highest political achievement was becoming the mayor of Cologne—the German equivalent of being, say, the mayor of San Diego. In that position, despite some local achievements, he was locally known for his financial mismanagement and was not very popular. Indeed, he had barely won his last (pre-Nazi, pre-Depression) mayoral election in 1929.[22] After WW2, despite his centrality in the creation of the CDU, he was a virtual unknown to the West German public. Indeed, one post-election poll, conducted shortly *after* Adenauer was named as the first Post-WW2 German chancellor, found that only 34% of the West German public even knew who he was.[23]

To this was added the age factor. Adenauer was already seventy-seven years old in 1953, an unusually old age for heads of government even by the standards of that era. Adenauer also suffered from various age-related illnesses. Indeed, in order to convince the CDU leadership to let him become chancellor in 1949 he had to bring a testimonial from his personal doctor confirming that he could do this job for about two years.[24] Therefore in early 1953, he was still widely seen as a temporary, transitional figure.[25] In this situation, any loss of power by the CDU was likely to completely end Adenauer's political career.

Due to all of these factors, in the run-up to the 1949 elections the SPD was widely expected to win and Schumacher was expected to become chancellor.[26]

---

[20] For example, despite declines in membership in both parties in the early 1950s for various reasons, the CDU's party membership dropped more drastically to a third of the SPD by 1954 (215,000 vs. 627,000) (Edinger 1965:107; Irving 2002:159).

[21] Heindenheimer 1960: 197, 200; Irving 2002:61, 64, 159–160.

[22] Irving 2002:34–37.

[23] Edinger 1965:217–218.

[24] Adenauer was the oldest member of the Bundestag after the 1953 elections. "Dr. Adenauer to Remain Foreign Minister," *The Guardian*, September 10, 1953; Granieri 1996:61–62.

[25] Kastner 1999:8; Schwarz 1995 (1): 413–414, 449.

[26] Kathleen McLaughlin, "Social Democrats Favored," *New York Times*, August 9, 1949; Flora Lewis, "The Hard-Bitten Herr Schumacher," *New York Times*, July 31, 1949; "Nationalism Is Ticket in Reich Today," *Washington Post*, August 14, 1949; see also Thayer 1957:138; Edinger 1965:139, 195; James Conant's unfinished draft book manuscript, "My Six Years in Germany," 3–4, 3–5, German ambassadorship drafts and diary entries/box 11/Conant Papers/Pusey Library, Harvard. Few people expected, of course, that the SPD would win an absolute majority. However, in multi-party parliamentary systems a party can be an effectively dominant party without needing to win

However, the CDU was able to eke out a bare victory (31% to 29.2%). Most likely, this was due to a major last-moment blunder by Schumacher—calling the German Catholic Church, of which a large number of Germans were still devout members, "the Fifth Occupation Power."[27] Despite their victory, Adenauer and the CDU had no illusions as to their true political situation. The weakness of the CDU's position was repeatedly noted in various internal post-election discussions by Adenauer and other CDU members.[28]

After the election the situation didn't improve for Adenauer and the CDU. Adenauer had to create a shaky, four-party coalition in order to have a majority in the Bundestag. It barely won its first vote of confidence by a majority of one (in a 402-member legislature); it was Adenauer's own vote.[29] One reason why the SPD refused to join the government was its (widely shared) belief that a CDU-dominated coalition wouldn't survive for long. Indeed, Adenauer's coalition was so shaky that one major reason why he successfully opposed the inclusion in late 1949 of West Berlin in the Federal Republic as the twelfth Lander (or state) was his fear that the addition of a few new MPs from Berlin (a SPD stronghold) would suffice to endanger his coalition.[30]

After an initial honeymoon period, Adenauer's unpopular domestic and foreign policies (such as support for early German rearmament)[31] as well as economic difficulties led to a collapse in public approval, with only 24% in support by the second half of 1950. The situation slightly improved by 1952 but then dropped yet again, and by the last quarter of 1952 only 34% were in support. On the question of party support, the main issue of significance in a parliamentary system, the situation was even more dire. The CDU fell behind the SPD by August 1950 and remained consistently behind the SPD in every poll taken until the spring of 1953 (when the U.S. intervention began).[32]

This dire electoral situation was not reflected only in the opinion polls. In the multiple Lander elections between 1949 and 1952 (the German variant of midterms), the CDU vote share greatly dropped, winning on average only 25%. The SPD repeatedly defeated the CDU in these elections. Even worse, fragmentation on the right increased and various new smaller parties, such as the refugee party, began to siphon votes away from the CDU.[33] Indeed, a 1952 study done

an absolute majority—as the examples of the Swedish Social Democrats and Mapai/Labor in Israel (until 1977) show quite well.

[27]   Edinger 1965:208, 248; Schwarz 1995 (1): 429–430.
[28]   Schwarz 1995 (1): 431, 441; Irving 2002:77.
[29]   Irving 2002:76.
[30]   Schwarz 1995 (1): 441, 449–450; Nicholls 1997:72; Trachtenberg 1999:131.
[31]   This was an initiative of Adenauer—not a policy encouraged or imposed by the U.S. which was not yet interested in 1950 in German rearmament (Schwarz 1995 [1]: 522, 527–528, 590).
[32]   Noell and Neumann 1967:256–257, 400; Drummond 1982:54–55.
[33]   Irving 2002:78; Drummond 1982:56–57, 70–71.

by the U.S. government based on the aforementioned Lander results estimated that, if these vote share trends continued, the SPD would decisively defeat the CDU in the next general elections. A similar conclusion was reached in a subsequent, widely propagated, West German study.[34] Many informed observers of the German political scene during 1952 saw Adenauer's political situation as precarious and the SPD's Schumacher as the likely next German chancellor.[35]

Economically, things weren't much better. Although the German economy (after an initial crisis in early 1950) had begun to recover from the effects of WW2 under Adenauer, by the beginning of 1953 it still hadn't reached the "economic miracle" stage for which it was to be known later in the 1950s. In public perception at that time, whatever economic gains were achieved were greatly offset by the great sudden jump in prices (of nearly 20%) due to the outbreak of the Korean War. Not surprisingly, by late 1952 polls have consistently shown a large plurality (47%) in support of the SPD's economic agenda while only 29%, a drop of 8% in comparison to a year before, supported the alternative proposed by the CDU.[36]

3.1.3 The U.S. View of the SPD and the Decision to Intervene

The American problem with the SPD in the early 1950s had little to do with either its democratic character or its position toward the Soviet Union or communism. The SPD was the only major German party which had opposed the 1933 enabling act that ushered in the Third Reich. Much of the SPD's postwar leadership was composed of people who had either spent much of the Nazi era in various concentration camps due to their open opposition to Hitler (such as Schumacher) or had been in exile, many actively aiding the allies during WW2 (such as Ollenhauer).[37] Likewise, the SPD's anti-communist credentials, despite its socialist ideology, weren't in doubt. Schumacher and the SPD leadership, as well as its rank and file, became well known for their complete rejection of communism in general and the USSR in particular, successfully resisting a Soviet attempt in the immediate aftermath of WW2 to amalgamate the SPD with the Communist Party throughout Germany.[38] This staunch anti-communist position was openly

---

[34] Edinger 1965:230; Bonn despatch 1775, December 29,1952/Central Decimal Files, file number 762a.00/Record Group 59 (hence RG59)/NARA. As late as July 1953, with the intervention in full swing, the CIA in an optimistic study on Adenauer's election prospects still expected the SPD to get more votes. See *Current Intelligence Weekly*, July 31, 1953, CIA Records Search Tool (hence CREST).

[35] Felix 1952:72; Lania 1952:13.

[36] Spicka 2007:96–98, 102. Not surprisingly, it was not until April 1953, after the intervention was already underway, that the percentage of Germans who believed that they were better off (24%) higher than that of those who felt like they were worse off (Spicka 2007:101).

[37] Mauch and Reimer 2003:174; Edinger 1965:48–53.

[38] Edinger 1965: 99–104; Schwartz 1991:54.

admitted even by senior U.S. policymakers such as Dean Acheson, who viewed Schumacher and the SPD as a major threat to U.S. interests.[39] The problem instead came from severe disagreements with it over the EDC.

In the beginning of the postwar era, the U.S. had no problem with the SPD being in power in West Germany. For example, in August 1949 the U.S. government secretly concluded that the best post-election result from its point of view would be a coalition between the SPD and the CDU. Indeed, a CDU-dominated coalition (as was eventually the result) was seen as an inferior, even problematic result in the U.S. view.[40] After the election, despite the fact that a contentious early November 1949 meeting between Schumacher and Secretary of State Acheson seems to have led Acheson to dislike Schumacher, the U.S., until at least the end of 1950, still saw a possible CDU-SPD coalition government as an acceptable, if not the preferable, option.[41] Indeed, after one rather stormy parliamentary debate between Adenauer and Schumacher in November 1949 the U.S. High Commissioner John McCloy described both of them in a secret cable as "problem children."[42]

From the point of view of the Truman administration, the final break seems to have occurred during 1951, mostly over U.S. plans for European integration, first over the European Coal and Steel Community (ECSC) and then over German rearmament and the EDC. Both treaties but especially the EDC were denounced in strong nationalist terms by the SPD. The EDC, for example, was opposed by the SPD as putting West Germany in a position of permanent inferiority vis-à-vis other European countries and, far more importantly, killing all chances at German reunification. As a result, as Schumacher declared in the Bundestag after the EDC treaty was signed in May 1952, "whoever approved" of the EDC "ceases to be a true German." The SPD then did everything possible to prevent the EDC's ratification. Likewise, in response to subsequent claims by McCloy in front of the Senate Foreign Affairs Committee that he (Schumacher) would nevertheless eventually accept the EDC, Schumacher declared that if in power he would not be bound by it.[43]

The SPD's continuing staunch public and private opposition to both treaties, but especially to the still unratified EDC, despite frequent attempts to enlist its support increasingly led the U.S. government to believe that Schumacher and the

[39] McAllister 2002:179; Brief, "Germany Policy and Problems," February 1953/CF136/box 21/lot/ RG59/NARA; Executive secretariat conference files; Memo, July 28,1953/762a.00/RG59/NARA.

[40] Report ORE 67-49, July 19, 1949/Papers of Harry S. Truman/PSF Intelligence File/box 257/ Harry S. Truman Library (hence HSTL).

[41] Schwartz 1991:185–186. Any negative impressions developed as a result of this meeting were probably milder than the effects of later developments; see FRUS 1949 3:312–314 vs. Princeton Seminars, October 10–11, 1953/box 75,767/Acheson papers/HSTL.

[42] FRUS 1949 3:353.

[43] Schwartz 1991:199, 276–277; Kisatsky 2005:45.

SPD were unacceptable. Accordingly, by mid-1952 Schumacher was viewed by the State Department as "the one man menacing the unity of Western Europe."[44] As Acheson described in a discussion with the French President Auriol in May 1952 following the signing of the EDC treaty the U.S., among other things, will need to "help him [Adenauer] to win the Bundestag elections of 1953," given "this alternative we have [to him]"—meaning Schumacher and the SPD.[45]

The SPDs staunch opposition to the EDC (and similar projects) came from a few sources. First, because of the strong Soviet opposition during this period to a reunified Germany with a pro-western orientation, the EDC was believed by many Germans to make German reunification, which required Soviet consent to give up its dominance over East Germany, impossible. As a result, joining the EDC was seen by many as akin to completely giving up on reunification in the short and medium terms.[46] Accordingly, the SPD's opposition to the EDC seemed to be based to a significant extent upon the genuine, deeply held preferences in many of the SPD leadership (shared by many Germans) for quick German reunification from patriotic or even personal motives. Ollenhauer, for example (like many SPD members), was born and grew up in what was, by the early 1950s, East Germany. Likewise, by late 1952, the only major thing that most of the party leadership could agree upon as to the SPDs foreign policy agenda was the primacy of doing everything possible to reunify Germany and opposing any acts which could prevent it.[47]

Nevertheless, this opposition also had a domestic political/strategic component. Schumacher, like other SPD leaders, believed that the main flaw in the SPD's policies during the Weimar era, a flaw that they saw as having enabled the rise of Nazism, was in permitting the other political parties to portray the SPD as insufficiently nationalistic. By taking up hard-line, nationalist positions in favor of German reunification it was thought that this would protect the SDP in advance from any attempts to use this card against it.[48] Likewise, such positions were expected to be useful in getting the vote of the nine million German refugees then residing in West Germany.[49]

[44] Schwartz 1991:199, 228, 245, 373; Edinger 1965:185.
[45] Schwarz 1995 1:687.
[46] For example, the March 1952 Soviet note explicitly made this demand a major prerequisite for its approval of German reunification (Steininger 1990:80). For an early expression of this SPD belief see Bonn despatch 1962 January 9,1952/EDC Germany to January 1953/Records Relating to the EDC 1951–1954/box 32/lot/RG59/NARA. See also Conant, "my Six years in Germany":3–8/German ambassadorship drafts and diary Entries/box 11/Conant Papers Pusey Library, Harvard. In private discussions some U.S. decision-makers agreed with this SPD assumption; Memo August 4, 1953/NSC 160.1(3)/box 6/WHO ONSNSA policy papers/Dwight D. Eisenhower Library (hence DDEL).
[47] Drummond 1982:93, 100–101.
[48] Vardy 1965:238–240, 242–243; Schwartz 1991:55.
[49] Schwartz 1991:55.

Given the reasons just stated, and despite some initial American hopes to the contrary, Schumacher's death in August 1952 did little to change the foreign policy positions of the SPD. Schumacher's replacement, Ollenhauer, was his trusted deputy and the man designated by Schumacher as his successor. Although more soft-spoken and mild-mannered, Ollenhauer seemed to completely agree with Schumacher's foreign policy views and policies. As a result, in the party congress conducted a month after Schumacher's death, the SPD readopted his foreign policy program, with Ollenhauer openly declaring that Schumacher's foreign policy was the SPD's policy "yesterday, today and tomorrow."[50] Not surprisingly, U.S. officials concluded that the death of Schumacher would lead to no significant change in the SPD's positions in the short or medium term. Indeed, Ollenhauer's milder political persona was initially seen by many as even a better vote-getter for the SPD than Schumacher's more aggressive persona and political style would.[51]

The following months showed little change in the SPD's position on the EDC. Using various political and constitutional delaying tactics the SPD forced Adenauer in December 1952 to not bring the EDC treaty to a third reading in the Bundestag as planned. Likewise, both publicly and in private talks, Ollenhauer and other SPD leaders reiterated their staunch opposition to the EDC and the SPD's intention, among other things, to reject and renegotiate the EDC if victorious in the upcoming elections.[52]

Not surprisingly, when the deputy high commissioner Samuel Reber was requested in mid-January 1953 to meet with Ollenhauer again about the SPD's foreign policy positions as to the EDC (and other related matters) Reber demurred, claiming that such a discussion would be ineffective and have no chance of changing the SPD's positions.[53] Likewise, when Eleanor Dulles, a high-ranking official in the State Department in charge of Berlin (and coincidentally John Foster Dulles's sister), visited Germany during January 1953 she concluded from the extensive conversations she conducted that the national SPD's foreign policy positions were "doctrinaire and unreasonable."[54]

The new Eisenhower administration, however, while strongly committed to the EDC, was initially more open-minded as to the political situation in West Germany. In sharp contrast to the attitudes which would later characterize the

---

[50] Drummond 1982:93–96.

[51] Bonn (telegram) 783 August 22,1952; Bonn 891 August 28,1952; Hamburg 116 August 29,1952, all 762a.00/RG59/NARA.

[52] Bonn 2873 December 19,1952/762a.00/RG59/NARA; Bonn despatch 1754 December 18,1952/762a.00/RG59/NARA; Bonn 3451 January 27,1953/740.5/RG59/NARA.

[53] Bonn 3355 January 21,1953/762a.00/RG59/NARA.

[54] Undated Report, "My impressions and comments on trip to Germany January 4–24, 1953"/Eleanor Dulles Papers/box 31/DDEL.

Eisenhower administration's relationship with Adenauer, it initially was quite wary and distrustful of him.

For example, Eisenhower's first meeting with Adenauer (as the commander of NATO) in January 1951 didn't go well, with Eisenhower coming out of the meeting quite angered by Adenauer's behavior and what he saw as a ham-handed attempt to get further American concessions in return for German military contributions to European defense.[55] Although later meetings went somewhat better, Eisenhower remained quite distrustful. Indeed, in early 1953 Eisenhower distrusted Adenauer and his claims to the point that one of the tasks that Dulles was given by Eisenhower during his visit and talks in Germany in February 1953 was to check whether Adenauer had actually hung up in his house a painting by Eisenhower as he had claimed when asked about it in late 1952. Eisenhower, an amateur painter, had given a painting of his to Adenauer, among other such paintings given to various European statesmen, when he had retired as NATO commander a year beforehand. When Dulles, during this trip to Germany, visited Adenauer's house and asked to see the painting, Adenauer—who indeed had Eisenhower's painting in storage—was able to distract Dulles in various ways until his staff got it hung up at the last moment in another room. Dulles failed to notice the deception.[56] Accordingly, the Eisenhower administration's decision in February 1953 to invite Adenauer to visit the U.S. in April (see later description) was initially just the fulfillment of a long-promised courtesy visit by the Truman administration going back to late 1951, a visit which was repeatedly delayed for various reasons.[57]

As for Dulles, the evidence indicates that prior to his first meeting with Adenauer in February 1953 he was still somewhat skeptical of Adenauer's full commitment to the EDC[58] and even afterward a certain level of distrust remained throughout 1953.[59] At the same time the SPD still seemed to Dulles to be a potentially acceptable option. Dulles seems to have initially thought that the SPD leadership's continued staunch opposition to the EDC was due to the SPD's belief (the result of various rumors circulating in Germany to that effect after

[55]   Schwarz 1995 (1): 621.

[56]   Schwarz 1995 (2): 46–48.

[57]   Maulucci 2003:578–579.The visit was also part of a preplanned set of visits by the major European leaders to the White House during March–April 1953, with Adenauer's visit being the final one (Maulucci 2003:579). One should note that at this point in time the Eisenhower administration was careful even at the minor protocol level to be impartial, making sure, for example, not to send to Adenauer an introductory letter for his meeting with Dulles in February 1953 which was warmer than the ones sent to other European statesmen. Memo January 22,1953/740.5/RG59/NARA.

[58]   State 3576 January 21,1953/762a.00/RG59/NARA; FRUS 1952–1954 7 (2): 1554.

[59]   See, for example, State 5049 April 27,1953/762a.00/RG59/NARA; State 4384 March 3,1953/762a.00/RG59/NARA; Hershberg 1993:669–673. The available evidence indicates that the famous Dulles-Adenauer friendship began, at the earliest, during the Berlin conference in January–February 1954 and probably much later (Grabbe 1990:110–111, 131).

the 1952 U.S. election) that the new Eisenhower administration would drop the Truman administration policy of strong support for the EDC, offering instead other, probably more palatable options, to the SPD. Accordingly, once this misunderstanding would be corrected, the SPD could be persuaded to change their position on the EDC to one more favorable to it and to the U.S.[60]

As a result of these American beliefs, the Eisenhower administration tried, at first, to reach out to and to clarify its position on the EDC to the SPD. After the new administration publicly affirmed its commitment to the EDC, Dulles decided to meet with the SPD leadership as part of his February 1953 visit to Germany in order to observe their position on the EDC and, if necessary, reiterate this point.[61]

The meeting did not go well. Despite the previously noted clarifications, Ollenhauer and the other two SPD leaders who accompanied him continued to oppose the EDC, proposing instead other, rather vague solutions for German defense. Dulles seems to have been so angered by the SPD's intransigence that he cut off Ollenhauer before he finished talking and gave a long monologue in which he described the SPD's proposals, as well as any other alternatives to the EDC, as unacceptable. He then repeated these positions in a subsequent press conference.[62]

Likewise, whatever hopes Dulles may have had for the effects of his harangue on the SPD's positions seem to have been quickly dashed. As multiple cables and analyses from the CIA and the High Commission in Germany indicated in the subsequent weeks, although after their meeting with Dulles Ollenhauer and the SPD leadership clearly understood the Eisenhower administration's position, their opposition to the EDC remained unchanged.[63] Accordingly, by mid-March 1953, a secret briefing paper accompanying the NSC 149/2 noted that a "Victory of the Social Democrats [in the upcoming elections] would mean control of [West] Germany by a party which is anti-EDC and which would be much less

[60] FRUS 1952–1954 7 (1): 399–400. Dulles's belief was shared by other officials in the State Department. Background paper December 13,1952/740.5/RG59/NARA. For reports on these rumors and the SPD's possible belief in them, see Bonn 3297 January 16,1953/762a.00/RG59/NARA; Bonn despatch 1718 December 17,1952/762a.00/RG59/NARA; Bonn despatch 1666 December 11,1952/762a.00/RG59/NARA. This rumor seems to have been made credible in the eyes of the SPD due to claims to this effect by former German chancellor Bruning, who was seen, due to his long American exile, as a U.S. expert, and other recent visitors to the U.S. Background paper, December 13,1952/740.5/RG59/NARA.

[61] FRUS 1952–1954 7 (1): 397–400; Telcom, Dulles to Conant January 23, 1953/Telephone call series/box 1/Dulles Papers/DDEL; FRUS 1952–1954 5 (2): 1554. Dulles's meeting with the SPD was preceded by a similar private meeting for this purpose by Reber (Bonn 3297 January 16,1953/ 762a.00/RG59/NARA).

[62] See the unsigned and undated memorandum of this meeting in CF137/lot/box 21/RG59/ NARA; Executive secretariat conference files and Schwarz 1995 (2): 46; Drummond 1982:101.

[63] Current Intelligence Bulletin, February 11,1953, CREST; Bonn despatch 2385 February 12,1953; Bonn despatch 2435 February 17,1953; Bonn 2871 March 19,1953 all 762a.00/RG59/NARA.

cooperative than the Adenauer government in contributing to the effective defense of the NATO area." Besides guaranteeing the death of the EDC, such an SPD victory would also mean, among other things given the general international context, that there would be no German military contribution to western defense in the foreseeable future and a general decline in European cooperation through other routes.[64]

Not surprisingly, when Adenauer requested in mid-March via a secret messenger to John McCloy, then-CEO of Chase Manhattan bank and a former High Commissioner to Germany, that the U.S. government intervene in his favor in the upcoming German elections through various measures to be provided during his upcoming trip to the U.S.,[65] the Eisenhower administration quickly decided to agree to his request and to help him in his upcoming election campaign. As Dulles described it, the Adenauer government needed to be helped in the upcoming elections because a SPD victory "owing to the SPD's strong anti-EDC position" would effectively kill the EDC.[66]

Despite Adenauer's desire to obtain at least some of the items on his "shopping list" of requested electoral aid (see subsections 3.2.1–3.2.2) as part of his April 1953 visit to the U.S., the Eisenhower administration was unable to immediately satisfy most of his requests, for various reasons. This made Adenauer's visit largely symbolic in nature.[67] For example, the Eisenhower administration, less than three months in office, was still in the process of getting its "sea legs," leading to various delays in getting some of the relevant requests done in time.[68] Likewise, during this period, the Eisenhower administration was facing heavy pressure from the Republican-held Congress to use the newfound Republican control of government to significantly cut foreign aid. This pressure was so severe that it led at one point to a shouting match between Eisenhower and Senate Speaker Robert Taft. As a result, the Eisenhower administration was politically incapable of granting one of Adenauer's requests for a new and very large grant or loan ($100 million to $250 million) for resettling German refugees, although

---

[64] NSC 149/2 background papers/Disaster file series/NSC Staff Papers/box 10/DDEL.

[65] The messenger, one of Adenauer's close personal aides, Herbert Blankenhorn, flew in especially for this purpose to the U.S., and then secretly met McCloy in his New York office. According to Blankenhorn, Adenauer justified his request for such electoral assistance by noting the continued opposition of the SPD to the EDC and warning of their advantage over him on the key German reunification issue (FRUS 1952–1954 7 (1): 405–408; Bonn 4340 March 24,1953/611.62a/RG59/NARA).

[66] FRUS 1952–1954 7 (1): 431–432, 434; FRUS 1952–1954 5 (2): 778; State 7236 May 7,1953/ 762a.00/RG59/NARA. See also Conant, "My Six Years in Germany":2–3, 2–5, German ambassadorship drafts and diary entries/box 11/Conant Papers.

[67] Although some relatively minor issues, like the long-planned return of 350 confiscated German ships, were nevertheless achieved.

[68] For examples see Telcon April 10,1953/White House Telephone conversations/telephone call series/box 10/Dulles papers/DDEL.

approximately $15 million in U.S. aid was eventually allocated before the election to German refugees in Berlin for this purpose.[69]

Nevertheless, partly as a result of the discussions during Adenauer's visit, over the following months the U.S. provided Adenauer with the costly requests on his list as well as later costly requests for electoral aid made by Adenauer.[70] The next section will describe the five major acts done by the Eisenhower administration for this purpose and the process by which they were accomplished.[71]

3.2 The Electoral Intervention

3.2.1 Reviving the U.S.–German Friendship, Commerce and Consular Relations Treaty

One significant way in which the U.S. aided Adenauer's reelection chances was by reviving the 1923 U.S.–German Treaty of Friendship, Commerce and Consular Relations a treaty which was suspended due to WW2. Despite its rather unimposing name, this treaty was quite significant, offering multiple commercial concessions which expedited trade between the two countries, such as equal treatment of exported products as to domestic taxes and the provision of treaty merchant visas to nationals of the other country.[72] The U.S. agreed to Adenauer's March 1953 request for the revival of this treaty which Adenauer believed would help his election prospects.[73] After speedy negotiations on an attached "small treaty," largely added in order to update the 1923 treaty to the conditions of the early 1950s, a draft was concluded.[74] Despite Adenauer's initial plans to have the

[69] Ambrose 1990:319–320; Inginmundarson 1994:470–471. See also FRUS 1952–1954 7 (1): 439–440, where this problem is implied to Adenauer.

[70] Other requests by Adenauer in the aforementioned memo which seem to have not been directly related to the West German election campaign, such as permitting Germany to start training some German soldiers in preparation for their later roles in western defense, seem to have been rejected by Dulles largely because of the fear of the possible effects that such acts may have upon the still-pending ratification of the EDC by France if/once they became public knowledge (FRUS 1952–1954 7 [1]: 416–417).

[71] Other, more minor acts included, for example, the ending of U.S. vesting of new German property in the U.S., the raising of the German chargé in D.C., as well as the U.S. high commissioner in Bonn, to a rank of ambassador and torpedoing a nearly successful attempt by the SPD to enable West Berlin, then under complete allied control, to send directly elected, voting members to the Bundestag. Due to space constraints, and in order not to tire the readers, these parts of the intervention are not discussed here in detail although they also fit my argument.

[72] Memorandum June 5,1953/320.1/RG466/NARA. Indeed, one major reason that the original version of this treaty in 1923 was negotiated and signed by the Harding administration was in order to help to stabilize the Weimar Republic at the height of the Ruhr crisis (Jonas 1984:173–175).

[73] Bonn 4340 March 24,1953/611.62a/RG59/NARA.

[74] Memo March 24,1953/611.62a/RG59/NARA; Brief April 2,1953/762a.00/RG59/NARA. For the interdepartmental fight within the U.S. government over the reactivation of some of these provisions, a fight eventually concluded in favor of Adenauer's requests; see the March 24 memo cited in note 73, and State 4761 March 31,1953/611.62a/RG59/NARA.

reactivation of the treaty signed during his April 1953 visit, the aforementioned "start of administration" difficulties of the Eisenhower administration prevented this from happening.[75] The reactivation of the treaty nevertheless was signed in an official ceremony in Bonn on June 5, three months before the elections, this action receiving, as was hoped by Adenauer, quite favorable domestic reactions.[76]

3.2.2 Establishment of Mixed Parole Boards for German War Criminals

Another significant way in which the U.S aided Adenauer's reelection was by the establishment of a mixed German-U.S. parole board for the early release of convicted German war criminals in U.S. and Allied prisons. Not long after the conclusion of the various war crime tribunals of the 1940s, a belief became widely entrenched in the general West German population that most of those Germans who were convicted for war crimes yet who weren't among Hitler's close associates were tried either as part of a vindictive "victors' justice" or as veiled political purges.[77]

Accordingly, despite some American public information efforts to explain the true nature of the crimes of those convicted on these charges, a survey conducted in October 1952 found that 63% of the West German population believed that those who were still imprisoned for war crimes in Allied jails were innocent. Indeed, by early 1953 American officials in Germany despaired of ever convincing them otherwise.[78] As a result, there was increasing public pressure within Germany for the release of the war criminals still imprisoned by the Allies and for the Adenauer government to do everything possible to achieve this goal. Indeed, at one point in 1952 this pressure was significant enough to endanger the continued survival of Adenauer's coalition.[79]

Not surprisingly, Adenauer searched for a way in which this hot-button issue could rebound to his electoral favor rather than to his disfavor. Accordingly, when asking for U.S. help in his reelection effort he requested that, prior to the election, a mixed parole board composed of German and Allied members be set up to consider the cases of the convicted German war criminals still imprisoned by the Allies. This was among the top of the items on his list, a request to which

---

[75] Bonn dispatch 3037 April 3,1953/320.1/RG466/NARA; FRUS 1952–1954 7 (1): 450.

[76] Memorandum June 5,1953/320.1/RG466/NARA; Bonn 4024 despatch, June 11,1953/762a.00/RG59/NARA.

[77] Schwartz 1991:157–160.

[78] Political brief 5, January 29, 1953, in Bonn despatch 2369 February 17,1953/762a.00/RG59/NARA. For some of the U.S. public information efforts see Bonn 1781 October 20,1952/321.6/RG466/NARA.

[79] Buscher 1988:164–165.

Adenauer attached "great importance" because, as he described it, of the significant electoral benefits which could be accrued from the public perception within Germany that this "problem" was on its way toward satisfactory resolution.[80] As a result of Adenauer's April 1953 talks during the visit about this topic (among other things), Dulles decided to agree to this request, promising Adenauer that the U.S. would " do all that it can in this regard."[81]

The release or the creation of methods by which convicted war criminals could be speedily released were already in the 1950s acts with significant potential political costs both domestically and internationally, costs which clearly worried the Eisenhower administration.[82] Internationally, any such early releases could lead to public condemnation of the U.S. in countries which had felt the wrath of Nazi Germany. Many of these countries were among the U.S.'s most important democratic allies in this period, such as France and Britain. Even worse, for such a mixed board to be applicable to many of these German war criminals it required the consent of France and Britain, yet the leaders of both, especially France, were opposed to such acts.[83] Domestically, such acts had the potential of leading to a major public outcry, especially from groups whose brethren had suffered greatly at the hands of many of these war criminals during WW2.[84]

The Eisenhower administration had a good reason to worry of such possible effects. For example, in January 1951 the Truman administration commuted the penalties of seventy-nine convicted war criminals in American prisons. That act led to widespread and intense condemnation of these commutations throughout Western Europe (sans Germany) as well as some highly negative reactions within the U.S.[85]

Nevertheless, following repeated reminders by Adenauer of how helpful a mixed board would be to his reelection chances,[86] the U.S., as promised, convinced Britain to consent to it. It then put increasing pressures over Spring 1953

---

[80]   FRUS 1952–1954 7 (1):420, 434, 442–443; Bonn 4340 March 24,1953/611.62a/RG59/NARA.

[81]   FRUS 1952–1954 7 (1): 443–444; FRUS 1952–1954 5 (2): 1589.

[82]   For the Eisenhower administration's fears in this regard and Adenauer's attempts to reassure them see FRUS 1952–1954 7 (1): 442.

[83]   FRUS 1952–1954 5 (2): 1629–1630; Negotiating paper April 1953/762a.00/RG59/NARA.

[84]   Schwartz 1991:161; FRUS 1952–1954 7 (1): 442–443. For the potentially explosive nature of some of these German war crimes, such as the murder of American POWs, see Bonn despatch 1658 December 22,1952/321.6/ RG466/NARA.

[85]   Schwartz 1991:168–171, 355. In theory this issue was already resolved with a special procedure (Article 6) in the May 1952 EDC treaty which was supposed to come into effect once the EDC treaty was ratified by all signatories. However, the delays in the full ratification of the EDC, which by early 1953 was not seen as occurring before early 1954 at the earliest, coupled with the increasing possibility that the EDC might fail nevertheless due to French actions, rendered this concession increasingly theoretical and meaningless (Buscher 1988:97). Furthermore, as shown in the earlier part of this section, creating a procedure for releasing war criminals earlier than would be the case if the U.S. just waited for the ratification of the EDC started anew the whole political/PR problem for those involved.

[86]   FRUS 1952–1954 7 (1): 468–469.

on the French government to consent to Adenauer's request as well.[87] In July 1953, right before the Tripartite talks, the French relented to U.S. pressure, offering, largely for face-saving purposes, a few slight modifications of Adenauer's proposed release method such as the creation of three separate mixed boards for the U.S., France, and Britain, respectively, rather than one joint board. During these talks the U.S. (and Adenauer) agreed to these minor face-saving changes.[88] A few days after the conclusion of the Tripartite talks, the announcement of this decision was made public.[89]

Following further pressure in mid-August 1953 from the West German government for concrete, visible pre-election evidence that the mixed commissions had begun to function, High Commissioner James Conant quickly announced the establishment of the three parole boards on September 1, five days before the elections.[90] The American desire to help Adenauer in this regard can be seen from the fact that this declaration was so hastily done that it came prior even to the internal approval of the rules of the board or, for that matter, the naming of the chairman of the American mixed board.[91]

After the elections, the mixed boards worked as planned, releasing in the following eighteen months more than 85% of the 525 German war criminals still imprisoned in early 1953 by the U.S., Britain, and France.[92]

3.2.3 Creating a Food Aid Program for East Germany

A third significant way in which the U.S. helped Adenauer's reelection chances was by agreeing to contribute $15 million ($111 million in 2016 dollars) to a food aid program for East Germans. This program was the result of a completely unexpected event, both on the communist and the western side—a first-of-its-kind popular uprising against a communist regime in Eastern Europe.

On June 16, 1953, the East German uprising began. A demand for a 10% increase in work requirements from East German industrial workers served as the last straw to the East German population. The East Germans were already quite angry at the crash collectivization conducted by the communist regime while,

---

[87] FRUS 1952–1954 5 (1): 1591; State 7236 May 7,1953; London 6144 May 18,1953 both 762a.00/RG59/NARA; Brief "German war criminals," July 9,1953/396.1-wa/RG59/NARA.

[88] Bonn 128 July 7,1953/321.6/RG466/NARA; FRUS 1952–1954 5 (2): 1629–1630. As the U.S. brief on this topic before the conference noted, the solution of the war criminal issue was "considered urgent and important [in order] to help Adenauer in [the] elections" (Brief, "German war criminals" July 9,1953/396.1-wa/RG59/NARA).

[89] Bonn 308, July 20,1953/321.6/RG466/NARA.

[90] Bonn 699 August 19,1953; Bonn 932 September 4,1953, both 321.6/RG466/NARA.

[91] Bonn 1249 undated; State 760 September 3,1953, both 321.6/RG466/NARA.

[92] Buscher 1988:110.

at the same time, they were encouraged by the rollback of some of the forced collectivization efforts which were included with this required increase in work requirements.[93] As a result, massive demonstrations and strikes erupted over much of East Berlin and East Germany and the East German regime temporarily lost control of parts of East Germany until the Soviet occupation troops intervened and fully repressed the uprising over the next few months, leading to the deaths and injuries of hundreds of East Germans.

With the uprising erupting less than three months before the West German elections, Adenauer was under growing West German public pressure to show (among other things) that he was "doing something" to help fellow Germans in East Germany who were suffering from the Soviet and East German crackdown.[94] A food aid program providing individual East Germans with large food packages and thus helping them deal with the frequent food shortages East Germany suffered from during this period was a good way to show that he "cared."[95]

In order, in Eisenhower's words, "to build Adenauer up" among other reasons, the U.S. decided to start a food aid operation to East Germany and provide $15 million) in food. This ultimately came to more than 33,000 metric tons of food of various types.[96] The U.S. also took a risk that such a plan, despite its nonviolent nature, would nevertheless be seen as so provocative to the Soviets that it would lead to a second blockade of West Berlin or to other aggressive Soviet reactions which, in turn, could bring about an unwanted superpower crisis.[97]

The decision to implement such a food aid program was a classic example of "great minds thinking alike"; both the West Germans and the Eisenhower administration came up with this idea simultaneously in the days following the uprising. The idea of providing food aid to the East Germans on humanitarian and/ or propaganda grounds was an idea which had long been discussed both within the West German government and within the Eisenhower administration, each rejecting it prior to the uprising for various reasons.[98] When the uprising began, both sides began thinking independently about such a program in order to help Adenauer's political chances, and in the American case, as will be seen later in this subsection, also to score propaganda points vis-à-vis the Soviet Union.[99]

---

[93] Inginmundarson 1996:388.

[94] See section 3.2.4 for the public pressure for more reunification efforts.

[95] "Adenauer Regime under Fire for Inaction on Riots in East," *New York Times*, July 29, 1953; FRUS 1952–1954, 7 (2): 1600–1603.

[96] Conversation August 1,1953/WH Telephone conversations/telephone call series/Box 10/ Dulles papers/DDEL; Bonn 1216 despatch November 3,1953/862b.49/RG59/NARA. Another 13,000 metric tons of food were taken out of the Allies' emergency food stockpile for Berlin, requiring subsequent replenishment by the U.S.

[97] FRUS 1952–1954 7 (2): 1620.

[98] Inginmundarson 1996:395.

[99] For the American idea see, for example, Memo June 19,1953/PSB 430(1)/Box 28/WHO NSC Staff papers/DDEL; for the German plan see Bonn 5456 June 25,1953/462a.62/RG59/NARA and

Indeed, the decisions of the U.S. administration and the Adenauer government to actually create such a program during the first week of July seems to have been made almost simultaneously with the German request for U.S. funding of such a program being sent as the U.S. government approved such a plan in principle.[100]

Nevertheless, once both sides began to coordinate in turning this general idea into action, the West Germans began to increasingly dominate how the food aid program was implemented in practice. Adenauer's initial plan was to have the food aid provided via the German churches and other private German relief organizations which had already been sending, long before the uprising, food and other private aid to the East Germans. The U.S. government decided to largely accept Adenauer's plan for the distribution of this aid, even formally adopting it when the detailed food aid plan came up for approval within the administration on July 7, 1953.[101] When Adenauer's plan was subsequently found to be unfeasible due to technical reasons as well as the refusal of the German churches and private relief groups to take part, the U.S. decided by mid-July 1953 to adopt a different West German government plan. This plan, using West Berlin and German government officials to give out food packages from special aid centers located in municipal facilities in West Berlin, was one of the four options proposed by the West German cabinet.[102] This plan was to be the principal way through which the food aid was distributed in practice in the following months.

With the food aid program starting to become a reality, a disagreement still remained over the way in which the program's publicity/propaganda aspects were to be handled. The West German government wanted as low-key an approach as possible toward the food aid operation. In order to deal with the West German public's sensitivity to any act which seemed like "cheap" propaganda, and to prevent a possible backlash to acts perceived in that manner, the food aid was to be, as much as possible, humanitarian in appearance, with the factual reporting of the "good deeds" in and of themselves providing most of the public relations benefits. Likewise, in order for Adenauer to get the credit (and

FRUS 1952–1954, 7 (2): 1600–1603. One should note nevertheless that when the Eisenhower administration was thinking about whether to implement such a plan it knew that the West German government was probably also thinking about similar ideas, making German agreement to such U.S. plans very likely. For its knowledge of similar German plans see Bonn 5456 June 25,1953/462a.62/RG59/NARA; State 5 July 1,1953/862b.03/RG59/NARA.

[100] State 20 July 2,1953/862b.03/RG59/NARA; FRUS 1952–1954 7 (2): 1600–1603.
[101] Memo July 7,1953/862b.49/RG59/NARA.
[102] Bonn 280 July 17,1953/CD Jackson records/box 3/DDEL; Bonn 254 July 18,1953/862b.49/RG59/NARA. Another local German actor, West Berlin Mayor Ernest Reuter, seems to have also had an important role in the process by which this option was developed and eventually approved.

the electoral benefit), they wanted the U.S. role in this operation to be noted but not emphasized.[103]

In contrast, the Eisenhower administration wanted far more publicity and propaganda operations involved. Initially, the other main goal of the food aid operation in the eyes of much of the Eisenhower administration (besides helping Adenauer's chances) was to achieve a major, European-level propaganda victory in the Cold War. Not satisfied with the natural, "local" (i.e., largely limited to the German population) propaganda benefits which were expected to be achieved from doing such an act in public, they wanted to step up the U.S. propaganda efforts in order to gain more large-scale results. By first emphasizing the U.S. role in the food aid operation and providing very high amounts of publicity around the world through all available means and then repeatedly forcing the Soviets to reject public American offers to permit such food aid into East Germany (after the initial U.S. offer was turned down on July 11), the administration was hoping to gain a major propaganda victory not just vis-à-vis Germany but in the general east–west struggle.[104] There was also significant pressure in the American media as well as within the Republican-dominated congress for such a "high key" approach.[105]

However, with the help of High Commissioner Conant, the low-key approach was nevertheless eventually chosen by the Eisenhower administration, largely because of Adenauer's electoral needs. As a result, the Eisenhower administration decided to drop most of the proposed high-key propaganda efforts (such as a second public offer of the food aid to the Soviets), largely leaving the food aid to "speak" for itself.[106] By the time the program ended in early October 1953, a few weeks after the elections, approximately 5.6 million food packages had been provided to needy East Germans with few significant problems and to near universal acclaim by the West German population.[107]

---

[103] FRUS 1952–1954 7 (2): 1600–1603, 1621, 1629–1630; FRUS 1952–1954 5 (2): 1588–1589; Bonn 353 July 23,1953 and Bonn 394 July 25,1953, both in 862b.49/RG59/NARA. For the importance of the program being done in this manner due to German electoral needs see Bonn 1216 despatch November 3,1953/862b.49/RG59/NARA.

[104] FRUS 1952–1954 7 (2): 1620, 1631; Memo July 8,1953/CD Jackson records/box 3/DDEL. Some in the administration, such as Jackson, seem to have even hoped to use the food aid operation in order to lead to the "peaceful liberation" of East Germany following Eisenhower's 1952 campaign rhetoric about "rollback" FRUS 1952–1954 7 (2): 1637.

[105] FRUS 1952–1954 7 (2): 1638; Secretary staff meeting July 31,1953/Minutes and notes of the secretary staff meetings/box 5/lot/RG59/NARA.

[106] Bonn 1216 despatch November 3,1953/862b.49/RG59/NARA; Inginmundarson 1996:400.

[107] Bonn 1216 despatch November 3,1953/862b.49/RG59/NARA.

3.2.4   Agreeing to a Four Power Conference with the Soviet Union

A fourth significant way in which the U.S. aided Adenauer's reelection was by publicly agreeing to a Four Power conference with the Soviet Union. In the context of the early 1950s such a meeting was far from being some kind of a "talking shop" or a costless gesture. Having a high-level U.S.-Soviet meeting of this kind was seen as an act that could have major effects in either positive or negative directions, as did the similar "Big Three" conferences in Yalta or in Potsdam in the mid-1940s. If successful, such a conference could lead to a major mutually beneficial agreement on any of the long list of major issues in dispute between the U.S. and the Soviet Union, a major reduction in superpower tensions, and perhaps eventually a true end to the Cold War and a "new world order." Failure, either due to being out-maneuvered or duped by the Soviets into signing a bad agreement harmful to U.S. interests or due, thanks to Soviet propaganda and diplomacy, to being held responsible for the failure by either the domestic and/or international public opinion in Western Europe, could have major political and national security costs to the administration. Accordingly, such meetings usually required months of intense preparations by all involved. Agreeing to hold one was considered quite a significant and costly act by the U.S.[108]

Not surprisingly, the Eisenhower administration had little desire to hold such a meeting with what it saw as a devious opponent who neither had any desire to negotiate honestly nor showed any real flexibility in its positions.[109] This position was further fortified by mid-March 1953 (when, following Stalin's death, this issue began to be seriously raised) by the fear that agreeing to such a conference might also undermine western unity and perhaps even the political positions of the various pro-American regimes in Western Europe.[110] As a result, the Eisenhower administration did all in its power to prevent such a meeting from occurring. For example, when the British government repeatedly proposed such a major power meeting in the winter and spring of 1953, first in private conversations and then in public announcements, the U.S. immediately rejected

---

[108] Boyle 1990:32; Gardner 2006:79–80. The opposite opinion, held by some in the administration in the immediate aftermath of Stalin's death, that such a four power meeting could be a useful propaganda tool for the U.S. (rather than a costly risk to be avoided) given the USSR's temporary weakness due to the formers death, was rejected by both Eisenhower and Dulles in March 1953 (136th NSC meeting March 11, 1953, in the Declassified Documents Reference System [hence DDRS]). For the major preparatory effort involved in such a meeting see FRUS 1952–1954 8: 1112.

[109] Boyle 1990:32; 139th NSC meeting April 8, 1953, DDRS. The administration's view of the Soviets changed little after agreeing to a Four Power conference. FRUS 1952–1954 5: 1761. By late April 1953 it was willing, in private, to consider such a meeting but only on the condition that it was clearly limited in advance to a relatively minor set of issues—an idea which went nowhere (141st NSC meeting April 29, 1953, DDRS).

[110] 136th NSC meeting March 11,1953, DDRS.

the proposal. Indeed, the initial American reason for proposing a meeting between the U.S., Britain, and France in the early summer, eventually the tripartite
Foreign Ministers meeting of July 1953, was in order to prevent the British from
doing any further acts that would make such a U.S.-Soviet conference with a significant agenda impossible to prevent.[111] The fact that Adenauer at the time had
little desire for such a conference, which was quite likely to focus on Germany,
reinforced an already staunch U.S. opposition to this idea.[112]

As a result, despite the British desire for such a meeting, the U.S. continued
to oppose the idea. The eruption of the East German uprising in mid-June 1953
and the use of Soviet troops to repress the demonstrations initially appeared to
the Eisenhower administration to further justify its opposition. In Eisenhower's
words, the uprising gave the U.S. "the strongest possible argument" against
conducting such Four Power talks any time soon.[113] Indeed, one of the objectives
listed in the American delegation's briefing book, completed a day before the tripartite meeting started on July 10, was achieving an agreement with the French
and British not to hold such a conference any time soon.[114]

This American position then dramatically changed because of Adenauer's
last-moment request. The holding of a Four Power conference to discuss, and
perhaps achieve, German reunification was a major and longstanding SPD demand. Prior to the uprising, Adenauer and the CDU publicly supported such a
conference in principle but only under very narrow and special circumstances.
In private, they were completely opposed to such a conference being held any
time soon.[115]

Then, on June 16, 1953, the East German uprising began (see section 3.2.3).
The news of the massive revolt of fellow Germans against the East German regime turned yet again the issue of German reunification into a burning issue for
the West German public. It accordingly greatly increased public pressure within
West Germany for the most plausible route in 1953 for achieving this goal—a
Four Power conference in which the issue of German reunification would be
seriously discussed by the U.S. and the Soviets.[116] Likewise, the SPD which, in
the search for a good election issue against Adenauer and the CDU, had already
prior to the revolt been making more insistent demands for such a conference,
raised the heat on Adenauer once the uprising began for not doing more to get
such a conference under way. The SPD accordingly described the post-uprising

[111] Larres 2006:144.
[112] Schwarz 1995 2:54.
[113] FRUS 1952–1954 7 (2): 1589.
[114] FRUS 1952–1954 5:1604; see also the planned draft communiqué in FRUS 1952–1954
5:1601–1602.
[115] Bonn despatch 3877 June 4,1953; Bonn 5280 June 10,1953; Bonn 5321 June 13,1953, all three in
762a.00/RG59/NARA.
[116] Bonn 5485 June 26,1953/762a.00/RG59/NARA.

situation as a rare window of opportunity for such a conference on German re-unification which must not be missed and attacked Adenauer for not caring and doing enough about German reunification.[117]

Adenauer accordingly, in the days after the uprising, began to declare in public his strong support for such a Four Power conference and he ostensibly started to make serious efforts to get such a conference to occur. However, in private he continued to staunchly oppose a Four Power conference, even requesting at one point from the U.S. to disregard a letter that he had sent a few days after the up-rising started in support of such a conference, a letter which he claimed was sent only for "public consumption" purposes.[118]

Then, in the last few days prior to the tripartite meeting, Adenauer abruptly changed his mind. In an attempt to neutralize the SPD's demand for a confer-ence and their attacks on him, Adenauer decided to request from the U.S. (and France and Britain) to agree to a Four Power conference on Germany during the tripartite meeting and, after its conclusion, to make a formal public offer to the Soviets to hold one. This was on the condition that this conference would only be held after the elections. He then secretly sent one of his personal aides, Herbert Blankenhorn, as a confidential messenger to Washington, D.C., where the tripar-tite meeting had just begun that very day to convey his request both verbally and in a letter. As Blankenhorn described it, this request by Adenauer, and his sudden change of mind on this topic "was a tactical move designed to improve his posi-tion in the election campaign."[119]

Although the U.S., as well as France and Britain, were quite annoyed at Adenauer's "crashing" of the meeting, the Eisenhower administration decided to agree to Adenauer's request in order to help him in the election. Dulles then con-vinced France and Britain to agree as well, even handing out during the meeting copies of Adenauer's letters requesting this aid to help in this effort.[120] The U.S., with British assistance, then even permitted Adenauer to go over both the new draft communiqué on Germany and the agreement to a Four Power conference and the note to the Soviets formally requesting this conference and amend it so as to fit his electoral needs.[121] As promised by the U.S., the Four Power confer-ence was eventually held in Berlin after the elections in January–February 1954. It failed to achieve any significant progress on German reunification or on other issues in dispute between the two superpowers.

---

[117] Bonn 5280 June 10,1953/762a.00/RG59/NARA; Bonn despatch 4222 June 25,1953/762a.00/RG59/NARA; Bonn 31 priority July 1,1953/762a.00/RG59/NARA.

[118] Bonn 5445 June 24,1953/762a.00/RG59/NARA; FRUS 1952–1954 5 (2): 1587; for the letter see FRUS 1952–1954 7 (2): 1591.

[119] FRUS 1952–1954 5 (2): 1606–1607.

[120] FRUS 1952–1954 5 (2): 1616–1617; FRUS 1952–1954 5 (2): 1628; for Dulles handing out of Adenauer's letter during the meeting see State 197 July 11,1953/396.1-wa/RG59/NARA.

[121] FRUS 1952–1954 5 (2): 1672; FRUS 1952–1954 5 (2): 1691.

3.2.5 Threatening "Disastrous Effects"

A fifth significant way in which the U.S. aided Adenauer's reelection was achieved by Dulles publicly threatening, in an American press conference which took place two days before the elections, "disastrous effects" for Germany if Adenauer was not reelected. This threat of punitive U.S. actions echoed throughout Germany, becoming front-page news in West Germany and the main issue of the election campaign in its final days, with the SPD strongly denouncing it and the CDU supportive of it.[122] As the administration knew quite well, making such a public threat was quite risky and put U.S. credibility on the line.[123]

I was unable to find the direct request by Adenauer for this threat. Furthermore, some historians who note this statement, which came in a response to a reporter's question, even claim that it was an uncoordinated and unplanned gaffe.[124] However, the lack of the direct request note is not very surprising given Adenauer's penchant on sensitive issues, as seen in multiple occasions here, to bypass regular diplomatic channels and instead use various backchannels utilizing multiple methods and people (such as through Allen Dulles, John Foster Dulles's brother and head of the CIA).[125] Such communication methods often leave little documentary record. Nevertheless, there is strong indirect evidence that this threat was intentional and was done at Adenauer's request.[126]

First, from the available notes of subsequent private conversations of Dulles with Eisenhower and Vice President Nixon, it is clear that this threat was done in accordance with the intentions of Eisenhower on this matter. Likewise, in one conversation with Nixon on this topic, Dulles briefly refers to a favorable previous exchange of messages which he had with Adenauer on this issue.[127]

Secondly, Dulles frequently used such calculated diplomatic "indiscretions" in an intentional manner. Some examples include the Yoshida letter in 1952

---

[122] "Dulles Pins Blame on Soviet Policies," *New York Times*, September 4, 1953; "Abroad," *New York Times*, September 7, 1953.

[123] As Nixon colorfully described it in a pre-election conversation with Dulles on the threat, "all our money" was now put on Adenauer. Conversation Dulles-Nixon, September 5, 1953/box 5/Dulles Chronological series/Dulles papers/DDEL.

[124] See, for example, Schwarz 1995 2: 79.

[125] For repeated complaints throughout 1953 within the administration about Adenauer's excessive use of such methods see telephone conversations of Dulles with McCloy, Allen Dulles, and Eisenhower in March 27, 1953, Dulles Chronological series/box 4/Dulles papers/DDEL; November 19, 1953/telephone call series/box 2/Dulles papers/DDEL; and November 20, 1953/telephone call series/box 10/Dulles papers/DDEL. One should also note that Dulles was, for much of the two weeks prior to this press conference, on vacation, as was Eisenhower, which means that such a backchannel message was even less likely to be preserved than usual.

[126] See Ninkovich 1988:102 for a similar argument.

[127] Memo September 8, 1953/White House Correspondence/Dulles Memorandum Series/Box 1; Conversation Dulles-Nixon, September 5, 1953/box 5/Dulles Chronological series/Dulles papers/ DDEL. Conant also believed at the time that Adenauer and Dulles coordinated this threat behind his back. Scrapbook entry September 6, 1953/box 35/Conant Papers.

(when he was a special envoy under Truman) and again in 1954, a few months after this election, when he publicly warned the French of an "agonizing reappraisal" of U.S. policy toward Europe if the French parliament were to refuse to confirm the EDC.[128]

Thirdly, Adenauer was quite pleased with Dulles's statement, which he saw as a useful boost. Indeed, after Dulles made his statement, Adenauer sent a private note thanking him for this statement. This note was sent a day *before* the voting began and, of course, two days before the election results were known.[129] Publicly, Adenauer even quoted Dulles's statement as part of a speech he made in one of the last pre-election campaign rallies.[130] Despite the complacency of Conant and the rest of the American diplomatic corps in Bonn, who believed by late August 1953 that the CDU's victory was all but certain,[131] Adenauer clearly perceived a need for extra help. In the days preceding Dulles's statement, the race between the SPD and the CDU had tightened considerably after a significant gap opened in favor of the CDU during the summer of 1953. The last pre-threat election poll by Adenauer's pollster showed the SPD coming within 1 point of the CDU and Adenauer's personal approval rating dropping by 6 points.[132]

Furthermore, in the run-up to the elections, Adenauer, both before and after Dulles's statement, showed no fear that over-identification with the U.S. might lead to a domestic backlash against him, although many in the State Department, the High Commission, and at one point in late July even Dulles showed such fears. Instead, Adenauer believed (as he described in one meeting with Conant) that the West German public were either so grateful for past U.S. actions or so certain of their dependence on it for their future security that the reverse would be the case. As a result, in the months preceding the threat Adenauer looked, among other things, for every possible opportunity to demonstrate to the German public the friendliness of the U.S. government toward him.[133] Indeed, Dulles's statement fit perfectly within the line promoted by the CDU's election

[128] Hoopes 1973:112–113, 189. For the way in which Eisenhower admitted in private conversations his part in this "unplanned" statement by Dulles toward the French see supplementary notes, "Legislative Leadership Meeting" December 18,1953/Staff notes January–December 1953/Eisenhower Papers/Whitman Files/DDE diary/box4/DDEL. For the way in which the State Department initially planned to use this method, an answer to an "unexpected" question during a press conference, for its overt intervention in the April 1953 Japanese elections see FRUS 1952–1954 14(2): 1405, 1409–1411.

[129] Bonn 937 September 5,1953/762a.00/RG59/NARA.

[130] "Dulles Pins Blame on Soviet Policies," *New York Times*, September 4, 1953.

[131] FRUS 1952–1954 7 (1): 531.

[132] Schwarz 1995 (2): 78.

[133] FRUS 1952–1954 7 (1): 495–496; FRUS 1952–1954 7 (1): 499–500; Bonn 937 September 5,1953 762a.00/RG59/NARA. Letter, Conant to Eisenhower September 8, 1953/Eisenhower Papers (Ann Whitman Files)/ administrative series/box 10/DDEL.

campaign in which Adenauer, in Conant's words, "virtually ran on an American ticket."[134]

Following all the previously described U.S. acts in Adenauer's favor, the CDU and Adenauer won a decisive victory in the September 1953 Bundestag elections. The CDU greatly increased its vote share to 45.2%, while the SPD's vote share slightly dropped (28.8%), thus enabling Adenauer to remain in the Chancellorship.[135]

3.3 Déjà Vu All Over Again? The 1958 Guatemalan Election

3.3.1 U.S. Interests in Guatemala in the Late 1950s

In the late 1950s, the Eisenhower administration had two closely related key interests in regard to Guatemala. The first was to deny control of Guatemala to any regime hostile to the U.S. Due to its strategic location in Central America near the Panama Canal, and its relative proximity to the continental U.S. (930 miles from New Orleans), control of Guatemala by an unfriendly regime was seen by the Eisenhower administration as a highly threatening situation both in the case of a wider military conflict and in peacetime. In the case of a wider military conflict (a quite plausible event in the 1950s) a hostile regime in Guatemala was expected to serve as a location for military bases from which strategically vital U.S. trade with Latin America could be seriously disrupted and air and submarine attacks could be launched on the Panama Canal and the continental United States. The need to prevent and counter such attacks near the home front would significantly reduce American military capabilities elsewhere in the world. In peacetime such a hostile regime, if dominated or controlled by the Soviet Union, would serve as an "ideological springboard" for the spread of communism throughout the region, disrupt U.S.-Latin American security and trade arrangements, and eventually lead to a significant Soviet military presence at the U.S. doorstep.[136]

Accordingly, the U.S. government wanted to prevent a rerun of the events under the Averalo and Arbenz presidencies in the late 1940s and early 1950s where such a situation was perceived to be emerging. In the Eisenhower administration's view of this period in Guatemalan history, after overthrowing a far-right dictatorship in 1944, these initially reformist and moderate left-wing

---

[134] FRUS 1952–1954 (6): 672.
[135] See Chapter 7 for an estimate of the effects of this intervention.
[136] Brief "Work Sheet Covering: On-The-Spot Survey Guide of Senate Special Committee" early 1957, Guatemala General/Geographic-Central Files/box 36/RG469/NARA; Immerman 1982:7–8, 103.

Guatemalan administrations had become increasingly radicalized due to the infiltration by local diehard communist party activists closely allied with the Soviet Union. The increasing subversion and takeover of important government ministries by these local communists led Guatemala under President Jacobo Arbenz to turn by 1954 into a communist-oriented regime on the verge of becoming a "beachhead" of Soviet influence in the western hemisphere. This extremely dangerous outcome was perceived as having been prevented at the last moment by the success of the U.S.-backed armed rebellion of Carlos Castillo Armas, a rebellion that removed Arbenz from power and then exiled him and many of his main communist supporters to other countries.[137] Avoiding a situation where it faced such an emergency again in Guatemala became, accordingly, the related U.S. interest vis-à-vis that country.

Secondly, these events led the U.S. government to see Guatemala during this period as a crucial showcase in its wider Cold War struggle. Due to this American view of Guatemala as the only country which had "ridden itself" of communism, positive political and economic developments in Guatemala were seen by the Eisenhower administration as having especially crucial effects on the prestige of the United States in general and on the brand of democratic capitalism that it championed during this era in particular. Given this recent history, if Guatemala eventually became a prosperous and open society, that would provide an especially powerful model of the benefits of the western way of life. In contrast, a "relapse" of Guatemala back into a communist, anti-U.S. regime after getting a "second taste" of the western way of life was expected to cause a severe blow to the attractiveness of the western economic/political model around the world in particular and to American prestige in general.[138]

3.3.2 On the Road to the 1957 Elections—The Unworried U.S. Government

In early 1957, the U.S. government was feeling cautiously optimistic about the direction of Guatemala under the leadership of Armas. After a difficult period

[137] Memo October 17,1957/Guatemala OCB/box 4/RG59/lot/NARA, Bureau of Inter-American Affairs, Records Relating to Guatemala; Eisenhower 1963:3, 424. For some of the heated historical debate over the accuracy of this view of the Eisenhower Administration of Guatemala see Immerman 1982; Schlesinger and Kinzer 1982; Rabe 1988; Gleijeses 1991; Grow 2008:chap. 1. The current scholarly consensus on this topic seems to be that while Arbenz and some key members in his administration did harbor Marxist or communist views by the early 1950s, the probability of Guatemala becoming a communist regime under Arbenz, and the threat that the Arbenz regime posed to the U.S., were both greatly exaggerated by the U.S. government (Gleijeses 1991:chap. 15).

[138] Handy 1984:185; Memo February 25,1957/Guatemala General/Geographic-Central Files/ box 34/RG469/NARA; Guatemala City 193 November 12,1957/350.211/Embassy, Guatemala City/ RG84/NARA.

of instability following the 1954 violent regime change operation in his favor, Armas was now seen by the Eisenhower administration as heading an increasingly consolidated and stable anti-communist regime.[139] The perceived communist influence and subversion problem which led to the regime change operation was now seen by the U.S. government as having been brought under short-term control.[140] Likewise, the Armas regime was seen as by the Eisenhower administration as making slow but steady progress toward improving the Guatemalan economy and democratizing the regime.[141]

The unexpected assassination of Armas by a member of his palace guard on July 26, 1957, did not initially change this positive American view. Likewise, the political developments of the following two months were mostly seen by the U.S. government as reassuring. Although the assassin, who committed suicide shortly afterward, was found to be a secret communist, the Eisenhower administration quickly determined that the assassination was not part of a wider conspiracy by communist or left-wing elements in Guatemala or abroad.[142]

In the immediate aftermath of the assassination, Armas was succeeded by his first vice president, Luis Arturo Gonzalez Lopez. After a few days of deliberation, senior officials from the military and from Armas's party (the Nationalist Democratic Movement or MDN) decided to follow the provisions of the 1956 Guatemalan Constitution and have a quick presidential election to replace Armas; they set it for October 1957. They then chose Miguel Ortiz Passarelli, the head of the Guatemalan Supreme Court and a strong supporter of Armas policies, as the MDN's presidential candidate. With the full resources of the Guatemalan government behind his candidacy, as well as some well-placed election fraud, they expected Passarelli to win the election with little difficulty. Holding an election to replace Armas was also seen by them as a way to avoid a possible American foreign aid cut-off due to a failure to uphold constitutional procedures.[143]

[139] Memo February 26,1957/Guatemala-Economic/box 3/RG59/lot/NARA, Bureau of Inter-American Affairs, Records Relating to Guatemala; Guatemala City Weeka 28 July 9,1957/714.00(w)/RG59/NARA.

[140] Report Guatemala July 5,1957/Guatemala 1958/box 7/lot/RG59/NARA, Records of the special assistant on Communism office files.

[141] Letter, Rubottom to Sparks July 9,1957/1957 Guatemala/box 2/lot/RG59/NARA; Records of Roy Rubottom, subject files; TOICA A-22 July 9,1957/Guatemala Monthly Summary/Geographic-Central Files/box 38/RG469/NARA. For similar views by contemporary scholars of Guatemala see Martz (1959:66).

[142] FRUS 1955–1957 6:210; FRUS 1955–1957 7:143–145. While unable to find any clear evidence either way, most American suspicions regarding a possible wider conspiracy behind Armas's assassination seem to have focused on one conducted by right-wing elements within the Guatemalan government using this guard as a useful foil. FRUS 1955–1957 7: 143–145.

[143] Ebel 1998:58; Guatemala City 41 August 3,1957/714.00/box 2961/RG59/lot/NARA.

As the Guatemalan political scene prepared for the elections in the following weeks, only one major competitor to Passarelli had emerged. This candidate, Miguel Ydigoras Fuentas, then the Guatemalan ambassador to Columbia, was a staunch anti-communist and a past opponent of the Arbenz regime. After losing the 1950 presidential election to Arbenz due to what he considered to be unfair methods by the Guatemalan government, Ydigoras went into exile in El Salvador and joined the underground resistance to the Arbenz regime. He there became one of the major opposition figures and was seriously considered by the CIA to lead the regime change operation against Arbenz in 1954 before it eventually settled on Armas.[144]

Similarly, when a group of Guatemalans on the center-left created a new party in August 1957 called the Revolutionary Party (or PR) and tried to run a presidential candidate in the 1957 elections, the U.S. government was not concerned. Despite its radical-sounding name, the new party was still seen as a grouping of non-communist leftists with no anti-American tendencies. Although a bit wary about the future possibility of communist infiltration into the PR ranks, it had little evidence of that occurring yet in practice. Claims by local Guatemalans, in meetings with U.S. embassy officials, that the PR was becoming a Trojan horse for communists and that, if victorious, it would lead to a quick communist takeover were dismissed by the U.S. government as "wild eyed."[145] Furthermore, U.S. government sources indicated that the PR had no significant popular following and would have virtually no chance of winning the upcoming presidential election.[146] Indeed, when the Guatemalan interim government decided in mid-September to reject the PR's application to register and run a presidential candidate in the 1957 elections the U.S. government even quietly tried, unsuccessfully, to convince it to reverse this decision.[147]

With both major presidential candidates seen as acceptable, the U.S. government saw no reason to worry about the outcome of the October 1957 elections.[148] Indeed, the only major American concern in the run-up to the 1957 elections was the possibility, based on secret information that it had received from various sources, of a pre-election coup d'état encouraged or organized by agents of the Dominican republic (then run by a far-right dictator)—a possibility which

[144] Ebel 1998:chap. 1.
[145] See handwritten note on Memcom September 11,1957/Guatemala political elections/box 4/ RG59/lot/NARA, Bureau of Inter-American Affairs, Records Relating to Guatemala.
[146] Guatemala City despatch 200 September 17,1957/714.00/RG59/NARA. The State Department's reports on the PR indicate that the CIA had, from a very early stage, informants within the party.
[147] State 170 September 23,1957/714.00/RG59/NARA.
[148] Guatemala City Weeka 36 September 3,1957/714.00(w)/RG59/NARA; Memo "Overseas Internal Security Program Guatemala," October 17,1957/1957 Guatemala OCB/box 4/RG59/lot/ NARA, Bureau of Inter-American Affairs, Records Relating to Guatemala. The U.S. also did not intervene in the selection of the MDN's presidential candidate (see Appendix D).

the U.S. government thought that it had succeeded in quickly discouraging by holding private discussions with some of the relevant actors.[149] As a result, when Ydigoras, who found out about some of the planned shenanigans by the MDN during September 1957, sent a trusted representative in the U.S. (a close American friend) to secretly request an electoral intervention in his favor, first from senior officials in the State Department and then from senior officials in the CIA, his request was promptly rejected.[150]

3.3.3 The 1957 Elections Aftermath and the Perceived Threat from the PR

The aftermath of the October 1957 Guatemalan elections turned out, however, very differently from what the U.S. or the Guatemalan governments expected. Certain of his victory, Passarelli, the MDN candidate, declared himself the winner on election night even before the polls had closed and any results were available. The next morning, again before any preliminary results were announced, Passarelli even called a press conference in which he discussed his plans once he was formally inaugurated.[151]

These acts of Passarelli, in conjunction with evidence of serious election-day shenanigans and election fraud in rural areas which reached the Ydigoras campaign, convinced Ydigoras that the government, as he expected, was going to rob him of his anticipated election victory.[152] As a result he decided to enact his pre-election plans for such an eventuality and start a wave of peaceful protests.[153] On the evening of October 21, after preliminary election results were announced which supposedly showed Passarelli with an insurmountable lead, Ydigoras held a mass rally in the central square of Guatemala City right across from the

---

[149] Memo, August 8,1957; Memo September 16,1957, both in Guatemala political-international/ box 4/RG59/lot/NARA, Bureau of Inter-American Affairs, Records Relating to Guatemala; Guatemala City 99 September 16,1957/714.00/RG59/NARA; Guatemala City Weeka 38 September 17,1957/714.00(w)/RG59/NARA. There were also some worries within the Eisenhower administration that the Dominican meddling may be designed instead to determine the election results—see, for example, FRUS 1955–1957 6:211.

[150] See Memcom October 2,1957/714.00/RG59/NARA; Memo October 3,1957/Guatemala-political/box 4/RG59/lot/NARA, Bureau of Inter-American Affairs, Records Relating to Guatemala. As this representative of Ydigoras noted in the request for electoral assistance, Ydigoras was sure that "the elections would be rigged against him." The U.S. rejected similar requests by another marginal candidate who later dropped out. Memcom August 26,1957/Guatemala-political/box 4/RG59/lot/ NARA, Bureau of Inter-American Affairs, Records Relating to Guatemala.

[151] James 1957:3–4. This was, of course, before the era of election or exit polling in Guatemala.

[152] One Guatemalan newspaper report claimed, for example, that an insufficient number of paper ballots were sent to some parts of Guatemala, leading to a very early end of the vote in some polling places (Najarro 2012:87).

[153] For these contingency plans of Ydigoras, described in a conversation with U.S. embassy officials, see Guatemala City despatch 198 September 13,1957/714.00/RG59/NARA.

presidential palace. During the rally he accused the government of conducting mass election fraud and of trying to steal the election and called in response for a sit-in demonstration with an unlimited duration to start the following evening in the central square. He also called for a general strike in Guatemala City starting the next morning. The PR party leadership, angry at their exclusion from the election, decided to independently join in with Ydigoras's protest activities, as did some local communist activists.[154]

The following morning Guatemala City was almost completely shut down by a general strike of most public and private businesses, a strike that continued for the rest of the week. That evening, despite a declaration of a state of siege by the Guatemalan government, more than 10,000 demonstrators tried to reach the central square and battled military and police forces which dispersed them using tear gas, fire hoses, and shots into the air. Ydigoras, undeterred, called for the demonstrations to continue and a repeat attempt to enter the central square the following evening.[155] The next morning (October 23), protests broke out across Guatemala City demanding the annulment of the election, the resignation of the interim government, and the installation of Ydigoras as president. More spontaneous groups of Ydigoras supporters, PR members, and communists rioted across the city, turning over buses and cars and breaking windows of government buildings and of the handful of businesses which violated the strike. That evening an even larger crowd was able to enter the central square and begin a sit-down demonstration where it remained in the following days.[156]

During meetings on that day, the leadership of the Guatemalan military concluded that the only way to restore order and end the demonstrations would be the heavy use of force by the military. Unwilling to kill and injure large numbers of peaceful demonstrators, many of whom were seen as coming from noncommunist backgrounds, the military decided instead to concede to some of Ydigoras's demands. That evening they declared that the 1957 presidential election would be annulled. Later that night the military forced the resignation of interim president Gonzalez and some of the senior military officers who had supported the interim government and declared the formation of a military junta. It then began to negotiate with Ydigoras over the next steps. It also, in complete secrecy, began to separately negotiate with representatives of the PR.[157]

[154] James 1957:4–5; Ebel 1998:85–86.
[155] James 1957:4; Guatemala City 147 October 22,1957/714.00/RG59/NARA; *New York Times*, October 23, 1957.
[156] USARMA 13-57 October 24,1957, Guatemala-political/box 4/RG59/lot/NARA, Bureau of Inter-American Affairs, Records Relating to Guatemala; Guatemala City 149 October 23,1957/ 714.00/RG59/NARA; "Guatemalans Try to Void Elections," *New York Times*, October 24, 1957.
[157] Ebel (1998:86–87); "Guatemalans Try to Void Elections," *New York Times*, October 24, 1957 and "Army Junta Seizes Power in Guatemala," October 25, 1957. For the Guatemalan military's unwillingness to use force against protesters see Guatemala City 152 October 23,1957/714.00/box 2961/RG59/ NARA; USARMA 16-57 October 25,1957/Guatemala-political/box 4/RG59/lot/NARA, Bureau of

Ydigoras first demanded that the new junta (seen by him as being too pro-MDN) dissolve itself, return power to the next-in-line interim leader under the Guatemalan constitution (Armas's second vice president, Guillermo Flores Avendano), and declare early new elections. Ydigoras then increased his demands, also asking to be declared by the Guatemalan Congress, once it was back in session, as the winner of the 1957 election and be installed as the new permanent president. The junta, a significant share of which disliked Ydigoras and his various antics during these demonstrations, refused to dissolve itself or to install Ydigoras in power. Then, following mediation efforts by the Vatican, ODECA (Central America's regional organization), and the U.S. government, the junta agreed to dissolve itself, let Flores assume power as interim president, and call a new presidential election, a proposal eventually accepted by Ydigoras.[158] In a separate, secret side deal with the PR, the junta also promised that the new interim government would legalize the party and permit it to run in the next election.[159] With these two agreements the demonstrations, strikes, and disturbances ended.

These post-election events dramatically changed the American view of Guatemalan politics in general and of the PR in particular. Ydigoras's strong second-place showing even according to the official results,[160] and his possible victory in the 1957 election, were seen by the U.S. government as being partly fueled by a protest vote by left-wing PR voters for Ydigoras over the refusal of the Guatemalan government to register the party and its candidate.[161] Likewise, a large share of Ydigoras's success in shutting down Guatemala City and turning out tens of thousands of demonstrators to protest the election results were

Inter-American Affairs, Records Relating to Guatemala. The presence of women and children among the demonstrators seems to have also been a factor. The military also seems to have blocked an attempt by the MDN to utilize its own secret militia for this purpose. Guatemala City despatch 308 November 12,1957/714.00/RG59/NARA.

[158] Guatemala City 155 October 24,1957/714.00/RG59/NARA; IR-114-57 October 25,1957/350/ Embassy, Guatemala City/RG84/NARA; USARMA 17-57 October 27,1957/Guatemala-political/ box 4/RG59/lot/NARA, Bureau of Inter-American Affairs, Records Relating to Guatemala. During its mediation efforts the U.S. government didn't attempt to discourage the junta from permitting Ydigoras from assuming power in the immediate aftermath of these demonstrations; indeed, it seems to have seen such an outcome as one of the acceptable solutions to the post-election crisis. See Guatemala City 159 October 24,1957/714.00/RG59/NARA.

[159] The negotiations and deal with the PR were kept secret from the U.S. which discovered it shortly afterward from its private discussions with Guatemalan politicians and subsequent secret inquiries (Guatemala City 159 October 24,1957; Guatemala City 177 October 30,1957; Guatemala City 215 December 1,1957, all three in 714.00/RG59/NARA). The PR initially also wanted a full-fledged constitutional convention in which the 1956 Guatemalan constitution would be replaced with a document more to their liking (Najarro 2012:89).

[160] According to the official preliminary results, Ydigoras got 37.1% of the vote, Passarelli got 51.7%, and a third minor candidate (Miguel Asturias Quinonez) got the remainder.

[161] Guatemala City Weeka 43 October 22,1957/714.00/(w)/RG59/NARA.

credited by it to the PR's decision to join the demonstrations and the declared general strike.[162] Furthermore, in the election's aftermath the PR was seen by the U.S. as being increasingly treated by the Guatemalan political scene as a legitimate political actor with significant influence on various political decisions.[163]

These events now indicated to the U.S. government that, contrary to its pre-election beliefs, the PR's left-wing ideology had widespread appeal among Guatemalans and a PR presidential candidate had a good chance of winning the 1958 elections if permitted to run.[164] By early November some secret U.S. government estimates even saw the PR as the strongest party in Guatemala.[165] Some subsequent estimates reached similar conclusions.[166] Given the PR's secret post-election deal, it was now all but certain to get permission to run. Any Guatemalan government attempt to ban the PR from participating in the 1958 elections was expected by knowledgeable Guatemalans, as well as by the Eisenhower administration, to lead to an even larger wave of demonstrations and possible outbursts of violence—a highly undesirable outcome for the U.S. and a completely unacceptable one to the interim government.[167]

At the same time, the Eisenhower administration was becoming increasingly worried about the PR. The local CIA station was finding growing evidence of significant communist infiltration into the lower echelons of the PR.[168] Indeed, even one PR leader, in a private conversation with U.S. embassy officials, felt forced to admit to its existence while trying (unconvincingly in American eyes) to minimize its scale.[169] As the U.S. ambassador to Guatemala noted, the danger was that Guatemalan communists "might be able to eventually control or substantially influence [the] PR just as they did [to] political parties supporting [the] Arbenz regime"—a dangerous possibility given the PR's new political position.[170]

[162] Memo November 5,1957/communism/box 1/lot/RG59/NARA Records of Roy Rubottom, subject files; for a secret admission by a PR leader during a conversation with U.S. embassy officials of a "tacit understanding" between the PR and Ydigoras before the election and in the post-election demonstrations see Guatemala City despatch 294 November 5,1957/714.00/RG59/NARA. This leader also claimed during the conversation that 40% of the demonstrators were from the PR.

[163] Guatemala City Weeka 46 November 12,1957/714.00(w)/RG59/NARA.

[164] Guatemala City despatch 294 November 5,1957/714.00/RG59/NARA. See also CIA Current Intelligence Bulletin November 15, 1957, CREST; INR intelligence brief 2217 December 2,1957/Guatemala Publications/box 39/RG469/NARA.

[165] CIA Current Intelligence Weekly Summary November 7, 1957, CREST.

[166] NSC briefing November 21, 1957, DDRS.

[167] Guatemala City 176 October 30,1957/714.00/RG59/NARA; NSC briefing November 21, 1957, DDRS; Guatemala City 215 December 1,1957/714.00/RG59/NARA. Due to the military's behavior in the post-election period, the U.S. government seems to have also thought, despite claims of some prominent Guatemalans to the contrary, that a victory by the PR in a free and fair election would be unlikely to lead to a post-election coup designed to prevent its candidate from assuming power; INR intelligence brief 2217 December 2,1957/Guatemala Publications/box 39/RG469/NARA.

[168] Guatemala City 166 October 26,1957/714.00/RG59/NARA; CIA Current Intelligence Bulletin October 27, 1957, CREST; Guatemala City 180 November 4,1957/714.00/RG59/NARA.

[169] Guatemala City despatch 294 November 5,1957/714.00/RG59/NARA.

[170] For quote see Guatemala City 166 October 26,1957/714.00/RG59/NARA. See also Guatemala City 193 November 12,1957/350.211/Embassy, Guatemala City/RG84/NARA.

The PR's leader and likely (and eventual) presidential candidate Mario Mendez Montenegro, although not seen as a communist, was nevertheless perceived as equally vulnerable to such influences.[171] In the Eisenhower administration's eyes an old danger seemed to be returning with a vengeance.

3.3.4 The Weakening Losers: Cruz Salazar and the MDN

In the aftermath of the annulment of the 1957 elections, Jose Luis Cruz Salazar, the Guatemalan Ambassador to the U.S., decided to run for the Guatemalan presidency. He knew he was facing very long odds in this attempt. This was due to a combination of personal and party-related political issues.

Cruz Salazar's party, the MDN, had suffered serious political damage as a result of the death of Armas and the 1957 elections. The assassination of Armas had led the MDN to lose its founder and, by mid-1957, relatively popular leader.[172] Rather than benefiting from a sympathy vote, some voters instead seem to have even held the assassination against the MDN in the 1957 elections. Many Guatemalans seem to have believed various widespread conspiracy theories which rejected the official explanation for the assassination and which claimed that a group of senior MDN officials had secretly hired the assassin, ostensibly in order to hide a corruption scandal that Armas exposed in the MDN and was trying to root out. According to this theory the official government investigation was then manipulated to cover up this fact.[173]

The 1957 election and the post-election protests caused further damage to the MDN. As noted, these protests brought a new interim government to power in Guatemala. The new interim government cut off the official government support for the MDN.[174] As a result, the MDN lost its access to government resources, significantly reducing its electoral capabilities. Already unpopular beforehand in some segments of the Guatemalan population due to its status as the

---

[171] State despatch 307 December 12,1957/714.00/RG59/NARA. Although not formally registered until early December Mendez Montenegro's high likelihood of being the PR's candidate was already known to the U.S. government (see Memcom October 29,1957/350/Embassy, Guatemala City/ RG84/NARA).

[172] For the mass turnout for Armas's funeral see Guatemala City despatch 88 August 1,1957/350/ Embassy, Guatemala City/RG84/NARA.

[173] Ebel 1998:76; "Guatemalans Try to Void Elections," *New York Times*, October 24, 1957. As noted, in private the U.S. government itself harbored significant doubts regarding some aspects of the official Guatemalan story of Armas's assassination.

[174] Sloan 1968: 88.Although it retained some support within the lower ranks of government bureaucracy, by the MDN leaders' own past admissions, the MDN's level of support there was relatively limited even prior to Armas's assassination and the 1957 elections. See, for example, Memcom June 7,1957/Guatemala-political/box 4/RG59/lot/NARA, Bureau of Inter-American Affairs, Records Relating to Guatemala.

official or government party and the previously noted conspiracy theories, the MDN's exposed and unusually blatant attempt to use election fraud in order to win the 1957 presidential election for Passarelli discredited the party in the eyes of much of the Guatemalan public.[175] As some MDN congressmen described it in private conversations, due to these developments their party was "washed up."[176] Likewise, Passarelli, the MDN's presidential candidate in the 1957 election, quickly reached similar conclusions, leading him to decide to not to try to run again in the 1958 election.[177] Accordingly, although the weakened MDN still retained some important parts of its political machine, a public association of a presidential candidate with it in the aftermath of the 1957 election was a major political albatross. Indeed, a major part of Cruz Salazar's election campaign consisted of finding and implementing various activities and strategies that would minimize any visible connection between him and the MDN in the eyes of the Guatemalan public while retaining, behind the scenes, its support for his candidacy.[178]

Cruz Salazar's personal political problems as a presidential candidate exacerbated his party-related ones. Although he played important political roles in Guatemalan politics during this period, first as a senior member in one of the short-lived post-Arbenz juntas and then as the Guatemalan Ambassador to the United States, Cruz Salazar was still in mid-1957 a virtually unknown figure within the Guatemalan public.[179] This was a major downside in Guatemala's highly personalistic political system and was worsened by two features of the 1958 elections: a relatively brief election period (ten weeks) and a ballot that used pictures of the candidates' faces in order to enable Guatemalan voters (most of whom were still illiterate) to identify the candidates.[180] This problem was further exacerbated by his age. In 1957 Cruz Salazar was thirty-six years old—too young in the eyes of many Guatemalans in that era for a president or ruler.[181]

Secondly, although he was a former colonel, Cruz Salazar was deeply disliked within the senior ranks of the Guatemalan army. This was mainly due to his past

[175] James 1957:6; Guatemala City Weeka 41 October 9,1957/714.00(w)/RG59/NARA.

[176] Guatemala City 159 October 24,1957; for Cruz Salazar's open acknowledgment of this problem see Memcom October 28,1957, both in 714.00/RG59/NARA.

[177] Ebel 1998:94.

[178] Memcom October 28,1957; Guatemala City 199 November 19,1957; for example, when Cruz Salazar formally registered his candidacy in early December 1957 he first registered it under the name of a minor Guatemalan party (the Partido Republicano). Guatemala City 229 December 8,1957, all three in 714.00/RG59/NARA.

[179] Sloan 1968:55; Clemente Rojas, Editorial *La Hora* (Guatemala) January 30, 1958.

[180] In 1954, 72.2% of Guatemalans were illiterate (Martz 1959:346). The importance of high levels of face recognition among Guatemalan voters given these circumstances was widely known among politicians in this era; see, for example, Guatemala City Weeka 35 August 27,1957/714.00(w)/RG59/NARA.

[181] See, for example, Guatemala City 270 December 22,1957/714.00/RG59/NARA; Clemente Rojas, Editorial *La Hora* (Guatemala) November 16, 1957.

support for a military faction that was believed to have been involved in the 1949 assassination of a chief of the armed forces who was then quite popular within much of the military.[182] As a result, the military top brass had repeatedly tried in the mid-1950s to block Cruz Salazar's political ambitions. For example, a secret plan by Armas in late 1956 to make Cruz Salazar into his designated successor appears to have been scrapped due to heavy pressure from senior military officers.[183]

Although one of Cruz Salazar's greatest opponents within the military, Colonel (and Defense Minister) Francisco Oliva, was forced into exile in the aftermath of the post-election demonstrations, significant resistance remained within the top ranks of the military to his candidacy.[184] With the Guatemalan military in effective control of the interim government in the aftermath of the annulled 1957 elections, and the MDN out of official favor, Cruz Salazar could expect no significant government help for his candidacy.

With these issues in view, Cruz Salazar quickly decided to ask for an American electoral intervention on his behalf. In late October, under the guise of a regular diplomatic meeting, he met with two senior officials in the State Department, described why he thought that he could win the election, and requested covert American funding for his election campaign.[185]

3.3.5 The 1958 Elections: The Rejections and Eventual Acceptance of the Intervention Request

However, to Cruz Salazar's dismay, the State Department rejected his request, ostensibly claiming that any such electoral intervention would be in contravention of the United States' non-intervention policy in regard to Guatemala and that, moreover, any American assistance of this kind could harm rather than help him. Undeterred by this rejection, Cruz Salazar promised to return once he could furnish the U.S. government with more information about his supposedly good chances of victory.[186] Two days later he visited again the State Department under a similar guise and provided some information on his chances.[187] Then, in

---

[182] See, for example, Memcom August 19/Guatemala political-local/box 4/RG59/lot/NARA, Bureau of Inter-American Affairs, Records Relating to Guatemala.
[183] Guatemala City despatch 230 October 15,1956/714.00/RG59/NARA.
[184] Guatemala City 180 November 4,1957/714.00/RG59/NARA. See also Letter, Minotto to Krebs December 19,1957/814.002/RG59/NARA for the private admission of a representative of Cruz Salazar of this problem.
[185] Memcom October 28,1957/714.00/RG59/NARA.
[186] Ibid.
[187] Memcom October 30,1957/714.00/RG59/NARA.

early November, Cruz Salazar secretly met with Alan Dulles, the director of the CIA, and repeated his request. Alan Dulles politely turned him down as well.[188]

The Eisenhower administration seems to have already believed by late October that, if feasible, an electoral intervention in the forthcoming 1958 elections in order to stop the threat emanating from the communist-infiltrated PR was necessary.[189] The administration's hand was temporarily stayed, however, by the situation within the Guatemalan center and right. Cruz Salazar was not alone in asking for such electoral assistance. Around this time another presidential candidate, the then-Guatemalan ambassador to El Salvador Enrique Peralta Azurdia, facing similarly serious political problems, secretly contacted the U.S. government with a request for an American intervention on his behalf in person and through a trusted messenger. He was then rejected in a similar manner.[190] When the Eisenhower administration assessed both candidates, it quickly concluded that neither Cruz Salazar nor Peralta had a significant chance of winning a competitive election in which multiple candidates of the Guatemalan center and right were running at the same time against the PR.[191]

A third candidate of the center-right, Ydigoras, was seen by the U.S. as having such a chance against the PR.[192] However, his belief that he was the true winner of the 1957 election seems to have led Ydigoras to become quite certain of his electoral chances in a cleaner "rerun." As a result, Ydigoras showed no interest in an American intervention in his favor.[193]

[188] Staff Meeting November 8,1957/box 7/RG59/lot/NARA, Minutes and Notes of the Secretary's Staff Meetings.

[189] See, for example, State 230 October 30,1957/714.00/RG59/NARA. See also Guatemala City 193 November 12,1957/350.211/Embassy, Guatemala City/RG84/NARA.

[190] Guatemala City 178 October 31,1957/714.00/RG59/NARA; Memcom November 12,1957/714.00/RG59/NARA. For a description of Peralta's equally serious political problems see Sloan (1968:231); CIA Current Intelligence Summary November 7,1957, CREST; and Memcom December 10,1957/350/Embassy, Guatemala City/RG84/NARA. One of Peralta's severest political handicaps during this period, rather ironically in view of his later actions as dictator in the mid-1960s, was the widespread belief among prominent Guatemalans of the center and right that Peralta, despite being on the right, would be too soft on communism and the far left if in power, a belief that seems to have eventually cost him his chances of being endorsed by the MDN (Schlewitz 1999:307; Memcom November 13,1957/350/Embassy, Guatemala City/RG84/NARA).

[191] Guatemala City 178 October 31,1957/714.00/RG59/NARA; CIA Current Intelligence Summary November 7, 1957, CREST.

[192] Guatemala City 178 October 31,1957/714.00/RG59/NARA.

[193] CIA Current Intelligence Bulletin October 27, 1957, CREST; Guatemala City 177 October 30,1957/714.00/RG59/NARA; Memcom November 27,1957/350/Embassy, Guatemala City/RG84/NARA; and Memcom January 13,1958 Guatemala-political/box 6/RG59/lot/NARA, Bureau of Inter-American Affairs, Records Relating to Guatemala. The only discussions that seem to have occurred in this regard, after the electoral intervention had already begun in mid-December, were complaints by official representatives of the Ydigoras campaign regarding evidence that reached them about the American assistance to Cruz Salazar (see, for example, Memo "Guatemala: Information Derived From Recent Interviews" December 23,1957 Guatemala-political/box 4/RG59/lot/NARA, Bureau of Inter-American Affairs, Records Relating to Guatemala). Ydigoras's lack of interest in an American electoral intervention on his behalf after the 1957 election didn't prevent, however, some private businessmen who supported his candidacy to "freelance" and secretly request an American

Facing two different electoral intervention options, neither of which was yet perceived as being able to provide the desired outcome, the Eisenhower administration decided in early November to temporarily choose a third option. It seems to have believed that Guatemalans from the political center and right, deeply worried (as the Eisenhower administration was) in the aftermath of the 1957 elections about the PR, would eventually be able to set aside their political differences and agree upon a single anti-communist candidate, either among the current presidential candidates or a different candidate. Such a candidate was expected to have far higher chances of victory against the PR presidential candidate and therefore be worthy of receiving U.S. assistance. Accordingly, the administration decided to wait for such a candidate to arise, limiting itself to quiet, behind-the-scenes encouragement of prominent Guatemalans of the center and right to agree on a unity candidate without directing them toward a particular person.[194]

Over the course of November and early December, the Eisenhower administration patiently followed this policy without deviation as some private Guatemalan citizens pushed, unsuccessfully, for the various factions of the Guatemalan center and right to settle on an anti-communist unity candidate and the presidential candidates jockeyed for support and began their election campaigns.[195] For example, when Cruz Salazar met again in late November with State Department officials, he complained about supposed attempts by secret agents of the PR to buy off some of his supporters and asked again, this time in an indirect manner, for covert funding for his campaign. However, the State Department ignored his request.[196]

Then, during the second week of December, the Eisenhower administration's view of the Guatemalan center and right shifted yet again. Based upon reports it was receiving from the U.S. embassy in Guatemala City and other sources,

---

intervention for Ydigoras on their own initiative and without consulting him. For examples see Memcom November 27,1957/714.00/RG59/NARA; Letter, Sparks to King December 30,1957/ Guatemala-political/box 4/RG59/lot/NARA, Bureau of Inter-American Affairs, Records Relating to Guatemala; and Memcom January 7,1958/Guatemala-political/box 6/RG59/lot/NARA, Bureau of Inter-American Affairs, Records Relating to Guatemala.

[194] State 230 October 30,1957/714.00/RG59/NARA; State 275 November 26,1957/714.00/RG59/ NARA; Staff Meeting December 6,1957/box 7/RG59/lot/NARA Minutes and Notes of the Secretary's Staff meetings. For the acceptability of both candidates to the U.S. see Staff Meeting December 9,1957 in the above location. For the planning work by the State Department in the interim of possible methods to assist the unity candidate when chosen, plans that were subsequently abandoned, see Staff Meeting November 13,1957 in the above location; Memo "Grant Aid to Guatemala" February 3,1958 Guatemala/box 4/RG59/lot/NARA, Bureau of Inter-American Affairs, Subject Files Relating to Regional Economic Affairs.

[195] For an example of one such private Guatemalan effort see Guatemala City Weeka 49 December 4,1957/714.00(w)/RG59/NARA.

[196] Memcom November 27,1957/714.00/RG59/NARA.

the U.S. government increasingly concluded that Cruz Salazar's chances were improving and that he now stood a real chance of winning the election. In contrast, Peralta's campaign was seen as being in serious trouble and suffering from growing defections to Cruz Salazar.[197] At the same time, the Eisenhower administration seems to have lost any remaining hopes of a unity candidate arising within the Guatemalan center and right.[198]

As a result, in mid-December 1957 the Eisenhower administration decided to support Cruz Salazar's presidential candidacy.[199] As Cruz Salazar requested, the U.S. then began to covertly provide him with funding for his election campaign, totaling around $97,000 ($655,000 in 2016 dollars).[200] From the available evidence a local Guatemalan movie house magnate named Ramiro Samayoa served as the conduit. Using as a cover his frequent trips to Hollywood for business purposes, Samayoa secretly met there with CIA agents in order to pick up the campaign funding and then delivered it upon his return to the Cruz campaign.[201]

Five weeks later, on January 19, Guatemalans came out again to vote without any incident or major election fraud.[202] Ydigoras won a decisive plurality of the vote (40.8%), with Cruz Salazar coming in second (29.6%), narrowly passing the PR's candidate, Mendez Montenegro (28.4%).[203] With no candidate getting an absolute majority, the Guatemalan Congress was constitutionally required to determine the identity of the winner among the top two candidates. After a few tense days, and secret, behind-the-scenes negotiations between the two candidates, Cruz Salazar agreed to concede the elections.[204] The Guatemalan Congress then confirmed Ydigoras's election victory in February 1958, leading to the inauguration of Ydigoras as president to a six-year term a few weeks later.

---

[197] Memo, December 5,1957/Guatemala Jose Cruz Salazar/box 3/RG59/lot/NARA, Bureau of Inter-American Affairs, Records Relating to Guatemala; Guatemala City 233 December 11,1957/ 714.00/RG59/NARA; Guatemala City Weeka 50 December 11,1957/714.00(w)/RG59/NARA. Eventually Peralta, reaching similar conclusions, dropped his candidacy and endorsed Ydigoras.

[198] For the U.S. government's frustrations in this regard see Letter, Sparks to Whelen December 20,1957/Guatemala Congress/box 4/RG59/lot/NARA, Bureau of Inter-American Affairs, Records Relating to Guatemala.

[199] Staff meetings notes, December 23,1957/box 7/RG59/lot/NARA Minutes and Notes of the Secretary's Staff meetings; 352nd NSC meeting January 22, 1958, DDRS.

[200] Kinzer 1982:237.

[201] Ebel 1998:115. Samoya also served at the time as a senior member of Cruz Salazar's campaign. Ebel also claimed (1998:114), citing here an earlier version of Streeter's argument, that the U.S. provided covert campaign funding to the PR as well. However, Streeter (2000) dropped this claim in the final version of his manuscript. Likewise, the documentary evidence that I found in regard to the PR, most of which were not available to Ebel when he wrote his book two decades ago, indicates the opposite to be the case.

[202] Although some isolated incidents of fraud in both directions by local government officials who supported either Cruz Salazar or Ydigoras seem to have occurred in this election (Sloan 1970:83–84), most scholars who have studied it agree that it was free and fair overall (Cehelsky 1967:115; Ebel 1998:108–109; Brockett 2002:106).

[203] A fourth minor candidate, Jose Ardon Fernandez, won 1.2%.

[204] Ebel 1998:108–109.

After five highly tumultuous years that saw, among other things, the beginning of a brutal thirty-six-year-long civil war, Ydigoras was deposed in a coup in March 1963.

3.4 A Populist Is Born: The 1946 Argentinean Election

3.4.1 U.S. Interests in Argentina in the Mid-1940s

During the mid-1940s, the U.S. government saw itself as having two key interests in regard to Argentina. The first was to prevent the rise of new fascist states in the western hemisphere. The United States believed that under the rule of the GOU[205] junta in general, and Colonel Juan Domingo Peron in particular, Argentina was being increasingly transformed into a fascist-totalitarian state similar in many of its domestic characteristics to Nazi Germany or fascist Italy. Indeed, in 1944 then–Secretary of State Cordell Hall even described Argentina as "the headquarters of the fascist movement in the hemisphere."[206] Due to its experiences with fascist regimes since the end of WW1, the U.S. at the time believed fascist states to be inherently war-prone, making any such state a major threat to American security.[207]

A supposedly fascist Argentina was seen as an especially "serious menace" to the U.S. government. As the one of the world's richest countries during this era, and the richest country in Latin America, Argentina had the potential ability to develop significant independent military capabilities for various aggressive purposes. Even worse, such a hostile Argentina could create an anti-American bloc of Latin American states, a goal which U.S. intelligence believed that the— Farrell-Peron regime was secretly pursuing for years. Such a bloc, either alone or with Ribbentrop–Molotov style outside Soviet backing, could pose a serious security threat to the U.S. in the western hemisphere.[208]

The second was to prevent the future return of Nazism to other key world regions. Despite its conclusive military victory over Nazi Germany during WW2, a victory already quite evident to the U.S. government by early 1944, it remained quite worried for many years of the possibility of a post-war return of Nazism.

---

[205] This acronym stands for the name of a secret military society within the Argentine military (Grupo de Oficiales Unidos) that was the main force behind the June 1943 coup.

[206] "Hull Says Fascism Nests in Argentina," *New York Times*, September 8, 1944.

[207] Memorandum February 1945/835.00/box 5517/RG59/NARA.

[208] Report "The fascist-totalitarian character of the present Argentine regime" October 1944/ 835.00/RG59/NARA; Memo, September 28,1945/box 16/lot/RG59/NARA,ARA memorandums; Speech, Spruille Braden War Department January 11, 1946/box 29/Spruille Braden Papers, Rare Books and Manuscripts Library, Columbia University. American fears of such future Soviet assistance to a fascist Argentina were already quite evident by mid-1945.

Regimes led by Nazi sympathizers or under secret Nazi influences, as Peron spe-cifically and senior GOU personnel in general were believed by the U.S. govern-ment to be, were especially dangerous in this regard. An Argentina led by such leaders and regimes could serve as a refuge for any senior Nazi leaders still at large and the resources they hid, giving them a secure location for regrouping and eventually recreating the Nazi war machine in Europe. Indeed, the long-standing ties between the two regimes made Argentina, in the U.S. government eyes, the most likely Nazi refuge.[209]

The exaggerated threat that the U.S. government perceived as emenating from Peron and the GOU was derived in part from past British black propaganda op-erations targeting the U.S., propaganda that frequently showed Nazi Germany as having an especially strong interest in Argentina.[210] It was also derived in part from Peron's unrelated actions as Secretary of War and of Labor during these years, actions which were designed to both build for himself an independent power base and deal with what he perceived as major flaws of Argentina's do-mestic and security policies. For example, as Secretary of Labor, Peron began decreeing and implementing a raft of pro-labor reforms and policies designed to improve the welfare of Argentina's marginalized working class. Many of these ec-onomic reforms were inspired, however, by Spanish and Italian state corporatist policies—which helped lead American decision-makers to mistakenly identify Peron as a committed fascist if not an "aspiring Hitler."[211] Likewise, as Secretary of War, Peron increased military spending, expanded the Argentine military, and put much effort into reforming the military and developing Argentina's mil-itary industries, efforts designed to deal with various longstanding deficiencies the military perceived in Argentina's defense policies. However, when that was occurring in an ostensibly neutral country far from the war theaters of WW2, it was perceived by the U.S. as evidence of Peron's and the GOU's inherently fascist and militarist tendencies.[212]

---

[209] Report "The fascist-totalitarian character of the present Argentine regime" October 1944/835.00/RG59/NARA; Memorandum "Colonel Juan D. Peron" February 1945/835.00/RG59/NARA; Macdonald 1980:378–379; Memcom, October 4,1945/800/Box 60/RG84/NARA.

[210] Dorn 2005:37. In the late 1930s, Nazi Germany had invested significant resources in completely unsuccessful attempts to subvert Argentina—giving this British black propaganda a patina of plausi-bility (Newton 1992:xv, chap. 7).

[211] Dorn 2005:33–35, 307; Memorandum "Colonel Juan D. Peron" February 1945/835.00/RG59/NARA.

[212] Potash 1969:240, 249–251; Report "The fascist-totalitarian character of the present Argentine regime" October 1944/835.00/RG59/NARA. Most of the modern scholarship on Peron has con-cluded that while some aspects of his political views were inspired by fascist ideas, and he was willing to temporarily ally with some Nazi sympathizers during various stages of his rise to power, Peron was not personally a Nazi or a fascist (Page 1988:35–36, 86–91; Wood 1985:142–143, 235; Crassweller 1987:142–143; Hedges 2011:66–67, 87–89).

This exaggerated threat perception was also buttressed by Argentina's un-friendly behavior toward the U.S. during WW2. In the aftermath of Pearl Harbor, then–Argentinean President Ramon Castillo refused to either abandon the Argentine policy of neutrality or break relations with the Axis. The Castillo re-gime then gave free reign to German espionage activities in Argentina, which used the German embassy in Buenos Aires and other means as cover. These German espionage activities collected intelligence that was quite useful to German submarine attacks on Allied shipping in the South Atlantic area. Castillo also turned a blind eye to German government subsidization of rabidly pro-Nazi newspapers and propaganda throughout the country.[213] In mid-1942, in re-sponse to a U.S. arms embargo designed to pressure Argentina to cut its relations with Germany, Castillo even secretly tried—unsuccessfully—to acquire weapons from Germany.[214] Indeed, the Castillo regime's behavior was so friendly toward Nazi Germany that the German ambassador to Argentina at the time, in private communications, described the Castillo regime as pro-German.[215]

The new GOU military regime that overthrew Castillo in June 1943, despite multiple reneged promises in this regard to the U.S. government, also refused to break diplomatic relations with Nazi Germany—making Argentina the only Latin American country still holding this position by 1943. Behind the scenes the new GOU government, led by General Pedro Pablo Ramirez, began a new round of secret negotiations with Nazi Germany for the sale of armaments. It also secretly aided a coup d'état in Bolivia in December 1943 that deposed the pro-Allied government and temporarily threatened American supplies of tin and wolfram—two major war materials during WW2.[216] When the U.S. govern-ment discovered these covert Argentine activities it gave a secret ultimatum to Ramirez to immediately break relations with Nazi Germany, threatening to pub-licly expose both acts otherwise.[217]

Ramirez complied with this American ultimatum and broke relations with Nazi Germany in January 1944. However, this decision led to his ouster a few weeks later by other members of the GOU led by Peron, an ouster perceived by the U.S. as having been done by the pro-Axis clique within the GOU.[218] The ouster of Ramirez led to the succession of General Edelmiro Farrell as president with Peron as the vice president and the de facto power behind the throne.[219] The

---

[213] Page 1988:43–44.
[214] Potash 1969:170–174.
[215] Frank 1980:15.
[216] Frank 1980:23–24; Potash 1969:218–223, 230–231. During these negotiations Ramirez prom-ised to remain neutral and claimed that any subsequent declaration of war on their side due to U.S. pressures would be merely pro forma (Newton 1992:287, 301–302).
[217] Potash 1969:231–232.
[218] For the source of this misunderstanding see Appendix D.
[219] Ibid.:232–237, 244.

Farrell–Peron regime then made at least one more unsuccessful attempt in late 1944 to acquire weapons from Germany.[220]

Clumsy attempts by the Argentinean government and Peron to change this negative American perception frequently backfired as well. For example, in one conversation in April 1945 with a U.S. State Department representative, Peron admitted that he was taught the tenets of fascism by a prominent Italian fascist during his visit to Italy in the late 1930s. He then argued that Italian fascism made only two major mistakes: persuading only a bit more than half of the Italian population in the correctness of fascism and creating a separate fascist militia side by side with the regular non-fascist army rather than creating a unified pro-fascist military. Peron concluded the conversation by noting his expectation that another global military conflict would erupt very soon. When the memo of this conversation reached the Truman administration, the administration's view of Peron further hardened.[221]

3.4.2   With No Elections in Sight: The Early American Regime Change Attempts

The growing alarm within the U.S. government about the GOU and Peron led it to decide to depose both of them. With no competitive elections expected or announced in the near future, the American regime change policy in Argentina initially began with other methods. After the ouster of Ramirez by GOU elements led by Farrell and Peron in early 1944, the U.S. government, conveniently defining it as a completely new regime for this purpose, refused to recognize the Farrell–Peron regime. Four months later it withdrew its ambassador from Argentina and forced Britain to do the same. It also imposed a whole new set of open and secret economic sanctions, freezing Argentina's assets in the U.S. and forbidding U.S.-flagged ships from visiting Argentine ports. These sanctions also included strict restrictions on U.S. exports to Argentina, restrictions so severe that they included, in one extreme case, a ban on exports of broken vinyl records for recycling.[222]

Then, in early 1945, with the Farrell–Peron regime still in place, this American regime change effort was temporarily stopped due to another, more urgent policy consideration. In the upcoming San Francisco conference scheduled for April–June 1945 the U.S. needed the votes and full cooperation of all other nineteen

---

[220]   Ibid.:252–253.

[221]   See the handwritten notes on Memorandum April 10,1945/835.00/RG59/NARA.

[222]   Macdonald 1980:380–381; Paz and Ferrari 1966:122–123; Memcom January 9,1945/lot/RG59/ NARA,ARA, Memorandums Relating to Individual Countries.

independent Latin American countries[223] in order to guarantee that the planned United Nations organization would be shaped in the desired manner, an organization which the U.S. government expected at the time to play a far more major role in world affairs than it eventually did. Given the serious misgivings of some Latin American countries regarding its policies toward Argentina, and the importance that many of them attached to this issue, the U.S. government had no choice but to relent on its regime change policy in order to secure their cooperation in regard to the U.N. Accordingly, in the Mexico City Inter-American conference of February–March 1945, the U.S. government agreed to a set of conditions by which the Farrell–Peron regime could gain American recognition. When the Argentine government consented to them, the U.S. recognized the Farrell–Peron regime on April 9, 1945, and agreed to send a new ambassador. It also removed its overt economic sanctions and promised to ship some surplus weapons to Argentina.[224] Later that month, during the San Francisco conference, again due to heavy Latin American pressure, the Truman administration assured Argentina's entry into the U.N. as a founding member over loud Soviet objections. As Secretary of State Edward Stettinius noted a few days afterward, had it not gotten Argentina into the U.N. "the [San Francisco] conference would not have continued."[225]

As the San Francisco conference concluded with a U.N. organization and charter to the liking of the U.S., its policy toward Argentina changed yet again. The Truman administration seems to have concluded by the first half of May 1945 that the Farrell–Peron regime, despite the inadvertent boost it received from both American acts, could be toppled in a few months due to growing domestic opposition to it within both the military and the civilian population. As a result the administration decided to return to a regime change policy in Argentina, one more aggressive than its predecessor.[226] Spruille Braden, the first new American ambassador after the restoration of relations, was designated as the main executor of this policy prior to his arrival to Argentina. As the British Ambassador to Argentina noted, Braden, with whom he was in regular contact, arrived in

---

[223] In 1945 the Latin American states made up nearly four-tenths of all then-independent countries, and the expected participants, at the San Francisco conference.

[224] Tulchin 1990:90–91; Schlesinger 2003:96–97. For Braden's support in private for this pause, given the "difficult conditions" that the U.S. faced in the Mexico City conference, see Letter, Braden to Rockefeller March 10, 1945/box 2/Braden Papers.

[225] Memcom May 4,1945/lot/RG59/NARA,ARA, Memorandums relating to individual countries; Schlesinger 2003:chap. 8.

[226] Memo May 15,1945/835.24/RG59/NARA. For the limitations of past attempts to analyze U.S. foreign policy towards Argentina in for the 1945 and early 1946 period using the bureaucratic politics models see Appendix D.

Buenos Aires with "the fixed idea that he had been elected by Providence to over-throw the Farrell–Peron regime."[227]

Initially, intervening in an Argentine election was not part of this renewed American regime change policy. Although the GOU military regime had made occasional public and private promises in this regard ever since it seized power in mid-1943, it continued in mid-1945 to refuse to set a specific date for national elections. A new election code decreed by the GOU on May 31, 1945, as a sup-posed step toward such an election was seen by the Truman administration as being intentionally written in an unusually cumbersome and obscure manner in order to provide the Peron regime with a "technical" excuse for not calling an election in the foreseeable future until the new code was fully "clarified."[228] Likewise, the Truman administration, based on information it received from various sources, expected such elections, if eventually called, to lack even the slightest modicum of true competitiveness and instead to be fully rigged in favor of a Peron presidential candidacy or a handpicked puppet.[229]

Instead, over the following five months the Truman administration and Braden developed and deployed a regime change policy against Peron using three major tools. First, the U.S. government maintained and strengthened the existing informal economic sanctions on Argentina which were conducted under the guise of the WW2 wartime economic controls and, when the war ended, under the guise of the preliminary reconstruction phase.[230] These sanctions were done in this low-key manner in order to reduce pressure on the U.S. government from American exporters to Argentina.[231] American civilian exports of various kinds to Argentina, including key economic resources such as rubber tires and oil, were denied export licenses, delayed through various bu-reaucratic procedures, or provided in very limited quantities.[232] Targeted WW2 sanctions on many major Argentinean firms and businessmen (the proclaimed list) believed to be trading with the Axis during the war, many of which were also

[227] Kelly 1954:307. See also Memo to the president July 1,1945/711.35/RG59/NARA. In the fol-lowing months Braden received multiple private messages voicing strong support for his activities from his superiors in the State Department (FRUS 1945 9:386, 404; Letter, Byrnes to Braden July 4, 1945/box 1/Braden Papers).

[228] Buenos Aires despatch 126 June 8,1945; Buenos Aires despatch 182 June 18,1945, both 835.00/ RG59/NARA.

[229] Buenos Aires 1416 July 3,1945; Buenos Aires 2066 September 4,1945, both 835.00/RG59/ NARA.

[230] Memo May 15,1945/835.24/RG59/NARA; Memcom September 14,1945/lot/RG59/ NARA,ARA, Memorandums relating to individual countries.

[231] Memo July 7,1945/835.24/RG59/NARA. The expected reaction of the Argentinean public was not in this case a major concern—indeed, the Truman administration believed that it would react favorably to overt economic sanctions designed to remove Peron (Buenos Aires 2048 September 3,1945/835.65/RG59/NARA).

[232] Dorn 2005:42; Memo May 15,1945/835.24/RG59/NARA.

believed to be supporters of the GOU, were extended into the post-war era.[233] The U.S. also restored its de facto military sanctions by canceling an arms shipment to Argentina, a shipment promised in April 1945 while it was trying to secure the cooperation of the other Latin American countries. These informal sanctions were expected to cause increased public and military dissatisfaction within Argentina with Peron.[234]

Second, shortly after his arrival, Braden began to regularly make public speeches in both English and Spanish throughout Argentina. These speeches were very critical in various indirect and direct ways of Peron and of the military regime and praised peaceful opposition activities against the GOU, frequently in front of audiences composed of opponents of the military regime.[235] For example, in one speech in late August 1945, Braden indirectly compared the behavior of the Farrell–Peron regime to that of European fascist regimes and promised that "the voice of freedom [that] makes itself heard in this land . . . the voice of the Argentine people—their authentic voice" would be heard by the U.S. government and no onewould "succeed in drowning it."[236] Braden's speeches were combined with efforts, with varying levels of success, to generate international criticism against the Peron regime in the non-Argentine press and at higher levels of the U.S. government and various foreign governments.[237] Both types of international criticism were intentionally designed and encouraged in order to further energize and mobilize the opposition to Peron.[238]

Third, Braden put heavy pressure on the Argentine government to permit more freedom of the press, to enable it in practice, and to release all of its political prisoners.[239] Many of Braden's meetings with the Argentine government officials focused on protecting and increasing the freedom of the press in Argentina both for domestic and for international media, the latter serving as a de facto outlet for domestic Argentine press criticism.[240] Braden also actively tried to protect

[233] Buenos Aires 1165 June 6,1945/740.00112ew/RG59/NARA; State 8769 August 28,1945/740.00112e/RG59/NARA.

[234] Potash 1969:258–259; Buenos Aires 607 May 30,1945/835.24/RG59/NARA.

[235] Letters, Braden to Briggs May 30, 1945 and June 7, 1945/Braden Papers. For a detailed description by Braden of how he used one of his public statements in this manner see Letter, Braden to Wright August 24, 1945/box 19/Braden Papers. For Braden's efforts to gain maximum coverage possible for his speeches within the Argentine public see Ray Josephs, "Iron-Gloved Diplomat," *The Inter-American*, October 1945.

[236] Speech (Braden) August 28, 1945/box 25/Braden Papers.

[237] Buenos Aires 1417 July 3,1945/711.35/RG59/NARA; Buenos Aires 2066 September 4,1945/835.00/RG59/NARA.

[238] Buenos Aires 2066 September 4,1945/835.00/RG59/NARA.

[239] The American demand for release of political prisoners also included the closely related demand to permit all Argentine political exiles to return without fear of imprisonment. Buenos Aires 1273 June 17,1945/711.35/RG59/NARA. For a closely related set of demands following a similar logic, demanding extremely high (and politically destructive) concessions from Peron in regard to the removal of Nazi influence, see FRUS 1945 9:409–410, 478.

[240] The Argentine media, still wary of criticizing Peron and the military too harshly after years of heavy censorship, frequently reprinted in full critical reports by American and foreign

press freedom in Argentina in various ways. For example, Braden offered the U.S. Embassy premises as a refuge to American journalists working in Argentina after Peron ominously warned Braden during a one-on-one meeting that he couldn't guarantee the safety of such "liars and troublemakers" from "spontaneous" violent attacks by his more "fanatical" supporters and then harassed some of them in various ways.[241] Likewise, Braden repeatedly pressured the Argentine government, right from his first public statement after landing in Buenos Aires, to release all of the political prisoners it held.[242]

Although these pressures and actions were described by the Truman administration, both in their private messages to the Argentine government and in their public statements, as being done out of a mixture of an idealistic desire to help liberalize Argentina and persuade the GOU to uphold the solemn commitments that it had made at the Mexico City conference, their goal was far more realpolitik in practice. In other words, these acts were designed to make it easier for the Argentine press to report on the international criticism of the GOU and the related economic difficulties and increase the domestic dissatisfaction with it. Likewise, the release of political prisoners was supposed to help the opposition organize and mobilize against Peron.[243] As Braden noted in one secret message to the State Department in July 1945, increasing and maintaining the freedom of the press was of the "utmost utility in weakening [the domestic] position of [the] Peron military-nazi dictatorship," and much of Peron's opposition to his activities has been because he correctly realized that such press freedom, combined with the release of political prisoners, would "place him in [an] untenable position leading to his downfall."[244]

These three techniques were expected to bring about regime change in Argentina through two possible routes or a combination of them. First, mass demonstrations and general strikes against the military regime, encouraged through these methods, could lead it to fall.[245] Alternatively, the Argentine military, increasingly cognizant of the widespread opposition to Peron and angered

---

correspondents about Peron as front-page news without any further comment. As a result, critical international reporting about the GOU often became a de facto supplement to such domestic press criticism (Frank 1980:62–63).

[241] FRUS 1945 6:508–513.

[242] Letter, Braden to Wright June 11, 1945/box 19/Braden Papers.

[243] Buenos Aires 1920 August 21,1945/835.00/RG59/NARA.

[244] Buenos Aires 1388 June 30,1945/Box 159/PSF/HSTL; Memo July 2,1945/811/RG59/NARA.

[245] See, for example, Memcom, October 4,1945/800/RG84/NARA. Braden also blocked the sale to the Argentinean government of a major crowd-control tool for demonstrations, tear gas, given that in his view the use of tear gas could "break the morals of a people where bullets would not" (Letter, Braden to Tausch July 15, 1945/box 19/Braden Papers).

by his inability to acquire new armaments from abroad, would stage a coup, removing Peron and his supporters from power.[246]

The second regime change operation came very close to success. The reduced restrictions on the freedom of the press and the release of some political prisoners due to these American pressures, combined with Braden's speeches, enlarged and encouraged the domestic opposition to Peron. Anti-regime demonstrations grew greatly in scale and frequency over the Argentine winter and early spring. The largest opposition demonstration, the "March of the Constitution and Freedom" in September 19, 1945, drew approximately 250,000 protesters.[247] Encouraged by these demonstrations, and by a secret understanding developed between them and the opposition, a group of officers under Argentine general Arturo Rawson launched a coup a few days later against Peron and the GOU regime. This first coup attempt failed, but Peron's subsequent harsh reaction, from the restoration of the state of siege to mass arrests of political opponents, failed to quell the public agitation against the increasingly shaky regime.

Then the Truman administration, in an attempt to provide "every encouragement" to the opposition, publicly declared on October 3 that it requested the indefinite postponement of the upcoming Rio Conference over the Argentinean government's post-coup behavior which, it claimed, led it to "not feel" that it could sign or negotiate a major defense treaty with "the present Argentine government." This major international conference, originally scheduled to occur later that month, was supposed to bring about the signing of a multilateral defense treaty between the U.S. and all other Latin American countries.[248]

A few days later a second, more successful coup was attempted. Although ignited by a minor incident, it was in practice a response by parts of the military to what was perceived as massive public opposition to Peron combined with their long-simmering resentment over his growing political power. Angered at Peron's decision on October 8, ignoring open army opposition, to appoint a political ally deeply disliked by much of the military to the director of Argentine mail and communications, a large anti-Peronist segment of the Argentine military decided the following day to demand his prompt resignation, threatening to take over Buenos Aires by force unless their demands were met. Peron, unwilling

---

[246] MacDonald 1989:143. Despite frequent public declarations to the contrary, in private the U.S. government was also quite skeptical of the ability of Argentina to succeed in transitioning to democracy in the near future, due to the passage of nearly fifteen years since the collapse of its previous democratic regime. Buenos Aires 1273 June 17,1945/711.35/RG59/NARA. The main U.S. goal was a Peron-free government of some kind rather than a democratic one in the short and medium term.

[247] Frank 1980:78–79, 85–86. The Truman administration also tried to directly help the opposition recruit protesters by secretly encouraging American-owned firms in Argentina to give their employees paid time off for such activities (MacDonald 1980:386).

[248] Circular, October 1,1945; Department of State Statement 728 October 3,1945; Memcom September 29,1945, all in 710 consultation/RG59/NARA. This treaty was eventually signed in 1947 and became known as the Rio Treaty.

to condone bloodshed between different factions of the military and mistakenly hoping that his close friend and ally, the nominal president Farrell, would find a way to eventually resolve this crisis in his favor, conceded to this demand and resigned. Four days later, Peron was arrested and sent to the island prison of Martin Garcia.[249]

Having achieved their first main goal, removing Peron from power, both the coup leaders and the democratic opposition lacked a clear blueprint for the next steps. After the coup occurred, the democratic opposition demanded the immediate transfer of all executive power in the interim to the Supreme Court, a proposal that was deemed deeply insulting to the military officers who forced Peron's resignation and was promptly rejected. On the democratic opposition's side, the official convocation of a new free presidential election by the interim junta, headed by General Eduardo Avalos, was seen as insufficient. Then, a long squabble ensued between the new junta and the democratic opposition over the interim holder of executive power, which delayed the formation of a new interim government. They also failed to adequately reassure the *descamisados*, the Argentine blue-collar workers who were the biggest beneficiaries of Peron's populist labor policies, that their gains would be protected by the new government. In the intervening ten days, Peron's allies in the labor movement, his remaining supporters in the government, and his girlfriend (and soon-to-be wife) Evita Duarte were able to mobilize the workers who benefited from Peron's populist policies.[250]

Those workers then began an escalating wave of protests in favor of Peron, culminating in a mass demonstration of about 300,000 workers in front of the Argentine presidential palace, the Casa Rosada, on the evening of October 17. Over the course of that day, Avalos, personally unwilling to use force in order to disperse the forthcoming demonstration due to the expected mass civilian casualties that it would require, chose to capitulate to their demands. Then, after brief negotiations with Peron, Avalos resigned his position and restored to power a pro-Peron government led by Farrell. Peron, out of a desire to better position himself politically for the upcoming election campaign, chose not to formally return to his previous government posts.[251] The Truman administration was back to square one with little to show for its efforts.

[249] Page 1988:chaps. 11–14; Potash 1969:268–271.
[250] Page 1988:chaps. 13–14; Potash 1969:271–275.
[251] Page 1988:chaps. 14–15; Potash 1969:276–282.

3.4.3 The Fearful Opposition: The Democratic Union
in Late 1945

The repeated declarations by the restored GOU regime in late October and November 1945 that they planned to maintain the decision of Avalos to convoke a new free and fair presidential election were greeted by the Argentine opposition with a mixture of deep skepticism and wary hope. In the event of a fully free and fair presidential election, the Argentine democratic opposition had strong reasons to be optimistic about its outcome. The main component of the democratic opposition, the radical party, was Argentina's dominant political party during its first democratic era, winning three consecutive presidential elections from 1916 to 1928 by large majorities.[252] Together with its allies in the Democratic Union, this coalition combined political parties which in the last competitive presidential election in Argentine history to that point (1928) had won 66.5% of the vote. Although all executive elections (and most local and congressional elections) conducted after the September 1930 coup by the various authoritarian regimes were non-competitive, when relatively competitive elections were permitted at the regional level or for non-executive positions the parties composing the Democratic Union did quite well in them. For example, in the 1936 midterm elections to the Argentine lower house, the parties which later composed the Democratic Union captured 58.1% of the vote.[253] Accordingly, the leaders of the Democratic Union, largely unaware of the changes in Argentine society that were quietly weakening their political support during this period, were quite certain of their chances of winning a fully free and fair presidential election.[254]

Instead, the opposition's concerns in regard to their electoral chances came from two different directions. The first were doubts regarding the fairness of the upcoming 1946 elections given recent Argentine history and the behavior of the GOU regime. The various military and civilian regimes that followed the 1930 coup usually followed the outer forms of democracy while using heavy government fraud and intimidation, especially on the election day, in order to win the two previous presidential elections (in 1931 and 1937). Among many other methods, large numbers of Argentine dead temporarily came back to life, fake ballots were printed and inserted in the ballot boxes, and known members of the political opposition were prevented from voting on election day by the police.

---

[252] Nohlen 2001:60, 108–109.

[253] Ibid.:85.

[254] Ciria 1974:89–90, 139–140, 221.Other contemporary observers held similar beliefs; see, for example, "New Moves in Argentina," *The Economist*, August 18, 1945.

The fraud was so massive in scale that it effectively rendered these elections completely uncompetitive.[255]

The democratic opposition initially had high hopes for the GOU military regime that came to power following the coup of June 1943. This coup was largely the result of the anger within elements of the military about two closely interrelated actions: the plans of incumbent president Castillo to impose his handpicked successor through yet another fraudulent election scheduled for late 1943 and Castillo's decision to fire his Secretary of War, whom he suspected was planning to enter as a candidate and disrupt these succession plans.[256] In the aftermath of this coup the democratic opposition initially expected, based on their secret pre-coup discussions with some of the coup leaders, and the GOU's statements in its immediate aftermath, a brief transitional military regime. The GOU was expected to remove the various existing restrictions on civil rights and political party activity and then quickly permit a free and fair election and the restoration of democracy.[257] They were to be sorely disappointed.

Instead of preparing the ground for a new, fair presidential election, the new GOU military regime under Ramirez eventually became, after a brief power struggle within the GOU, even more authoritarian. Ramirez dissolved the Argentine Congress and enforced existing restrictions on civil rights with greater zeal than his predecessors had, firing civil servants and professors who called for the restoration of democracy, dissolving pro-democratic student organizations, and reimposing existing restrictions on the press. A new election was indefinitely delayed and the GOU began to talk of itself as a permanent authoritarian right-wing dictatorship, even dropping the term "provisional" from its official title. In December 1943, the GOU went further than the previous post-1930 authoritarian regimes ever had, ordering the dissolution of all political party organizations, confiscating their property, and imposing an even harsher set of restrictions on the press.[258] When Ramirez was ousted in an internal GOU reshuffle in February 1944, Farrell and Peron maintained and deepened these harsh authoritarian policies, which also now included mass arrests and extended imprisonment of "politically dangerous" elements.[259]

In early 1945, due to a variety of domestic and international factors, the behavior of the GOU regime began to veer back and forth between repression and liberalization. The year started with a deeper government crackdown on any opposition activity.[260] In February–March 1945 the Farrell–Peron regime made a

---

[255] Blanksten 1953:43; Ciria 1974:13, 19, 35–42. For a colorful description of the specific fraud methods used by the government during this period see (Rennie 1945:227–228).
[256] Potash 1969:191–193.
[257] Potash 1969:207–208, 217; Cane 2011:93–94.
[258] Potash 1969:216–218, 225–224; Cane 2011:92–93.
[259] Frank 1980:50, 115; Potash 1969:245–246.
[260] Ciria 1974:89.

few liberalizing moves such as restoring opposition figures fired from their government and university jobs to their positions. Then, in late April, in response to some opposition demonstrations and suspicions of a planned coup, the GOU returned to a policy of harsh repression. A new wave of arrests of civilian opposition figures and of military opponents was initiated which was combined with the tightening of restrictions on demonstrations.[261]

The subsequent behavior of the restored GOU in late October and November 1945, although increasing the opposition's hopes for a relatively free election, nevertheless failed to dispel many of the opposition's fears in this regard. Following its repeated promises to enable a free presidential election, the GOU did permit the political parties to operate legally and restored to the political parties the property confiscated from them two years beforehand. It also promised the opposition to permit it to have observers in all ballot stations during election day.[262] However, the military government, despite multiple requests by the opposition, refused to lift the state of siege that had been reimposed in late September 1945. The continuance of the state of siege, under which many run-of-the-mill electioneering activities could be theoretically declared illegal, gave the GOU the legal right to resume its repressive practices toward the opposition any time it so pleased.[263] The GOU also continued during this period to impose some significant restrictions on the ability of the opposition to broadcast and distribute its election propaganda. Likewise, some parts of the Argentine government, still dominated by strong supporters of Peron in the GOU, continued to provide significant assistance of various kinds to the Peron campaign.[264] As a result, although the Democratic Union saw by late November 1945 the upcoming Argentine presidential election as being more likely to be relatively competitive than its recent predecessors, its fears of the GOU heavily tilting the electoral playing field in favor of Peron in some manner continued into the last days of the election campaign.[265]

[261] Potash 1969:255–257.

[262] Potash 1980:22; Buenos Aires 3017 December 3,1945/835.00/RG59/NARA.

[263] Potash 1980:26. The state of siege was eventually only removed for 48 hours—for the election day and the day that preceded it.

[264] Ibid.:20–26. As the GOU's censorship on the propaganda efforts of the opposition effectively stopped in mid-December, a new concern took its place in the eyes of the Democratic Union—whether the GOU would protect it in practice from occasional violent attacks by pro-Peron gangs on its outdoor campaigning activities (ibid.:27–28).

[265] Potash, for example, doesn't find the "atmosphere of skepticism" about the honesty of the presidential elections within the Democratic Union "beginning to dissipate" until at least early February (Potash 1980:37). From private conversations of senior Democratic Union members in this regard, it is clear that their fears of a last-moment success by Peron to force the GOU to tilt the playing field against Tamborini (or their outright annulment) continued into the second week of February (FBI report February 11,1946/835.00/RG59/NARA).

Second, the exigencies of building a broad political coalition between parties with very different political platforms forced the Democratic Union to choose two less-than-optimal candidates for this task. The presidential candidate, Jose Pascual Tamborini, was a grey, undistinguished politician with little popular appeal or charisma. This was a major handicap against a candidate already widely known for his charisma and spellbinding speeches.[266] Likewise, the vice presidential candidate, Enrique Mosca, except for being equally grey and uncharismatic, was quite unpopular among voters in his own region (the Argentine province of Santa Fe) due to his use of paramilitary troops to crush a strike when he served as its governor.[267] As a result, the Democratic Union was led by candidates that weakened its hand. In that problematic political situation the democratic opposition began to look for help from abroad.

3.4.4 The American Decision to Intervene
October–December 1945

In the aftermath of the failure of the second coup attempt in October 1945, the Truman administration initially continued its pre-coup policies. These policies were now led by Braden after he was appointed in August 1945, as a reward for his efforts in Argentina, as the new assistant secretary of state for Latin America—the fourth-highest policymaking position in the U.S. government during this era for this region after the president, the secretary of state, and his deputy.[268] Sure that its regime change policies came quite close to success, the administration continued looking for ways to create heavy international pressure on the Argentine government that would reignite massive anti-regime protests or another coup attempt against Peron. Accordingly, the Truman administration's initial post-coup focus was on convincing other Latin American states to join an American multilateral pressure campaign on Argentina through various diplomatic initiatives and quietly encouraging members of the democratic opposition to go on lobbying trips for this purpose throughout the western hemisphere. Creating a united front against Argentina in Latin America was expected to give the U.S. the ability to impose multilateral economic sanctions or at least generate

---

[266] Luna 1969:350, 362–364. Although the formal selection of Tamborini as the Democratic Union's presidential candidate was not concluded until late December 1945, by early November, two weeks before the creation of the Democratic Union, he was already the informally agreed choice by all of the constituent parties (ibid.:350).

[267] Alexander 1951:46–47. Furthermore, Mosca's name (which means "fly" in Spanish) was an open source for effective mockery among political opponents (ibid.:46).

[268] Not surprisingly, changes in the identity of assistant secretaries of state were seen in this era as events worthy of front-page articles. See, for example, "Byrnes Expected to Drop 4 Top Aides," *New York Times*, August 6, 1945.

mass multilateral condemnations of the GOU regime—either act was expected to have the desired destabilizing effects.[269]

The U.S. government made, however, no progress in these efforts over the following six weeks. Most Latin American governments showed no interest in joining such anti-Argentine efforts.[270] Likewise, even the long-existing American informal sanctions on Argentina largely collapsed in late 1945 due to the effective counter-pressures by the GOU regime (such as restricting its food exports to U.S. allies) after it became increasingly aware of their existence.[271]

In early December the Truman administration shifted to a completely new policy. This was due to two key developments. First, during November and early December 1945 the U.S. government was receiving an increasing number of reliable reports from multiple sources that the upcoming Argentinean election, now set for February 24, 1946, would likely be conducted in a relatively free and fair manner.[272] Then, in early December, Braden received a visit from Hugo Stunz, the editor of an Argentinean newspaper and a prominent member of the democratic opposition to Peron.[273] Stunz requested that the U.S. intervene in the elections in the Democratic Union's favor by releasing a statement about the information it had from captured German archives about Peron and the GOU's ties to Nazi Germany approximately twenty days before the elections. He also requested for this purpose that the U.S. government impose sanctions on American fuel exports to Argentina.[274]

Braden was forced, due to the previously noted success of the Argentine government's countermeasures, to immediately reject the second request.[275]

---

[269] Memcom October 18,1945/835.00/RG59/NARA; Macdonald 1980:388. For the encouragement of the lobbying trips see State 1488 October 23,1945/835.00/RG59/NARA.

[270] For example, during this period the Uruguayan government, after quiet American encouragement, proposed the enactment of a new regional doctrine. Under this new doctrine a collective Latin American intervention in a fellow state's affairs would be an acceptable activity when that state heavily and repeatedly violated the human rights of its population or broke its international commitments, a thinly veiled reference to events in Argentina. This Uruguayan proposal was quickly rejected by most Latin American states (State 404 [Montevideo] October 24,1945/835.00/RG59/NARA; Whitaker 1946:206).

[271] Dorn 2005:42–47.

[272] Buenos Aires 2800 November 7,1945; Memcom November 21,1945, both 835.00/RG59/NARA; ONI estimate r-786-45 December 5,1945/800/RG84/NARA.

[273] In early October 1945, for example, Stunz had to temporarily seek refuge in the Chilean embassy in Buenos Aires in order to avoid arrest by the military government (Buenos Aires 2439 October 5,1945/891/RG84/NARA). The prominence of Stunz's newspaper (El Dia) within the democratic opposition can be seen in the fact, for example, that it was one of the first three opposition newspapers to be suspended by the GOU during the political crisis of early October 1945 and it was among the handful of opposition newspapers to be violently attacked by Peron supporters on the night of Peron's return from imprisonment and the failure of the second coup attempt on October 17 (U.S. Department of State 1946:82; Despatch 1098 October 17,1945/891/RG84/NARA). For the close ties of Stunz to prominent members of the Radical Party see, for example, Fascetto (2014:50–51). See also n. 306.

[274] Memcom December 3,1945/835.00/RG59/NARA.

[275] Ibid.

However, the first request was more feasible and over the next two-and-a-half months the Truman administration began to intervene for the Democratic Union in the 1946 election in the requested manner.

3.5 The Electoral Intervention

3.5.1 The Initial Blast: The Thirteen Nazi Telegrams

After deciding to intervene in the 1946 Argentinean elections, the Truman administration, which seems to have become quickly aware of the rather embryonic state in which the planned requested compilation of such information, called the Blue Book, (see subsection 3.5.2), remained, began thinking of an early release during the pre-election period of some evidence of the ties between Peron and Nazi Germany. For this purpose it turned to some documents already readily available—thirteen captured telegrams from the German embassy in Buenos Aires documenting German government subsidies to multiple Argentine media organs during WW2, some of which were now strong supporters of Peron's presidential candidacy.[276]

Even before the U.S. government decided to intervene in these elections, the use of these telegrams to affect Argentine domestic developments had been considered but rejected. For example, in mid-November 1945 the Argentine Catholic Church published a pastoral letter that was widely seen as a de facto endorsement of Peron's economic policies and an indirect rejection of his democratic opponents.[277] The American chargé in Buenos Aires, and the effective replacement of Braden as ambassador, John Cabot, then proposed publishing some of these telegrams, which showed Nazi support for the Argentine Church's official newspaper (*El Pueblo*), as one major way to blunt this letter's potential effect on Argentine voters and discourage it from further aiding Peron.[278] However, in late November 1945, the Truman administration rejected this intervention option, or any other pressure on the Argentine Church, out of a desire to preserve this information for later use in its then-ongoing attempt to attract multilateral Latin American support for pressure on Argentina.[279]

However, the interest of the opposition in exposing such materials for electoral purposes changed the U.S. government's calculus in regard to those documents. In mid-December it began picking possible German telegrams to use for this

---

[276] State 1791 December 14,1945/835.00/RG59/NARA.
[277] Buenos Aires 2893 November 19,1945/835.00/RG59/NARA.
[278] Buenos Aires 2909, November 20,1945/835.00/RG59/NARA.
[279] Buenos Aires 1694, November 29,1945/835.00/RG59/NARA.

purpose and in early January it settled on what it perceived as the best possible way of exposing them—handed to the Argentine foreign minister in a private diplomatic meeting followed by a press conference by Cabot in Buenos Aires in which these documents would be released to the Argentine press and public. As it noted in one telegram on this topic, the method of exposure it proposed—releasing the Nazi telegrams in Argentina itself—was "calculated to achieve main objective, i.e. affecting Arg[entine] public opinion and creating confusion in Peron campaign."[280] It then asked Cabot to check with the Democratic Union whether such a release would indeed be of electoral use to them. After receiving a very positive reaction from the opposition, Cabot released these telegrams, in translation into both English and Spanish in this manner on January 17, 1946.[281] The telegrams received wide exposure in the Argentine press. Nevertheless, they seem to have had little effect on the election campaign.[282]

3.5.2 The "Atomic Bomb": The Blue Book

A few weeks later, the Blue Book was finally ready for use. The idea of publishing an official statement describing and summarizing the evidence that the U.S. had about the ties of Peron and the GOU to Nazi Germany in order to weaken and discredit it in a non-electoral setting had been percolating within the U.S. government since at least late 1944.[283] However, no concrete action had been taken in this regard. In August 1945, Braden's predecessor as assistant secretary of state, Nelson Rockefeller, had begun planning to start such a compilation, combined with documentation of Argentine violations of its Mexico City promises, in order to generate multilateral pressure within Latin America on Argentina.[284] This was part of the wider American effort during this period to look for ways to generate international criticism of the GOU for the regime change campaign. When Braden arrived back in the U.S. in late September to start his new position, he took up this idea with the same goal in mind, and further developed these

---

[280] See erased line in State 22 January 5,1946/835.00/RG59/NARA; State 1791 December 14,1945/835.00/RG59/NARA. The Truman administration also seemed to hope that these documents would serve a secondary yet related purpose—to discourage the Argentine government from favoring pro-Peron newspapers through increased supplies of newsprint, a possibility about which it was receiving increasing reports in late December 1945.

[281] State 48 January 10,1946/800/RG84/NARA; Buenos Aires 194 January 18,1946/835.00/RG59/NARA.

[282] Luna 1969:369; Letter, Cabot to Boal, January 21, 1946/Cabot Papers, Tufts (microfilm).

[283] MacDonald 1980:388.

[284] State 6964 August 14,1945/800/RG59/NARA. In response to this request, and Braden's support for this idea when he still was the ambassador to Argentina, the U.S. embassy in Buenos Aires had begun to slowly collect and prepare some such materials (Memo September 27,1945/800/RG84/NARA; Despatch 1116 October 20,1945/835.00/RG59/NARA).

plans.[285] After the eventual failure of the second coup in mid-October 1945, Braden convinced Secretary of State James Byrnes to start the collection of information for this purpose, leading Byrnes in October 26, 1945, to order the setting-up of a special ad hoc working group in the State Department for this purpose and request assistance for it from other U.S. government agencies.[286]

Although Braden and other State Department officials frequently expressed a desire to complete the Blue Book quickly, in practice work on it moved quite slowly over the following five weeks. For example, almost a month after the formal creation of the Blue Book working group in late October, many key positions in it were yet to be filled.[287]

The opposition's request for electoral assistance of this kind in early December 1945, and the American decision to accordingly utilize the planned Blue Book for this purpose, shifted the work on it into high gear, greatly increasing the amounts of manpower, effort, and resources dedicated by the Truman administration to this project.[288] The U.S. embassy in Buenos Aires, for example, was informed on December 7, 1945, that given the importance and the urgency of the Blue Book, now described as "the most important undertaking confronting this government in the hemisphere today," it had to immediately suspend all other non-urgent political and economic work until further notice. It was then to transfer all freed personnel to work on collecting information and preparing summaries for the Blue Book team in Washington, D.C. Likewise, all vacations, including for the upcoming holidays, were canceled.[289]

The Truman administration then began to transfer temporarily personnel from other embassies and U.S. missions to the Buenos Aires embassy. Due to the U.S. government's heavy manpower needs in Asia and Europe during this era, U.S. embassies in Latin America suffered from severe manpower shortages which hampered their ability to function effectively.[290] Nevertheless, in order to speed up work on the Blue Book, the U.S. government in the second week of December temporarily transferred personnel from multiple embassies in Latin America to its embassy in Argentina. As it described in its requisition requests, these personnel from other embassies were "urgently" needed because of the "utmost importance" of the Blue Book which now had to "be released before

[285] Memorandum October 11,1945/835.00/RG59/NARA.

[286] Departmental Order 1353 October 26,1945/box 29/lot/RG59/NARA, Memoranda on preparation of Argentine Bluebook.

[287] Memo November 23,1945/box 29/lot/RG59/NARA, Memoranda on preparation of Argentine Bluebook.

[288] For the approval of Braden's decision to redirect the Blue Book for this purpose see Letter, Braden to Dawson February 26, 1946/box 20/Braden Papers.

[289] Buenos Aires 1736 & 1737, both December 7,1945/box 16/lot/RG59/NARA, Memoranda on preparation of Argentine Bluebook.

[290] Memo, undated Braden to Russell/box 24/Braden Papers.

Argentine Elections scheduled for Feb[ruary] 24."[291] It also reassigned a U.S. Treasury Department team in Argentina which was working on unrelated economic matters to full-time work on the Blue Book.[292]

On the same day in which these requests were made of the U.S. embassy in Argentina, the State Department also sent an urgent request to the U.S. occupation authorities in Germany. It now demanded "maximum amounts of materials immediately" for the Blue Book. Over the following three months the U.S. occupation authorities, giving "all possible emphasis" to the Blue Book, sifted through four hundred tons of captured German government and corporate documents, microfilming any useful documents found and sending them to the U.S. by air.[293] A special team of dedicated investigators, supplemented by personnel flown directly from the U.S., began in mid-December 1945 to crisscross Germany, hunting for additional documents and relevant former members of the Nazi regime. Over the following three months the team interrogated dozens of former Nazi officials and directors of German corporations with extensive operations in Argentina.[294]

No expenses were spared in the search for and quick provision of information to the Blue Book working group. For example, one of the documentary sources inspected for this purpose was a collection of 26 million Nazi party membership cards captured by the U.S. army in Germany at the end of WW2. Following the State Department's request, the process of going through these membership files in search for useful information was sped up considerably with a team of 135 Germans and thirty German-speaking Americans working in ten-hour shifts in search of files from Latin America, eventually locating 1,489 such Argentine members.[295] When the microfilmed copies of these Argentine membership files were found to be difficult to read by the Blue Book working group, the State Department had all of the original files flown directly to Washington, D.C.[296]

[291] State 473 (Montevideo) December 7,1945/box 19/lot/RG59/NARA, Memoranda on preparation of Argentine Bluebook; Buenos Aires 1737 December 7,1945/box 16/lot/RG59/NARA, Memoranda on preparation of Argentine Bluebook.

[292] Despatch 1945 February 2,1946/box 10/lot/RG59/NARA, Memoranda on preparation of Argentine Bluebook.

[293] Rawls 1976:435. According to the available documentation, more than 90% of the documents arriving from Europe for the Blue Book were sent after mid-December (Index to telegraphic information February 26,1946/box 1/lot/RG59/NARA, Memoranda on preparation of Argentine Bluebook).

[294] State 397 (Berlin) January 4,1946/box 20/lot/RG59/NARA, Memoranda on preparation of Argentine Bluebook; according to the available documentation, at least forty people were interrogated for this purpose (Memo, "Record of documentary material from Germany sent directly to Mr. Spaeth from Mr. Blanke," undated/box 1/lot/RG59/NARA, Memoranda on preparation of Argentine Bluebook).

[295] Berlin 1333 December 27,1945; A-357 (Berlin) December 28,1945/box 20/lot/RG59/NARA, Memoranda on preparation of Argentine Bluebook.

[296] State 195 (Berlin) January 23,1946; State 752 (Berlin) March 26,1946, both box 20/lot/RG59/NARA, Memoranda on preparation of Argentine Bluebook.

Despite all American efforts to expedite the Blue Book, the large amount of work that it involved led it to be delayed. The deadline chosen for completing the expedited Blue Book, February 1 or around the time frame requested for the release of the Blue Book by the opposition, could not be followed.[297] After another massive push by the working group it was nevertheless completed eight days later, at 4:00 a.m. on Saturday, February 9.[298]

When Braden informed the embassy about the upcoming completion of the Blue Book and the Administration's plan to publish it, a last-minute debate arose about using it.[299] Cabot, the U.S. chargé, opposed its publication prior to the election. Cabot argued that recent developments in the election campaign had made a Peron victory unlikely and the pre-election publication of the Blue Book, the "atomic bomb" in his colorful description, could have unpredictable effects.[300] The Argentinean opposition, however, disagreed with Cabot. Mosca, the Democratic Union's vice-presidential candidate, when secretly asked by Cabot in this regard, strongly supported the publication of the Blue Book.[301] It then secretly sent, through the FBI representative in Buenos Aires, a recommendation to publicly release the Blue Book on February 12, the day in which Peron was scheduled to deliver his formal nomination speech as presidential candidate.[302]

Braden decided to accept the advice of the opposition and publish the Blue Book prior to the elections in the manner that they recommended. After copies of the Blue Book were given, as a formality, to representatives of all Latin American states except Argentina in a closed meeting, Braden had the Blue Book leaked to the Argentine press in the morning of February 12, a day earlier than the original date in which the U.S. government planned to release it to the general public.[303] As Peron was making the final preparations for his formal nomination speech that evening, detailed reports about the contents of the Blue Book began to appear in special evening editions of major Argentinean newspapers.[304]

For the remainder of the election campaign, the Blue Book became the key topic. Coverage of the Blue Book and reactions to it completely dominated the

[297] Despatch 1351 January 16,1946; Memo January 23,1946, both 835.00/RG59/NARA.

[298] Attachment to Blue Book offprint copy February 13,1946/box 1/lot/RG59/NARA, Memoranda on preparation of Argentine Bluebook.

[299] State Niact 222 February 8,1946/835.00/RG59/NARA.

[300] FRUS 1946 9:201–202.

[301] Niact 435 February 9,1946/835.00/RG59/NARA.

[302] See FBI Report February 11,1946/835.00/RG59/NARA and the handwritten notes on it. Argentine political traditions during this era had presidential candidates accepting formally the nomination a short period before election day, long after their nomination was a settled fact. FBI representatives in the western hemisphere served in this era, prior to the creation of the CIA in 1947, as de facto intelligence agents under the guise of being "legal attachés."

[303] See a copy of the text in U.S. Department of State (1946),

[304] Buenos Aires 462 February 12,1946; State Niact 222 February 8,1946, both 835.00/RG59/NARA.

Argentinean media with the anti-Peronist media giving prominent, daily coverage to extracts and summaries taken from it while the Peronist press countered these reports by publishing various denials of the charges contained in it combined with attacks on the decision by the U.S. government to publish it. As one historian noted, as a result of the widespread coverage "it is difficult to conceive of a voting age person who had not heard of the Libro Azul [Blue Book] in one context or another" prior to election day.[305]

Peron didn't remain silent about the Blue Book. In a last-moment addition to his prepared nomination speech, Peron claimed that he is a staunch defender of Argentine sovereignty and, unlike the Democratic Union, he will not "bend the knee" in front of the U.S. He then accused Braden of creating, inspiring, and organizing the Democratic Union in an attempt to create "a puppet government" of "quislings" which would harm Argentina. Peron concluded with the claim that "Let those who vote on the twenty-fourth for the Oligarchic-Communist alliance [the Democratic Union] know that they are simply voting for Mr. Braden. The question of the hour is this: 'Braden or Peron!' "[306] In the following days the Peron campaign gave out handbills and pasted campaign posters on walls throughout Argentina with this slogan. In subsequent speeches Peron denied the allegations in the Blue Book and even published a few days before the elections a brief booklet, called the "Blue and White book" after the colors of the Argentine flag, in which he claimed to refute the charges made in the Blue Book.[307] In contrast, the Democratic Union initially came out in open support of the Blue Book, with one senior leader even describing it in one of his campaign speeches as a "friendly gesture" by the U.S. toward the people of Argentina.[308]

To the great annoyance and surprise of the Truman administration, the electoral intervention didn't have the effect that the administration expected.[309] After a few days of shock about the claims made in the Blue Book on Peron and the GOU's supposed ties to Nazi Germany, a wave of nationalist backlash seems to have begun within significant segments of the Argentine public against the Democratic Union and Tamborini.[310] In the last few days before the election, a growing number of members of the opposition, based on the largely unfavorable reactions they were increasingly receiving from the general public, concluded

[305] Potash 1980:42.
[306] English-language translation taken from Buenos Aires 465 February 13,1946/835.00/RG59/NARA.
[307] Potash 1980:43.
[308] Cueno 1982:115; Luna 1969:378.
[309] One subsequent U.S. government intelligence memo, expressing surprise at the adverse effects of the Blue Book, blamed the Democratic Union for its failure to gain "political capital" out of the book's release although "prior to its release there had been considerable clamor" by the Democratic Union for the U.S. government to do that (Memorandum April 4, 1946/box 1/Braden Papers).
[310] Whitaker 1954:148.

in private that the timing of the release of the Blue Book was "poor."[311] Likewise, when a Democratic Union activist on election day questioned the people standing in line to vote about their voting intentions, one of them answered, "Peron is not my cup of tea. But I will vote against Braden."[312]

Despite the opposition's fears in regard to the election, and the increased political tensions over the Blue Book, the election eventually passed without any special incidents or shenanigans, leading to nearly universal acclaims in its aftermath—including from the Democratic Union—for its overall fairness and cleanness. When the votes were counted over the next few weeks, Juan Peron was found to have won the election with 53.7% of the popular vote and 304 to 72 votes in the Argentinean Electoral College. He then, together with his wife, Evita, transformed Argentine politics and society over the following nine years. All the U.S. government could do was to cry for Argentina.

3.6   Conclusions

As can be seen here, the archival evidence from the three in-depth case studies of electoral interventions follow overall the theoretical expectations of my theory. In the first case, the 1953 West German elections, the SPD, because of the strong preferences of its leadership for German reunification as well as their hope to protect themselves from attacks of being insufficiently nationalist, decided to staunchly oppose the creation of the EDC—an organization seen by the Eisenhower administration as the best policy solution to its three main interests in regard of Germany. The SPD's opposition, in combination with Adenauer's decision to request U.S. electoral help because of his and the CDU's weak political position, led the U.S. to agree to intervene in the elections in Adenauer's favor. The U.S. then, in full cooperation with Adenauer and his election "shopping list," assisted him in various costly ways during the campaign: from restarting a trade agreement, to setting up a commission to release German war criminals, to spending $15 million ($111 million in 2016 dollars) in a food aid program for East Germans, to agreeing to call for a risky Four Power conference with the USSR, and finally to issuing a public threat a few days before the elections warning Germans of severe consequences if Adenauer were not reelected.

---

[311] Buenos Aires 555 February 21,1946/820.02/RG84/NARA. The Democratic Union's growing fears about the effectiveness of the "Braden or Peron" retort even led it to come out in the campaign's final days with a new counter-slogan: "Tamborini or Hitler" (Scenna 1974:90).

[312] Cueno 1982:184. Likewise, one U.S. member of Congress who visited Argentina at the time became "sure" from his conversations and observations there that the Blue Book had "helped to elect" Peron (Letter, Baldwin to Truman April 14, 1946/Box 144/PSF/HSTL).

In the second case, the 1958 Guatemalan election, the U.S. had remained largely uninvolved in a preceding competitive presidential election in October 1957 due to its view of all major candidates and parties as acceptable. That, in turn, led it to reject some requests of electoral assistance in the 1957 election. However, the annulling of the results of these elections and the scheduling of new presidential elections due to large post-election protests—protests that indicated to the U.S. the significant electoral power of a new left-wing party, the PR, as well as growing communist infiltration into the party—led the Eisenhower administration to become increasingly worried of the possibility of the PR winning power. Such a victory by the PR was expected to lead to the administration's worst-case scenario—that is, a slow slide of Guatemala into communism as had supposedly occurred earlier that decade there under Arbenz. Nevertheless, after receiving requests of electoral intervention from two relatively weak candidates (Cruz Salazar and Peralta) and no interest from a third, now far stronger one (Ydigoras), the Eisenhower administration chose initially to bide its time, hoping for a stronger center-right unity candidate to arise. Only when one of these candidates (Cruz Salazar) showed some tentative signs of improvement in his political chances, and no such stronger unity candidate arose, did the U.S. government decide to choose between the two intervention requests, accept Cruz Salazar's request, and covertly give him the campaign funding that he asked for.

In the third case, the 1946 Argentinean elections, the United States long perceived the GOU regime under the de facto control of Juan Peron as an unfriendly, increasingly fascist-totalitarian dictatorship whose continued existence in power gravely threatened U.S. security in the western hemisphere and increased the chances of a future return of Nazism to Europe. It initially tried, when no competitive elections were in sight, of its own volition to remove Peron and the GOU through a regime change operation—the imposition of sanctions combined with the encouragement of a coup and/or mass anti-regime protests. However, that method, despite some temporary near-successes, failed to bring about the removal of Peron from power, as did attempts to enlist multilateral support for such efforts.

In that situation, the decision of the GOU in late 1945 to hold what was increasingly believed to be a relatively competitive executive election, and a request by the long-repressed Argentine opposition, fearful of yet another rigged election, for electoral assistance, led the Truman administration to decide to change its policy and shift toward an electoral intervention instead. It then, following the request and subsequent strong encouragement of the Argentine opposition, began to search for, prepare, and release captured Nazi documents and other information allegedly proving the ties of the GOU and Peron to Nazi Germany—culminating in the release of the Blue Book twelve days before the elections. Table 3.2 summarizes the key aspects of these three cases. In the next chapter, I investigate three cases where the two theoretical conditions are missing in part or in full.

Table 3.2 Causes of Electoral Intervention (H1–H2): Full Summary of Key Aspects of the Three Main Intervention Case Studies

Case Study	Assisted Actor Wants/ Requests Aid	Domestic Political Situation of Assisted Actor	GP Sees Implacable Actor	Collusion During Intervention	Support of Theory?
West Germany 1953	Yes—request by Adenauer	Fragile Victor Low membership and severe political and organizational weaknesses of CDU; Adenauer's advanced age (77) and his and CDU's high, persistent unpopularity, etc.	Yes—SDP/ Ollenhauer	Yes—all five main int. methods result of an Adenauer proposal and/ or closely coordinated/ deployed w/him	Yes
Argentina 1946	Yes— request by democratic opp.	Blocked/ Weakened Loser Credible expectations of heavy fraud, manipulation, by GOU, etc.	Yes—Peron/ GOU	Yes—aid type (dirty tricks) proposed by and deployed in requested manner by opp.	Yes
Guatemala 1958	Yes—request by Cruz Salazar (and Peralta)	Blocked/ Weakened loser (both requestors) For Cruz Salazar—badly damaged and unpopular party (MDN) due to 1957 elections and aftermath; low name recognition, etc.	Yes (after annulment of 1957 election)— PR	Yes—aid type (campaign funding) requested by Cruz Salazar and provided w/his knowledge	Yes

4

Staying on the Sidelines

When Intervention Opportunities Are Declined

In the previous chapter I began to examine my argument about the causes of electoral intervention. Investigating three cases of partisan electoral interventions, I found that the two critical concurrent factors that my argument notes—a request or agreement to receive such aid by the assisted side and a perception by the great power of a certain actor in the target to be a serious threat to its interests—were indeed critical factors in the process that led to a decision to intervene. I also found, as expected, that cooperation and coordination between the target and the intervener once the intervention had commenced, played a key role in what specific methods were used as part of the intervention and exactly how they were provided.

However, only investigating cases in which both conditions were present (and in which electoral interventions have occurred) is not sufficient to support this argument. It is possible, for example, that one or both of these concurrent conditions are superfluous. In other words, the fact that the three cases that were examined so far included both conditions makes one wonder whether, in situations in which only one (or neither) of these conditions is present, we would see processes and outcomes that diverge from my theoretical predictions. Failing to analyze some such situations as well will leave a permanent question mark over the conclusions derived from the cases analyzed in Chapter 3.

Accordingly, in this chapter I investigate three additional case studies—the 1967 Greek election, the 1965 Philippine election, and the 1958 Venezuelan election. As can be seen in Table 4.1, each one of these cases shows the other three possible combinations of conditions according to my argument. In the 1967 Greek Election case, neither condition is present. In the 1965 Philippine Elections case, only the second condition (desire of a domestic actor for electoral aid) is present, and in the 1958 Venezuelan elections case, only the first condition (the great power perceiving its interests as being seriously threatened by another domestic actor) is.

These three cases are also analyzed using structured-focused comparison[1] checking, via process tracing and congruence, for the same set of observable

[1] George and Bennett 2005.

Meddling in the Ballot Box. Dov H. Levin, Oxford University Press (2020). © Oxford University Press.
DOI: 10.1093/oso/9780197519882.001.0001.

Table 4.1 The Case Studies (Possible Targets) by Selection Criteria (Investigated Cases in This Chapter Are Shaded)

		Great Power Sees Implacable Actor B	
		Yes	No
Actor A Wants Aid	Yes	West Germany 1953 Guatemala 1958 Argentina 1946	Philippines 1965
	No	Venezuela 1958	Greece 1967

implications in each process in which a would-be intervening country decides whether to intervene in an election. As noted, in situations where only one or neither of the previously noted conditions is present we wouldn't expect any significant electoral intervention to occur. A great power which sees all of the significant political actors in a given country as "acceptable" is expected to not be interested in intervening nor to allow itself to be pulled into an intervention by one of the domestic actors requesting its help in an upcoming election. Likewise, if the great power sees one of the domestic actors as one with whom "they can't do business" but is unable to locate domestic help within the target, it is expected to usually prefer to "sit out" the election, waiting to see the election results before taking any significant actions. As for the domestic actor, it is expected not to accept an offer to intervene on its behalf nor make a request for a significant intervention when it perceives its political situation as relatively good or at least as acceptable. We also expect the lack of these conditions to play key roles in the decision by the great power to not intervene in the election in question.

4.1. By Mutual Disinterest: The 1967 Greek Elections

4.1.1 U.S. Interest in Greece in the 1960s

Unlike in the days of the Truman Doctrine of the late 1940s, when the Greek government was in the midst of a difficult civil war against a communist-dominated insurgency, Greece was not a burning, daily concern to U.S. decision-makers during the 1960s. Nevertheless, the U.S. government still saw itself as having very important interests in Greece throughout this period and kept its watch over events there. First of all, Greece occupied an important strategic position both in the geographic sense and in the American Cold War alliance network. As a member of NATO, the U.S.'s main military alliance during (and after) the Cold

War, Greece played an important role in maintaining NATO's cohesion during a period of fragility.[2] It likewise occupied an important strategic location on NATO's southern flank, limiting Soviet access to the Eastern Mediterranean, the Middle East, and Africa.[3]

Second, as a result of Greece's strategic position, the U.S. had major facilities in Greece whose continued and unhindered activities was considered vital to U.S. national security. For example, the U.S. military bases in Greece (with nearly 7,000 U.S. personnel by late 1965) were of primary importance in serving the U.S. Sixth Fleet in particular and U.S. force projection capabilities in the Eastern Mediterranean and the Middle East in general. These were both areas where the U.S. saw (and still sees) such capabilities as very important to its security.[4] Likewise, as the only Balkan state in this era which was also a NATO member, Greece hosted a large CIA station which played a key role in CIA intelligence-gathering and covert espionage activities throughout the Balkans.[5] Greece also hosted important overt "Voice of America" relay stations for open propaganda activities by the United States Information Agency (USIA) in Eastern Europe.

The number and importance of these U.S. (and NATO) facilities were increasing throughout this period. For example, during the first four years of the Lyndon B. Johnson (LBJ) administration, the U.S. completed the construction of two important communications facilities, one of which solved a major communications problem with the U.S. Sixth Fleet while on missions in the Eastern Mediterranean, and was in the process of trying to expand a third communications facility in Marathon for CIA purposes.[6]

Third, the U.S. saw a cooperative Greece as an essential component, through its influence over the Greek Cypriots, in achieving favorable results in the Cyprus peace process and preventing a conflagration from erupting there. This issue was considered quite important to the U.S. For example, following a low-level civil war within Cyprus between the Turkish Cypriots and the Greek Cypriots which almost ignited into a regional war in early 1964, LBJ invested significant amounts

[2] For the fragile condition of NATO in the mid-1960s in the eyes of American and European contemporaries following the withdrawal of France from its military component in early 1966, a situation which made any potential anti-NATO acts by any other alliance members all the more worrisome to the U.S., see Schwartz (2003:96–97, 105, 147, 229).

[3] John Owen Oral History (hence OH) at the Association for Diplomatic Studies and Training Oral History program website (hence ADST); Memorandum December 1,1965/box 2/lot/RG59/NARA, NEA/GRK 1964-1966.

[4] Memorandum to the President July 22,1967/Greece memos/Country File Greece/box 126/LBJ Presidential Library (hence LBJL); Memorandum December 1,1965/box 2/lot/RG59/NARA, NEA/GRK 1964-1966; Suggested Talking Points to the Secretary September 1,1965/box 2/lot/RG59/NARA, NEA/GRK 1964-1966.

[5] Miller 2009:73.

[6] A-1010 (Airgram) March 20, 1964/Greece cables/Country File Greece/box 126/LBJL; Memo, April 22,1966/box 8/lot/RG59/NARA,NEA/GRK 1964-1966.

of time and effort throughout 1964 to resolve this conflict.[7] After this attempt failed in late 1964, the U.S. continued with private, behind-the-scenes encouragement of secret negotiations between the Greek and Turkish governments in the hopes of reviving the peace process and resolving this incendiary dispute.[8]

4.1.2 The U.S. Embassy's Changing Views of Andreas Papandreou and the Proposal to Intervene

When the Center Union party (hence EK), a moderate center-left party headed by a staunch anti-communist named George Papandreou, came to power in Greece following its electoral victories in 1963 and 1964, American officials saw initially little reason to worry.[9] American officials were also quite pleased when Andreas Papandreou, George's son, decided to enter Greek politics on his father's side in early 1964. Indeed, Andreas Papandreou (hereafter "Andreas" to prevent confusion) was initially seen by the U.S. as a "positive" influence on his father.[10] During much of 1964, Andreas was also seen by U.S. officials as providing much-needed aid in countering the increasing anti-American tide within the Greek public.[11] These American views of both the Center Union being in power (hence referred to by its Greek acronym, EK) and the Papandreou men in general changed, however, when Andreas, following a humiliating failure in his first entry into politics, decided to radically remake his political persona.

Andreas's initial foray into electoral politics didn't go well. First elected to the Greek parliament in a safe district as part of the EK's February 1964 election victory, he immediately joined his father's cabinet, first as a minister in the prime minister's office and then as the alternate minister of economic coordination. His quick rise at a relatively young age (forty-four) by the Greek political standards of that era, as well as his father's obvious efforts to groom him as his eventual successor, raised the ire of fellow politicians at the EK who were themselves hoping to eventually succeed George.

Likewise, much of the Greek public initially was quite wary of Andreas. Although born and raised in Greece, Andreas had spent more than two decades in the U.S. (largely detached from the events within Greece), had served in the U.S. military during WW2, and had even temporarily acquired an American

---

[7] Miller 2009:chap. 4

[8] FRUS 1964–1968 16:494–496, 525–526.

[9] Keeley 2010:xxiii. Indeed, George Papandreou was considered so pro-western that the British, when liberating Greece in 1944, appointed him as the prime minister of the first interim, post-liberation Greek government (Rousseas 1967:76).

[10] A-1120 February 19,1964/box 1/lot/RG59/NARA, NEA/GRK 1964-1966; A-915 January 20,1964 Subject numeric files, file designation Pol2-1/RG59/NARA.

[11] State 990 March 3,1964/Pol7/RG59/NARA; Athens 1356 March 5,1964/Pol7/RG59/NARA.

citizenship. He returned to Greece in 1959 with an American wife and as the head of an American-funded economic research institute. For a Greek public which was becoming increasingly anti-American in the mid-1960s, such significant American connections led to strong suspicions as to his "true" loyalties. Accordingly, within a short time (with the behind-the-scenes encouragement of fellow EK politicians), he became widely seen as an alien imposter, a "parachutist" into Greek politics, with persistent rumors about him being a CIA agent circulating within Greece.[12] Then, eight months after his appointment, he was forced to quickly resign from his cabinet position in order to avoid being hit by a bribery scandal.[13]

In such a problematic political situation, Andreas made a calculated strategic decision to shift to strident anti-American positions on various foreign policy issues such as the Greek membership in NATO, the U.S. military and other official presence in Greece, and the issue of Cyprus.[14] By becoming "more Catholic than the Pope," he seems to have hoped to conclusively prove to the Greek public that he was a true Greek patriot and not an American "stooge."[15]

Likewise, such a foreign policy shift, combined with a change toward a more left-wing "social justice" agenda on domestic issues, was seen by Andreas as a shift which could provide major political dividends. Such a platform could appeal to a significant slice of Greek voters which had been largely neglected by other EK politicians—from the left of the EK as well as many voters of the United Democratic Left (hence EDA), the far left (de facto)[16] Greek Communist party. By "stealing" much of the EDA's foreign and domestic policy agenda while making it seem more achievable in the context of a major governing party like the EK, Andreas seems to have believed that he could create his own significant political power base, a base which would make an eventual succession to his father's position as the head of the EK more likely.[17]

For example, already in the final weeks prior to his resignation from the cabinet, Andreas began to publicly display more anti-American attitudes, sharply attacking the proposed U.S. settlement in Cyprus in an interview to a French

---

[12] Stern 1977:28; Keeley 2009:28; Daniel Brewster OH, ADST.

[13] Miller 2009:118.

[14] Many Greeks felt betrayed and disappointed at what they perceived as the American responsibility for blocking the Greek government in 1964 from achieving the long-dreamed enosis (or unification) of the majority ethnically Greek Cyprus with Greece (Miller 2009:106, 108).

[15] Keeley 2010:28; Stern 1974:28.

[16] Following the Greek Civil war, in which many of the insurgents (and losing side) were members of the Greek Communist Party (KKE), the communist party was formally outlawed. However, many sympathizers of the Communist Party were nevertheless able to legally contest the elections under the banner of the EDA, a party which adopted much of the Communist Party's domestic and foreign policy platform (Rousseas1967:21).

[17] Keeley 2010:29–30, 51. For a U.S. despatch (based on a still classified U.S. intelligence report) describing these plans by Andreas see A-854 April 22,1965/Pol12/RG59/NARA.

newspaper and claiming, among other things, that its membership in NATO had turned Greece into a "satellite" and that Greece needed to stop "taking orders."[18] A few days after resigning from his cabinet position, Andreas tried to present his resignation as being supposedly due to heavy American pressure on the Prime Minister, George Papandreou, secretly using a friendly Greek newspaper to spread this spurious claim. This claim got such wide currency within Greece, thanks among other reasons to the initial refusal of George to deny it, that the U.S. Ambassador to Greece was forced to officially deny it, angering much of the American embassy personnel in the process.[19]

Andreas's new, vehement anti-American positions began to worry U.S. officials in Athens in both the embassy and the CIA station by the start of 1965. Nevertheless, during early 1965 they still thought that a modus vivendi may be possible and tried during this period, through private meetings and quiet diplomacy, to resolve the disagreements between them and disabuse Andreas of his new anti-American views.[20] They also still saw the continuation of the George Papandreou government as an acceptable situation.[21]

The decisive shift in the embassy and the local CIA station views occurred during the Greek political crisis of summer 1965. Following the dismissal of George Papandreou on July 15, 1965, by the King of Greece, Constantine II, due to the latter's attempt to fire the defense minister and the non-partisan chief of staff of the Greek military in order, among other reasons, to protect Andreas from possible prosecution in a military scandal known as ASPIDA,[22] Greece descended into a period of political turbulence. The conservatives, who successfully pressured the king into making this move, tried to get enough defectors from the EK to create a new government without the Papandreous which could survive a vote of confidence in parliament while the remaining EK parliamentary delegation, headed by George Papandreou, tried to create enough public

---

[18] See translation in A-284 October 9,1964/Pol12/RG59/NARA. As one contemporary journalist noted, in the context of the mid-1960s, Andreas's words in this interview could be understood "as an attempt to fly the kite of neutralism in Greek foreign policy" (David Holden, "The Greek Colonels Are Part of an Old Tradition," *New York Times*, May 31, 1970).

[19] FRUS 1964–1968 16:332–334. For Andreas all but admitting his culpability in spreading these claims see his discussion with an embassy official on December 18,1964, in A-928 May 13,1965/ Pol12/RG59/NARA.

[20] A-568 January 19,1965/pol12/RG59/NARA; A-928 May 13,1965/Pol12/RG59/NARA. The embassy was also still uncertain whether Andreas, given his recent political setbacks, even had the popularity or political acumen necessary for playing any independent long-term role in Greek politics.

[21] For the way in which both the embassy and the Greek desk in the State Department saw it in a sufficiently favorable light as late as June 1965 to, for example, push for the maintenance of an aid program critical to a pet project of George Papandreou see Memo June 3,1965/box 2/lot/RG59/NARA, records relating to Greece 64-66.

[22] An acronym in Greek for "Officers Save Fatherland Ideals Democracy Meritocracy" (the word shield in Greece), the name of the controversial Greek military group at the center of this scandal.

pressure of various kinds (such as via mass demonstrations) to force the king to reinstitute him.[23]

As this Greek political crisis progressed during the summer of 1965, American officials in Athens became increasingly convinced that the U.S. had to prevent the return of the Papandreous. While George Papandreou was still seen as "acceptable," the problem lay with Andreas and his possible influence upon his father. Andreas was now seen as a "neutralist" whose "policies constitute [a] threat to [the] present U.S. position in Greece and U.S. policy objectives in Greece." With the defection of most of his political opponents within the Center Union, Andreas was now expected to dominate the party. Likewise, as George's senior advisor and number two, he was likely to push a new George Papandreou government in a neutralist direction, loosening its ties with NATO and greatly warming up Greece's relationship with the Soviet Union.[24]

The embassy and the CIA accordingly, in September 1965, jointly proposed a covert action program to be carried out by the CIA. The currently available information on this proposal indicates that this plan, among other things, was supposed to destabilize the Center Union by encouraging further defections and weaken Andreas's position within the rump EK by locating and eliminating his financial resources. At the same time, it was also supposed to help the first wave of EK defectors (who quickly became known within Greece as the "Apostates") and the center-right, conservative-dominated, National Radical Union party (hence ERE) in their efforts to cobble together a majority through, for example, guiding the new wave of induced defectors from the EK into their proposed coalition.[25] This proposal was, however, rejected by the top echelons of the U.S. government (see subsection 4.1.4).

The rejection of the proposed intervention proposal, however, didn't diminish the aforementioned fears of the U.S. embassy, the local CIA station, and, increasingly, the Greek Desk in the State Department (headed in 1966 by a former senior member of the embassy) of the Papandreous' possible return to power.[26]

---

[23] Miller 2009:120–123.

[24] Athens 369 September 5,1965/Pol15/Greece/RG59/NARA. This version (like other documents noted here) includes sections still sanitized in the FRUS version; A-321 November 8,1965/Pol15/Greece/RG59/NARA.

[25] Athens 369 September 5,1965/Pol15/Box 2242/RG59/NARA; Athens 401 September 10,1965/Pol15/Box 2242/RG59/NARA. Another component of the plan involved the weakening of the EDA—which the CIA station and embassy seem to have suspected was one of Andreas's sources of financial support Athens 369 September 5,1965/Pol15/Box 2242/RG59/NARA; Athens 401 September 10,1965/Pol15/Box 2242/RG59/NARA.

[26] Memorandum   December   23,1966/box   8/lot/RG59/NARA,NEA/GRK1964-1966; Memorandum October 19,1966/Pol15-1 Andreas Papandreou/box 12/lot/RG59/NARA, NEA/GRK 1964-1966. See also Stern (1977:36–37) for the CIA's view. The increasing fear of the Greek Desk in the State Department of Andreas can be seen in the fact that from 1966 onward a special "Andreas Papandreou" folder, solely dedicated to his recent utterances and activities, was being kept by the desk, a highly unusual treatment for someone who was formally just a common member of parliament and moreover a part of the opposition.

Indeed, the subsequent developments within Greece caused them to see such an option as even more threatening.

First, by late 1966 and early 1967, Andreas's public rhetoric had become more and more anti-American and the embassy now believed that, despite not being a communist himself, he would become, if in power, completely dominated by the EDA.[27] For example, in a February 18, 1967, speech, Andreas accused the U.S. government of, among other things, being behind Greece's political ills and demanded the reduction of Greece's NATO Alliance obligations.[28] In another speech a week and a half later Andreas claimed that American foreign policy was, in practice, under the control of the Pentagon, the CIA, and the U.S. business community and that the U.S. needed to undergo a major domestic shift in order to change its existing negative nature. He also accused the U.S. government of constantly interfering in Greece's internal affairs, relegating Greece to a neo-colonial status, and trying (unsuccessfully) to impose on it a forced solution on the Cyprus issue. Andreas also hinted that the CIA was the real manager of Greece's foreign and domestic policies and promised that an EK government would put a stop to that situation. Indeed, the latter speech even led the American embassy officials, who were in attendance, to walk out in anger due to what they perceived as its anti-American content.[29]

Second, despite the hopes of Andreas's opponents, the EK seemed likely to win in the next election, now expected in May 1967. A third factor which increased the embassy's worries was George Papandreou's age and health. By early 1967, George was eighty years old and was believed to be in failing health. In that situation, a victory of the EK in the polls and the return of George Papandreou to the prime ministry was likely to lead, within the next government's term, to the death or retirement of George Papandreou and his replacement by Andreas.[30]

In December 1966 the Greek government, headed by the "Apostates," which was eventually created (without U.S. aid) in late September 1965 after the previously noted political crisis, fell. It was replaced two weeks later by a service government which was expected to lead Greece to an election in May 1967. Accordingly, by the start of 1967 the U.S. embassy as well as the CIA station in Athens decided to propose a covert intervention designed to prevent Andreas from gaining power as a result of an EK victory in the expected upcoming Greek elections. From the currently available information about this proposed intervention plan, it appears to have involved the covert funding of legislative

---

[27] FRUS 1964–1968 16:541.

[28] For a translated version of this speech see A-444 February 18,1967/Pol15-1/RG59/NARA.

[29] Keeley 2010:44–48.

[30] FRUS 1964–1968 16:575; FRUS 1964–1968 16:541. Likewise, by late 1966 Andreas was seen by the embassy as being increasingly successful in solidifying support for himself within the EK; A-215 October 25,1966/Pol6 Greece/RG59/NARA.

candidates opposed to the EK in what were perceived as "swing" districts in this forthcoming election to the tune of around $300,000 ($1.7 million in 2016 dollars).[31]

4.1.3 The Preferences of the Greek Conservatives

The U.S. embassy quickly discovered, however, that there was little desire for a U.S. electoral intervention on the side of the Greek conservatives. The ERE could certainly have used such help. It had already lost twice in a row, in 1963 and 1964, to the EK, in the latter case the EK getting an absolute majority of the vote (53%). Despite the previously noted dismissal of George Papandreou and the defection during the summer 1965 crisis of forty-nine EK MPs, the popularity of George Papandreou and the EK was undiminished. Indeed, a secret CIA poll taken in early 1967 had found that in the upcoming election the EK was likely to do even better than in 1964 and, from their own sense of the electorate's preferences, most Greek politicians believed that as well.[32]

Likewise, the conservative Greek politicians had no moral compunctions against such interventions on the side of the U.S. For example, in the 1961 election the U.S. had covertly intervened against the de facto communist EDA following a request for such help by the ERE prime minister, Constantine Karamanlis.[33] However, due to the nature of Greek politics, the Greek conservatives seem to have believed that they had at their disposal what they saw as better, more effective domestic tools than an American electoral intervention to defeat the Papandreous. One group of conservative politicians within the ERE, as well as some of the advisors to the Greek King, thought that in response to the electoral threat posed by the Papandreous they should encourage the Greek military, much of its upper echelons deeply conservative and personally loyal to the King, to do some kind of a "soft" or "hard" coup. After a Turkish-style "resetting" of the political system following such a coup, the electoral chances of the conservatives would be much better.[34]

A second group of conservatives, headed by the leader of the ERE, Panagiotis Kanellopoulos, preferred another domestic solution. In order to prevent the incumbents from abusing their office to assure their reelection, Greece had a political tradition of appointing non-partisan, apolitical service governments to run the country in the months preceding the elections.[35] Kanellopoulos wanted

---

[31] Minutes, 303 Committee March 16,1967/NSF intelligence files/box 10/LBJL.

[32] Stern 1974:35; A-456 February 27,1968/Pol12/RG59/NARA.

[33] Miller 2009:77–78. From the available evidence it appears that the CIA, with George Papandreou's consent, also gave then-covert electoral aid to the EK (Miller 2009:78).

[34] FRUS 1964–1968 16:528; Athens 4335 March 24,1967/Pol15/RG59/NARA.

[35] Keeley 2010:57.

to ignore this tradition and replace the non-partisan service government with a partisan ERE service government headed by himself. With all of the organs of the government at their disposal in the run-up to the elections (and, if possible, a modification of the electoral law so as to favor the ERE), Kanellopoulos seems to have thought that the political landscape would be sufficiently tilted in the ERE's favor to enable it to win the election.[36]

After the U.S. refused in private talks to passively countenance a coup, a temporary consensus seems to have developed among the conservative politicians, and they all decided to support Kanellopoulos's proposed option and contest the elections in that manner.[37] However, if the ERE's chances in the final days of the campaign (or during the counting of the votes) continued to be bleak, the military would be nevertheless encouraged to carry out a coup.[38]

As a result, despite efforts by some American officials in this regard, there were no requests for or desire among any significant Greek conservative politician for a U.S. electoral intervention.[39] Indeed, the only people outside of the aforementioned U.S. government officials who seem to have desired such an intervention was a group of arch-conservative, well-connected Greek-Americans with significant social and/or commercial interests in the "old country."[40]

---

[36] FRUS 1964–1968 16:569; Athens 4451 April 4, 1967/Pol15/RG59/NARA; Memo April 8,1967/Pol14/box 7/lot/RG59/NARA, NEA/GRK 1963-1974. For an example of the ways in which the power of the Greek state could be used for that purpose see Memo January 17,1967/Pol14/box 7/lot/RG59/NARA,NEA/GRK 1963-1974. Interestingly enough, no evidence was found that the Greek public's increasing anti-Americanism played a role in the ERE's lack of desire for such a U.S. electoral intervention—perhaps due to the fact that the ERE knew quite well that a covert electoral intervention was a possibility that they could utilize as well.

[37] This partisan ERE service government was eventually created, as planned, in the beginning of April 1967.

[38] FRUS 1964–1968 16:528, 569.

[39] For an unsuccessful attempt by supporters of such an electoral intervention in the State Department's Greek Desk to recruit the former PM Karamanlis to run in the upcoming Greek elections (and by implication become the receiver of such electoral aid) see Keeley 2010:16; Letter, Brewster to Rockwell March 6,1967/Pol12/box 7/lot/RG59/NARA, NEA/GRK 1963-1974; Interview with Robert Keeley November 28, 2011. Likewise, after a thorough search in the relevant archives (LBJ Library and NARA) I could not find any request for such U.S. aid by a Greek politician in the months preceding the U.S. intervention proposal (or withdrawal sheets hinting of such requests that are still classified).

[40] This group probably included, for example, Tom Pappas, a wealthy Greek-American businessman who owned a network of gas stations in Greece (Interview with Robert Keeley November 28, 2011). The lack of requests for support for such an American intervention among Greek politicians may have also been quite ironically due to the fact that one of Andreas's main public claims was that the ERE were U.S. stooges brought to power in the past largely thanks to CIA support. In such a situation, any later exposure of U.S. covert aid would have had especially high political costs to their political standing within Greece. See Athens 3894 February 17,1967/Pol15/RG59/NARA.

4.1.4 The Majority U.S. View of Andreas and the Rejection of the Electoral Intervention Proposal

Furthermore, the Athens embassy's dark threat assessment as to the dangers of an EK election victory in general and of Andreas Papandreou in particular seems to have been the minority position even within the higher echelons of the LBJ administration. While agreeing that Andreas Papandreou was neither very friendly now to the U.S. nor their most preferred candidate for leading Greece, they nevertheless saw him as a leader with whom the U.S. could deal and live with on the major issues of relevance.

Within the State Department, the INR (Bureau of Intelligence and Research) seems to have consistently disagreed with the Greek Desk as well as with the U.S. embassy in Athens as to the level of threat that Andreas posed to U.S. interests.[41] A similar position was held also by some of the lower level officials in the U.S. embassy, some of whom viewed Andreas's ostensibly threatening behavior and rhetoric as being no more than cynical political moves to promote his political career.[42] The highest echelons of the White House and the State Department, while often disliking Andreas on a personal level (partly from their experiences with him and his father during the 1964 Cyprus peace negotiations),[43] shared this more benign view of Andreas as well. For example, when the previously noted September 1965 CIA station and embassy proposal for a covert destabilization program against the Papandreous was brought for their approval in the 303 Committee (the high-level body then in charge of approving covert operations), the NSC staff as well as top officials in the state department were extremely skeptical of the embassy's (and CIA's) claims that Andreas was a grave threat to U.S. interests (see previous descriptions). From the limited evidence available on the proceedings of the 303 Committee on this particular plan (only a brief summary of which has been declassified), they seemed to have disagreed with the embassy's threat assessment, rejecting the embassy's and CIA station's proposals on the grounds that the available evidence from the embassy's own reporting didn't support their claims.[44]

When the embassy and the CIA station proposed in February 1967 a covert U.S. intervention in the May 1967 Greek elections against the Papandreous, this more benign view of Andreas Papandreou remained. When the proposal

---

[41] Letters, Talbot to Spain February 10, 1966, and Owen to Barnham May 6, 1966, both Pol15-1 Andreas Papandreou/box 12/lot/RG59/NARA, NEA/GRK 1964-1966.

[42] August Valneti, OH, ADST.

[43] See Stern 1977:26; Lucius Battle, OH, LBJL.

[44] FRUS 1964–1968 16:430. For the skeptical manner in which these proposals were received see Memo September 11, 1965/Greece memos/NSF Country Files/box 126/LBJL; State 260 September 9, 1965/Greece cables/NSF Country Files/box 126/LBJL.

was brought up for debate in the 303 Committee over two separate meetings in early March 1967, much of the debate centered on the level of threat that Andreas Papandreou posed to U.S. national security. NSC Advisor Walt Rostow, as well as the representatives of the State Department, sharply disagreed with the portrayal of Andreas by the Athens CIA station head Jack Maury as, among other things, having "percolating animosity" toward the U.S., claiming that he was greatly exaggerating the threat that Andreas posed to the U.S. and that if Andreas were to be elected, he would be likely to "settle down" and be someone with whom the U.S. could live. However, given Maury's continued insistence as well as that of the Greek Desk in the State Department on the need for a U.S. electoral intervention to stop Andreas, they decided to send the decision up to Secretary of State Dean Rusk for his final decision on the matter.[45]

Rusk seems to have agreed with those who didn't see Andreas as a significant threat. He was also (as was at least one member of the 303 Committee) greatly troubled by the fact that the only ones who were willing to cooperate with the U.S. within Greece on an electoral intervention were the aforementioned group of Greek-Americans. As a result of these two factors, Rusk decided to reject the proposal and, with it, the possibility of any U.S. intervention of any kind in the expected May 1967 Greek elections.[46]

Following the U.S. decision to not intervene, a partisan ERE service government was eventually created, as planned by the Greek conservatives, in the beginning of April 1967. A few weeks later (on April 22), a coup was done by a group of henceforth unknown Colonels in the Greek army (the "colonels'" coup), surprising both the various political groups within Greece as well as the U.S.[47]

---

[45] FRUS 1964–1968 16:551–552, 554–555; see also the secret letter to U.S. Ambassador in Athens Talbot on this decision reproduced in (Keeley 2010:41–43). The representatives of the Defense Department were also opposed to such an intervention, probably for the same reasons as those described earlier. The LBJ administration thought that it could, if necessary, effectively exercise its leverage (via its military aid, etc.) to moderate Andreas's behavior; see Q&A for the NEA advisors April 20,1967/Pol15-1/NEA/GRK 1963-1974/lot/RG59/NARA. From that letter it is clear that the "divided councils" in the State Department noted during the discussion refer to the previously noted Greek Desk.

[46] Minutes, 303 Committee meeting March 16, 1967/Greek coup 1967/NSF intelligence files/box 10/LBJL and the previously noted document in Keeley (2010:41–43).

[47] The U.S. expected the May 1967 Greek elections to occur as planned (see, for example, FRUS 1964–1968 16:611–612). Despite some Greek claims that the LBJ administration was behind the coup or quietly encouraged it, the American archival documents declassified over the past two decades have led to an academic consensus that the U.S. government had nothing to do with it (Klarevas 2006:471–508; Miller 2009:253–254). For the surprised reaction of the Director of the CIA at the time, Richard Helms, to this coup see Weiner (2007:331).

4.2 The Uninterested Patron: The 1965 Philippine Elections

4.2.1 U.S. Interests in the Philippines in the 1960s

During the mid-1960s, as during much of the Cold War, the U.S. saw itself as having multiple important interests in the Philippines. First, the Philippine Islands were seen as occupying an important strategic location in Asia in regard to the American defensive and power projection requirements. Defensively, the Philippines were located right next to the major ocean approaches from Asia to the U.S. As for power projection, the Philippines provided the U.S. with effective power projection capability toward the Far East in general and Southeast Asia in particular through its geographic location and the existence of a half-dozen major U.S. naval and air bases (and numerous smaller ones) and the relatively free hand the U.S. had in using them. As a result, if to give one example of their importance in official American eyes, these bases were seen as "indispensable" for the support of the escalating U.S. military operations in South Vietnam and its neighbors during this period.[48]

Not surprisingly, the control of the Philippines by a friendly government was defined in secret internal policy analyses during this period as an "irreducible minimum" for the American strategic position in Asia and the Pacific.[49]

Second, a democratic and prosperous Philippines which was also closely allied with the U.S. was seen as important for American prestige and influence throughout Asia. This was due to the unique history of the Philippines as the U.S.'s only significant former colonial possession.[50]

Finally, the U.S. needed a friendly, cooperative government in the Philippines also in order to get a significant Philippine military contribution for the Vietnam War.[51] Such a contribution, while of limited direct military benefit, was nevertheless expected to be very important for U.S. goals in this conflict in three major ways. First, every further significant participation by a "free world" country in the Vietnam War effort on the American side was expected to increase its international legitimacy. This was seen as important given that the Vietnam War, from its very start, was quite controversial although not as much as it would become by the late 1960s.[52]

---

[48] NPP draft November 1964 part I:2-3/Bureau of Far Eastern Affairs, Records Relating to the Philippines 1964-1966/Pol1/box 3/lot/RG59/NARA; military assistance reappraisal FY67-71 draft report June 1965 VI:10-11,22-24NSF agency materials/box 20/LBJL.

[49] Ibid.

[50] NPP draft November 1964 part II: 2-3, part I: 1-2/Pol1/box 3/lot/RG59/NARA, Bureau of Far Eastern Affairs, Records Relating to the Philippines.

[51] Interestingly enough, this Philippine troop contribution idea seems to have begun with such a secret offer by Philippine president Macapagal in September 1964 rather than a U.S. initiative in this regard vis-à-vis the Philippines; FRUS 1964–1968 26:656–657).

[52] Colman and Widen 2009:486.

Second, more specifically, such participation by a Southeast Asian country such as the Philippines, one of the countries on the "line of dominos" which was believed to eventually fall if South Vietnam were to go communist, was expected to be especially valuable in providing credibility to the Johnson administration's effort to legitimize the war as an effort to protect the future of Asia from communism both at home and abroad.[53] Likewise, such Asian troops would help reduce the negative image that a largely non-Asian, "White" U.S. military force fighting indigenous Asian forces would be expected to create by the mid-1960s.[54]

Third, significant support from a fellow Southeast Asian country like the Philippines was seen as especially valuable in raising the morale and willingness to fight among the South Vietnamese population which, by the mid-1960s, was already quite weary after two decades of almost non-stop warfare.[55]

Accordingly, and given the increasing U.S. interest and involvement in this region during this period (during this Philippine election year, 1965, the U.S. began the major escalation of its combat involvement in Vietnam), the importance of the Philippines to the U.S. was rising.

4.2.2 The "Blocked and Weak Losers": The PPP's Difficulties and the Decision to Request U.S. Aid

In 1964, increasingly disappointed by their political marginalization under the Macapagal administration and its failure (in their view) to promote its promised reform agenda, two Philippine senators, Raul Manglapus and Manuel Manahan, together with a small cohort of like-minded reformists quit the reigning Liberal Party. Manglapus and Manahan then decided to run for the presidency and vice presidency under their reconstituted third party (the Party of Philippine Progress, hence PPP) as well as present a slate for the Philippine Senate.[56]

Success in this endeavor was, given the Philippine political context of the era, a quite remote prospect. The Philippines during this period had a two-party system. While party loyalties weren't very strong, several features of the political system and of Philippine society made it extremely difficult for a third party such as the PPP to win an election.

First, the Philippines had, probably due to American influences, an electoral system very similar in many of its features to that of the U.S. For example, the Philippine president was selected using a one-round plurality method and the

---

[53] Hess 2007:56; Logevall 1999:182.
[54] Colman and Widen 2009:486, 503.
[55] Logevall 1999:183; State 29 July 6,1965/Pol27-3/RG59/NARA; FRUS 1964–1968 26:656–657.
[56] Joaquin 1990:157–161; Pinckney 1971:134–135.

lower house of the Philippine Congress was chosen with first-past-the-post. This kind of electoral system isn't very conducive for third-party victories.[57] This anti–third party institutional feature was further buttressed by various Philippine election laws and regulations. For example, in the local election boards, the bodies responsible for the actual counting of the votes in Philippine elections, only members of the two largest parties in the previous election were legally permitted to have representatives. That, in turn, enabled the representatives of the two main parties to collude, when necessary, in various shenanigans to reduce a third party's vote share.[58] The 1965 presidential election was expected by knowledgeable contemporaries to be no exception in this regard.[59]

Second, and more important, victory in a nationwide election in the Philippines, in other words in the presidential, vice presidential, or senate contests (Philippine senators were elected at large), required having nationwide "machine" or patronage networks throughout the country in order to get out the vote and get the voters to vote in the "right" way. The local politicians, who controlled the various patronage networks, as well as many of their clients, were primarily interested in the various material benefits bestowed by those in control of the government machinery. As a result, a candidate/party which couldn't provide this patronage through the power of incumbency, or through the provision of large amounts of pre-election funding (and/or past electoral record) make a credible case for having a good chance of being victorious and providing this patronage in the future, had a very limited ability to gather enough votes to have a plausible chance of victory.[60]

Thirdly, due to various sociological reasons, Philippine politics at the local level was traditionally divided in a strong bifactional manner, with only two major rival factions competing with each other for the various local offices. That, in turn, left very limited political space for politicians (or parties) trying to build grassroots support but operating outside of the two major parties.[61]

Not surprisingly, the record of third-party runs in national-level Philippine elections was quite dismal. The record of third-party runs by reformist groups (such as the PPP) was, if anything, no exception to the rule with not a single independent victory in a run for any national-level office (president, vice president, senator) since such parties (and candidates) began their efforts in the aftermath of Philippine independence in 1946.[62]

---

[57] Wurfel 1988:94.
[58] Pinckney 1971:99–103.
[59] Members of the leading parties openly admitted in private conversations that such "discrimination" against the PPP by the observers of the major parties was likely to occur in this election; A-1053 June 17,1965/Pol political affairs and relations/RG59/NARA.
[60] Lande 1964:86–87; Wurfel:83, 85–87, 94–96.
[61] Lande 1964:86.
[62] Wurfel 1988:96; Pinckney 1971.

The leading members of the PPP knew these facts quite well from their own personal political experiences. Manahan, after a failed but respectable third-place showing (20.9%) in the 1957 presidential election under a similar reformist third-party run (also named the PPP), was not even able, despite widespread name recognition, to win a senate seat under the same party's ticket (now renamed the "Grand Alliance")[63] in the 1959 midterms. Manglapus suffered a similar fate when he ran for a senate seat under that ticket in 1957 and again in 1959. Both were able to win their senate seats in 1961 only after the PPP temporarily joined the Liberal Party and its patronage networks in the hope that this would finally enable them to win a political office from which they could advance their reform agenda.[64]

Furthermore, over the following months, the factors which Manglapus and Manahan seem to have believed that would give them a decent chance to mitigate these expected difficulties failed to materialize. For example, despite his secret promises to that effect before they quit the Liberal Party, the sitting vice president, Emmanuel Paleaz (who had a considerable patronage network and political following), decided not to join the PPP or support their candidacies.[65] Likewise, they were largely unsuccessful in raising campaign funds from various private sources, such as from U.S. firms active in the Philippines.[66]

Finally, while the PPP was able to receive support from some elements in the Philippine Catholic Church hierarchy, the Philippine church had, during this period, very limited ability to affect the average voter's behavior or vote choice.[67] Even worse, other elements of the Philippine church openly supported Macapagal.[68]

As a result, the leadership of the PPP decided to request U.S. assistance in the upcoming election for the presidential and vice presidential campaigns as well as for the building of the renewed party. Manahan, together with two prominent civilian supporters of the PPP, first approached the U.S. government in March 1965, using for this purpose a visit to the Philippines by Paul Kattenburg, a senior

---

[63] One should note that the Grand Alliance's failure in the 1959 midterms seems to have occurred despite the fact that the CIA intervened in favor of its senate ticket with $200,000 in covert election funds ($1.3 million in 2016 dollars) among other assistance, a fact that seems to have been known at least to Manahan, if not to Manglapus as well (Smith 1976:299–300, 315).

[64] Joaquin 1990:159–160; Pinckney 1971:133–134. As part of the pack leading to unification of the PPP with the Liberal Party before the 1961 elections, the united party's platform was amended to include much of the PPP reform planks on various issues, and Macapagal promised to promote these reforms if elected (Pinckney 1971:130–131, 135).

[65] Joaquin 1990:160.

[66] Memcom October 13,1964/Bureau of Far Eastern Affairs, Records Relating to the Philippines 1964-1966/Pol2/ box 3/lot/RG59/NARA; A-52 July 20,1965/Pol12/RG59/NARA.

[67] Memcom March 10,1965/Pol Political affairs and relations Phil-U.S/RG59/NARA; A-358 November 3,1965/Pol13-6/RG59/NARA; A-810 (election report 5) October 28, 1965/Pol19/RG59/NARA; A-182 September 11,1964/Pol14/RG59/NARA.

[68] Carlos and Banoloi 1996:108–109.

State Department official, a visit which included a private informal meeting that Kattenburg arranged in order to elicit the views of prominent friendly Filipinos about U.S. foreign policy toward the Philippines and Southeast Asia.[69] During this meeting they requested covert campaign funding for the forthcoming election.[70] After admitting that their electoral chances at present weren't very good, Manahan and the two PPP supporters nevertheless justified a U.S. electoral intervention in their favor (as its "true friends") as being necessary in order to counter the increasingly negative effects of the "enemies" of the U.S. (defined as the two major parties and their presidential candidates) on the Philippines' domestic situation. The continued control by the leaders of either party would, they argued, eventually lead to disastrous effects on U.S. interests in the Philippines akin to those it was then seen by them as facing in South Vietnam and perhaps even eventually requiring a similar, costly military intervention on the U.S. side.[71]

Kattenburg was non-committal but promised that the U.S. government would study their intervention request. As few months later, after receiving no response, Manglapus and Manahan seem to have secretly contacted the local CIA station in Manila and repeated this request.[72]

4.2.3 The U.S. Threat Assessment as to the Philippines and the Rejection of the Intervention Request

To the PPP's misfortune, the U.S. government felt no serious need or desire to intervene in these elections. The Johnson administration had no aversion to partisan electoral intervention, intervening in this manner at least ten times during the five years in which it was in power.[73] Nor did the U.S. show any compunctions in the past about intervening in Philippine elections. In 1953, for example, fearing that president Elpidio Quirino's extremely corrupt ways and overall incompetence (and repeated staunch refusal to reform) was, Batista-style, pushing the Philippines into the hands of a major communist-inspired insurgency raging

---

[69] Memcom March 10, 1965/Pol Political Affairs and Relations Phil-U.S/RG59/NARA. This visit by Kattenburg, then a member of the Policy Planning Council (and a former Manila embassy official), was part of the State Department's internal policy process for creating a new national policy paper on U.S. policy toward the Philippines; Paul Kattenburg, OH, ADST.

[70] Likewise, they seem to have also asked for some funding for a development project survey in the Philippines by a Philippine NGO affiliated with the PPP, a survey which they hoped to use as a de facto way of identifying potential PPP supporters. Memcom March 10,1965/Pol Political Affairs and Relations Phil-U.S/RG59/NARA.

[71] Ibid.

[72] Memorandum for the 303 Committee "CIA Action in the 1965 Philippine election" September 13, 1965, Author's FOIA request. From the currently available information it appears that the second meeting probably occurred sometime in June or July 1965.

[73] PEIG.

then in the Philippines (the Huks), the U.S. covertly intervened in the presidential election. This intervention was done after it was able to secure the cooperation of a candidate, Ramon Magsaysay, who was seen as being both more honest and more capable of defeating the Huks.[74] Four years later, after President Magsaysay died in a plane crash, the U.S. covertly intervened in the presidential elections in order to prevent the election of a candidate, Claro Recto, who it saw as having dangerous nationalist and anti-American tendencies.[75]

However, by the mid-1960s, thanks to the efforts of Magsaysay and others, the Huk insurgency was long vanquished for all practical purposes, with the Huk forces down to a minor, irrelevant remnant. No other major internal threat took its place.[76] Indeed, the Philippines was seen by the LBJ administration as having one of the more stable and democratic regimes in Asia, a relative "bright spot" in an otherwise troubled region.[77] While there were some significant longer-term American concerns about the direction in which the Philippines was heading, neither of the two main presidential candidates was seen, if (re)elected, as jeopardizing the chances of future political/economic reforms or bringing about the (re)ignition of a communist insurgency.[78]

Nor were the two other candidates seen as having policy positions and/or preferences which would threaten U.S. interests. As for the incumbent, President Diodaso Macapagal, the U.S. government saw him in a quite favorable manner by 1965. The relations between the U.S. and Macapagal were quite rocky at the start of Macapagal's term, with the two sides getting into multiple public disputes over compensation for WW2 Philippine war claims as well as over the best ways to deal with neutralist Indonesian President Sukarno (among other issues). However, the LBJ administration and Macapagal were able to resolve their disagreements on these issues during 1963 and 1964. With their resolution, the bilateral relations improved and with them the American view of Macapagal. Accordingly, by 1965 he was seen by the LBJ administration as a pro-American leader and a reliable and cooperative ally.[79]

The other major presidential candidate, Senate President Ferdinand Marcos, was also seen by the U.S. government in a favorable manner although somewhat less favorably then Macapagal. Marcos's somewhat inscrutable and slippery

[74] Smith 1975:106–107.

[75] Ibid.:254–255.

[76] FRUS 1964–1968 26:713–714.

[77] Letter, Usher to Service June 2,1964/Pol political relations U.S./box 5/lot/RG59/NARA, Bureau of Far Eastern Affairs, Records Relating to the Philippines.

[78] Ibid.; A-67 July 31,1964/Pol 6/RG59/NARA; CIA intelligence memorandum oci 2343/65 October 28,1965/box 278/NSF Country Files Philippines/LBJL.

[79] For a description of the controversies and the later improvement in relations see A-1011 June 8, 1965/Pol1/RG59/NARA; Gleeck 1993:273–275, 294–296; Gleeck 1988:135–136, 145–146. For the American view of Macapagal by 1965 see FRUS 1964–1968 26:651, 699; A-576 December 21,1965/Pol14/RG59/NARA.

character led some American diplomatic and CIA personnel in the Philippines to have more reservations about his plans, if victorious, then about Macapagal's.[80] Likewise, the fact that Marcos was running on the Nationalist Party presidential ticket, a party which despite its overall pro-American orientation had, by the mid-1960s, some of the more nationalistic elements in Philippine politics (which, in turn, could exert some influence on his future administration), led the LBJ administration to believe that cooperation with Marcos could become somewhat more difficult than with Macapagal.[81]

Nevertheless, Marcos was seen overall by the LBJ administration as a friendly, "solidly Pro-U.S." candidate who would, if elected, maintain the Philippines' pro-western orientation.[82] Accordingly, cooperation with Marcos on various issues important for the U.S. was expected to be quite feasible. For example, although in public Marcos at times opposed a Philippine troop commitment to Vietnam, from private discussions with him and his close associates (in which they were more open to such a commitment) U.S. officials believed that they could eventually convince Marcos, if he became president, to agree to provide one.[83] Not surprisingly, the LBJ administration expected these elections to result in a friendly and cooperative pro-American government, regardless of which of these candidates won.[84]

Given these factors, even the CIA saw little pressing need for an electoral intervention in favor of the PPP and its presidential candidate, identifying no significant short- or medium-term threats to U.S. interests in the upcoming Philippine elections or in general. It was also wary of unnecessarily disrupting an overall acceptable political status quo in the Philippines. Nevertheless,

[80] FRUS 1964–1968 26:696. For the CIA's view of Marcos see Smith 1976:311; Richardson 2005:136.

[81] FRUS 1964–1968 26:695; for a description of some of those elements see A-779 April 8,1965/Pol 12/RG59/NARA. One should note that even most of the demands of many of those elements were seen as ones which the U.S. could probably accommodate. For one example in which the U.S. gave the Philippines a preemptive concession on one of their planned nationalist party election planks see Manila 1601 March 3, 1965/Pol 12/ RG59/NARA.

[82] A-67 July 31,1964/Pol6/RG59/NARA; A-779 April 8,1965/Pol 12/RG59/NARA; CIA intelligence memorandum oci 2343/65/October 28, 1965/box 278/NSF country files Philippines/LBJL; Memorandum to the President November 12, 1965/box 19/NSF files of McGeorge Bundy/ LBJL; FRUS 1964–1968 26:694–699.

[83] Memorandum of conversation with Romualdez May 24,1965/Philippine aid to South Vietnam/ box 6/lot/RG59/NARA, Bureau of Far Eastern Affairs, Records Relating to the Philippines; State 29 July 6,1965/Pol27-3/RG59/NARA; FRUS 1964–1968 26:695. As the LBJ administration hoped, a few months after defeating Macapagal, Marcos changed his mind and agreed to send two thousand Philippine troops to South Vietnam. The U.S. embassy also received private assurances by Marcos that some of the previously noted elements in the Nationalist Party, such as its vice presidential candidate Fernando Lopez (nominated and elected separately from the presidential candidate under the Philippine presidential system), would not be put in foreign policy–related positions if victorious. A-363 November 5,1965/Pol14/RG59/NARA.

[84] CIA intelligence memorandum oci 2343/65 October 28, 1965/box 278/NSF Country Files Philippines/LBJL (pp. 1, 6); Manila 866 November 8,1965/Pol14/RG59/NARA.

after a discussion with the U.S. Ambassador to the Philippines about this intervention request, the CIA, with the ambassador's endorsement, decided to recommend the provision of personal electoral aid (covert campaigning funds)[85] to both Manglapus and Manahan in the upcoming election campaign. Such covert aid was recommended by them in order to keep such reformist politicians within the Philippine political system after the elections and their expected defeat. The CIA seems to have hoped that Manglapus and Manahan's continued presence in Philippine politics would provide a future nucleus for a moderate democratic reform movement, a movement that would help push for reforms of the various long-term socioeconomic ills plaguing the Philippines.[86]

The CIA's proposal didn't impress the 303 Committee, and after two different meetings discussing it in September 1965 it was rejected. From the very brief summary of the debates over this intervention proposal it appears that it was rejected in full because, agreeing with the CIA's assessment, the members of the 303 Committee perceived no serious threats to U.S. interests in these elections.[87]

As a result, the U.S. did not intervene in the November 1965 Philippine elections in any covert or overt manner.[88] Two months later, Marcos defeated Macapagal 51.9% to 42.9%. This victory began a two-decade-long rule by Marcos, first as a democratic leader and then, after a fraudulent election victory in 1969 and the imposition of martial law in 1972, as a dictator.

Both Manglapus and Manahan ended in poor third places in the presidential and vice presidential contests, with 5.2% and 3.4% of the vote, respectively. As the CIA expected, these two candidates, following their heavy defeats, decided to retire from electoral politics in the late 1960s when their senate terms expired.[89]

---

[85] The proposed amount was excised from the declassified documents released on this intervention.

[86] Memorandum for the 303 Committee "CIA Action in the 1965 Philippine election" September 13, 1965; 303 Committee minutes September 23, 1965, Author's FOIA request. If approved, the CIA expected close coordination with both candidates in this intervention, including on secure ways of using these funds. For a description of those ills from the U.S. view see ibid. and FRUS 1964–1968 26:707–708.

[87] 303 Committee minutes September 23, 1965, FOIA request.

[88] See the CIA memorandum in FRUS 1964–1968 26:688; Manila 866 November 8,1965/Pol14/ RG59/NARA; Memorandum to the President November 12, 1965/box 19/NSF files of McGeorge Bundy/LBJL. For examples of U.S. subsequent efforts not to intervene, even in an inadvertent manner, in this election see FRUS 1964–1968 26:686–687. A few months beforehand, the Johnson administration seems to have also rejected a proposal coming from a member of the NSC (Chester Cooper) to intervene in favor of Macapagal as part of a quid pro quo meant to speed up the process of Philippine congressional approval of the sending of troops to Vietnam (FRUS 1964–1968 26:672–675)—for reasons similar to those described here.

[89] Manglapus eventually returned to electoral politics in the late 1980s after the fall of Marcos, first as a senator and then as foreign minister.

4.3 Just Saying No: The 1958 Venezuelan Elections

4.3.1 U.S. Interest in Venezuela in the Late 1950s

During the first part of the Cold War, the United States saw itself as having multiple important interests in Venezuela. First, Venezuela's natural resources, but especially oil, were seen as "essential" to U.S. national security and economy. For example, Venezuela's role as an oil producer was far more important in the 1950s than it is nowadays, being at the time the world's biggest oil exporter and second-largest oil producer (after the U.S.)—or in a position similar to that of Saudi Arabia presently. The U.S. was, during this period, Venezuela's chief client, with about two-thirds of all U.S. oil imports coming from Venezuela. Most of this oil was being produced by U.S. companies.[90] Furthermore, the Eisenhower administration even hoped during this period that Venezuelan oil production would become sufficiently large to reduce Western European dependence on the Middle Eastern oil with its already volatile regional politics.[91] As a result, Venezuela's importance as a reliable oil producer both in peacetime and possible wartime was quite high to the Eisenhower administration.[92]

Second, Venezuela was seen as very important economically to the U.S. For example, Venezuela was a major market for U.S. exports as well as the second-highest recipient of American foreign investment (after Canada) in the late 1950s.[93]

Third, Venezuela, which was going in the 1950s through a period of rapid economic growth, was seen by the U.S. as an important public showcase of the benefits of capitalism and private enterprise in Latin America, an example repeatedly used by Eisenhower as part of his ideological campaign in the Cold War in general and his administration's efforts to help Latin American countries mainly through the encouragement of foreign investment and private enterprise in particular.[94] "Losing" such a prominent example of how capitalism could help

---

[90] "Mutual Security program Fiscal year 1958 estimates for Latin America" undated WH central files/confidential files/box 97/DDEL; VP Nixon South American trip, brief on Venezuela May 58 economic situation-petroleum/box 23/lot/RG59/NARA, Maurice Bernbaum files; Rabe 1982:158. The U.S. still imported only 16% of its oil needs in 1958. Nevertheless, given the high share of Venezuelan imports, that meant that one tenth of all of American oil demand in that era was supplied by Venezuela (Rabe 1982:198)—an amount quite sufficient to cause significant economic pain to the U.S. if it were to be suddenly cut off, or other possible smaller disruptions.

[91] Memo February 24, 1958/1958 Petroleum folder/box 8/lot/RG59/NARA, Records of Roy Rubottom.

[92] Rabe (1982:120–121). See also, for example, Memo November 12,1958/ARA deputy/box 25/lot/RG59/NARA, Maurice Bernbaum files, where Venezuela is discussed in Saudi Arabian terms.

[93] "Mutual Security program Fiscal year 1958 estimates for Latin America" Undated, WH central files/confidential files/box 97/DDEL; Rabe 1982: 128.

[94] "Mutual Security program Fiscal year 1958 estimates for Latin America" Undated, WH central files/confidential files/box 97/DDEL; Rabe 1988:92–94.

the world would naturally have been quite problematic to U.S. foreign policy during this period.

Finally, Venezuela had geostrategic importance in two major ways. First, it was located in an important strategic position in which it dominated the southern Caribbean and the approaches to the Panama Canal, the U.S.'s most important strategic installation in the region.[95] Second, as a country in the American "backyard," any situation in which Venezuela came under communist domination or influence was seen as especially threatening to U.S. interests.[96]

4.3.2 The Growing Threat, Part 1: The PCV

During the eight years of the Perez Jimenez military dictatorship (1950–1958), the U.S. had little to no concerns about Venezuela. The relations between the U.S. government and Jimenez were, despite a few minor tensions, quite good and it was seen by the Eisenhower administration as a friendly government under which U.S. interests were maintained.[97] Likewise, the possibility of a communist takeover was seen as very low with the Venezuelan Communist Party (hence the PCV) outlawed and believed to be quite weak.[98] Indeed, in early January 1958, three weeks before Jimenez's downfall, the U.S. intended to cancel a planned internal security program for Venezuela because, among other reasons, Venezuela was believed to be facing "no real communist threat."[99]

The wave of public protests and general strikes which brought down the Jimenez regime on January 23, 1958, came largely as a surprise to the U.S. government which, as late as December 1957, still saw it as very stable.[100] Nevertheless, the coming to power of a new regime, a transitional military junta headed by Admiral Wolfgang Larrazabal, didn't initially bring about a significant increase in U.S. concerns about Venezuela. Both Larrazabal and the transitional regime he headed were seen as having moderate conservative and strong pro-American tendencies, and the Eisenhower administration was quite pleased with their democratic transition plans.[101] Likewise, although the decision by the transitional

---

[95] "Mutual Security program Fiscal year 1958 estimates for Latin America" Undated, WH central files/confidential files/box 97/DDEL; Rabe 1988:35.

[96] Rabe 1988:30–31, 39–40.

[97] See, for example, FRUS 1955–1957 7:1138–1139.

[98] Caracas 347 November 15,1957/731.001-8-1055/RG59/NARA.

[99] Memo January 2,1958/Internal Security Venezuela 1958/box 7/lot/RG59/NARA, records of the special assistant on Communism.

[100] For example, the CIA informed Eisenhower that Jimenez's overthrow was likely only one day before it actually occurred; 352nd NSC meeting, January 22,1958/Eisenhower Papers/NSC series/box 9/DDEL.

[101] FRUS 1958–1960 microfiche supplement 5: VE-1; briefing memo "Political Situation: Venezuela" February 25,1958/Venezuela/box 10/lot/RG59/NARA, Records of Roy Rubottom. See also the biographical sketches in Vice President Nixon South American trip, briefs

government to permit in practice the PCV to openly operate within Venezuela (due to its role in the previously noted demonstrations against Jimenez) was of concern to the Eisenhower administration, the PCV and its activities were nevertheless still seen as a quite secondary problem for the U.S.[102]

This U.S. view of Venezuela, of the interim junta, and of the PCV began to change as a result of Vice President Nixon's visit to Caracas in May 13, 1958. This visit was the final leg of a Latin American goodwill trip in which Nixon and his entourage were subjected to an increasing number of anti-American demonstrations and various hostile acts by local civilians as it progressed through the various Latin American capitals. In Venezuela, however, the reaction to Nixon's arrival was hostile in an unprecedented manner up to that point in time.

As soon as the vice president's plane landed in Caracas, Nixon was greeted by hundreds of angry demonstrators which, during the landing ceremony organized by the Venezuelan government, threw garbage at and spat on him and on his entourage. After the landing ceremony ended, Nixon and the American delegation ignored the demonstrators and continued to their next destination—laying a wreath on Simon Bolivar's tomb in downtown Caracas. As the delegation's motorcade made its way to Bolivar's tomb, it was stopped by a large, angry mob in downtown Caracas, a mob organized by PCV activists for a second, larger demonstration against Nixon's visit. However, the PCV activists quickly lost control of the angry, agitated mob. Then this mob, unhindered by the Venezuelan police, attacked Nixon's limousine with rocks and pipes, broke the windows and nearly overturned the car while yelling *Muera Nixon* ("Death to Nixon"). Only the timely arrival of some Venezuelan military units enabled Nixon and his entourage to escape with their lives. Then, with anti-American riots continuing throughout Caracas for the whole night, Nixon canceled all of his planned events and hunkered down in the U.S. embassy until he flew out of Venezuela the next day.[103]

on Venezuela May 1958 "Venezuelan Government officials and other prominent persons"/briefing papers for Vice President South American tour/box 23/lot/RG59/NARA, Maurice Bernbaum files.

[102] For example, in the briefing papers for Nixon for his May 1958 visit to Venezuela, getting the Venezuelan government to deal more forcefully with the PCV threat was listed as the last of five of U.S. policy objectives vis-à-vis Venezuela—behind, for example, various economic objectives such as preventing Venezuelan efforts to broaden its economic base through increasing tariffs on American goods. Likewise, the topic of Venezuelan communism was noted as one which was not even a scheduled part of Nixon's talks with the leaders of the junta during his visit but rather as an issue for him to raise at his discretion. See briefs "U.S. policy towards Venezuela" April 9,1958 and "The Communist threat" May 1958, both in briefing papers for Vice President South American tour/box 23/lot/RG59/NARA, Maurice Bernbaum files.

[103] Zahnisher and Weis 1989:170–183; Nixon 1962:217–220. For the U.S. government's conclusions about the PCV's role, and the later public admission by the PCV, see DRA report June 19,1958/Nixon trip followup/box8/lot/RG59/NARA, records of the special assistant on Communism office files; Memo October 5,1958/731.001-8-1055/RG59/NARA. Nixon and the Eisenhower administration

Shocked and concerned by the levels of public hostility expressed toward Nixon throughout Latin America, and by the ability of local communist activists to organize such protests and exploit this hostility, the Eisenhower administration began to put significant efforts into finding the underlying causes of the hostility as well as devising ways to combat this problem in general and local communist agitation in particular.[104] While the Eisenhower administration's concerns as to the vulnerability of most Latin American countries to communism quickly receded in the subsequent weeks and months,[105] its worries as to Venezuela just increased.

These new American anxieties about Venezuela came from two main sources. First, despite U.S. hopes that the events transpiring during Nixon's visit would lead to prompt action by the Venezuelan government against the PCV in general and the communist activists responsible for organizing them in particular, very little was done by the transitional junta to either investigate the causes of these demonstrations or crack down on the PCV besides the arrest of some protestors.[106] Nine days after Nixon's visit the transitional junta formally legalized the PCV.[107] Furthermore, Larrazabal, during a mid-June press conference, even openly dismissed the claim that the PCV posed in any way or manner a threat to Venezuela or to the U.S.[108]

At the same time, the Eisenhower administration was receiving indications from various reliable sources of increasing communist influence in the Venezuelan press, universities, and labor unions—three components of civil society that were seen by the U.S. as being frequently utilized by communist revolutionaries in order to take over countries around the world. Even more worrisome was the increasing evidence of the PCV's successful infiltration into

were so unconcerned about domestic developments in Venezuela prior to these events that Nixon initially asked for his visit to Caracas to have a car with an open roof. Only the strong protests of the embassy seem to have led Nixon to accept a car with a closed roof (McPherson 2003:28), a change that probably saved his life.

[104] Memo May 17,1958; Memo May 14,1958, both in Nixon trip to South America/box7/lot/RG59/NARA Records of Roy Rubottom, subject files; 366th NSC meeting May 23,1958/Eisenhower Papers/NSC series/box 10/DDEL.
[105] Memo for the OCB Planning board July 15, 1958 in NSC 1958/box 7/lot/RG59/NARA Records of Roy Rubottom, subject files; Telcon, Foster Dulles to Allen Dulles June 19,1958/box 8/telephone calls series/Dulles papers/DDEL. As Rabe notes, only after Fidel Castro came to power in Cuba in the following year (1959) and began to move in a more communist direction did the Eisenhower administration start to seriously worry about the possibility of a communist takeover in most Latin American countries (1988:113-115).
[106] DRA report June 19,1958/Nixon trip followup/lot/box 8/RG59/NARA, Records of the special assistant on Communism; Memo August 14,1958/Venezuela 1958/box 8/lot/RG59/NARA, Records of the special assistant on Communism.
[107] CIA Central Intelligence Bulletin June 23, 1958, CREST.
[108] Caracas 857 June 20,1958/731.001-8-1055/RG59/NARA.

the transitory government, where communist sympathizers were believed to occupy major positions within the cabinet.[109]

As a result, anxiety about the developments within Venezuela became widespread within the administration during the summer of 1958. For example, in a secret speech at the National War College on August 25, 1958, the acting secretary of state, Christian Herter, described the Eisenhower administration as having "considerable apprehension" about the "very serious situation" in Venezuela because of the aforementioned reasons.[110] Subsequent political developments in Venezuela, such as the failure of another military coup attempt in September 1958, were seen by the U.S. as further increasing the PCV's influence.[111] Due to these growing concerns the Eisenhower administration even started, during the summer of 1958, a set of various covert and overt activities (through multiple government agencies) designed to improve its image within Venezuela and reduce communist influence in Venezuelan universities and trade unions.[112]

Nevertheless, these concerns (and actions) by the Eisenhower administration about Venezuela didn't extend at that point to the electoral sphere. This was due to two main reasons. First, although the PCV showed worrisome signs of quick growth in party membership and overall public support, it was still believed to be far too small, in electoral terms, to have any chance of seriously contesting an executive election in the near future.[113]

Second, the initial democratic transition plan agreed upon (at least in public) by all of the main political parties (AD, URD, COPEI)[114] after the ouster of Jimenez called for the selection of a single joint presidential candidate in the first post-Jimenez elections. As a result, much of Venezuelan politics during 1958 was consumed with negotiations between these three parties over the exact identity of this "unity" candidate and various power-sharing formulas. The PCV was excluded from these negotiations.[115] The Eisenhower administration believed

[109] Memo July 2,1958 731.001-8-1055/RG59/NARA; Memo August 14,1958/Venezuela 1958/ box 8/lot/RG59/NARA, Records of the special assistant on Communism; CIA current Intelligence Weekly Summary July 24, 1958, CREST. At one NSC meeting in July 1958 CIA director Alan Dulles even described the Venezuelan government as "Communist Infiltrated"; 371st NSC meeting July 3,1958/Eisenhower Papers/NSC series/box 10/DDEL.

[110] Speech, Christian Herter, National War College August 25,1958/box 15/Herter papers/DDEL; see also Letter, Rubottom to Sparks August 15,1958/350.21/Embassy, Caracas/RG84/NARA.

[111] See, for example, memo September 16,1958/1958 Venezuela/box 8/lot/RG59/NARA, Records of the special assistant on Communism.

[112] Memo November 12, 1958/Anti-communist campaign task force 1958/Box 1/lot/RG59/ NARA, Records of the special assistant on Communism; Memcom November 5,1958/memoranda file/box 3/lot/RG59/NARA, records relating to Venezuela.

[113] An embassy estimate from August 1958 expected the PCV to win at most about 5% in the upcoming elections. Report August 14,1958/731.001-8-1055/RG59/NARA;CIA current Intelligence Weekly Summary July 24, 1958, CREST; FRUS 1958–1960 microfiche supplement 5:VE-13.

[114] Democratic Action/Accion Democratica (AD), Democratic Republican Union (URD) and the Social Christian party (COPEI).

[115] Alexander 1982:418–423.

that any candidate agreed upon by these three parties, all seen as having largely friendly attitudes toward the U.S., would, after easily winning the elections, be unlikely to be one who would endanger U.S. interests in Venezuela, or, once firmly established, continue giving the PCV a free hand.[116]

4.3.3 The Growing Threat, Part 2: The Electoral Aid Offer to Betancourt

However, new unexpected turns of events in Venezuela during October and November of 1958 led to an extension of the administration's concerns about the increasingly threatening situation in Venezuela to the one of the major candidates contesting the 1958 Venezuelan presidential race (Larrazabal). That, in turn, led the Eisenhower administration to seriously consider an intervention in those elections on the side of one of his competitors, Romulo Betancourt.

During October 1958 the negotiations over the identity of a unity candidate between the three main parties finally collapsed. As a result, all three parties decided to run separate candidates, making the expected presidential race, now set for December 7, 1958, into a highly competitive match.[117] Then Larrazabal, after agreeing to contest the elections as the presidential candidate of the URD, decided to also formally accept the endorsement of the PCV. Larrazabal, as part of accepting this endorsement, seems to have also received, as the CIA discovered sometime in mid-November, some covert Soviet funding for his campaign.[118]

This decision by Larrazabal completed the ongoing shift in the Eisenhower administration's view of him. In the months following Nixon's visit, the

[116] Briefing memo "Political Situation: Venezuela" February 25,1958/Venezuela/box 10/lot/RG59/ NARA, Records of Roy Rubottom; FRUS 1958–1960 microfiche supplement 5:VE-13. The U.S. was, as late as October 1958, so unconcerned with the upcoming election results that it was canceling some planned activities in Venezuela in order to avoid even the possibility of being inadvertently pulled into the election campaign and alienating any of the sides contesting them; Letter, Sparks to Bernbaum October 1,1958/320/Embassy, Caracas/RG84/NARA; Memo November 12, 1958/task force 1958/Box 1/lot/RG59/NARA, records of the special assistant on Communism.
[117] Alexander 1982:423, 426. The demise of the unity candidate plan was not fully clear to the U.S. government until at least late October with the signing of the Funto Pijo pact between the three main parties. Memcom October 25,1958/731.00-10-358/RG59/NARA; Caracas 229 November 1,1958/731.00-10-358/RG59/NARA.
[118] Diary file November 24, 1958/1958 diary/Box 219/Adolph Berle papers/FDR Library (hence FDRL). Berle's source was his close friend J. C. King, the head of the CIA's Latin American division at the time. See also "Updating supplement major developments in Latin America since the issuance of the OCB special report on Latin America (NSC 5613/1) dated November 26, 1958" December 22, 1958/Who OSANA records/NSC series briefing notes subseries/box 12/DDEL. The CIA's intelligence seems to have been quite accurate in this case. The available evidence from the Soviet archives shows a one-time transfer by the CPSU (one of the bodies used at times to finance such interventions) of an additional $100,000 (about $660,000 in 2016 dollars) in covert funding to the PCV for 1958 (Riva 1999:50), at least some of which was probably used also for Larrazabal's election campaign.

Eisenhower administration was developing an increasingly negative opinion about Larrazabal over what they saw as the failure of the transitional junta that he headed to deal in any serious manner with the increasing threat posed by the PCV and his rather naïve view of the threat that the U.S. believed that they posed (see previous examples).[119]

Larrazabal's decision to accept PCV, and through them Soviet, endorsement and aid seems to have fully convinced the Eisenhower administration that he would be an unacceptable candidate. Larrazabal's unacceptability was due to the administration's belief that his excessively friendly and/or staunchly naïve position toward the PCV (and the Soviets) if he stayed in power, as conclusively shown in this decision, would make any significant cooperation with the U.S. on this issue very difficult if not impossible. At the same time, due to the likely future PCV participation in such a Larrazabal government, a victory by Larrazabal would open Venezuela to communist domination and takeover through its common infiltration techniques—as had supposedly almost occurred in Guatemala under Arbenz in the early 1950s.[120]

As a result, the Eisenhower administration decided to offer electoral assistance to the other main candidate in this race, Romulo Betancourt.[121] Trying to keep this proposal completely secret, the State Department asked Adolf Berle to serve as a trusted intermediary. Berle, during this period a law professor at Columbia, was a former senior White House advisor and assistant secretary of state for Latin America under FDR, as well as a close personal friend of Betancourt.[122]

---

[119] Memo July 2,1958/731.001-8-1055/RG59/NARA; FRUS 1958–1960 microfiche supplement 5:VE-13; see also Nixon (1962:222).

[120] The Eisenhower administration believed that in the most likely scenario of a Larrazabal victory, a narrow win over Betancourt, Larrazabal would probably appoint members of the PCV or public figures approved by it to important cabinet positions. Larrazabal would then, given his domestic political needs and general attitude toward them, be loath to do anything to keep the PCV under check. That, in turn, would open Venezuela to being slowly taken over by the PCV in a manner similar to what it thought had almost occurred under Arbenz; Memo November 21, 1958/Herter papers/Chronological files/box 6/DDEL; Memo December 4,1958/Venezuela 1958/box 8/lot/RG59/ NARA, Records of the special assistant on Communism; CIA Current Intelligence Weekly Summary November 26, 1958, CREST. Indeed, some members of the Eisenhower administration were increasingly worried about such a "Guatemalan" scenario in Venezuela occurring even before Larrazabal accepted the PCV's endorsement. See, for example, Memo August 14,1958 in Venezuela 1958/box 8/ lot/RG59/NARA, Records of the special assistant on Communism.

[121] From the available information we can see that the assistance offer was completely open-ended in regard to the types of possible electoral assistance to be provided; Letter November 24, 1958/Box 219/Berle papers/FDRL. The third candidate, Caldera, was seen in an even more favorable light than Betancourt was by the U.S. government. However, the U.S. government thought that Caldera had no chance of winning; Memo November 19,1958/63/box 3/lot/RG59/NARA, Records relating to Venezuela 1948–1963. Not surprisingly, I could find no evidence of the Eisenhower administration contacting Caldera in some manner with such an offer or providing any assistance to his candidacy.

[122] Diary file November 24, 1958/1958 diary/Box 219/Berle papers/FDRL. Berle became, long before the Eisenhower administration thought of intervening in this election, an important informal channel of communication with Betancourt when the latter returned to Venezuela in early 1958 from his Puerto Rican exile and resumed his involvement in Venezuelan politics; see, for example, Memo

4.3.4 Betancourt's Political Position and the Rejection of the Electoral Intervention Proposal

Betancourt, however, decided to reject this American electoral aid offer.[123] Betancourt's decision to reject this American offer seems to have been the result of the strength of the party which he founded and led—the Accion Democratica (AD). The AD was the first of its kind of party in Venezuela, a mass party which had developed widespread grassroots support. Using that support, as well as a successful military coup in its favor, Betancourt and the AD took over Venezuela in 1945 and delivered on some of their socio-economic promises over the next three years. As a result of both factors, the AD was able to consolidate a mass public following within Venezuelan society, winning more than 70% of the votes in three overall fair nationwide elections conducted between 1946 and 1948, including one for the presidency.[124]

Although the AD suffered under the Jimenez regime, during which it was banned and many party members were heavily persecuted, it nevertheless was largely able to maintain its party organization and political strength within Venezuela over that decade. Indeed, when Jimenez called an election in 1952 to legitimize his rule, he banned the AD from participation given its expected strength. When the AD decided to clandestinely support the URD, that was sufficient to lead the URD (which beforehand was getting less than 5%), despite heavy restrictions on URD campaigning and large-scale government harassment, to an overwhelming victory over Jimenez's "government" party, the FEI, 63% to 21% according to one later estimate, forcing Jimenez to stop the counting in the middle and issue "corrected" returns a few weeks later.[125]

As a result, when the Jimenez regime fell in early 1958, Betancourt and AD leadership quickly rebuilt the party organization and membership and reclaimed its dominant political position in Venezuelan politics. For example, by August 1958 the AD already had 600,000 registered party members—around 10% of the Venezuelan population at that time and far more than any other party.[126] Indeed, in private conversations before the attempt to find a unity candidate collapsed and the election campaign began, there was a general consensus among

July 21,1958/731.001-8-1055/RG59/NARA; Diary files October 24, 1958/1958 diary/Box 219/Berle papers/FDRL.

[123] Letter, Betancourt to Berle December 6, 1958/1958 diary/Box 219/Berle papers/FDRL.
[124] Kornblith and Levine 1995:41–43; Martz 1966:72–78.
[125] Martz 1966: 146, 327–329; Nohlen 2005 (2): 568.
[126] Report August 14, 1958/731.001-8-1055/RG59/NARA.

Venezuelan politicians (including some of their harshest political opponents) as to AD's continued political dominance.[127]

The only thing that could still have stopped the AD and Betancourt from a decisive election victory and coming to power in the first post-transition months was the Venezuelan army. As previously noted, the Venezuelan army had removed the first freely elected AD government in late 1948. Despite the overthrow of Jimenez in January 1958, the army still included some senior, far-right officers who detested the AD, seeing it as little better if not worse than the Communists. These officers were widely believed to be willing and able to execute a coup if a member of the AD and/or Betancourt were to win the election. Indeed, the initial willingness of Betancourt to agree, at least in theory, to the idea of the unity candidate, was probably because of his fear of such a coup occurring if he dared to propose his own candidacy.[128]

However, two failed coup attempts in July and early September 1958, attempts which failed largely because of cross-party civilian opposition to the return of a military dictatorship, weakened the military's political position and therefore its ability to meddle in Venezuelan politics. More importantly, as a result of the coups, most of the senior military officers who opposed the AD and Betancourt, the main participants in both coup attempts, were exiled by the transitional junta and lost all of their influence over the military. With their removal, the remaining military hierarchy had a friendlier attitude toward the AD. As a result, Betancourt seems to have become certain by late September 1958 that the Venezuelan military would not carry out a coup in the case that he won or that it looked like he was about to win the presidential elections.[129]

As a result, when Betancourt openly announced his candidacy for the presidency in the middle of October 1958, he seems to have been very certain of his chances of winning it.[130] Likewise, unlike the Eisenhower administration, Betancourt seems to have had very little worry about Larrazabal's candidacy and his subsequent reception of the PCV's endorsement, seeing Larrazabal as a

---

[127] One example was Rafael Caldera, the leader of COPEI at the time. For his and other such admissions see Caracas despatch 610 February 24,1958 in 731.00-2-358/RG59/NARA; Caracas despatch 913 June 6,1958/731.00-5-558/RG59/NARA; and FRUS 1958–1960 microfiche supplement 5:VE-13.

[128] Alexander 1982:424; Caracas despatch 24 July 8,1958/731.00-6-1758/RG59/NARA; FRUS 1958–1960 microfiche supplement 5:VE-13; Caracas despatch 364 November 6,1958/731.00-10-358/RG59/NARA. For some examples of the views of the military officers see Caracas despatch 95 July 28,1958/731.00-6-1758/RG59/NARA. For Betancourt's (private) desire to be a candidate in these elections see his conversation with Adolf Berle in Diary file January 31, 1958/1958 diary/Box 219/Berle papers/FDRL.

[129] Caracas Despatch 364 November 6,1958/731.00-10-358/RG59/NARA; Caracas despatch 311, October 13,1958/ 731.00-10-358/RG59/NARA.

[130] Alexander 1982:426; Caracas despatch 311, October 13,1958/731.00-10-358/RG59/NARA.

political neophyte with little real chances of beating him.[131] Indeed, Betancourt, when rejecting this American aid offer, indirectly noted his good chances of winning this election as the reason for rejecting it.[132]

As a result of Betancourt's rejection of this electoral intervention offer, the Eisenhower administration decided to largely drop this attempt to intervene in the Venezuelan presidential elections.[133] Two weeks later, Betancourt nevertheless won the Venezuelan presidency in a landslide with 49.9% to Larrazabal's 35%.[134] Betancourt's election to the presidency inaugurated a forty-year period of democratic politics in Venezuela, not interrupted, despite the eruption of a short-lived communist insurgency in the early 1960s, until the coming to power of Hugo Chavez in December 1998.

4.4 Summary and Conclusions

A few years ago, when the author went to the LBJ Presidential Library and informed the archivists of his interest during his research trip of investigating two cases of possible non-intervention by the U.S. government, one of them, only half in jest, responded that he didn't know that such situations ever occurred in practice. This chapter indicates that such situations do indeed sometimes happen. As can be seen here, the documentary evidence from these three cases of non-intervention follows overall the theoretical expectations of my theory.

In the first case, the 1967 Greek elections, Andreas Papandreou, as part of a cynical political "remake" designed to restart a faltering political career, adopted increasingly left-wing, anti-American positions on Greek membership in NATO and the U.S. bases (among other things). These anti-American positions, combined with the fear of his potential effects on his father (the leader of the EK), led the Athens embassy as well as the local CIA station to first recommend in September 1965 a destabilization operation against the Papandreous. It then, when a new election was in the offing, recommended a covert electoral intervention designed to prevent Andreas and the EK from winning the elections. However, there was little desire among Greek conservative politicians for such a U.S. intervention (despite some unsuccessful efforts by supporters of such an intervention within the U.S. embassy to find them) due to the their belief that

---

[131] Caracas despatch 311 October 13,1958/731.00/10-358/RG59/NARA; FRUS 1958–1960 microfiche supplement 5:VE-15.

[132] As Betancourt described it in his rejection of this offer, given that he (Betancourt), once elected, would never let the PCV in his government, the U.S. had "no rational reason" to worry about them; Letter, Betancourt to Berle December 6, 1958/1958 diary/Box 219/Berle papers/FDRL.

[133] Memo December 1,1958/63/box 3/lot/RG59/NARA, Records relating to Venezuela; Memo December 16,1958/350/Embassy, Caracas/RG 84/NARA.

[134] A third candidate, Rafael Caldera, received 16%.

they had in this case better, more effective domestic tools to deal with their political problems. The American knowledge of this fact, combined with the widespread belief within the higher echelons of the LBJ administration that Andreas
was not a major threat to U.S. interests, led the administration to twice reject the
embassy's recommendations, and not intervene in the expected elections.

In the second case, the 1965 Philippine elections, the weak political position
of the PPP and its presidential candidate Manglapus led them to secretly ask the
U.S. government for electoral aid in this election. However, the U.S. government
also saw the other two main candidates in the presidential race, Macapagal and
Marcos, as overall friendly candidates who, if victorious, would cooperate on issues of importance to it—such as getting a Philippine troop commitment for the
Vietnam War. As a result, the U.S. government, seeing no good reason to intervene, decided to reject the PPP electoral intervention request and did not interfere in any way or manner in that election.

In the third case, the 1958 Venezuelan elections, the Eisenhower administration became increasingly concerned, following the violent attack by an angry
communist agitated mob on Vice President Nixon's motorcade during a visit
to Caracas, by the growing strength and influence of the PCV which began to
operate freely in Venezuela after the fall of the Jimenez dictatorship in the beginning of that year. It also became concerned by the unwillingness of the transitional junta, under Admiral Larrazabal, to do much in order to keep the PCV in
check in the following months.

These increasing American concerns spilled over into the electoral sphere
when Larrazabal decided to run in the presidential elections and then chose to
accept the endorsement of the PCV (and covert Soviet funding). That, in turn,
led the U.S. concerned about Larrazabal's attitude toward the PCV and his expected unwillingness, as a result, to cooperate with the Eisenhower administration in suppressing PCV activities (and prevent a possible future communist
takeover attempt) if he were to win the elections, to offer his main opponent in
these elections, Romulo Betancourt, to intervene in these elections in his favor.
However, Betancourt, who was quite confident of his chances of winning the
presidential election due to the political and organizational strength of his party,
the AD, chose to reject this American offer. That, in turn, led the Eisenhower administration to "sit out" this election and not significantly intervene in it. Table
4.2 summarizes the key aspects of these three non-intervention cases.

The results in this and the preceding chapter demonstrate the utility and
strength of the theoretical framework proposed here for explaining the causes
of partisan electoral intervention. For example, as expected, the would-be client
played a key role in the decision whether to undertake the intervention. If the
foreign power chose eventually to intervene, the client played a key role in the
decision-making process as to what forms of electoral aid to provide, and how

Table 4.2 Causes of Electoral Intervention Argument (H1–H3): Full Summary of Key Aspects of Case Studies - the Non-Intervention Cases

Case Study	Actor Wants/ Requests Aid	Domestic Political Situation of Would-Be Assisted Actor	GP Sees Implacable Actor	Key Reason(s) for Non-Intervention	Support Of Theory?
Philippines 1965	Yes Request by PPP	Blocked/ weakened loser	No	Both other major candidates (Macapagal, Marcos) acceptable to U.S./ No threat	Yes
Venezuela 1958	No U.S. offer rejected by Betancourt	Good/likely winner (after Sept. 1958)	Yes (after Oct. 1958)— Larrazabal	Rejection of U.S. intervention offer by Betancourt	Yes
Greece 1967	No Greek conservatives prefer other domestic options	Bad/weak—but full extent unclear	No	Most U.S. officials don't see Andreas as a major threat; no interest in such intervention on side of Greek conservatives	Yes

exactly to provide them with its own view playing a key role, whenever there was an internal debate in this regard within the intervener, as to the exact course of action chosen.

These results also have further implications as to some claims and/or arguments made about such interventions in the literature. First, a high level of strategic importance of the country in question (in the eyes of a would-be intervener) is far from sufficient to lead a great power to intervene in this manner in its electoral processes. All six countries were perceived by the U.S. government, at the time of their relevant elections, as countries in which the U.S. had important interests, the "loss" or "continued intransigence" of any one of them during the period in question likely to have been seen as a major setback to the U.S. Nevertheless, that fact didn't suffice to lead American decision-makers to intervene in three of the six elections investigated here in depth. That, in turn, indicates that being the target of a partisan electoral intervention is not some nearly automatic result of being a "country of interest" to a great power while having relatively competitive elections. Instead, the way in which the various major political actors in the target are perceived by the great power and the willingness of one or more of them to accept (or request) such aid are far more important factors in leading (or not leading) to such interventions.[135]

Nor was evidence found for the existing theoretical (and aggregationist) approaches. As for O'Rourke (2018), many of the key factors that led to the conduct of an electoral intervention were found here to be very different from those that, according to her argument, might lead to a covert FIRC. First, in contrast to her expectation, the political alternative chosen in all three electoral intervention cases was, prior to the start of the intervention, significantly weaker than the side the U.S. tried to remove or prevent from coming to power. When it had more than one potential client (as in the Guatemalan case), the U.S. did choose the candidate perceived as the strongest of the two available options—but that chosen option (Cruz Salazar) was still significantly weaker than the undesirable side (the PR) as well as its initial hopes in this regard. In another case (Venezuela), it indeed tried to recruit a candidate (Betancourt) which was significantly stronger than the undesired side (Larrazabal), but that candidate rejected its offer, thus preventing an electoral intervention from occurring. Likewise, in at least two of the electoral intervention cases (West Germany and Argentina), the U.S. government had a rather low or skeptical view of its chosen client and its preferences.[136]

Second, as could be seen in Chapter 3, the choice of a covert electoral intervention versus an overt one in all three cases had little to do with the overall material or reputational costs of each method to the intervener. Instead, the choice of intervention largely depended on what exact types of assistance or level of covertness were desired by the client. That, in turn, explains the major differences in the relative frequencies of overt electoral interventions versus overt FIRCs noted in Chapter 1—the underlying factors that determine the overtness of the foreign intervention in each case are usually very different.

As for Bubeck and Marinov's argument (2019), as could be seen in the detailed analysis of the decision-making process in these six cases, neutral and partisan electoral interventions were not usually seen by policymakers as policy alternatives or substitutes to each other. This is despite the fact that the U.S., as a liberal power, would be expected according to their argument to be especially

---

[135] Likewise, although I found some secret efforts by business and ethnic lobbies get the U.S. to intervene on behalf of a particular side in two of the cases analyzed here, in neither case was this pressure able to determine whether the U.S. intervened (Greece) or the exact side that the U.S. intervened for (Guatemala).

[136] For the American skepticism in regard to Adenauer's preferences see Chapter 3. In the Argentinean case, for example, the U.S. chargé Cabot described Tamborini in early 1946 as having "the general appearance of and rather less than the intelligence of a tame teddy bear"; Buenos Aires despatch 1747 January 9,1946/835.00/RG59/NARA. Likewise, Braden, based on his firsthand interactions with the Argentine opposition, described them as "nincompoops" (Frank 1980:98).

open to such neutral activities. Likewise, as could be seen in the Philippine case, the U.S. government also rejected the option of using a partisan intervention for a neutral goal—encouraging various needed domestic reforms in the Philippines.

Finally, these cases provide no significant evidence for claims that electoral interventions are the result of bureaucratic inertia or become, after done once in a particular country to deal with a particular problem, an ingrained "Standard Operation Procedure" by the intervener for dealing with any new issue which arises with that country.[137] Two of these cases (Greece and Philippines) had experienced U.S. electoral interventions in past national-level elections. This past intervention record may have indeed been a secondary factor in increasing the chances that a domestic actor in the target in deep political trouble would think of the possibility of requesting electoral aid from the U.S. as a way to resolve its political difficulties (Philippines), or for some members of the local U.S. embassy and CIA station to propose this option when encountering what they saw as an increasingly threatening domestic actor in the target (Greece).[138]

Nevertheless, the available evidence indicates that their past electoral intervention record in a particular country isn't usually a significant consideration for decision-makers when deciding, when such proposals arrive at their desk, whether to intervene or not in an upcoming election there. Indeed, the fact that the U.S. had electorally intervened in the past in the Philippine and Greek cases seems, from the available documentary evidence, to have had little "pull" or effect on the relevant American decision-makers' calculus, rejecting in both of these cases a proposal to intervene in this manner.[139]

Instead, the available evidence shows that the decision-making process on whether to intervene or not in a particular election in a given country is usually a discrete, separate new decision by the relevant decision-makers for each election in question, the decision largely based on the existing conditions in the target in the months prior to that election and requests for aid (and/or lack of desire for it) from political elements within it.[140] Past conditions in potential targets, or

---

[137] This is an accusation made at times against CIA/covert U.S. interventions of various types (including electoral ones). For one recent example see Prados (2006:381). Given that 44% of the interventions in PEIG are repeat interventions (see Chapter 5), the possibility that this was indeed the case couldn't be dismissed out of hand.

[138] For a complaint by one of the opponents of the proposed intervention in this regard in Greece see Minutes of the 303 committee March 16, 1967/NSF intelligence files/box 10/LBJL. Likewise, another kind of U.S. meddling, the covert coup d'état in 1954, probably played an important role in the decision of Cruz Salazar to request an electoral intervention in the 1958 Guatemalan election.

[139] Similarly, past use of other methods of regime change (Argentina, Guatemala) do not automatically lead the intervener to choose an electoral intervention—indeed, as could be seen in the Guatemala case, the first competitive post-FIRC election (1957) did not have an American intervention of this kind.

[140] While the U.S. government did significantly overestimate the threat from the relevant actor in some electoral intervention cases (such as Argentina), as can be seen in the case of Germany such threat inflation was by no means a prerequisite for such an intervention to occur.

whether previous electoral interventions were done in the country in question, seem to usually play a very small to no role in the making of the intervention (or non-intervention) decision.[141] Situations where we see repeated electoral interventions by the same foreign power in a certain target are accordingly usually because the underlying conditions that led to a previous intervention persisted in the interim—not because of any perverse bureaucratic dynamics.

The next chapter (Chapter 5) will be a descriptive overview of my new dataset describing additional results and general patterns found as to the American and USSR/Russian interventions.

---

[141] The nature of national-level elections in most democracies—that is, discrete events temporally separated from one another by a few years rather than an ongoing, continuous process (like say most civil wars)—may be a factor in that.

5

Surveying the Landscape

An Overview of U.S. and Soviet/Russian Partisan Electoral Interventions, 1946–2000

When an unexpected event takes place in one's country, many people want to know more about past occurrences of such affairs. The 2016 Russian electoral intervention was no exception, leading to numerous attempts by American journalists and scholars to describe particular examples of previous interference of this type by Russia and other actors. However, as insightful as delving into particular past meddling cases can be, without a wider systematic dataset of partisan electoral interventions it is much harder to develop a full understanding of this phenomenon.

Accordingly, this chapter will provide a brief overview of PEIG, the dataset of U.S. and Soviet/Russian electoral interventions constructed by the author and the first scholarly database of this kind. It will try to answer some general questions many readers may have about electoral interventions—such as when and where they have been most likely to occur, their most frequent targets, and the most common methods used (and not used) as part of such meddling. It will then discuss some additional evidence already visible from this overview for the arguments made here and for other perspectives.

When feasible or analytically useful, some of the general patterns described in the following sections are examined using two forms of table statistics: the cumulative binomial probability test (see Gaubatz 1999:chap. 6) and the Chi-square test. Accordingly, any reference in the following sections to certain patterns being statistically significant (or not) refers to results found using these two methods.

5.1 When, Where, and Who Is Targeted

Overall, 117 partisan electoral interventions have been done by the U.S. and the USSR/Russia between January 1, 1946, and December 31, 2000. Eighty-one (or 69%) of these interventions were done by the U.S. while the other thirty-six cases (or 31%) were conducted by the USSR/Russia. To put this number in the proper perspective, during the same period 937 competitive national-level executive

Meddling in the Ballot Box. Dov H. Levin, Oxford University Press (2020). © Oxford University Press.
DOI: 10.1093/oso/9780197519882.001.0001.

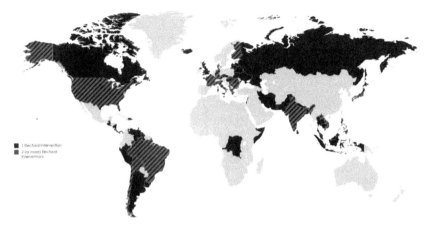

Figure 5.1 U.S. and USSR/Russian interventions, 1946–2000 (black= one electoral intervention, stripes= two or more interventions).

elections, or plausible targets for an electoral intervention, were conducted within independent countries.[1] Accordingly, 11.3% of these elections, or about *one of every nine competitive elections* since the end of WW2, have been the targets of an electoral intervention.

Even in absolute numbers, electoral interventions have been a more common form of intervention by these two powers than other, better known methods. For example, during this period there were fifty-three significant military interventions (including the deployment of at least five hundred soldiers) by either the U.S. or the USSR/Russia (Sullivan 2007). Likewise, during the Cold War era (1946–1989) the U.S. conducted fifty-nine covert foreign-imposed regime changes, or FIRCs (via assassinations, sponsoring of coup d'états, or arming or aiding of dissident groups) and six overt ones (via military invasion, etc.) (O'Rourke 2018:77).[2]

As can be seen in Figures 5.1 and 5.2, electoral interventions have occurred in every world region except for Oceania, although their relative frequency has greatly varied.[3] Overall, given the number of competitive elections in existence in

---

[1] For the definition of an intervenable election, see Chapter 6. Four cases of partisan electoral interventions occurred in elections which weren't competitive following my criteria (Bolivia 1964, Chile 1988, South Vietnam 1961 and 1971), usually due to last-moment boycotts of the elections by one of the major sides which were widely expected to contest them or (in the Chilean case) a rare example of a relatively competitive plebiscite. These cases are nevertheless included in the subsequent calculations unless noted otherwise.

[2] Excluding sixteen or so cases of covert electoral interventions noted by O'Rourke.

[3] See Appendix C for the definition of the regions. The number of competitive elections in each region varied depending upon various factors such as the number of states, the number of democracies, and the subtype of democratic regime (and existence of fixed elections terms or not).

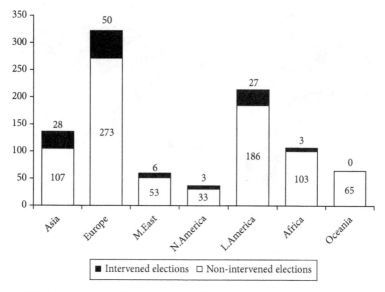

Figure 5.2 Intervened elections by region: all interveners, 1946–2000.

every given region, elections in Europe and Asia were significantly more likely to be targets of such interventions ($p < 0.05$ and $p < 0.001$, respectively). In contrast, elections in sub-Saharan Africa and Oceania were significantly less likely to be targets of electoral intervention ($p < 0.001$ in both cases), perhaps due to the relative marginality of many of the states in both regions. As for specific interveners (Figures 5.3 and 5.4), the main statistically significant differences between them were as to the most preferred target region. The Russians mostly intervened in Europe ($p < 0.01$). In contrast, given the number of elections in each region, the U.S. was more likely to intervene in Asia ($p < 0.001$).[4]

As to specific countries in which electoral interventions occurred, sixty different independent countries have been the targets of such interventions since 1946. As can be seen in Figure 5.1, the targets came from a large variety of sizes and populations, ranging from small states such as Iceland and Grenada to major powers such as West Germany, India, and Brazil. As can be seen in Table 5.1, with the unique exception of Italy, each great power tended to most frequently target different states in its electoral interventions.

---

[4] Calculated using the cumulative binomial probability test (both directions). The finding noted in this paragraph about the U.S. is congruent with Prado's (2006:627) analysis, based on qualitative research on CIA activities, as to overall rate of covert electoral interventions in different world regions.

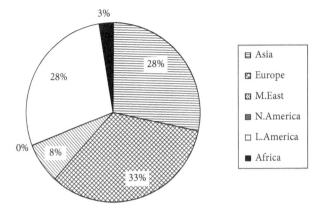

Figure 5.3. U.S. Electoral interventions by region, 1946–2000.

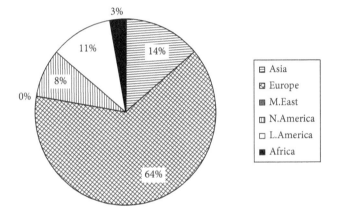

Figure 5.4 USSR/Russia electoral interventions by region, 1946–2000.

As for the subtypes of national-level elections targeted by interveners, about 19.5% of all electoral interventions have occurred in founding elections. Given the number of founding elections overall during this period, no significant difference has been found between the chances of an electoral intervention occurring in founding versus non-founding elections.[5]

---

[5] For these calculations I excluded the three intervention cases noted as occurring in non-competitive elections (see footnote 1 in this chapter). If one counts the fourth exception, Chile's 1988 plebiscite, as a founding election (whose criteria it fully fits except for its plebiscitary nature), the U.S. (at marginal significance of $p < 0.1$) is more likely to intervene in such elections.

Table 5.1 Top Five Targets of Partisan Electoral Interventions by the U.S. and the USSR/Russia

	U.S	Number of Intervention Attempts		USSR/ Russia	Number of Intervention Attempts
1	Italy	8	1	West Germany	5
2	Japan	5	2	Finland	4
3	Israel	4	2	Italy	4
3	Laos	4	4	France	2
3	Sri Lanka	4	4	India	2

About 44.4% of all intervention cases (40.6% with the exclusion of the Italian cases) are repeat interventions—in other words, cases in which the same great power, after intervening once in a particular country's elections, decided to intervene again in (one or more) subsequent elections.[6] Of course, a situation of "returning customers" may fit the argument as to the causes of electoral interventions proposed in Chapter 2. In other words, a repeat intervention may simply indicate that the initial underlying conditions which led to an electoral intervention in one election weren't "solved" by the first electoral intervention and persisted into later elections, sparking similar requests for electoral aid by the target and/or perceptions of threat by the great power. For example, in both the 1964 and 1970 Chilean elections, the U.S. faced a similar threat—the plausible possibility of Salvador Allende, a presidential candidate who was perceived by the U.S. as an implacable foe, winning the Chilean presidential elections (Gustafson 2007). The plausibility of this being the case is strengthened by the fact that 71% of the repeat interventions are in consecutive elections.[7]

Furthermore, elections are also discrete events, each usually separated from the next (or previous) election by three to six years. Given that fact, one would expect each such decision on whether to intervene or not in a particular election to be taken independently, many times with different decision-makers in charge in the great power in each new election in the target. That, in turn, should

---

[6] U.S. and Soviet/Russian interventions have equal shares of "repeat customers." During the data collection process, whenever an intervention was found in a peculiar election in a given country, special effort was put into checking later and previous elections for further possible interventions. Accordingly, it is highly unlikely that this percentage of "repeat customers" is underestimated.

[7] The exclusion of the Italian intervention cases has little effect on the results of this calculation.

discourage new electoral interventions from being done merely due to the fact that in the previous election in the target such an intervention was done.[8]

Nevertheless, given this finding, the possibility of bureaucratic inertia (on the side of the intervener)[9] or an "addiction" (on the side of the aided candidate/party) to outside aid being in these cases a significant cause for such repeat interventions can't be completely dismissed out of hand. However, as can be seen in two of the qualitative case studies in this study—the 1965 Philippine elections and 1967 Greek elections in the preceding chapter (Chapter 4), both of which were past targets of electoral interventions—such bureaucratic processes do not seem to be at work in such meddling. Another possible effect, the possibility that the great power's past experience in conducting electoral interventions in a particular country will affect the effectiveness of its most up-to-date intervention will be examined in Chapter 6.

As for the specific characteristics of the electoral interventions, one important fact that stands out is the covertness of most such interventions. Like the proverbial iceberg, the vast majority of electoral interventions (64.1%) were covert and were not known to the target country's public prior to election day.[10] Likewise, about a quarter of the overt interventions (23.8%) also had some clearly covert components.[11] Covert electoral interventions are rarely exposed before the conclusion of the intervened election or while the secret activity is occurring—only five of the covert interventions found here, or 6.6% of the covert interventions in the dataset were caught "red handed" in this manner.[12] The situation which occurred in the 2016 U.S. election, where credible evidence of the covert Russian intervention for Trump became public prior to election day, is accordingly quite unusual in the annals of partisan electoral interventions.[13]

A second finding of interest is that incumbents and challengers are almost equally likely to be recipients of an electoral intervention on their behalf. Of the 111 intervention cases in which the identity of the aided candidate/party is known, and there is a clear incumbent in the election, about 52.2% of the interventions were done in favor of the incumbent and 47.8% in favor of the challenger.[14]

---

[8] For descriptions of the overall decision process which led to many of the covert electoral interventions that indicate that the decision to intervene electorally indeed tended to be discreet, see the secret internal CIA study of Jackson (1973 [3]:94–98) and, for the Soviet case, Andrew and Mitrokhin (1999:295–297, 468–469; 2006:71–72).

[9] This is an accusation made at times against CIA/covert U.S. interventions of various types (including electoral ones). For a recent example see Prados (2006:381).

[10] The average for each intervener is roughly the same, with 65.4% of U.S. interventions being covert while 61% of USSR/Russian interventions are of this type, a statistically insignificant difference (Chi-square test insignificance at 0.65, test statistic 0.2).

[11] See a further discussion of such interventions in Chapter 6.

[12] Two additional cases of exposure occurred in an overt intervention which had a covert part.

[13] See Chapter 8 for a further discussion of the 2016 Russian intervention.

[14] For the definition of incumbents and challengers see Chapter 6.

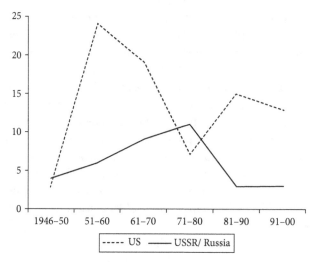

Figure 5.5 U.S. and USSR/Russia Number of electoral interventions by decade, 1946–2000.

Turning to the temporal patterns exhibited by the electoral interventions (Figure 5.5), they seem to be roughly congruent with the overall behavioral patterns of each power on other, heavily studied, dimensions during the Cold War. In the American case, the pattern of its partisan electoral interventions found here is concomitant overall with the way U.S. behavior during the Cold War is usually described by historians: a burst of activity during the early Cold War followed by a decline usually ascribed to the combined effects of Vietnam and Détente and then a renewed burst of activism during "The Second Cold War" of the early to mid-1980s (Gaddis 1990; Westad 2005). In the Soviet case, these patterns are also concomitant with the way historians nowadays usually describe Soviet behavior on other dimensions during the Cold War: an overall increase in international activism over time, peaking in the 1970s, followed by a decline in overall activism ascribed first to the war in Afghanistan and then to Glasnost and Perestroika (Westad 2005; Zubok 2007). Likewise, as in other types of intervention, the end of the Cold War does not seem to have resulted in the stoppage of partisan electoral interventions. They continue to be frequently done by both great powers.

5.2. The Main Electoral Intervention Methods

A wide variety of costly methods was used by the great powers in order to help the preferred side. The specific methods of intervention noted in Table 2.3 in

Chapter 2, as well as many other, less common methods used, can be grouped under six main categories:

1. **Campaign Funding:** Providing campaign funding to the favored side. Such funding can be given directly through, for example, the provision of cash, in-kind material aid (office equipment, newsprint for party newspaper/leaflets, vehicles for the parties' campaign, etc.), or via a "padded" contract with a firm affiliated with that party. It can also be given indirectly such as, for example, via "independent" organizations bringing likely voters of the preferred side to the polls on election day and so forth.

2. **Dirty Tricks:** The intervention included acts which were designed to directly harm one or more candidate(s) or parties competing against the preferred candidate/party. Examples of such acts include: the dissemination of scandalous exposés/disinformation on the rival candidate/parties, physically harming/disabling rival candidates, damaging/destroying a rival's offices or campaigning materials, breaking in/spying on rival's campaign activities and plans, disruption of rival's fundraising efforts by threatening would-be donors, encouraging the breakup of the rival side's political coalition/party in the run-up to the election/bribing some rival candidates to leave/stay in the race, etc.[15]

3. **Campaigning Assistance:** Increasing the capabilities/effectiveness of the assisted side's election campaign through the provision of non-monetary/non-material assistance to the election campaign. Examples include training locals (of the preferred side only) in advanced campaigning, party organization, and get out the vote (GOTV) techniques, designing (for the preferred side only) of campaigning materials, sending campaigning experts to provide on-the-spot assistance to the preferred side's campaign in messaging, strategy, polling analysis, etc.[16]

4. **Threats or Promises:** Public and specific threats or promises by an official representative of intervening country to provide or take away a thing of value to the target/significantly harm it in the future.

5. **Giving/ Taking Aid:** Giving: Sudden new provision of foreign aid or a significant increase in existing aid and/or other forms of material or economic assistance (such as loans/improved loan conditions/loan guarantees, trade treaties/preferred trading conditions, etc.) either directly or indirectly via a multilateral International Organization heavily funded by the intervener.[17]

---

[15] It also includes assistance to the preferred side (usually an incumbent) in conducting voter fraud such as "creating" fake voters or manipulating voter rolls.

[16] The direct provision of expert campaigning advice by officials of the intervener's government is also included.

[17] This also includes the provision (or increased provision) of various kinds of food aid.

Taking: the withdrawal of part or whole of aid, preferred trading conditions, loan guarantees, etc.

6. **Other Concessions:** The intervention included the provision of a costly benefit by the intervener to the target which was non-economic/material in its nature/main value. Some examples include the evacuation of a military base, supporting a highly contentious claim by the target for a particular piece of disputed territory, release of POWs or war criminals, or signing/revising an alliance treaty with the target.

7. **Other:** The electoral intervention included other kinds of costly assistance which do not fall under the preceding categories (see later examples).

Given, as previously noted, the large number of interventions which were covert (with some details still remaining classified), a full accounting of all of the specific methods used in order to help a client in a particular election, beyond the most general characteristics of the intervention, cannot yet be done in many of the intervention cases. With that kept in mind, some conclusions can already be drawn from the available information. First, as can be seen inFigure 5.6, the most commonly known method of electoral intervention by far, used in nearly two-thirds of all electoral interventions, is the provision of campaign funding in some manner. The mother's milk of politics is also, it seems, the mother's milk of foreign meddling in politics.[18]

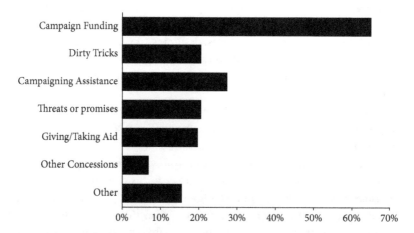

Figure 5.6 Main electoral intervention methods used, 1946–2000. *Note:* More than one method has been used in many elections, so the numbers don't sum to 100%.

---

[18] As for the methods of supply of this electoral aid, the U.S. in a small number of known cases (12.1%) gave campaign funding openly—but in most of these interventions it was in in-kind material aid (such as office equipment) rather than in cash, probably in order to reduce the chances of such aid

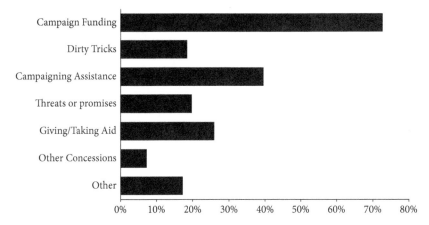

Figure 5.7 Main electoral intervention methods used by the U.S., 1946–2000. *Note*: More than one method has been used in many elections, so numbers don't sum to 100%.

Second, the U.S. and the USSR/Russia (Figures 5.7 and 5.8) greatly differ in the provision of one important method of electoral intervention—campaign assistance. While the use of such methods is the second-most common intervention technique used by the U.S., it is not known to have been used by the USSR/Russia in this era.[19] The highly authoritarian nature of Russia during much of this period, without even a semblance of competitive elections until the end of the Cold War, seems to have made it unable to effectively provide this form of assistance to its clients during this period.[20]

Third, there is great diversity in the character of electoral interventions done in different countries. From the available evidence we can see that at least 45.2% of all interventions involved the use of intervention methods out of more than one of these categories. Likewise, nearly a fourth of all interventions are known

being "misinterpreted" by the target public. Campaign assistance was given in an overt manner by the U.S. a bit more frequently (21.8% of known cases). With a few exceptions, dirty tricks were provided by either power in a covert manner.

[19] This difference is of course highly significant (Chi-square test significance at $p < 0.001$, test statistic 19.57). The differences between the two interveners regarding the use of other electoral intervention methods were insignificant other than the withdrawal or giving of aid, which was more commonly used by the U.S. This difference seems to exist largely due to the U.S. being a provider of foreign aid of various kinds to far more countries and in larger quantities, regardless of such meddling, than the USSR/Russia was in this period—which made threats of withdrawal of existing foreign aid more available to the U.S. in would-be targets when "needed."

[20] Instructively, the first known case of the use of this electoral intervention method by Russia (in an intervention beyond the temporal scope of PEIG at present) came after a decade of relatively competitive Russian elections in the 1990s—the Russian intervention in the Ukraine in 2004 (Kuzio 2005:37).

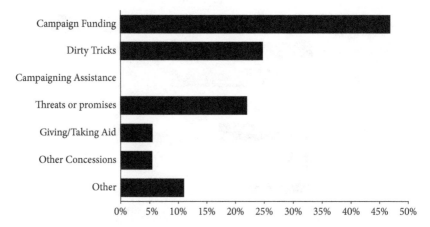

Figure 5.8 Main electoral intervention methods used by the USSR/Russia, 1946–2000. *Note*: More than one method has been used in many elections, so numbers don't sum to 100%.

to have used methods which are hard to categorize (the "other" or "other concession" categories. For example, in some such interventions the assistance also included, among other things, surrendering a strategically important military base to the target (Finland 1956), coming out in support of a highly contentious claim by the target for a particular disputed territory (Italy 1948), or enabling the release of convicted Nazi war criminals (West Germany 1953).

Likewise, even those methods of intervention which fit under the five other categories were frequently quite varied in their application or goals. For example, in a few cases of intervention (such as Guyana 1968 and Chile 1964) key components of the intervention seem to have been designed to serve as pre-election "pork" (i.e., for roads and other infrastructure) for particular constituencies in order to help the incumbent attract support. In at least one case (Malta 1971), one component of the intervention seems to have been designed to "goose" the economy in the months preceding the election—an example of what might be called the "transnational" form of the political business cycle. Indeed, in the previously noted Chilean case, one of the components of the American intervention seems to even have included smuggling frozen meat into Chile in order to deal with a severe shortage that had developed there in the pre-election period. Even the campaign funding sometimes involved (or also involved) the provision of various things other than money, from loudspeakers and portable movie projectors (Laos 1955), to a printing press for a party newspaper (Romania 1990), to five thousand graffiti spray cans and 2.5 million bumper stickers (Yugoslavia/Serbia 2000).

This great variety indicates that many electoral interventions were "customized" by the intervener to fit a particular client's needs—in a manner similar to what was observed in the three cases of intervention studied in Chapter 3. This is unlike the common manner in which many forms of foreign aid are frequently characterized. This variety also provides one indirect piece of evidence for one of the key components of the argument made here as to the causes of electoral interventions—that such interventions involve (and require) cooperation between the intervener and a particular candidate/party in the target.[21]

This data also indicates that on one key aspect the Russian intervention in the 2016 U.S. elections was not unusual or special. The types of intervention methods used by Russia in this case, the collection and subsequent release of documents designed to embarrass a certain undesirable candidate and the spreading of "fake news" in their regard, belong to a subtype of intervention, dirty tricks, used by both great powers in about a fifth of all interventions conducted between 1946 and 2000. Many of those interventions, in turn, used pre-internet or "analog" versions extremely similar to those known to have been known to have been used by Russia in 2016.

For example, in the 1980 West German elections the Soviets spread disinformation against the CDU supposedly linking it to Nazis in the German intelligence services. Likewise, in the Japanese elections in 1958, the U.S. secretly provided the Liberal Democratic Party political intelligence of various kinds about its main political rival, the Japanese Socialist Party, using paid informants that the CIA had in that party. In the 1990 Nicaraguan elections, the CIA secretly leaked damaging information on alleged corruption by the Sandinistas to German newspapers. The U.S.-backed opposition candidate, Violetta Chamorro, then used those "independent" foreign exposés against the Sandinista candidate, Daniel Ortega, during its election campaign.[22] When Putin ordered the GRU to intervene in this manner in the 2016 U.S. elections, they were using a tried-and-true meddling technique.

One final aspect of interest is that partisan electoral interventions seem to rarely include attempts to inflict physical harm on particular candidates or other related persons.[23] Nor does such meddling usually involve symbolic or actual use of military force by the intervener.[24] In only one intervention case in PEIG, the

---

[21] Furthermore, it is clear from the nature of virtually all of these interventions that, even if they weren't successful, it was not due to a "desire" by the great power to fail in this regard. In other words, there is little to no evidence that electoral interventions are done with the purpose of harming or giving a "kiss of death" to the aided side (even if, in some cases, that is indeed the unintended result).

[22] Author's data.

[23] Such acts, if they occurred, would be counted as a type of "dirty tricks."

[24] Bubeck and Marinov (2019:93) claim to have found such use of force as part of 5% of all partisan interventions in their dataset. However, a careful look at these supposedly violent electoral intervention cases indicates that nearly all of them refer to acts which began many years beforehand and for reasons completely unrelated to the election in question. Likewise, no evidence is given in their

1953 Philippine elections, was there any attempt to physically harm the undesirable candidate—and in this case it was limited to drugging Philippine president Quirino before a major speech so he would temporarily appear to listeners and observers as completely drunk.[25] Indeed, the infamous "track 2" American intervention in Chile (which included the kidnapping and assassination of General Rene Schneider) occurred only *after* the 1970 election was concluded (Gustafson 2007).[26] Likewise, in only two cases (Italy 1948 and Nicaragua 1990) is there any evidence that the intervener tried to use military force for this purpose in a "symbolic" or "real" manner—and in both cases this was just one secondary component of a larger, multifaceted electoral intervention. Although partisan electoral interventions are, of course, a severe, blatant, and frequently coercive violation of the target country's sovereignty, such meddling does not usually involve acts of violence on the intervener's side.[27] When great powers intervene in elections, the sword and the dagger are left in their sheaths.

5.3 Additional Evidence for Arguments

As noted in the introduction, an overview of PEIG (or the universe of cases) may enable us to do an additional examination of some of the arguments proposed in this study as well as some, or components of, plausible alternatives. Firstly, the dataset provides some strong yet indirect evidence for the argument in the first part of this study on the causes of partisan electoral interventions. As noted in Chapter 2, I argued that one of the key factors required for an intervention to occur is the existence of a significant domestic actor within the target who wants or is willing to be aided in this manner. An overall overview of the universe of cases enables us to check a proxy measure of this component—that is, whether the supported candidate and/or party is a fragile victor or a blocked/weakening

sources for an election-related shift in these activities in the run-up to the elections. For example, the U.S. military aid to the Mujahedin in Afghanistan as part of its proxy war there (which began back in 1979) is coded in their dataset as an American electoral intervention on their behalf in the 1988 Afghan elections—an election which the Mujahedin (or any affiliated party), moreover, never even bothered contesting in the first place.

[25] This intervention also included the torching of offices and storage areas of the Quirino campaign which were believed to be storing fake ballots. However, these acts of arson, according to the available sources, were conducted at night when no people were present (authors' data).

[26] If the case of the Russian intervention in 2004 Ukrainian election (outside of the time frame of PEIG at present) indeed included the attempted poisoning of opposition candidate Yuschenko with dioxin (Kuzio 2005:38), that was a very unusual exception to this rule.

[27] This is another important difference between electoral interventions and the other covert FIRC methods described by O'Rourke (2018), nearly all of which involve the direct use of force by the U.S. or the direct inducement of such violence in the target through the provision of weapons or other methods.

loser.[28] Overall, out of the 114 intervention cases in which enough data is available to indicate who exactly was supported by the great power, at least 76.3% of the receivers of such support (or eighty-seven cases) belong to one of these subtypes. The share of supported domestic actors which fit these criteria on the Soviet/Russian side (72.2%) is a bit lower than U.S.-supported actors (78.2%)— however, this difference isn't statistically significant.[29]

Second, little evidence is found to back up other plausible alternative explanations. In the case of O'Rourke's (2018) argument, as noted in Chapter 1, I find forty-two cases of overt electoral interventions during the 1946–2000 period, twenty-seven of which were done by the U.S. This is in comparison to only six overt FIRCs by the U.S. during this period. Although overt electoral interventions are less common than covert ones, they are more than three times as common compared to covert electoral interventions than overt FIRCs are compared to covert FIRCs—a statistically significant difference indicating major differences between these two phenomena.[30]

Similarly, contra the expectations of Bubeck and Marinov (2019:210),[31] no evidence exists that countries with fragile democratic institutions are more likely to be the targets of such interventions than "full" democracies. In order to test this claim I used, as is the standard in the field, a 6-or-above polity2 score in the year in which the electoral intervention occurred to indicate a fully democratic polity. When the share of electoral interventions in democratic polities under this definition was compared to the probability of competitive elections occurring in such polities during the same period, no statistically significant chances of such interventions overall occurring in such countries was found.[32] The same thing was found (no statistically significant relationship) when this test was repeated for each separate decade in the dataset. This result is far from surprising, given that in seventy-two cases (or 64.3% of all interventions) the target had a 6 or higher polity score. Indeed, in forty-three cases (or 38.4% of all interventions) in which an intervention had occurred, the target had the combined polity2 maximum score of 10—a score usually reserved for countries whose democratic credentials are beyond doubt (such as Sweden or Canada).[33]

Third, under similar threat environments (or eras) little difference is found between Democratic and Republican presidents as to their electoral intervention

---

[28] See Chapter 2 for the definitions of both subtypes.
[29] Using the Chi-square test (insignificance at 0.48, test statistic 0.49).
[30] Chi-square test significance at $p < 0.001$, test statistic 15.3.
[31] See also Corstange and Marinov (2012:658) for a similar suggestion.
[32] Using the cumulative binomial probability test (both directions). This analysis only includes cases in which polity has scores. For the analysis of this result by intervener see Appendix C.
[33] In other words, fully democratic countries aren't any less or more likely to be targets of such interventions than countries with less consolidated democratic regimes, given the number of competitive elections during this period.

propensity.[34] During the Cold War, Democratic presidents would intervene electorally on average 1.35 times per year in power while Republican presidents did 1.37 electoral interventions per year, a minor substantive difference which isn't statistically significant.[35] Similar results are found as to Soviet General Secretaries until the end of the Cold War.[36]

When publicly justifying their partisan electoral interventions long after they took place, policymakers and "on the ground" operatives frequently claim that they did those electoral interventions largely because the "other side" was intervening in this manner as well (see, e.g., Colby 1978:109–113).[37] However, as can be expected from Table 5.1, only seven (or 6.3%) of the intervened elections in PEIG are cases of a double electoral intervention—that is, that the U.S. was backing one side while the USSR/Russia was backing another side during the same election.[38] This percentage of double interventions is but slightly higher (7.8%) if only Cold War interventions are counted. This is despite, as noted, a special effort made in the data collection process to check the behavior of the other superpower whenever clear evidence of intervention by one of the great powers was found in a particular election. Two of the most famous cases of intervened national-level elections prior to 2016—the 1948 Italian elections and the 1970 Chilean elections—were double interventions, but they are not typical. Accordingly, Bubeck and Marinov's hypothesized scenario of "election wars" for such situations (2019:58–65) seems to be a quite rare occurrence in practice in the post-WW2 era.[39]

[34] For some claims of variance in regard to military activities see Bertoli, Dafoe, and Trager (2019).

[35] Using the cumulative binomial probability test (both directions). A slightly different metric of the probability of intervention of U.S. presidents of each party in a given foreign election (as from the number of foreign competitive elections open to intervention in each year in power) during the Cold War gives the probability of a democratic president intervening during this period in a given foreign election as 10.78% and a Republican president at 10.35%—the difference again being insignificant. In the post–Cold War era Democrats are significantly less likely than Republicans to intervene. However, given that this dataset ends in December 2000, this is largely the function of the Clinton presidency—which occurred during an unusually low-threat environment (which famously was an important factor in enabling his presidency in the first place).

[36] Using the cumulative binomial probability test (both directions). If the last three years of Gorbachev's rule (which coincide with the end of the Cold War) are included, he is found to be significant less likely to intervene in this manner ($p < 0.01$).

[37] Some scholars of electoral interventions have made similar arguments (Corstange and Marinov 2012:658).

[38] In another half-dozen cases (such as the U.S. interventions in Mauritius 1982 or Israel 1996), claims were made by some of the sources that were consulted that another country, one hostile to the intervener (such as Libya under Qaddafi and Iran, respectively) was aiding the other side in the elections. However, even if these claims were true (and the evidence is frequently quite weak), the overall number of double interventions would remain quite low.

[39] It is, however, in congruence with my explanation for why interventions are accepted by local actors—that is, that only parties/leaders in a very bad political shape (blocked weak/loser or fragile victors) will be usually willing to take the risks/costs involved in asking or agreeing to such a foreign intervention on their behalf. Usually only one major actor is in such a situation in a given country at a given time.

Of course, during the Cold War the bipolar rivalry had an important role in the way in which each great power defined "dangerous" or "unacceptable" leaders/parties in third countries. Likewise, one cannot completely dismiss the possibility that in a few cases of electoral intervention mistaken beliefs about the plans of the other superpower were an important factor in the decision-making process. Nevertheless, the relative dearth of such double interventions seems to indicate that this factor (the decision of the other superpower to electorally intervene) was usually a relatively minor part of the decision process which led or didn't lead to an electoral intervention. Indeed, in some cases there is even evidence that claims of such interventions—that is, creating an impression of a double intervention occurring when only one country is intervening—was sometimes made as part of a disinformation campaign so as to hide the actual covert intervention in one's favor and/or to "muddy the waters" in overt ones.[40]

5.4 Conclusion

This brief overview chapter illustrated some of the main patterns found in the PEIG dataset. Some indirect "first cut" evidence was found for the explanation proposed here for why electoral interventions occur, with more than three-fourths of the interventions (76.3%) being done for the type of actors that it would expect (fragile victor or a blocked/weakening loser). Likewise, clear evidence was found that many of these interventions are, as my explanation would expect, usually "customized." In the following chapter I will begin to analyze the effects of electoral interventions on the targeted election results using PEIG directly via an in-depth analysis of six cases where an electoral intervention was seriously considered by the great power.

---

[40] For example, in the 1953 West German election (Chapter 3), Adenauer made intentionally spurious charges that some SPD members were receiving covert funding from the GDR—this while he was being overtly aided by the U.S. (Schwarz 1995:77–78).

6

Dragging Them over the Finish Line

The Effects of Partisan Electoral Interventions on Election Results

> In the midst of these pleasing ideas we should be unfaithful to our-
> selves if we should ever lose sight of the danger to our liberties if
> anything partial or extraneous should infect the purity of our free,
> fair, virtuous, and independent elections. . . . If that solitary suffrage
> can be obtained by foreign nations by flattery or menaces, by fraud
> or violence, by terror, intrigue, or venality, the Government may not
> be the choice of the American people, but of foreign nations . . . and
> candid men will acknowledge that in such cases choice would have
> little advantage to boast of over lot or chance.
>
> —U.S. President John Adams, Inaugural Address March 4, 1797[1]

As the target of a French electoral intervention in 1796, John Adams was among the first modern leaders, but by no means the last, to be wary of foreign electoral meddling in their country. Partisan electoral interventions are a quite common phenomenon. As I described in Chapter 5, such interventions have occurred in approximately one of every nine competitive national-level executive elections between 1946 and 2000 and have been done in sixty different independent countries around the world.

Nevertheless, the mere ubiquity of partisan electoral interventions may not necessarily indicate, in and of itself, that they are of any significant "real life" importance. For that purpose, this chapter will examine one important, basic criterion determining whether electoral interventions "matter." It will inves- tigate whether electoral interventions are truly able to significantly affect the election results in the targeted country—and therefore, as John Adams warns in the chapter's opening quote, determine the identity of the target's leader- ship. Given what we know about the effects of leaders (see Chapter 1), if elec- toral interventions frequently enable great powers to wield such influence on

---

[1] Online by Gerhard Peters and John Woolley, *The American Presidency Project*, available at http://www.presidency.ucsb.edu/ws/?pid=25802.

Meddling in the Ballot Box. Dov H. Levin, Oxford University Press (2020). © Oxford University Press.
DOI: 10.1093/oso/9780197519882.001.0001.

the target through this pathway, they may have other major effects on the target as well.

Great powers frequently believe that they can indeed determine the election results, and therefore the leadership of a given country, by conducting a partisan electoral intervention. For example, the CIA and the KGB when reviewing their electoral intervention records claimed, in secret classified reports, that they were quite effective in this goal. One such analysis in 1969 by the CIA maintained that "there have been numerous instances when, facing the threat" of a hostile party achieving an "election victory," the CIA "met the threat and turned it successfully."[2] The KGB made similar claims (Andrew and Mitrokhin 2005:72, 318, 350). This possible effect, however, is by no means certain. John Adams himself, after all, became president despite a French electoral intervention against him.

This investigation will also be of value in two other major ways. First, one usually assumes, prima facie, that policymakers choose a particular policy tool given that it is, in most cases, quite effective in its main purpose. Finding out whether this is indeed the case will enable us to see how accurate that underlying presumption is. Second, this examination will also provide some further indirect evidence as to the strength of my argument about the causes of such interventions. As was described in Chapter 2, the first three hypotheses on the effects of electoral interventions (H4–H6) are directly derived from the model of the causes of such intervention (H1–H3). Accordingly, the findings on these three hypotheses may buttress or weaken any conclusions noted in previous chapters.

In Chapters 3 and 4, I investigated the first three hypotheses in regard to the causes of electoral interventions (H1–H3). Four major hypotheses about the effectiveness of electoral interventions will be examined in this chapter. Briefly stated, my first hypothesis as to the effects of partisan electoral interventions on election results (H4) is that such interventions will overall increase the electoral chances of the aided candidate/party. My second hypothesis (H5) is that overt public interventions are more beneficial to the aided candidate/party than covert interventions. The third hypothesis (H6) is that electoral interventions will be less helpful to the aided party/candidate in founding elections than in later elections. Finally, the fourth hypothesis (H7) expects the effects of electoral interventions to differ between interventions that favor of challengers and those in favor of incumbents with contrary predictions. A full in-depth description of these four hypotheses can be seen in Chapter 2.

This chapter will be divided into five main parts. In the first section, the method by which the aforementioned four hypotheses are operationalized and tested is described. Then these hypotheses are tested using PEIG and the results

[2] FRUS 1969–1976 12: Document 149.

described. The third section examines the possible effects of the specific subtypes of electoral intervention methods used and the magnitude of the overall intervention. The fourth section tries to estimate these effects in particular intervention cases. Finally, the concluding section summarizes the findings and notes some of their implications.

6.1 Variables and Definitions

In order to investigate these four hypotheses about the effects of electoral interventions (H4–H7), a plausible model of the factors which affect cross-national voting, of the type frequently used in the economic voting literature, is required. Accordingly, I use the approach recently employed by two major scholars in this subfield, Timothy Hellwig and David Samuels (2007), and then add the relevant electoral intervention variables. As a further check I also employ (with two exceptions)[3] a second cross-national economic voting model, that of Mark Kayser and Michael Peress (2012), with the inclusion of the electoral intervention variables.[4]

Besides the inclusion of the variables specified for each of these economic voting models (such as GDP growth rate, party fragmentation,[5] trade openness,[6] country wealth, etc.), I also add, for further robustness checks, relevant control variables. These controls are, for example, for various kinds of national security/foreign policy factors (Civil Wars, Interstate Wars, and major foreign policy crises), the level of democracy in the target (polity scale) and the time period involved (Cold War era or later). Appendix E, sections E.1 and E.2, provides further description of the control variables and their construction as well as of the subsequent robustness checks.

All models analyzed here use the standard tool used in cross-national aggregate studies of the economic vote (Wilkin et al. 1997; Samuels 2004; Benton 2005), as well as the two previously noted replicated studies—OLS with PSCE (panel corrected) robust standard errors (Beck and Katz 1995). It is also the best technique to use when the dependent variable (as in this study) is incumbent

---

[3] The first-noted variable, unemployment, is unfortunately not available for many countries. Furthermore, the differences in its measurement and reliability in non-OECD countries make it a problematic tool for cross-national comparisons outside of the OECD (see Hellwig and Samuels 2007:303). Indeed, even in the models of Kayser and Paress, local unemployment has no significant effects in eight of the nine models tested. The second missing variable, coalition size, is unfortunately either unavailable, irrelevant, or an inapplicable concept as to many of the presidential and semi-presidential systems included in our dataset.

[4] The author wishes to thank Michael Peress for the kind aid provided in replicating this model.

[5] This is a measure of the number of effective (e.g., significant) parties or candidates contesting that election. See Appendix E for further details.

[6] Trade as a percentage of GDP in constant terms. See Appendix E for further details.

vote share, a variable which usually exhibits an approximately normal distribution and, due to its bounded nature, has few influential outliers.

An outside partisan intervention in an election will only be invited by a domestic actor and/or seriously considered by a foreign power if there is some plausible prospect of success in this endeavor. I therefore begin by compiling the universe of cases—a list of national-level competitive elections in which an electoral intervention could potentially occur.[7] I define an intervenable/competitive election as one that receives 7 out of 7 on the 2010 DPI's (Database of Political Institutions) executive electoral competiveness index (Beck et al. 2001) with a small modification. For an election to get that score, multiple parties (in parliamentary systems) need to have won seats in the election and the largest party must have received less than 75% of the vote, or, in presidential or semi-presidential systems, multiple candidates need to have run and the winning candidate has to have won less than 75% of the votes.[8]

Following this criterion and extending the coverage of this index back to 1946 using Nohlen's data on elections (see description in the next paragraph), 937 national-level executive elections with a population of above one hundred thousand have been found. These elections come from 148 different countries. Australia, Denmark, New Zealand, Greece, and Japan have the most competitive elections in this dataset (between 22 and 18) while another 23 countries have only one competitive election. Because of missing data of various kinds on the independent and dependent variables, the number of elections (and countries) on which the statistical analysis can be done is somewhat smaller in practice.

The dependent variable in all of the models estimated here, as is common in models of economic voting (including in the two approaches adopted here), is the vote share of the incumbent's party (in parliamentary systems) or of the incumbent's party's presidential candidate (in presidential and semi-presidential systems with direct elections).[9] Nearly all of this data came from the edited

---

[7] Such elections can occur, of course, even in many regimes which are far from being democracies if not largely authoritarian, such as the Philippines under Marcos (after the imposition of martial law), Yugoslavia under Milosevic, or Argentina under Peron. As a result, even elections in such "competitive authoritarian" regimes, so long as they are expected to be overall competitive (even if the playing field is significantly tilted in favor of one of the sides), can be and often are tempting targets for interveners. Accordingly, no criteria for the country's level of democracy, beyond the election's competitiveness, are used in order to exclude or include particular elections.

[8] For examples of use see Brownlee 2009; He 2007; and Triesman 2007. The list of competitive elections according to these criteria can be seen as part of the PEIG dataset at the author's website www.dovhlevin.com. For further explanation of the reasons for choosing the DPI measure see Appendix E. Elections to Constitutional assemblies if one of their explicit purposes is to select an executive are included, as are partial/supplementary elections in parliamentary systems so on the number of seats contested in them is at least 10% of the total (i.e., usually enough to potentially affect the parliamentary majority of the executive).

[9] Besides its ubiquitous use in the cross-national economic voting literature in order to investigate the effects of various factors on election results, incumbent voter share was chosen as the dependent variable for this analysis for three other reasons. First, it is widely recognized, as a result, as a

volumes by Dieter Nohlen and colleagues (1999, 2001, 2005, 2010) on elections around the world. These scholars, over the course of the last two decades, have painstakingly assembled data on national-level election results from all independent states from at least 1946 to the present. The data on election results in different countries is standardized into one common format, making it an ideal source for cross-national comparisons.[10]

In this and other variables where this distinction is used, an incumbent is defined as the party and/or candidate which held the highest elected executive position (president in presidential and semi-presidential systems, prime minister in parliamentary systems) in the period preceding the elections and/or received the endorsement or backing of the holder of the highest executive position during that period.[11] A challenger is a party and/or candidate which does not fall under these criteria.

The main independent variables, partisan electoral interventions and, in subsequent models, various subtypes of such interventions, are taken from PEIG—a new dataset constructed by the author of all such interventions between January 1, 1946 and December 31, 2000, which were done by the US and the USSR/Russia. As noted, a total of 117 American and Soviet/Russian interventions have been found during this period: 81 by the U.S. and 36 by the USSR/Russia. Chapter 5 provides a detailed description of PEIG and what intervention methods are included and Appendix B describes the method of its construction.

An electoral intervention is coded as covert when all of the significant acts done in order to help a particular party/candidate were a secret and/or when the connection between those acts and the election was not known to the average voter in the target. An intervention is coded as overt when at least some of the significant acts done in order to aid a particular candidate/party were known to

---

valid tool for such purposes. Furthermore, any findings discovered while utilizing it would be harder to contest with claims that this particular independent variable was used just because it happened to provide the "right" results. It also makes it easier to compare the findings on the variables emphasized by the economic voting literature (economic growth, etc.) to the findings on my variables of interest.

[10] For the small number of election results missing from these volumes (usually those occurring right before or after the publication of these volumes) I used other reliable sources such as the African elections database and the reports on election results by the Inter-Parliamentary Union. For a small number of parliamentary systems in which vote share was repeatedly missing, seat share was used instead. Cases in which the elections were clearly competitive but the elections were invalidated before the results became fully available and/or the data sources indicate that election fraud was so massive as to make the results completely unreliable were excluded from the dataset.

[11] In countries in which it is common to install a neutral non-partisan caretaker government in the run-up to the elections (like Greece or Bangladesh since 1996), I code the party of the last pre-caretaker executive as the incumbent. As some researchers on the economic vote have noted, while voters can also hold (in multiparty parliamentary systems, etc.) other coalition partners accountable for the executive's performance, the evidence seems to show that, in most cases, the party/candidate which holds the top executive position prior to the election receives nearly all of the credit and/or blame for the executive's performance (Duch and Stevenson 2008:59).

the average voter in the target to have been done in order to help or hinder a particular candidate/party in the elections.[12]

To investigate my first hypothesis on effectiveness (H4) I include in the first set of models an electoral intervention variable (*Electoral Intervention*). In order to model the fact that electoral interventions can be done in order to help or to harm the incumbent,[13] this variable is constructed as trichotomous,[14] coded as 1 if an intervention is for the incumbent, –1 if it is for a challenger, and 0 when no intervention occurs.[15] If this hypothesis is correct, I would expect a positive and significant effect.

In order to test the second hypothesis (H5) I include in the second set of models two trichotomous variables, one of overt interventions (*Overt Int.*) and one of covert interventions (*Covert Int.*) following my coding of my electoral intervention dataset. If hypothesis 2 is correct, I would expect the Overt Interventions variable to have a positive and significant effect as well as an effect larger in substantive terms than the effect of the Covert Interventions variable. Electoral interventions can include both significant overt and covert components (say, a public threat/promise as well as covert campaign aid). However, most of the overt interventions do not include a covert component.[16] Accordingly, I also include a variable (*Covert & Overt*) for such cases.

In order to investigate the third hypothesis on effectiveness (H6), I create in the third set of models an interaction (*Int*Founding Election*) between a founding election dummy (*Founding Election*) and the electoral intervention variable from

---

[12] To examine whether a certain known intervention was overt, I examined pre-election mass-media descriptions of these acts (and/or reliable secondary sources describing these reactions). If these acts are described by the media as being part of such a foreign electoral intervention, then it is assumed that the average voter knew about this intervention. Given that overt interventions are designed to affect public opinion in the target, there was rarely any ambiguity in this regard in practice as to the main components of these interventions.

[13] As can be seen in Chapter 2, I do not expect any differences in the effects of electoral interventions based upon whether the intervention is for the incumbent or for the challenger. Accordingly a trichotomous intervention variable closely approximates my theoretical arguments for these three hypotheses. See the results for H7 for the findings when this theoretical assumption is relaxed and empirically examined.

[14] Electoral interventions for either side by a great power are seen as inherently identical—the operational differentiation here is only due to the nature of the independent variable (incumbent vote share) which requires such an operationalization in order to estimate their effects.

[15] Given that in cases of double intervention (the Soviets helping one side, the U.S. another) there are effects in both directions, I exclude these interventions as well (except in the models for Hypothesis 7 4). As noted in chapter 2, such interventions are quite uncommon in practice. Also excluded are cases in which the identity of the incumbent is unclear.

[16] Only ten of the overt interventions (23.8% of all overt interventions) in the dataset fall into this category. Given the good data availability in most cases of overt interventions as to any covert activities also being done by the intervener in regard to that election, it is clear that covert components aren't an "automatic" part of most overt interventions. As will be later described in this chapter, the exclusion of the mixed category is done in order to help more clearly identify the separate effects of each subtype—and the inclusion of these interventions as part of the overt interventions does not affect the main results.

the first hypothesis.[17] In order to prevent possible bias, together with the inter-action I also include its two previously noted main effects. All three variables are then included in the third set of models. If Hypothesis 6 is correct, then the inter-action term should be negative and significant.

One should note that I code founding elections here somewhat differently than some other scholars do (see, e.g., O'Donnell Schmitter and Whitehead 1986).[18] The theoretical logic behind this hypothesis is that the quality of in-formation which the aided candidate/party can provide to the intervener about the target country's preferences, etc., information usually acquired through the aided candidate/party's previous electoral experience, has a major effect on how effective the intervention is. Accordingly, in order to be coded as a founding elec-tion, in the previous six years there had to be no competitive, national-level ex-ecutive election in that country. The six-year time range was chosen because it is the longest gap that modern democracies (with one past exception) permit between executive national-level elections.[19] For longer periods, the information available to the local politicians from a previous competitive election is expected to degrade to the point of being of little value.

For periods shorter than six years, the information about how to effectively campaign in their country or the preferences of the electorate is unlikely to vanish from the minds of the local politicians simply because there was a short, non-constitutional "interruption." Indeed, when such a relatively short inter-ruption ends, the subsequent election usually has the same pre-interruption politicians and parties reentering politics and contesting the elections.[20]

Accordingly, except in cases in which the data indicated that all or most of the pre-interruption politicians (and parties) had been exiled, executed, and/

[17] The incumbent in such elections was coded, in a manner similar to my coding incumbency in democratic regimes, as either the effective (unelected) leader/member of the leadership group of that country (if running in the elections) or whichever party/candidate was endorsed/supported by the current effective leadership. In order to enable this interaction, the founding election dummy is constructed as 1 for non-founding elections and 2 for founding elections. An alternate way of creating the interaction—having the founding election dummy as 0 for non-founding and 1 for founding and turning the trichotomous election variable into a 1-to-3 scale (each respectively of the original −1, 0, and 1 scale) had no effect on the subsequent substantive results.

[18] These scholars define a founding election as the first competitive multiparty election following a period of authoritarian rule (regardless of its length).

[19] Some fully democratic countries with presidential systems (post-1987 South Korea, Chile pre-1973 and post-1989) have an executive election only once every six years. Likewise, some parliamen-tary systems have a maximum term of five years (the U.K). In practice, while coding this variable for countries which suffered from non-constitutional interruptions, etc., there were no more than three or four cases in which the coding would have differed if a four-year range were chosen instead. For the one past exception to this rule in modern democracies, France between 1958 and 2002, I code the relevant presidential elections as non-founding.

[20] Likewise, the fact that the previous competitive national-level election was done prior to inde-pendence (or under foreign military occupation) should not usually reduce the value of the know-ledge acquired from it for the participating politicians for the purposes of campaigning.

or banned from running in the post-interruption elections (as was the case of Turkey in the 1981 elections or in Argentina in the 1963 elections), I don't code the second of two competitive elections with less than a six-year gap as a founding election even if there was a successful coup (or autocoup) in the interim or the first of these competitive elections was done prior to independence.

To investigate the fourth hypothesis (H7), I include two dummy variables, one for the interventions done for the purpose of aiding the incumbent (*Int. for Incumbent*) and one for interventions done for the purpose of helping a challenger (*Int. for Challenger*). Given that successful interventions in favor of a challenger would reduce an incumbent's vote share and vice versa, if the fourth hypothesis is correct I would expect the absolute substantive effect of the challenger aid variable to significantly differ from that of the incumbent aid variable.[21]

6.2 Results: Hypotheses 4 through 7

Tables 6.2 and 6.3 present the statistical results for the first hypothesis about the beneficial effects of such interventions on the aided side (H4). For improved readability, these and all regression tables henceforth noted are at the end of the chapter. As can be seen from Model 1 in Table 6.2, I am able to replicate Hellwig and Samuels' (henceforth HS) main result—that the interaction of economic growth and trade openness significantly reduces the incumbent's vote share. However, under some robustness checks, such as fixed effects (Model 2) and fraud limit (Model 5), this result becomes insignificant. This also occurs in many subsequent models where the electoral intervention variables are included as well.[22]

In Model 1, I also include the electoral intervention variable. The effect is in the predicted positive direction and has significant effects both statistically and substantively. A Wald test also indicates (at the 0.01 level) that it significantly increases overall model fit. On average, an electoral intervention in favor of one of the sides contesting the election will increase its vote share by about 3%. That is quite a significant effect. For example, such a swing in the vote share from the winner to the loser in the fourteen U.S. presidential elections occurring between 1960 and 2012 would have been sufficient to change the identity of the winner in seven of these elections.[23] Its effects also stack up quite well in comparison to

---

[21] This operationalization for H7 also indirectly serves as an alternative specification to the trichotomous construction of the electoral intervention variables as used in previous hypotheses.

[22] In a "clean" replication (without the electoral intervention variable) of HS (see Appendix E, section E.4.3, table E5.15), this interaction becomes insignificant under fixed effects as well (0.11).

[23] Assuming, of course, a similar shift in the relevant "swing states" and, accordingly, the Electoral College.

another well-known major effect on election results—the state of the economy. As can be seen in Model 3 (where the interactions of the economic growth variable with two other variables are excluded), a 1% increase in the real GDP per capita would increase incumbent vote share by about 0.4%. To illustrate its effects, had Carter in 1980 run for reelection with the economy which Reagan had in 1984 (+6.6%) rather than the economy he actually had in 1980 (−1.9%), our model would have predicted Carter's vote share to have increased by about 3.4%. An illustration of the effects of electoral interventions in "real life" cases of such interventions is provided in section 6.4.

The following models include a battery of various robustness checks. My results hold under country fixed effects (Model 2) as well as when elections in which evidence exists that significant election fraud had occurred (i.e., possible "measurement error" on the dependent variable) are excluded from the dataset (Model 5). In Model 4 I attempt to replicate the Kayser and Peress (2012) study (henceforth KP) on the cross-national economic vote and then include the electoral intervention variable. This is done in order to make sure that my finding of a positive, significant, and substantive effect for electoral interventions was not the result of an unusually well-fitting economic voting model. I am able to replicate KP's main result—that once one controls for the tendency of the public to compare (or benchmark) the economic performance in their country to that in other relevant countries (or global growth) the effects of the local economic performance on the incumbent's vote share will consistently be affected by the performance of the local economy.[24] The results regarding electoral interventions, however, are similar to those found in the HS models.[25]

Model 6, Table 6.3 includes a control for whether the intervention in a particular case is a repeat intervention on the side of that intervener. In other words, this robustness check tries to examine, among other things, the effects of any possible experience accumulated by the intervener from intervening in elections in that target in the past. This control is not significant, nor does it have any effects on my result.

In Model 7, I examine the robustness of the effects found in Model 1 as to possible temporal patterns in the data. A dummy variable for the Cold War period does not have a significant and substantive effect and an interaction between this variable and the electoral intervention variable (not shown) is not significant. Similar non-significant results are found when the time trend variable in Kayser and Peress's models is included (see Model 4) or when an interaction between

---

[24] In the various robustness tests conducted for the electoral intervention hypotheses, this result by KP was found to be quite robust to alternate specifications, although it also, in some subsequent robustness checks, becomes insignificant.

[25] Similar results are found when minimal (or bare-bones) models are run for all of the four main hypotheses checked here (see Appendix E).

this variable and the electoral intervention is added as well (see Appendix E, section E.5). These results indicate that, at least as to the post-WW2 era, there is no significant relationship between the time period in which the intervention occurred and the effectiveness of the intervention. In Model 8, I check for the effects of a potentially significant international factor—the presence of international election observers in the country prior to the elections. This factor has, in contrast to some scholars' theoretical expectations (Bubeck and Marinov 2019), no significant effects.[26]

My theoretical argument about the effects of electoral interventions expects the U.S. and the USSR/Russia to be equally effective.[27] Nevertheless, some may wonder whether these general patterns are indeed what one finds in practice given the significant differences between the U.S. and the USSR/Russia (such as regime type, areas of influence, etc.). Accordingly, in Model 9, I disaggregated the electoral intervention variable by U.S. and USSR/Russian interventions. The results for the disaggregated Russian and American electoral intervention variables are essentially the same as for the aggregated variable, although the results for the Russian interventions are not significant. This is probably due to the relatively small number of Russian interventions (as low as twenty-two cases in some models here and in Appendix E, section E.4) which haven't been dropped due to missing data on some covariates.[28]

This finding does not, of course, necessarily foreclose the possibility that the electoral interventions of the U.S. and the USSR/Russia each differently affected the target after the intervened election. Indeed, elsewhere (Levin 2018b) I find such significant differences, regarding, for example, post-election cooperation between the intervener and the (victorious) client. Nevertheless, these results do show that both powers had an equal ability overall to affect electoral outcomes in elections around the world.

---

[26] Similar results are found when, in an alternate specification, I include only western-based international monitors. This control is in a few models significant and in the opposite direction, but this result is not robust (see Appendix E, section E.6.2). The sending of election observers is also, of course, one of the major non-partisan methods by which democracy is promoted—so this factor (together with the robustness checks for period, etc.) should also capture any separate effect, if any, such efforts have on election results if done in conjunction with a partisan intervention. This result also may indicate why, contra Bubeck and Marinov (2017, 2019), neutral interventions are not usually seen as a major policy alternative to a partisan intervention by major powers—many of the neutral methods, whatever other effects they have on the target, are not very good in tilting the playing field toward the opposition.

[27] Given the logic of H1 through H6, I expect the various great powers to be equally adept overall in avoiding giving electoral support to "lost causes." Likewise, as will be seen in the second hypothesis, I argue that the exact method of intervention is determined by the great power based upon the information it receives from the supported candidate or party. Accordingly, I do not expect the identity of the intervener to matter as to the effects its intervention has on the election results.

[28] Similar results are found in the KP approach as well as when a similar disaggregation is done in Hypotheses 5 and 6 (see Appendix E, section E.4).

As for the argument presented here, my trichotomous electoral intervention variable continues to have significant effects both statistically and substantively. A Wald test indicates here as well (at the 0.01 level) that the electoral intervention variable significantly increases model fit.[29] In subsequent models in Appendix E, I examine the effects of other factors such as, for example, the target's level of democracy, of clarity of responsibility, and of other foreign policy/national security factors (such as interstate wars, civil wars, and crises). None of these factors has major effects on the results.

Table 6.4 presents my results regarding the second hypothesis on the differing effects of covert and overt electoral interventions (H5). As can be seen from Model 1, the results support Hypothesis 2, with overt interventions on average increasing vote share by 3% more than covert interventions do—a major substantive difference in the effects of each subtype.

Models 2 through 4 in Table 6.4 (and Appendix E) include some robustness checks for this result, similar to those done for Hypothesis 1. These models show essentially the same results as to the effectiveness of covert and overt intervention variables as Model 1. Model 5 examines the possibility that the differences found in effectiveness between covert and overt interventions in favor of the latter are simply due to the cases in which the covert interventions were exposed prior to the election and the resulting political "fallout." Accordingly, in this model I exclude the small number of cases of covert interventions for which clear evidence about this activity by the intervener was exposed and became well known to the public prior to election day. As can be seen from Model 5, this has little effect on the results.[30] Some may wonder whether interventions which combine both overt and covert components should actually be coded and included as overt interventions. Given the nature of the hypothesis investigated here (i.e., that overt and covert interventions differ in their effects), separating the mixed category from overt interventions is required in order to fully identify any differences in the effects of these two subtypes. Nevertheless, as an additional robustness check, I included in Model 6 such interventions together with the fully overt intervention. As can be seen from Model 6, while the effect of overt intervention is a bit smaller in substantive terms, the results are otherwise the same.[31]

---

[29] The inclusion of various additional control variables shown here in KP's approach leads to similar results as in the HS (see Appendix E, section E.4). Other robustness checks using these two approaches utilizing, for example, other controls (such as for economic sanctions or the target's relative power (Cinc) showed no significant effects (see Appendix E, section E.6).

[30] Likewise, when put as a separate control variable the exposed covert interventions have a similar effect to that of their unexposed brethren, although given the small number of these cases (five) this measure is insignificant.

[31] Interestingly, electoral interventions which combine both covert and overt components are insignificant when included as a separate control. This result may be due to the nature of the domestic actors receiving assistance of both types. In other words, actors receiving both types of aid simultaneously may be in an unusually weak political situation (which may be why they requested components of both types of aid), making it quite hard for the great power to provide them with useful assistance.

Table 6.5 (and Appendix E) presents the models which evaluate the third hypothesis, that electoral interventions will be less beneficial to the aided party/candidate in founding elections than in later elections (H6). As previously noted, in order to enable such a comparison I include, besides the electoral intervention variable, a dummy variable for founding elections and an interaction term between them and exclude the control variable for previous vote share.

In results which support this hypothesis, the interaction variable between my intervention variable and a measure of founding elections is both negative and statistically significant. A joint Wald test also indicates (at the 0.01 level) that this interaction significantly increases overall model fit. Because such interactions are not easy to interpret, to estimate the substantive differences between the effects of electoral interventions in both situations, I generate the predicted absolute mean effect of electoral interventions in founding versus non-founding elections in Model 1, Table 6.4 (the benchmark for this hypothesis).

As can be seen in Figure 6.1, while interventions in non-founding elections usually benefit the aided side, increasing its predicted mean vote share by 3.2% on average, this is not the case in founding elections. In founding elections, the interventions appear to usually *harm* the aided side, reducing its predicted mean vote share by 6.7% on average. These are quite significant substantive differences in the effects of interventions in founding versus non-founding elections which I further discuss in the chapter's conclusions. In Models 2 through 5 (and Appendix E) I conduct some robustness checks for this result similar to those done for the previous two hypotheses. The results show that the interaction between founding elections and electoral interventions essentially retains the same direction, statistical significance, and effect as in Model 1 of Table 6.6.[32]

Models 6 and 7 in Table 6.6 show the results pertaining to the fourth hypothesis (H7). As can be seen in these models, electoral interventions for the incumbent and interventions for the challenger have nearly identical effects on election results, leading to the rejection of this hypothesis.[33]

There are two possible types of selection problems that could exist in my results. The first would be selection bias due to missing cases of covert electoral interventions. The second would be selection on the "easy"

---

[32] An alternative interaction between the electoral intervention variable and a logged electoral experience variable shows similar results with aided candidates/parties benefiting more from such interventions as their (and their country's) experience with competitive elections increases. Unfortunately, this interaction is significant only at the 0.1 level and the results were not robust under certain robustness checks—probably due to the fact that the number of interventions at many levels of electoral experience was relatively small (see Appendix E, section E.6.4).

[33] Inclusion in the model of a control for double intervention leads interventions for the challenger to have a stronger effect—but that result is not robust to later specifications.

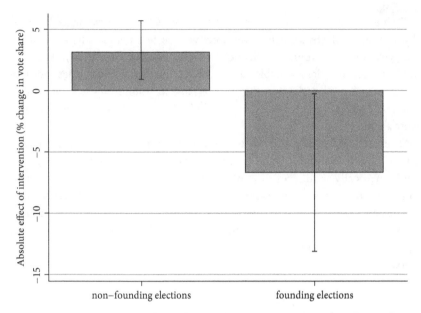

Figure 6.1 Predicted mean effects of electoral interventions (non-founding and founding elections—absolute effect).

cases with the great powers helping "likely winners"—that is, candidates or parties which are highly likely to win the elections anyway, perhaps as a way by which it can curry favor with the likely would-be winner. Likewise, the differences found in the effectiveness of covert and overt interventions may be simply due to overt interventions being more likely to be used in "easier" situations.

As for the first bias, the data collection strategy of PEIG was carefully designed to prevent missing cases of covert interventions. As for the second selection bias, as could be seen in the case of Venezuela in Chapter 4, "likely winners" are quite unlikely to become the recipients of electoral aid, frequently rejecting such aid when offered. Nevertheless, to examine for these two possibilities, in the case of the first possible selection bias I did a simulation of my results in which I randomly dropped some known cases of covert electoral interventions, examining the possible effects of such missing data. For the second bias, in order to check for the possibility of a selection bias toward "likely winners," I used matching. After using these two methods I found similar results to those shown here—which can be seen in Appendix E, sections E.7.1–E.7.2.

6.3 The Effectiveness of Different Tools and Magnitudes of Electoral Interventions

Given the finding here about the overall effectiveness of electoral interventions, it would also be of interest to examine whether there are any significant differences in the effectiveness of specific aid provided and/or its magnitude. Accordingly, I also tried to disaggregate the electoral intervention variable into the seven main categories noted in Chapter 5 (Campaign Funding, Dirty Tricks, Campaigning Assistance, Threats or Promises, Giving/Taking Aid, Other Concessions, Other) entering them as multiple trichotomous variables (Table 6.6, Models 1 and 2). Most subtypes have, on their own, no significant effects. This result is not surprising given the high correlations between the various methods due to the fact that 45.2% of the electoral interventions utilize methods from more than one category as well as the relatively small number of cases (in statistical terms) where some techniques were used (N of below or around 25).

One interesting exception is the case of other concessions—which have a very strong and statistically robust effect on election results, increasing the assisted side's votes share by 8.7%.[34] This result provides a tentative indication that carefully tailored public concessions by the intervener to the target on significant non-economic issues of concern to the target public can have especially strong effects on the results. However, given the relatively small number of such interventions in PEIG (eight cases), the very diverse nature of the concessions in question, and the use of other methods as well in some of these cases, this conclusion must be seen as preliminary.

Some may also wonder whether the overall size of the electoral intervention may have an effect upon the magnitude of its effect on election results. Unfortunately, the most plausible and frequently used metric for size for election-related activities, some scaled or unscaled economic metric capturing the monetary cost to the intervener or potential economic benefit/harm to the target, is unfeasible at present. Some important subtypes of interventions cannot be easily quantified in monetary terms, such as openly threatening severe consequences if the "right" candidate is not elected or agreeing to release war criminals—two of the ways by which the U.S. aided Adenauer in the 1953 West German elections case described in Chapter 3. Likewise, even when the method in question is quantifiable in such terms, such as campaign funding, the data on the exact amounts of covert campaign funding provided

---

[34] This result is robust to a variety of robustness checks as well as matching (see section 6.4) not shown here out of space considerations.

in many cases of U.S. and Soviet interventions is missing or still classified.[35] Indeed, even the amount of proposed funding in *rejected* electoral intervention proposals (such as the case of the 1965 Philippine elections noted in Chapter 4) is frequently excised from declassified documents on those proposed interventions.[36]

Instead I tried, as a proxy to magnitude, to check whether the use of electoral intervention methods from more than one of the seven categories noted here leads to larger effects for the preferred side. For that purpose I interacted the electoral intervention measure with a 0-to-7 scale with 0 signifying cases of non-intervention, 1 signifying an electoral intervention in which methods out of only one category were used, and 7 signifying the use of methods out of all seven categories.[37] As can be seen in Models 3 and 4, such an interaction is indeed significant with the use of each additional method from a different category (after the first one) increasing the target's vote share by an additional 1.4%. However, the significance of this result is highly dependent on the handful of cases (seven) in which a very large range of methods were used (more than four categories). When those cases are excluded this interaction becomes insignificant (Model 5).[38] These results provide some rough, preliminary evidence that very large-scale electoral interventions may have larger effects than "run of the mill" ones—but in most cases otherwise, the exact magnitude of the electoral intervention is of little consequence to its overall effects on the election results.

[35] Likewise, from the testimonies of CIA agents who were part of some of these interventions, it seems that the official sums approved for the operation, even when available, may not be an accurate measure of the actual amounts provided to the target in some cases, given the use of various methods (such as converting the covert funding to the local currency in the black market using an unusually favorable exchange rate) in order to increase the funds available for this purpose (see, e.g., Smith 1976:211, 316). Furthermore, as various recent studies indicated with regard to a partly related domestic phenomenon (the relationship between pork "brought home" and congressional vote share), exact dollar amounts of such pork, even when fully available, fail to usually capture the true effect on subsequent vote share unless one accounts for the manner in which it influences in practice the voters (Grimmer, Messing, and Westwood 2012:717).

[36] Memorandum for the 303 Committee "CIA Action in the 1965 Philippine election" September 13, 1965, FOIA request.

[37] I thank Wilfred Chow and Kai Quek for suggesting this method.

[38] Similarly insignificant results are found when I graph the whole range of this interaction with the exclusion of those cases. One should note that this result is not due to the possible influence of the "other concession" category—the result remains significant if intervention cases where such concessions were used are excluded, but cases using multiple methods otherwise are kept (not shown).

6.4 Estimated Effects in Particular Election Cases

Of course, a question may be raised as to how much the estimated electoral intervention effects found here apply in practice as to specific elections in which such an intervention had actually been done. Accordingly, in order to illustrate some of the "real life" effects of electoral interventions, Table 6.1 gives the estimated effects on election results in six cases of intervened elections, all of these elections (and their results) widely considered to be important turning points in retrospect in these nations' histories.

As can be seen in Table 6.1, in most cases (in non-founding elections), the electoral intervention had an important and decisive effect on the outcome in the "desired" direction. In the 1972 West German parliamentary elections, for example, my model estimates that the Soviet intervention in favor of chancellor Willie Brandt and the SPD was an important factor in its winning a narrow 5-seat margin (in a 496-seat lower house or Bundestag) over its main rival, Rainer

Table 6.1 Estimated Effects of the Electoral Intervention on Election Results—Selected Real Intervention Cases (Interventions in Favor of Challengers in Bold)

Election	Aided Side	Intervener	Actual Incumbent Vote Share	Estimated Incumbent Vote Share without the Intervention	Did the Intervention Have the Desired (and Decisive) Effect?
W. Germany, Nov. 1972	Incumbent	USSR	45.8	43.6	Yes
India, Aug. 1977	Incumbent	USSR	34.5	32.3	No
Israel, June 1992	**Challenger**	**U.S.**	**24.9**	**30.3**	**Yes**
Yugoslavia/ Serbia, September 2000	**Challenger**	**U.S.**	**38.2**	**43.4**	**Yes**
Founding Elections					
Argentina, Feb. 1946	**Challenger**	**U.S.**	**53.7**	**47.2**	**No (reverse)**
Bulgaria, 1990	**Challenger**	**U.S.**	**47.2**	**40.8**	**No (reverse)**

Note: This table was created by deducting from the true election results the predicted electoral intervention effects in that election. The predicted intervention effect was estimated by generating the predicted vote share from our model for that election and then recoding that case as a non-intervention on the intervention variable, generating a second prediction and deducting this result from the first prediction. The predicted results of Hypotheses 5 and 6 were used for estimating the effects in cases of non-founding and founding elections, respectively.

Barzel and the CDU (230 to 225).[39] Without the increase in vote share due to this intervention, and given West Germany's electoral system, I estimate that the SPD would have narrowly lost the election to the CDU, 216 to 236, probably leading to Willie Brandt's loss of the chancellorship.[40] Had Brandt lost this election, his Ostpolitik policy (normalization of relations) toward Eastern Europe and the Soviet Union would have probably collapsed as well prior to its consummation.

Likewise, the American intervention against the incumbent, PM Yitzhak Shamir, in the 1992 Israeli parliamentary elections is estimated, according to my model, to have cost Shamir's right-wing Likud party the amount of votes equivalent to about 5 or 6 seats in the 120-seat Israeli parliament (the Knesset).[41] Given that in this election, the left-wing opposition parties won a narrow, 1-seat absolute majority in the Knesset for the first time since the 1973 elections, this intervention was likely an important factor in enabling the coming to power of Yitzhak Rabin following this election as the head of a center-left coalition and the start, a year later, of the Oslo peace process with the PLO (Quandt 1993; see also Chapter 7).

Of course, like any other domestic or international factor known to affect elections, an electoral intervention in one's favor does not always guarantee success to its intended beneficiary. In the 1977 Indian parliamentary elections, the covert Soviet intervention in favor of Indira Gandhi and the Congress Party is estimated by my model to have done little to prevent, or to even much soften, the crushing blow that it had suffered from the Janata Party. In this defeat, which led the Congress Party to lose power for the first time since India's independence, the Soviet intervention is estimated to have assisted the Congress Party in keeping only 11 or so seats[42] from being lost to the Janata Party and/or other parties. This

---

[39] Shift estimated given Germany's electoral system (and assuming a uniform shift in the PR component) and that most votes shifted from the SPD to the CDU—the two major parties. The seats of West Berlin representatives whose status (and ability to be full voting members in the Bundestag) was one of the hotly contested issues in this election are excluded, but their inclusion would not significantly affect this estimate.

[40] Given the nature of coalition forming in parliamentary systems, and West German election laws, it is of course theoretically possible that the SPD's main coalition partner, the FDP, would have nevertheless agreed to recreate their pre-election coalition. However, such defeats usually lead to the largest party gaining power. Indeed, it is instructive that the most recent exception to the largest party gaining power norm in German politics, the 1969 West German elections, came only after the CDU lost some votes and the SPD made significant electoral gains.

[41] Seat share change given this shift in vote share estimated based on the Israeli election law in force during 1992. Israel had (and has) a single-district PR system.

[42] Estimated using the SMD district-level results in the 1977 statistical report of the Indian electoral commission on this election and assuming a uniform swing in all districts. Many districts had more than two significant candidates (and eighteen parties won seats in the Lok Sabha in this election), so no estimate of where the votes could have otherwise gone (besides being lost to the Congress Party candidates) could be plausibly made in this particular case.

is a number too small to have any serious effect on the election results given that the Congress Party lost more than a 150 seats in this election and the Janata Party won 295 seats and a solid, 24-seat absolute majority in the 542-seat lower house (the Lok Sabha).

In contrast, the American intervention against Slobodan Milosevic in the 2000 Yugoslav election is estimated by my model to have been decisive in bringing about his final downfall. Without this U.S. intervention my model predicts that Slobodan Milosevic would have run neck to neck with his main rival, Vojislav Kostunica (43.4% to 46.5%).[43] If the first round of the Yugoslav elections had concluded in this inconclusive manner, rather than in an outright Kostunica victory (51.7%), Milosevic would probably have been able, as he had done in the past, to "steal" the elections without bringing about the massive wave of demonstrations which eventually forced him to acknowledge his defeat and resign from the presidency.

In the two founding elections, the effects were also quite significant and decisive, but in the direction opposite of that desired by the intervener. In the 1946 Argentinean election, my model estimates that the overt American intervention against Peron (see Chapter 3) backfired badly, enabling him to win this election with a comfortable, absolute majority of the popular vote (53.7%) rather than a narrow loss to the other presidential candidate, Tamborini (47.2% to 50.1%). In the Argentine electoral college system this shift, in turn, would change an overwhelming Peron victory (304–72) into a comfortable victory by Tamborini (146–230).[44] Due to the close margins in some Argentine provinces in this election, even a far smaller backlash effect away from Tamborini in the right provinces could have sufficed to make the critical difference for Peron. For example, a shift back of merely 39,584 votes in this election in five Argentine provinces (or 1.5% of the total valid votes) from Peron to Tamborini would have sufficed to give Tamborini a narrow electoral college victory, 194 to 182, over Peron.[45] The quip by historian Enrique Menocal in 1986 about Peron being "the son of an American Ambassador" (in Vannucci 1987:49) seems, given these findings, to be painfully close to the truth on one key part of his rise to power.

---

[43] Assuming that most of the votes which Milosevic lost went to Kostunica, a reasonable assumption given that Kostunica was the only other major candidate as well as the main beneficiary of the U.S. electoral intervention.

[44] Assuming a uniform swing in the Argentinean electoral college. The Argentine electoral college in this era gave each province one EC vote for each of their two senators and two EC votes for every deputy they had in the lower house.

[45] The provinces of Buenos Aires, Jujuy, La Rioja, Mendoza, and Entre Rios. Estimate made using Canton 1969. For a similar past estimate using less accurate voting data see Potash (1980:45).

Likewise, the American intervention for the UDF in the 1990 Bulgarian elections seems to have caused it significant harm, the resulting backlash enabling the ruling communist party now under a new name (the BSP) to remain in power with an absolute majority in the 400-seat Bulgarian Constitutional Assembly (211 to 144) rather than narrowly lose to the UDF (168 to 176), leading Bulgaria into a far more protracted and torturous transition to democracy than it would have had otherwise.[46]

6.5 Discussion and Conclusion

The results found here indicate that John Adams was quite justified in his worries about the likely effects of foreign electoral interventions on the targeted elections results. Three of the four hypotheses tested here were supported. Overall, electoral interventions seem to substantively benefit the aided candidate or party (H4). Of the two main subtypes of electoral interventions, overt interventions are significantly more effective than covert interventions in both the substantive and the statistical sense(H5). However, no significant robust differences have been found between interventions in favor of challengers versus incumbents (rejecting H7). Likewise, interventions done in founding elections (such as the U.S. 1796 elections),[47] unlike in later elections, do little to benefit and in fact usually harm the aided candidate/party (H6). Some preliminary evidence was found that the overall magnitude of such interventions may matter with very large interventions having perhaps greater effects. Furthermore, as to the specific subtypes of intervention, some very preliminary and tentative evidence was found for the special effectiveness of tailored public concessions to the target.

These results indicate that electoral interventions, with some exceptions, seem to be an effective foreign policy tool benefiting those they are designed to help. Given the average effect found here (of about 3% change in vote share), an electoral intervention will not always assure victory for the great powers' preferred candidates. Likewise, as in all statistical averages (or average treatment effects), actual effects in particular cases may vary. However, as shown in some

---

[46] For the inadvertent electoral problems caused to the UDF during this campaign due to the assistance it received from the U.S. see, for example, Melone 1998:chap. 5; Blaine Harden, "Bulgaria Lifts Curtain on Its Stalinist Gulag," *Washington Post*, May 26, 1990. Shift estimated given Bulgaria's mixed electoral system in 1990 assuming a uniform swing across both components and that most votes shifted between the BSP and the UDF. District-level data used for this estimate was taken from the IRI's post-election report.

[47] George Washington famously ran unopposed in the 1789 and 1792 elections.

examples in Table 6.1, under many commonly occurring situations at national-level elections, partisan electoral interventions can and do swing elections. The evidence presented in this chapter, showing little change in the effectiveness of electoral interventions over time, suggests that in the foreseeable future, partisan electoral interventions will continue to be an effective way for great powers to determine the leadership of other states, regardless of whether their targets are governed by "competitive authoritarian," partially democratic, or fully democratic regimes. These results also provide further—and cross-national—support for the finding of Corstange and Marinov (2012:664–669) that no popular backlash effect existed in their survey experiment of an overt intervention.

Those things said, these results also indicate, quite ironically, that the "model scenario" for electoral interventions, the one deemed by many as the most morally acceptable for such interventions by the U.S. (e.g., see Carothers 1996:102–103), is the one when it will be unable to do much to "tip the scales." In other words, when the U.S. helps inexperienced yet well-intentioned pro-democracy parties facing long odds in a competitive election either against an entrenched competitive authoritarian regime or strong and more authoritarian forces within their society, they are unlikely to actually benefit in practice from such help.

To give a recent illustration: after the fall of the Mubarak regime in February 2011 some members of the U.S. foreign policy community called on President Obama to intervene in favor of the liberal groups in the May 2012 Egyptian presidential election, the first competitive executive elections in Egypt since 1950 (Takeyh 2011; Krauthammer 2011; Satloff 2012; see also quotes in Carothers 2011). The available evidence seems to indicate that in this case, the Obama administration eventually concluded that the main faction of the Moslem Brotherhood (the expected winners) could be an acceptable option to U.S. interests. As a result, it seems that the Obama administration rejected these calls and did not significantly intervene in favor of any side in these Egyptian elections.[48]

However, the statistical evidence found here indicates that had the Obama administration, in a hypothetical alternate universe, listened to these calls[49] and decided to intervene in favor of the Egyptian liberals in these elections, it

[48] David Kirpatrick and Steven Lee Myers, "Overtures to Egypt's Islamists Reverse Longtime U.S. Policy," New York Times, January 3, 2012; Josh Rogin, "State Department Training Islamic Political Parties in Egypt," Foreign Policy, November 3, 2011; Satloff 2012.
[49] Given how recent these events are, it is of course quite possible that a U.S. covert intervention for the more liberal forces did occur in this presidential election but is still unexposed. For example, according to one reputable source, the impartial technical aid provided by the U.S. to Egypt for the conduct of the Egyptian parliamentary elections in late 2011 was in practice only being funneled to the liberal parties (Stephan McInerney, "Building on Sand," Campaigns and Elections, October 22, 2011). If true, such partisan aid may have occurred also in the presidential campaign the following year. However, given the results of the presidential elections, in which the liberal candidates were unable to reach even the second election round, such a failed electoral intervention would be in congruence with the point made here.

would have been unable to help them in an effective manner. Indeed, it would have probably harmed their chances rather than benefiting them. Partisan electoral interventions are not a tool that can be usually used for "idealistic" goals.[50]

Finally, these results provide strong indirect support for my model of the causes of electoral interventions. The three hypotheses about the effects of electoral interventions which received statistical support here (H4–H6) were also "observable implications" developed from the author's model of the causes of electoral interventions. Accordingly, besides supporting the main arguments provided here for the effects of electoral interventions, these results also provide some strong indirect statistical evidence for the argument tested in the first part of this study.

In the next chapter I will examine three cases of electoral intervention and attempt to determine whether the patterns we see at the aggregate, large-N level fit the evidence available in election surveys from particular intervened elections.

Table 6.2 First Effects Hypothesis (H4): Electoral Intervention Effects

	(1)	(2)	(3)	(4)	(5)
	HS & Electoral Int.	Fixed Effects (HS)	No Interactions (HS)	KP Model 4 & Elect. Int.	Fraud Limit (HS)
Electoral Intervention	3.190** (1.226)	2.976* (1.307)	3.280** (1.218)	3.413** (1.181)	3.115* (1.228)
Previous Vote	0.368** (0.0509)	0.373** (0.0558)	0.368** (0.0503)	0.394** (0.0527)	0.389** (0.0552)
Growth	0.564** (0.106)	0.523** (0.102)	0.391** (0.0685)		0.525** (0.142)
Trade Openness	0.315 (1.384)	−2.073 (2.176)	−0.829 (1.273)		0.945 (1.592)
Growth * Trade Openness	−0.291* (0.134)	−0.183 (0.122)			−0.257 (0.171)
Presidential Election	−1.737 (1.964)	−5.509 (3.370)	−1.661 (1.954)		−2.925 (2.135)

---

[50] See also my findings elsewhere on the negative effects of electoral interventions on established democracies (Levin 2019b).

Table 6.2 *Continued*

	(1)	(2)	(3)	(4)	(5)
	HS & Electoral Int.	Fixed Effects (HS)	No Interactions (HS)	KP Model 4 & Elect. Int.	Fraud Limit (HS)
Growth*Pres. Election	0.0367 (0.164)	0.156 (0.184)			0.0495 (0.200)
Re-election	8.315** (1.662)	8.732** (1.813)	8.316** (1.700)		8.723** (1.890)
Effective No. of Parties (logged)	−14.30** (1.929)	−13.40** (2.238)	−14.22** (1.916)	−14.67** (2.037)	−13.24** (2.128)
GDP per Capita (logged)	0.935 (0.722)	1.239 (1.135)	0.916 (0.730)		0.653 (0.810)
Africa	2.881 (3.170)	‡	2.920 (3.200)		0.139 (3.626)
Asia	−3.178 (2.030)	‡	−3.032 (2.025)		−4.437+ (2.397)
Central & E. Europe	−4.710* (1.903)	‡	−4.715* (1.900)		−6.211** (2.133)
L. America & Caribbean	−1.608 (1.478)	‡	−1.534 (1.488)		−1.659 (1.663)
Global Growth				0.620 (0.398)	
Local Growth				0.147* (0.0724)	
Population (logged)				0.320 (0.307)	
Year				0.00400 (0.0337)	
Constant	28.85** (7.493)	26.42** (10.08)	29.52** (7.569)	31.21** (4.636)	29.51** (8.110)
Elections (N)	698	698	698	700	634
Countries	121	121	121	122	113
R-squared	0.548	0.521	0.544	0.488	0.525

Notes: These and later models were calculated using Stata 11. Standard errors in parentheses.

$+p < 0.10$; $*p < 0.05$; $**p < 0.01$.‡ Omitted when calculating country fixed effects due to being country invariant.

Table 6.3 First Effects Hypothesis (H4): Electoral Intervention Effects—Various Controls (HS)

	(6)	(7)	(8)	(9)
	& Repeat Elect. Int.	**& Cold War Control**	**& Elect. Observers**	**Separate U.S. & Russ. Int.**
Electoral Intervention	3.194** (1.231)	3.198** (1.227)	3.192** (1.226)	
US Elect. Int.				3.111** (1.106)
Rus. Elect. Int.				3.324 (2.822)
Repeat Int.	0.971 (2.273)			
Cold War		0.227 (0.893)		
Elec. Observers			0.0377 (1.243)	
Main Control Variables	√	√	√	√
Constant	28.48** (7.657)	27.91** (7.590)	29.01** (7.543)	28.89** (7.534)
Elections (N)	698	698	697	698
Countries	121	121	121	121
R-squared	0.549	0.549	0.548	0.548

Note: Standard errors in parentheses. To make the table more user-friendly the main control variables are excluded from the presentation—although they were, of course, part of these models.

$^{+}p < 0.10$; $^{*}p < 0.05$; $^{**}p < 0.01$.

Table 6.4 Second Effects Hypothesis (H5): Effects of Covert and Overt Electoral Intervention

	(1)	(2)	(3)	(4)	(5)	(6)
	HS & Covert/ Overt Int.	& Fixed Effects (HS)	& Fraud Limit (HS)	KP Model 4 & El. Int.	& No Exposed Int. (HS)	& Overt Combined w/Mixed (HS)
Overt Int.	5.424* (2.277)	5.423* (2.410)	5.181* (2.350)	5.507* (2.292)	5.478* (2.283)	4.381* (2.375)
Covert Int.	2.255 (1.425)	1.921 (1.420)	2.298+ (1.365)	2.559* (1.293)	2.023 (1.322)	2.368 (1.453)
Covert & Overt	−10.13+ (6.102)	−13.35 (8.719)	−9.976 (6.161)	−9.953 (6.217)	−10.23+ (6.086)	
Main Control Variables (HS/KP)	√	√	√	√	√	√
Constant	30.17** (7.593)	29.04** (10.46)	30.87** (8.206)	31.33** (4.67)	31.24** (7.646)	29.08** (7.500)
Elections (*N*)	698	698	634	700	695	698
Countries	121	121	113	122	121	121
R-squared	0.549	0.526	0.525	0.490	0.551	0.549

Note: Standard errors in parentheses. To make the table more user-friendly the main control variables are excluded from the presentation—although they were, of course, part of these models.

$^{+}p < 0.10$, $^{*}p < 0.05$, $^{**}p < 0.01$.

Table 6.5 Effects Hypotheses 3 and 4 (H6 and H7): Effects of Electoral Intervention in Founding vs. Non-Founding Elections and Electoral Intervention for Challengers vs. Incumbents

	(1)	(2)	(3)	(4)	(5)	(7)	(8)
	& Founding Election Interaction	& No HS Interactions	& Fixed Effects	& Fraud Limit	KP Model 4 & Interaction	HS & Incum./Challenger	KP Model 4 & Incum./Challenger
Electoral Intervention	13.16** (4.244)	13.18** (4.163)	13.59** (4.664)	13.85** (4.323)	12.30** (3.782)		
Int.*Founding Election	-9.908* (3.652)	-9.797** (3.547)	-10.63* (4.147)	-10.59** (3.746)	-8.948** (3.117)		
Founding Election	3.059* (1.474)	2.952* (1.468)	3.460* (1.637)	2.387 (1.646)	3.845** (1.420)		
Int. for Challenger						-3.137+ (1.657)	-3.480* (1.541)
Int. for Incumbent						3.074+ (1.592)	3.183+ (1.640)
Main Control Variables (HS/KP)	√	√	√	√	√	√	√
Constant	49.77** (7.473)	51.38** (7.346)	50.57** (11.12)	49.88** (8.288)	84.66 (68.85)	30.37** (7.717)	31.86 (71.23)
Elections (N)	839	839	839	739	841	705	707
Countries	144	144	144	131	145	121	122
R-squared	0.457	0.452	0.438	0.417	0.390	0.543	0.483

Note: Standard errors in parentheses. To make the table more user-friendly the main control variables are excluded from the presentation—although they were, of course, part of these models.

$+ p < 0.10$; $* p < 0.05$; $** p < 0.01$.

Table 6.6 Additional Analyses: By Subtypes of Electoral Intervention Methods and Effects of Scale of Intervention (Interaction)

	(1)	(2)	(3)	(4)	(5)
	Subtypes (HS)	Subtypes (KP 4)	Interaction w/Scale (HS)	Interaction w/Scale (KP)	Interaction w/Scale (HS) & No High Methods Int.
Campaign Funding	1.108 (1.728)	0.994 (1.732)			
Campaigning Assistance	3.987 (2.853)	4.880[+] (2.688)			
Dirty Tricks	3.328 (3.198)	3.863 (3.382)			
Threats or Promises	1.221 (2.460)	1.866 (2.626)			
Giving/Taking Aid	−3.040 (2.856)	−4.310[+] (2.405)			
Other Concessions	9.046** (3.320)	8.697** (3.342)			
Other	0.741 (3.812)	0.571 (3.782)			
Electoral Intervention			−0.687 (2.250)	−0.687 (2.410)	0.699 (2.923)
Electoral Int.* Scale			2.325** (0.858)	2.440** (0.917)	1.262 (1.573)
Scale			−0.904[+] (0.537)	−0.958[+] (0.512)	−1.143 (0.801)
Main Control Variables (HS/ KP)	√	√	√	√	√
Constant	30.05** (7.793)	39.31 (69.78)	30.22** (7.910)	32.16 (71.21)	30.06** (8.016)
Elections (N)	698	700	698	700	693
Countries	121	122	121	122	121
R-squared	0.557	0.500	0.550	0.493	0.550

Note: Standard errors in parentheses. To make the table more user-friendly the main control variables are excluded from the presentation—although they were, of course, part of these models.

[+]$p < 0.10$; *$p < 0.05$; **$p < 0.01$.

7

Delving In

Single Election Level Analysis of the Effects of Electoral Interventions

> If Adenauer wins a resounding election victory . . . it will have been
> due in a large part to the [U.S.] food program.
>> —C. D. Jackson, Senior Assistant to President Eisenhower,
>> 1953–1954[1]

> [The] undisguised [American] attempt to bring down the democrat-
> ically elected government of Israel . . . contribut[ed] to the downfall
> of the [Likud] government led by Yitzhak Shamir.
>> —Moshe Arens, number two on the Likud party slate in 1992 (and
>> Secretary of Defense)[2]

As can be seen in the preceding quotes, in the 1992 Israeli elections and the 1953 West German elections, decision-makers within the intervener and/or knowledgeable locals credited the electoral intervention with significant effects on the election's results. In the previous chapter, I began to empirically examine how seriously one should take such claims. Utilizing PEIG, I found, in the aggregate, that electoral interventions are indeed quite effective in helping the preferred candidate/party in non-founding elections.

However, a large-N aggregated statistical analysis of multiple elections is only one major way by which the effects of certain factors on voters' choice is estimated by scholars in comparative politics. The other frequently used method is analyzing election surveys with relevant questions. Indeed, some scholars in this literature, uncertain of the accuracy of results derived from large-N aggregated analyses, see election surveys as a superior way to estimate the effects of the economic vote and other factors (Paldam 1991; Lewis-Beck and Stegmaier 2000:191). While this method cannot be used in order to examine some of my hypotheses (which require the simultaneous comparison of two different

---

[1] Letter, C.D. Jackson to Smith August 18,1953/C.D. Jackson records/Box 6/DDEL.
[2] In Arens (1995:9).

Meddling in the Ballot Box. Dov H. Levin, Oxford University Press (2020). © Oxford University Press.
DOI: 10.1093/oso/9780197519882.001.0001.

subtypes of electoral intervention), it can be used to conduct a second test of the first key hypothesis on the effects on elections (H4)—that is, that electoral interventions usually significantly increase the vote share of the preferred side.

A second advantage of analyzing survey data is that it enables the examination of some of the mechanisms predicted by my argument about the effectiveness of electoral interventions. One reason why I would expect overt electoral intervention elections to benefit the assisted side is that the public in the target knows about the statements and actions of the great power, understands them correctly, and then at least some of the voters decide, as a result of this message, to vote in the way preferred by the intervener. In other words, if my argument here is correct, I would expect factors measuring voter knowledge of the intervener's position and/or activities to be good predictors of their vote choice in the "preferred direction."

I would also expect, for both overt and covert interventions, to find evidence indicating that the particular issues which the intervener's statements and/or actions affected (or threatened to affect) tended to be bigger "vote getters" for the preferred side than for the unwanted side or, at least, better vote getters than they were expected to be in the past. As a bonus, by questioning a representative sample of voters directly rather than estimating the effects of the intervention from the aggregate election results I can reduce the concerns some readers may have about whether the large-N analysis accurately identified the causal effect that electoral interventions usually have.

Testing, however, the effects of partisan electoral interventions using election surveys is easier said than done. For obvious reasons, such surveys don't usually ask about factors related to covert electoral interventions—which are 64.1% of all electoral interventions. In many elections in which overt interventions had occurred, either no election surveys were conducted or no surveys asking respondents questions related to the intervention in particular were done.

Nevertheless, after some effort, I have been able to find such surveys in three cases of intervention. The first two, which will be examined in this chapter, come from overt electoral interventions—Israel 1992 and West Germany 1953. In Chapter 8 I examine a rare case where we have survey data on a key aspect of a covert intervention due to one of the methods used in it (i.e., the leaks of stolen documents) and its inadvertent exposure—the 2016 U.S. elections.

7.1 Waiting for Rabin: The 1992 Israeli Elections

7.1.1 Overview of Intervention

From what is known at present, the intervention of the George H. W. Bush (hence Bush Senior) administration in the June 1992 Israeli elections in favor of the Israeli Labor party (hence Labor) and Yitzhak Rabin included two major components. The first, in March 1992, was the U.S. president's final public rejection of the Israeli government's request for $10 billion in loan guarantees ($15.5 billion in 2016 dollars). This rejection followed an increasingly angry public spat on this issue in the preceding six months. These loan guarantees were requested by the Israeli government in order to help it absorb the large wave of new immigrants from the former Soviet Union (375,000 by 1992—or about 7% of Israel's population in the early 1990s) that had begun to arrive en masse after Mikhail Gorbachev legalized Jewish immigration from the USSR in 1989. The Bush Senior administration publicly made the future reception of these guarantees conditional on the complete freezing of the Israeli government of any further construction in Jewish settlements in the West Bank and Gaza (with the exception of houses already in construction)—a condition that it knew a Likud government (during this period) could never accept (Ben-Zvi 2013:200, 204; Ross 2004:83–84; Rubin 1995:196–197).[3]

The second main component consisted of various acts designed to further strengthen the impression that the Israeli public had drawn from the argument over the loan guarantees that U.S-Israel relations were in a deep crisis in the months preceding the elections and were likely to worsen further (with various negative effects) if a right-wing government headed by the Likud (and Yitzhak Shamir) were to remain in power. To give three examples, in January 1992 the U.S. voted in the U.N. in favor of a resolution that "strongly condemn[ed]" the deportation of Palestinian terrorists—the harshest resolution of this kind that it had ever supported up to that point. Two months later, the Bush Senior administration leaked two classified reports accusing Israel of supposedly selling American weapon systems to various countries (including parts of American Patriot missiles to China)—an illegal act on Israel's side if it were true. If Israel were found guilty, that was widely known to be also, of course, a potential basis for future U.S. sanctions of various kinds. A subsequent U.S. investigation (the pre-election part) only partially cleared Israel of this accusation (Rubin

---

[3] Indeed, after the victory of Rabin in these elections, the Bush Senior administration, in the final months before its defeat in the 1992 U.S. elections, agreed to give Rabin the full loan guarantees under far less restrictive conditions as to construction in the West Bank than it demanded of Shamir (Ben-Zvi 2013:204).

1995:197).[4] Then, in mid-May 1992, one month before the Israeli elections, the State Department's senior spokesperson announced that U.N. Resolution 194 from December 1948, which guaranteed a right of return to Palestinian refugees from the 1948 war, was seen by the U.S. government as still relevant and valid to any peace talks between Israel and the Palestinians—an act seen as supportive of the PLO's claims in this regard (Steinberg 1995:194).

7.1.2 Analysis of Effects: Methodology

To analyze the effects of the U.S. intervention in this case, I turned to a pre-election Israeli survey which happened to have a suitable question. This survey, the 1992 Israeli National Election Study (INES), was designed by two of Israel's premiere political scientists, Asher Arian and Michal Shamir. This ANES-style survey was carried out in the two weeks preceding the 1992 election (June 8–18) by a reputable Israeli polling firm (Dahaf Research Institute) among a nationally representative sample of the adult Jewish population within the 1949 borders (1,192 respondents).[5]

In order to check the effects of the U.S. intervention in this case, I utilized one of the questions asked in this survey about U.S.-Israel relations (*US-IL relations*). This question, one among a battery of questions about the two main parties' performance evaluations on various topics, asked the respondents to which of them, the Likud or Labor, was the characteristic "can maintain good relations with U.S" more suitable. The respondents could then choose whether this characteristic suited Labor more, suited the Likud more, or if both were equally suited/neither. I then operationalized this question into a trichotomous measure with 1 for those who saw Labor as better in this regard, –1 for those who saw the Likud as better in this regard, and 0 for those who saw both parties as being the same on this characteristic.

In the analysis that follows, I use this question as an indicator of the effect of knowledge about U.S. attitudes on vote choice. While this question isn't a perfect proxy of the U.S. intervention in this case[6] it nevertheless, given the characteristics of the intervention in this particular case, should capture enough of the possible effect of this overt U.S. intervention to enable us to determine whether this intervention "mattered" and at least provide the lower bound of its effect.

---

[4] The full investigation, completed after the election, fully cleared Israel of these charges.
[5] Given the vote preferences of the excluded populations and the nature of this intervention, the effect of these exclusions is expected to be minimal (see Appendix F).
[6] A question asking directly about the U.S. intervention and/or one of its components (such as the loan guarantees) would have been, of course, better.

Following Shachar and Shamir (1995:chap. 2), I operationalized the vote choice facing the voters (or independent variable) as a dichotomous variable with 1 coding a vote for left-bloc parties (including Labor) and 0 a vote for right-bloc parties (including the Likud).[7] To analyze the resulting models I used probit.

Of course, other variables besides the U.S. electoral intervention may have had significant effects on vote choice in this election. Accordingly, I use the general approach employed by Shachar and Shamir (1992:chap. 2) to model the main factors affecting vote choice in this election to which my variable about voter knowledge of U.S. attitudes is added.[8] A detailed explanation for the inclusion of these variables and for their operationalization is included in Appendix F.

7.1.3   Results

Figure 7.1 illustrates the substantive effects of the variables in the main model (Model 1) which were statistically significant in it as well as in other robustness checks. The full regression tables and various robustness checks can be seen in Appendix F. Overall, the other factors in the model are in the expected directions and magnitude and are largely in conformity with the results of Shachar and Shamir.

As my hypotheses would expect, the proxy factor for the U.S. intervention (*US-IL relations*) has significant effects both statistically and substantively.[9] On average, a shift by an Israeli voter from believing that both parties are equally good in maintaining Israel's relations with the U.S. to believing that Labor would perform better in this regard (a one-unit shift) increases his or her probability of voting for a left-bloc party by about 2.8%. This is a medium-sized yet significant effect substantively.

This effect also stacks up quite well compared to other important factors in this model. For example, the factor that has the most effect on increasing the probability of vote choice for the left bloc, the performance evaluation of security and foreign policy (*Sec. & FP Performance*) increases, in a similar one-unit shift, the probability of voting for the left bloc by about 5.6%. A similar one-unit shift toward a more hawkish position on the best way to resolve the West Bank and Gaza Strip territories issue (*Territories issue*) reduces the probability of voting for

---

[7] Following Shachar and Shamir's coding (1995:73), I exclude the small number of votes (around 5%) to parties which couldn't be clearly designated at the time as being in either bloc, such as two of the religious parties (Shas and United Torah Judaism). See Appendix F for the full listing of which parties were put in which bloc.

[8] The author wishes to thank Michal Shamir for the kind aid provided in replicating this model.

[9] The inclusion of this variable increases the model's ROC score versus a version which excludes it. A Wald test also indicates (at $p < 0.0001$) that this variable significantly increases overall model fit.

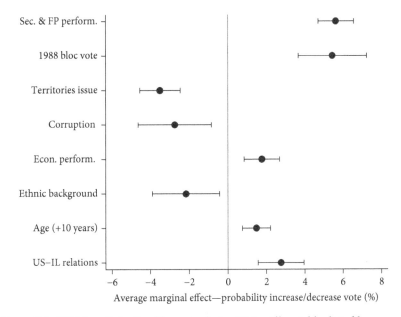

Figure 7.1 1992 Israeli election bloc vote choice. Note: All variables listed here (except for ethnic background and age) are scaled between –1 and 1, with the higher score denoting past vote for the left bloc, performance evaluation in favor of Labor, evaluation of Labor as corrupt and hawkish positions on the territories issue. The size of effect for age is for a 10-year increase in the respondent's age. The effect for ethnicity is the difference in the probability of voting for the left bloc when the respondent comes from a Sephardic background rather than an Ashkenazi (or non-Sephardic) one.

the left bloc by 3.5%. Likewise, the economic vote (*Econ. perform.*)[10] has a some-what *smaller* effect than the intervention, with a similar one-unit shift leading to only a 1.8% increase in the probability of voting for the left bloc. This result is also robust to the further inclusion of various additional control variables noted earlier, such as (to give a few examples) income, specific questions about ability to promote peace or post-materialist values, and party ideology (see Appendix F).[11]

---

[10] This was derived from a question asking, "Who do you think will take better care of the country's economic problems—the Labor team or the Likud team?"; see Appendix F for further details on its construction.

[11] Similar results are also found in separate analyses of subsamples composed only of respondents who voted for a right-wing party in the previous election (1988) or of first-time voters—indicating that this result is not merely the function of supposed partisan biases by the more dedicated left-wing respondents in this survey that were encouraging them to see "their side" as better on this aspect as well (see Appendix F).

It is also clear from the responses to other questions in this survey that this statistical finding reflected a factor that truly "mattered" to Israelis at the time.[12] For example, when respondents were asked about eight "worst case" scenarios that Israel may face in the future and the ability of the country to cope with them, the only scenario which a majority of Israelis thought Israel would be unable to cope with (51% to 49%) was a situation in which the U.S. government ceased to provide support to Israel.[13] Likewise, when asked in later follow-up questions how much different issues affected their vote, 62% of those responding to this question said that the state of Israel's relations with the U.S. would affect their vote. These responses indicate that the respondents' answers as to the performance evaluation question on this issue probably reflected an underlying factor that at least some Israelis indeed took very seriously when casting their votes a few days later.

Likewise, the pre-intervention trends as to Labor's chances in the upcoming elections didn't seem to show any indication that it was about to win. The opposite seemed to be true. Labor had lost already four elections in a row (1977, 1981, 1984, 1988). While a Gallup-style tracking poll unfortunately didn't exist at the time in Israel, intermittent polls conducted by various Israeli pollsters prior to the U.S. intervention showed a party highly likely to lose for the fifth time. For example, one survey conducted in November 1991, before the U.S. intervention began in full force, found that if the Israeli election had occurred then, Labor's vote share would have dropped by 9.5%, to 22%. In contrast, the Likud would have seen its vote share increase by 1% and the right-wing bloc overall would have gotten 54% of the vote. Other polls conducted during this period found similar results (Mandilow 1992: 217).

As one knowledgeable commentator noted in December 1991, "all the indications are that the image of Labor is so besmattered with self seeking corruption and division, that the long-suffering population will turn once again to the Shamir-led Likud."[14] Although the American intervention in favor of Labor was not the only thing that had changed in its favor in the following months,[15] it is quite likely, given the previously noted results, that it was one of the key factors that helped lead to the turnaround in its fortunes.

---

[12] One should also note that the crosstabs of this question show that Labor was seen in this regard (U.S.-Israel relations) as being far better than the Likud (47% to 24%).

[13] In comparison, 65% of Israelis thought that Israel could cope with a total Israeli–Arab war (i.e., with all other Arab states in the Middle East) and 87% with a significant increase in terrorist activity.

[14] See also Joseph Finklestone, "Israel Politics Goes Critical," The Guardian, December 30, 1991.

[15] For example, in March 1992, three months before the elections, the more popular Rabin replaced Shimon Peres as the Labor's leader (and PM candidate)—although one must note that the control variable included in order to capture the differences on candidate evaluation between Rabin and Shamir in my statistical analysis becomes statistically insignificant under certain situations (see Appendix F).

7.2 Part 2—The Effects: The 1953 West German Elections

7.2.1 Overview of the Intervention

This section focuses on the effects that the American intervention in the 1953 West German election had on its final results. As noted in the case study in Chapter 3, the U.S. intervention in favor of Adenauer, following his request for U.S. aid in March 1953, included five major components. The five major components of this intervention, all done between April and September 1953, will be analyzed here. The first was reviving the 1923 U.S.-German Friendship, Commerce and Consular Relations treaty, a treaty which was suspended as a result of WW2. The second was the establishment of mixed parole boards for the purpose of releasing German war criminals. The third was supplying West Germany with $15 million worth of food in order to enable Adenauer to give out food to East Germans civilians, following a revolt against the East German regime which began on June 17, 1953 (the June 17 uprising). The fourth was agreeing to a Four Power conference in which the topic of German reunification would be discussed. The fifth was an open threat by U.S. Secretary of State John Foster Dulles of "disastrous effects" if Adenauer were not reelected.

In order to analyze the effects of this electoral intervention the major tool that I use are two post-election exit surveys with some relevant questions that I located during my archival research at the U.S. National Archives. These two exit surveys were conducted by a reputable German firm (DIVO) under a secret contract with the U.S. government on a nationally representative sample of the West German population in September 14–27 and October 22–November 2 with 1,270 respondents in the first survey and 907 in the second one. While the underlying data for both surveys seems unfortunately to have been lost, tables summarizing many of the results for the main questions, and for some questions even full-scale crosstabs, have nevertheless been located in a classified report by the U.S. High Commissioner's office written about these findings (hence HICOG 191) in late 1953. These surveys enable us, in regard to some of these methods in particular and to this intervention in general, to draw some general conclusions about the specific effects of three components of these interventions and the intervention overall and even use some basic table statistics (such as Chi-square) in some cases.

Of course, one must note that this American intervention was not the only factor benefiting the CDU and Adenauer in the 1953 elections. The CDU also, as will be later seen, benefited from the fact that the effects of what was later known as the German "economic miracle" finally began to be felt by the average West German voter by the late spring and summer of 1953 (Spicka 2007:101–102, 197). Likewise, the SPD made some serious errors during the election campaign such as deciding, as a cost-cutting measure, to forgo the use of a polling firm. In contrast, the CDU avoided this and other errors and ran a better campaign (Friedal 2007:116, 122–123). Nevertheless, as will be seen in the subsequent sections, the U.S. intervention was an important factor in enabling the victory of the CDU in this election.

7.2.2   Agreeing to a Four Power Conference with the Soviet Union

As noted in Chapter 3, the June 17 revolt in East Germany turned yet again the issue of German reunification into a burning issue for the West German public. It accordingly greatly increased public pressure within West Germany for the most plausible route for achieving reunification in 1953—a Four Power conference in which this issue would be seriously discussed by the U.S. and the Soviets.

For example, when asked, in a poll conducted in July 1953, as to the most important question that the country should deal with, the issue of reunification was noted by 38% of the respondents—the most highly ranked on the list of options. This was also an increase of nearly 15% in its perceived importance over the preceding time this question was asked in July 1952. Not surprisingly, when asked in early July about their view of holding a Four Power conference, before the decision to hold it was made by the U.S., no less than 75% of the West German public were in support (Noelle and Neumann 1967:464).

The American decision to hold a Four Power conference (at Adenauer's request) in order to help the CDU's electoral chances accordingly paid significant dividends in the ballot box. When asked in the second post-election exit poll about the various factors or issues that affected their vote choice, 7% of voters to the CDU claimed that the foremost reason for their vote choice was that the CDU was the best advocate for German reunification, and another 15% claimed that it was the second-most important reason. In contrast, only 2% of the SPD voters claimed that German reunification was the foremost reason for their vote, and 8% claimed that it was the second-most important reason—a statistically significant difference (HICOG Survey 191).[16]

This was especially effective among one of the main groups seen as "swing voters" in this election—the nine million German refugees from East Germany and from the areas annexed by Poland and the USSR east of the Oder-Neisse line after WW2 (Bretton 1955:55, 142). Among these swing voters, 13% of those who voted for the CDU claimed that this was the most important reason why

---

[16]   Chi-square test significance at 0.001, test statistic 10.99.

they voted for it, and another 23% claimed that this was the second-most important factor. Only 3% and 11%, respectively, of refugee voters to the SPD from this group made a similar claim—a statistically significant difference (HICOG Survey 191).[17]

Given what we know about German public opinion on this topic prior to the announcement of the Four Power conference, the CDU's ability to predominate among, and gain votes from, voters who strongly cared about the German reunification issue was completely unanticipated. Indeed, the CDU and Adenauer were at a distinct disadvantage. Over the preceding four years the SPD had constantly presented itself, among other things, as the champion of German reunification and had repeatedly accused Adenauer (with some justice) of not really caring about reunification (Handrieder 1967:129; for Adenauer's views see Trachtenberg 1999:131, 231, 277–278).

This effort by the SPD made significant inroads, prior to this U.S. intervention, in achieving the preferred "branding" of each side in the mind of the West German public. For example, in an October 1951 poll only 36% of the respondents were completely certain that Adenauer was indeed interested in the reunification of Germany (Noelle and Neumann 1967:243). Likewise, in an April 1952 poll the SPD was seen by more respondents as being for the reunification of Germany (24%) than the CDU (19%). Similar results were found in other questions comparing Adenauer versus the then-head of the SPD, Schumacher (Noelle and Neumann 1956:314). The main method repeatedly proposed by the SPD to achieve reunification, a Four Power conference, was also polling quite well even prior to the revolt. For example, by early 1953, a plurality of the West German public (44% to 48% in various polls conducted in April 1953) thought that a Four Power conference on this topic would benefit West Germany (HICOG Survey 193).

Not surprisingly, the SPD leadership decided in early 1953, long before the revolt, to make the issue of German reunification the centerpiece of its election campaign. Convening a Four Power conference for this purpose became the central foreign policy prescription in the SPD's pre-election platform, a platform otherwise largely lacking in specific foreign policy prescriptions (Drummond 1982:105). After the revolt began, the SPD naturally tried to press its advantage even further and succeeded in embarrassing Adenauer in parliamentary debates on this topic in late June and early July.[18] In contrast, Adenauer, given his aforementioned image as to reunification and the fact that he publically and repeatedly

---

[17] Chi-square test significance at 0.035, test statistic 4.4.
[18] For two examples see M. R. Handler, "Adenauer Defeats Bid for Big 4 Talk," *New York Times*, July 2, 1953; and M. R. Handler, "Bonn House Votes 2 Rebuffs to Paris," *New York Times*, July 3, 1953.

opposed a Four Power conference until after the revolt was long under way (see Chapter 3), was likely to be far less successful on this potent issue.

This American intervention, announced following the Three Power Meeting in mid-July 1953, dramatically changed the situation in Adenauer's favor. By being able to provide what seemed like a concrete achievement on the road toward German reunification—achieving an American (and western) agreement to convene a Four Power conference—Adenauer was able to clearly prove, to significant parts of the West German public, his (supposed) true desire for prompt German reunification and disprove the SPD claims about him in this regard. That, in turn, turned this issue from a negative into a positive, enabling the CDU to take from the SPD its dominance on this topic (Friedel 2007:129–130; Schwarz 1995:69).

For example, a survey in August 1953 already found a 9% gap in favor of the CDU (30% to 21%) when respondents were asked whether a CDU-led government or an SPD-led government would be more likely to achieve reunification (Noelle and Neumann 1967:463). Likewise, by "stealing" from the SPD its main positive foreign policy demand, Adenauer left the SPD little to campaign about on foreign policy issues beyond various nit-picking arguments over the exact details of this conference's planned agenda or taking credit for Adenauer's shift— now on a topic on which the CDU was stronger (Friedel 2007:130).

7.2.3 Creating a Food Aid Program for East Germany

As noted in Chapter 3, Adenauer, in the weeks following the June 17 revolt, was under growing West German public pressure to show (among other things) that he was "doing something" to help fellow Germans in East Germany suffering from the Soviet and East German crackdown and was repeatedly attacked for his passivity in this regard. Adenauer was also under increasing SPD attacks that he didn't really care about the East German population—a line of attack which seems to have begun to resonate among many West Germans before the food aid program started.[19]

From the available survey data we can see that there was widespread sympathy among the West German population toward the East German protesters with only 19% of West German respondents claiming that their protests were "in vain" (Noelle and Neumann 1967:480). This was despite the obvious, well-known fact that the protesters had no real chance of defeating the Soviet occupying troops

---

[19] See, for example, Kisatsky (2005:55); "Adenauer Regime Under Fire for Inaction on Riots in East," *New York Times*, June 29, 1953; and "Adenauer Defeats Bid for Big 4 Talk," *New York Times*, July 2, 1953

or the East German police. As a result, this line of attack by the SPD could have seriously harmed Adenauer's electoral chances.

The food aid program clearly helped to blunt this attack by the SPD in its infancy. The DIVO survey done in late July 1953, a week after the food aid program had begun and a few weeks after the initial West German and American request for the provision of food was rejected by the Soviets, found that 89% of the West German respondents fully approved of the food aid program.[20] Likewise, the food aid program, together with the Four Power conference proposal (see previous subsection), seems to have also convinced most West Germans that all that could be feasibly done by Adenauer (and the west) for their East German brethren was indeed being done. The same survey found, for example, when asking whether more could be done to help the East German population that only 13% of West German respondents believed that anything more was possible.[21]

As Adenauer had hoped, the initial food aid request and subsequent food distribution program received widespread, overwhelmingly favorable coverage by the West German media, probably thanks to its "humanitarian," relatively low-key nature (Schwarz 1995:65).[22] As a result, the food aid plan seems to have helped Adenauer deflect SPD charges that he "didn't care," causing the subsequent (accurate) SPD accusations that it was done for selfish electoral purposes make the SPD, rather than Adenauer, look bad (Kisatsky 2005:54–55).

7.2.4 Threatening "Disastrous Effects" if Adenauer Were Not Reelected

The final act of U.S. intervention in this election was done with a statement by U.S. Secretary of State John Foster Dulles in an American press conference which took place two days before the elections. As noted in Chapter 3, Dulles publicly threatened in this statement "disastrous effects" for Germany if Adenauer were not reelected. This threat echoed throughout Germany, becoming front-page news in West Germany and the main issue of the election campaign in its final days, with the SPD strongly denouncing it and the CDU supportive of it.[23]

---

[20] See a brief description of this aspect of the DIVO survey in Bonn 550 August 6,1953/862b.49/ RG59/NARA.

[21] Ibid.

[22] For a description of the initial German media coverage, see also Bonn 202 July 13,1953; and Bonn 418 July 30,1953, both in 862b.49/RG59/NARA. The shift toward less favorable West German media coverage of this aid program noted by Inginmundarson (1996:406) was largely a post-election phenomenon.

[23] "Dulles Pins Blame on Soviet Policies," *New York Times*, September 4, 1953;"Abroad," *New York Times*, September 7, 1953.

No direct questions were asked about this public threat. Nevertheless, we can gauge indirectly its impact from other questions made in the DIVO post-election surveys. First, this threat by Dulles was indeed widely noticed by the West German public. One of the DIVO post-election surveys found this threat to be the most frequently noted example of the intervention by respondents in open-ended questions on the American electoral intervention (HICOG Survey 191).[24] Second, this threat was the only component of the intervention that involved some kind of negative inducement to vote for Adenauer and the CDU. All other components of this intervention (see the introduction) involved various kinds of carrots and "goodies."

Given these facts, if this threat by Dulles had been counterproductive we would expect the respondents overall to have seen the intervention in a more negative light than they had beforehand, or to see at the minimum no shift in their views in its regard. However, the American intervention was seen in a sig-nificantly *more favorable light* in mid-September (in both the substantive and statistical senses), or shortly after the threat was made, than in a previous pre-threat poll in late July 1953 by DIVO in which the same question was asked (HICOG Survey 191).[25] Likewise, their overall view of the American interven-tion was favorable in mid- to late September 1953. Furthermore, the last pre-threat (and pre-election) poll available showed the race tightening and the CDU vote share about 7% lower than what it actually received in the election after the threat (Schwarz 1995:79). An ineffective or counterproductive threat would not have shown such differences between pre- and post-threat surveys nor led to final election results better than the final pre-election polls.

7.2.5 Overall Evaluation of the Intervention's Effect

Of course, the question can be asked as to how much, overall, did all of these components help the Adenauer campaign. This can be indirectly ascertained through a key question in the second exit survey (HICOG Survey 191). This question listed various reasons for voting for a particular party and then asked the respondents to note which of these reasons affected their vote choice for the CDU (and other parties) the most and then the second- and third-most

---

[24] These questions asked respondents when did they notice the U.S. intervention and/or for examples of the U.S. electoral intervention. Estimate made based on the listing of the most frequently given/representative responses given by respondents in the report about these two post-election polls (HICOG Survey 191).

[25] Its overall favorability rose from 40% in late July to 53% in September 1953—a statistically sig-nificant difference (Chi-square test significance at 0.01, test statistic 6.33); data derived from HICOG Survey 191.

important reasons. Unfortunately, with the exception of the German reunification advocacy reason which I noted in section 7.2.2, the other factors which
were part of the U.S. intervention (or in this question as to the intervention itself) were not listed among the reasons available for the respondents to choose
from. Nevertheless, some of the most important reasons noted in this poll which
led the respondents to vote for the CDU are indeed closely related to many
components of this intervention.

In this poll, the top two reasons noted by respondents for choosing the
Christian Democrat Union, following the main socio-demographic factor that
defined it (i.e., being a Christian party),[26] were the prestige, friends, and respect
Adenauer had acquired for Germany around the world (with 18% reporting it as
the first reason and 24% reporting it as the second reason) and Adenauer being
a great leader (with 16% and 20%, respectively) (HICOG Survey 191).[27] Both
of these reasons why people voted for the CDU were clearly influenced by the
U.S. intervention.

For example, according to the available polling data, few West Germans saw
Adenauer as a particularly great or good leader prior to 1953 with Adenauer
having, for example, an average approval rating of 28.7% in the preceding three
years (Noell and Neumann 1967:256–257).[28] Given that fact, if Adenauer's leadership was a significant factor in the German voters' minds, that was the result (at least in part) of Adenauer's major foreign policy achievements during
1953—achievements which were due to the U.S. intervention noted here. In
other words, a perception (and resultant vote choice) of Adenauer as a great
leader probably had much to do with the fact that in the six months prior to
the election Adenauer was suddenly able to present to the electorate a series
of important achievements such as signing a significant trade agreement with
the U.S., getting from the U.S. two things widely desired by many within West
Germany (a Four Power conference and a procedure for the release of German
war criminals), finding a way for West Germany to help their oppressed East
German brethren, etc.

As for the other major reason for voting for the CDU, gaining friends and
prestige for Germany, there is little reason to doubt that the U.S. intervention in
Adenauer's favor greatly contributed to this being such a major factor for voting
for Adenauer and the CDU. The average German getting all of his or her news

[26] Forty percent noted this as their top reason for voting for the CDU.
[27] In contrast, when asked a similar option about the leadership skills of the leader of the SPD,
Ollenhauer, virtually no one (less than 1% overall) seems to have voted for the SPD due to this factor.
[28] Likewise, when asked in an August 1952 poll about who are (or were) the greatest Germans,
Adenauer was only listed by 3% of the respondents—or within the survey's margin of error. It is instructive to note that when asked this question again two months after the elections in November
1953 (the start of his ascent, by the mid-1960s, to the greatest German ever in this survey), Adenauer
was listed by almost three times as many people (9%) (Noelle and Neumann 1967:241).

from the West German media (without any access, of course, as we currently have to archival documents) would have received, thanks to the U.S. intervention in Adenauer's favor, numerous significant examples of how Adenauer had found friends and increased Germany's prestige around the world.

To describe the view from the perspective of the average West German voter, in April 1953 Adenauer made a visit to the U.S. (a first ever for a German chancellor), was received in an official ceremony and a very warm manner by President Eisenhower and other officials from the administration, and returned from the talks with clear promises, listed in the resulting communiqué,[29] for various benefits for Germany. These benefits included the trade agreement and the parole committee. As one could expect from a friend, many of these promises were actually fulfilled afterward.

A few months later, after the June 17 revolt erupted, the U.S., Britain, and France sent friendly letters showing their sympathy with West German anguish over events in East Germany in response to Adenauer's telegrams. President Eisenhower even sent afterward, on his own initiative, a letter endorsing the West German government's positions as for how German reunification should occur (Hirsch-Weber and Schurtz 1957:130; Schwarz 1995:65).[30] The U.S. shortly afterward upgraded the German representative in the U.S. (and its own representative, Conant) to the rank of an ambassador. Then, after a personal letter from Adenauer to Eisenhower asking for American help with feeding East Germans, President Eisenhower showed that U.S. friendship toward Germany was not limited to mere words but also included "real help" (to quote the report in one German newspaper) by kindly agreeing to offer American food to feed the East Germans. This food was then sent over the following weeks (Hirsch-Weber and Schurtz 1957:129).[31]

Two weeks later, following the request and efforts by Adenauer's messengers, whose role was widely reported afterward in the German media,[32] Germany was able to determine much of the agenda of the meeting of the three western great powers in Washington, D.C., in July 1953. This was despite the fact that Germany was not actually invited to it. Adenauer's efforts also led the U.S., after consulting with Britain and France, to agree to a Four Power conference and to the setting up of parole committees for German war criminals.

---

[29] "U.S. to Help Arm Bonn When Europe Implements Act," New York Times, April 10, 1953.

[30] These were other significant components of the U.S. intervention which, in order not to overwhelm the reader, were not discussed in much depth here or previously.

[31] Quote from one German newspaper (FAZ) in Bonn 418 July 30, 1953 /box 5263/862b.49/RG59/ NARA. Other newspapers included headlines in response to this program such as "Americans Want to Help."

[32] See, for example, "Ulbricht kann nicht denken," Der Spiegel, July 22, 1953; "Die Stunde von Seoul," Der Spiegel, July 22, 1953—both from a major West German magazine which was not very friendly to Adenauer.

In other words, many of the costly acts of intervention done by the U.S. also showed to many West German voters that the U.S. had become, thanks to Adenauer, a friend of Germany. As one scholar, and observer of this election, noted, the various aforementioned American acts designed to help Adenauer's reelection "contribut[ed] further to the identification of the Adenauer regime with good German-American relations" (Bretton 1955:153).[33]

West Germany's friendship with the U.S. was especially important to the average German voter. For example, when asked prior to the start of the intervention in March 1953 with which country Germany should seek the closest possible cooperation, 83% noted the U.S.—the most of all nine countries listed (Noelle and Neumann 1967:510, 550). This could be also seen in a related open-answer question as to this factor in which many of the preserved responses noted Germany's relations with the U.S. in this regard.[34]

Accordingly, at least some of the 42% who mainly voted for the CDU either because of Adenauer's leadership skills or because of his acquisition of prestige, friends, and respect to Germany did so due to the American intervention in his favor. If one includes also the 7% whose foremost reason for voting for the CDU was directly connected to one of the U.S. intervention acts (i.e., the Four Power conference) noted in subsection 7.2.2, the overall effect of the American intervention is quite sizable. In comparison, according to this question only 11% of CDU voters noted the economic achievements of the CDU as the most important reason why they had voted for it (HICOG Survey 191), making that the fourth-most important reason.[35]

7.3 Conclusions

As can be seen from the single election level analysis of two intervention cases, the effects of the partisan electoral interventions were in congruence with large-N results on the first effects hypothesis (H4) in Chapter 6. In the 1992 Israeli elections the results of the statistical analysis indicate that this factor increased the probability of voting for the left-wing bloc (the one supported in this intervention) by at least 2.8%—a medium-size effect which stacks up quite well in comparison to important factors which determined vote choice in this election. This finding is in accordance with the estimate in Chapter 6 on this election

---

[33] Indeed, the previously noted threat by Dulles can be seen in this context as helpful also by showing that voting for Adenauer would guarantee such good relations.

[34] HICOG Survey 191. In the first exit poll asking about this issue in an open question, four of the six responses related to the component "Adenauer's . . . prestige in the world" noted in some manner relations with the U.S. as a reason why they voted for the CDU.

[35] Seventeen percent noted it as a second reason.

derived from the large-N analysis in section 6.4 where the effects of the electoral intervention were estimated to have been large enough to have enabled the coming to power, as a result of this election, of Rabin as the head of a center-left coalition.[36] The analysis here, using local-level survey data, further buttresses this conclusion.

In the case of the 1953 West German election, clear evidence has also been found for significant direct effects of at least three of the five major components of the U.S. intervention in favor of Adenauer and the CDU. For example, one of these components—agreeing to hold a Four Power conference—probably contributed about 7% of the overall CDU vote in this election. When one also includes at least some of the indirect effects of this intervention on other key factors noted by voters in post-election surveys as leading them to vote for the CDU (such as, for example, the view of Adenauer as a great leader), the overall electoral benefits of the American assistance to Adenauer were large and substantial.

This analysis accordingly provides additional support to some of the findings of the aggregate large-N statistical analysis in Chapter 6. The congruence between the findings in the election surveys and the results of H4 in Chapter 6 (i.e., a significant electoral benefit to the assisted side) provides further evidence that the large-N analysis correctly identified the usual causal effects of electoral interventions. These findings also provide strong support for one of the key mechanisms proposed here as to how overt interventions may affect vote choice in non-founding elections, indicating that voters in the target usually pay attention to such interventions, modify their opinions on the relevant issues accordingly, and at least some of them do change, as a result, their voting choices in the desired direction as well. In the following chapter I will discuss another case of an electoral intervention and analyze its effects—the Russian electoral intervention in the 2016 U.S. elections.

[36] Given the different statistical methods used (OLS in Chapter 6, probit here), the different independent variables (incumbent party vote share vs. left/right bloc), and the different ways used to interpret the results of each method, the absolute magnitude of these effects aren't directly comparable. Nevertheless, both methods indicate an effect large enough to have significantly affected this election's outcome in the direction that this intervention was supposed to have (i.e., a Rabin and a Labor/left-wing bloc victory).

8

The (In)famous Election

Analyzing the Russian Intervention in the 2016 U.S. Elections

> The election of a President of America some years hence will be
> much more interesting to certain nations of Europe than ever the
> election of a king of Poland was . . . they will interfere with money
> & with arms. A Galloman or an Angloman will be supported by the
> nation he befriends.
>
> —Thomas Jefferson on the new U.S. Constitution, 1787[1]

Naturally, many readers may wonder about how the research presented here
on partisan electoral interventions applies to one such recent and already notorious case—the Russian intervention in the 2016 U.S. elections. Aside from
satisfying this interest, an analysis of this case can provide two other empirical
benefits. First, as an "out-of-sample" case, occurring after the draft versions of
my arguments were already written,[2] the Russian intervention in 2016 is an especially strong test of these. Second, as for the causes of electoral interventions,
it provides us with an in-depth analysis of a case from a great power intervener
other than the U.S. and from a more recent time period—thus enabling us to conduct a preliminary test of the wider applicability of these arguments. Although,
of course, in such a "brand new" case, we need to accept far more ambiguity than
in older cases where archival documents of the decision-making process is available, it may nevertheless still give us an idea of whether these arguments are indeed germane.

Accordingly, this chapter will analyze two key aspects of this intervention, first
its causes and then its effects on the results. It will use the theoretical framework
presented throughout this book and the best available qualitative and quantitative information, as similar whenever possible to that used in the other cases,

---

[1] Letter, Jefferson to Madison December 20,1787, founders online https://founders.archives.gov/.
[2] For a preliminary version of the first two hypotheses on the effects, as well as a brief summary of
the argument regarding the causes, see Levin 2016a.

Meddling in the Ballot Box. Dov H. Levin, Oxford University Press (2020). © Oxford University Press.
DOI: 10.1093/oso/9780197519882.001.0001.

checking in each aspect what has exactly occurred and how pertinent this frame-work is to this case.

8.1. The Causes of the Russian Intervention

8.1.1 The "Existential Threat" to Russia: Hillary Clinton in 2016

As first lady during Bill Clinton's presidency (1993–2001), and then as a promi-nent politician in her own right, Hillary Clinton (hence Clinton) developed quite hawkish preferences on many key foreign policy issues facing the United States—more hawkish than those of most democrats. Russia was one key area where Clinton developed such inclinations. By the second half of the 2000s she seems to have reached the conclusion that Putin was a throwback to the old, hostile Soviet Union and that a Russia under his rule would be a foe of the United States. She also seems to have quickly concluded that Putin's decision to step down in May 2008 after two presidential terms and let his protégé, Dmitry Medvedev, re-place him was merely cosmetic and that Putin, now Medvedev's prime minister, remained the true key decision-maker in Russia (Landler 2016:263–265).

These beliefs were frequently expressed by Clinton in various private and public conversations. For example, during a January 2008 town hall meeting, in a riff on George W. Bush's famous remark in this regard, she half-jokingly doubted that Putin, as a former KGB agent, has a soul (Clinton 2018:327). Then, as Obama's first secretary of state, Clinton seems to have been the most hard-line member of Obama's foreign policy team regarding Russia and a major opponent in in-ternal debates to its reset policy toward Russia. For example, during the first high-level meeting of the Obama administration on Russia in February 2009, Clinton strongly rejected the idea, raised by some aides to Obama, that the U.S. should make some symbolic concessions to Russia as a goodwill gesture, claiming that Obama should not concede anything whatsoever without getting something in return (Landler 2016:54). Nevertheless, after losing the internal policy debate on Russia, Clinton, as a member of the Obama administration, dutifully helped im-plement the "reset" policy on both the symbolic and the substantive levels.

Although the Russian government was well aware of Clinton's hawkish views in their regard, they initially didn't seem to have been unduly worried about her. From our limited knowledge of the views of the Russian government about Clinton in 2007–2008, when she ran for the first time for the presidency, she seems to have been seen as an acceptable option to the Russian government.[3]

---

[3] Not surprisingly, no evidence exists that the Russian government tried to intervene against Clinton during the 2008 primaries.

Indeed, as secretary of state Clinton seems to have been initially able to de-velop a working relationship with the Russian government (Landler 2016:279). At the same time, she earned a reputation for toughness among her Russian interlocutors, many of whom came to refer to her with grudging respect as "a lady with balls."[4]

From the available evidence thus far, it appears that two developments began to shift the Russian government's view about Clinton. The first was the American humanitarian intervention in Libya in mid-2011. When events in Libya led the U.S. to decide to do a humanitarian intervention, the Obama administration decided that it needed a U.N. Security Council resolution authorizing the in-tervention in order to legitimize it. After heavy American lobbying, the Russian government under Medvedev agreed to abstain in the U.N. Security Council when this resolution came up for a vote. The Russian agreement to abstain was largely due to what it perceived as quiet assurances by Clinton and other American officials that this planned humanitarian intervention, and the request for a "no-fly" zone, would not become a cover for an outright regime-change op-eration in Libya (Myers 2015:382–384; Ehrlich 2016).[5]

The eventual expansion nevertheless of the U.S.-led humanitarian interven-tion into a regime-change operation that removed Kaddafi from power and brought about his gruesome death by the U.S.-backed rebels made a profound impression on Russian government officials, significantly increasing their fears of the United States.[6] It also led Putin and much of the Russian foreign policy establishment to conclude that the U.S. government had duped them as to their true intentions in this intervention (Myers 2015:381–384; Ehrlich 2016). Clinton's well-known key role in pushing for this intervention within the Obama administration, her subsequent role in the prewar negotiations in persuading the Russian government to not veto the UNSC resolution, and her later boast, "We Came, We Saw, He Died," when asked about Kaddafi's death, led much of the Russian foreign policy establishment to perceive Clinton as a "duplicitous war-monger" (Ehrlich 2016).[7]

---

[4] Michael Crowley and Julia Ioffe, "Why Putin Hates Hillary," *Politico*, July 25, 2016.

[5] For the debate about what exactly the U.S. has promised in this regard to Russia (and China) see Vilmer (2016) and Carpenter (2017).

[6] For example, according to one report, Putin became "obsessed" with this case, watching re-peatedly the video of Kaddafi's death. Julia Ioffe, "What Putin Really Wants," *The Atlantic*, January/February 2018. According to another source, Medvedev's perceived failure on this case and Putin's and much of the Russian foreign policy establishment's fears about the future plans of the U.S. in their regard even played an important role in Putin's decision to force Medvedev to retire from the presi-dency after his first term and to return to the presidential chair (Zygar 2016:204–205).

[7] Clinton's role in pushing for this intervention within the Obama administration received wide-spread contemporary media coverage. See, for example, Helene Cooper and Steven Lee Myers, "Obama Takes Hard Line with Libya after Shift by Clinton," *New York Times*, March 18, 2011. For

The second development occurred in the aftermath of the December 2011 Russian parliamentary elections. Following credible evidence of fraud occurring in that election, small-scale protests began to erupt in its immediate aftermath. Over the course of the following two months, these protests snowballed into mass protests in Moscow which, at various points, seriously threatened Putin's chances of returning to the presidency in the March 2012 Russian presidential elections. Two days after these parliamentary elections, as the protests began to metastasize, Clinton, during a visit to nearby Lithuania for the OSCE Conference, publically denounced the irregularities. In her public denunciation she described the elections as "neither free nor fair" and called for a "full investigation" of the "fraud and manipulation" in it.[8]

This immediate American denunciation of the election, which was far harsher than what the Russian government expected from its ongoing direct interactions with the White House, as well as from its subsequent conversations with other senior White House officials, seems to have led Putin to believe that Clinton was the principal author of a secret American scheme designed to bring him down through Arab Spring–style mass protests.[9] Accordingly, Putin in his public reactions to Clinton's remarks directly blamed her for the growing protests, claiming that she "gave . . . a signal" and the Russian opposition leaders then "heard the signal and with the support of *the US state department* began active work" on this plan (my emphasis) (Myers 2015:396–397). He later made similar claims in private conversations as well (Seipel 2015:36).

The Obama administration was able to temporarily mollify the Russian government in this regard. As a result, the Russian government resumed its regular interactions with both Clinton and the U.S. government. However, Clinton's subsequent pronouncements seem to have brought back and further enhanced Russian fears about her. For example, in December 2012, during a farewell meeting with the Russian foreign minister followed by a speech at the Organization for Security and Co-operation in Europe (OSCE) conference, Clinton declared that the planned Eurasian Union, Russia's main foreign policy scheme in the early 2010s prior the 2014 Ukrainian revolution, was an attempt to "re-Sovietize" parts of Eastern Europe and Central Asia, and she

Clinton's version of her role in pushing for this intervention and of her prewar interactions with Russian officials over Libya see Clinton (2014:369–372).

[8] U.S. Department of State, "Secretary Clinton's Comments on Russia's Elections," (press release), December 6, 2011.

[9] From the available evidence it appears that a miscommunication occurred in the White House, with Clinton's post-election message being approved by the senior White House Russia advisor without Obama and other senior White House personnel, who seem to have preferred a far softer initial reaction, being consulted first. Mark Landler, "Russia, Suspected in Hacking, Has Uneasy History With Hillary Clinton," *New York Times*, July 28, 2016.

promised to "figure out effective ways to slow down or prevent it." This led to angry complaints by the Russian government that Clinton had a completely "wrong understanding" of its plans.[10]

As U.S.-Russian relations worsened during Obama's second term due to Putin's takeover of Crimea in the aftermath of the overthrow of Ukrainian President Yuschenko in early 2014, and his subsequent assistance to Russian separatists in Eastern Ukraine, Clinton took a far more hawkish position on Russia than did the rest of the Obama administration. The events in Ukraine seem to have further hardened Clinton's already negative views on Putin and Russia. Likewise, it was also probably seen by Clinton as a good policy issue for her to differentiate herself from Obama as well as to protect herself from possible Republican attacks in the general elections.[11] For example, in a private charity event in March 2014 she compared Putin's actions in Ukraine to those of Hitler in Eastern Europe in the 1930s.[12] When those comments leaked to the press, they led to an uncharacteristically harsh public response from Putin.

Although Clinton walked back the Hitler analogy afterward, her subsequent foreign policy proposals and pronouncements reflected similarly strong negative beliefs about Putin and Russia. For example, in a CNN interview in July 2014 Clinton claimed that it would be "next to impossible" for the U.S. to have "positive" relations with Russia so long as Putin was in power.[13] In a speech given during a private fundraising event that month (later stolen by Russian hackers), Clinton talked about using the U.S.'s growing natural gas and oil production in order to counter Russian gas exports to Europe, reducing Russia's key export and tool of geostrategic influence.[14] In September 2015, in the Q&A session after her first foreign policy speech as a declared presidential candidate, Clinton promised, when asked about her planned policies for dealing with Russia, enhanced sanctions and a return to Cold War–style policies toward Russia. Those were seen by Clinton as necessary for dealing with a power that she thought planned "to stymie, to confront, and to undermine American power whenever and wherever they can." Her aides in the subsequent days leaked to the press that such Cold War–style policies would also include the provision of defensive weapons to the Ukrainian government (Landler 2016:283–284). As one scholar of Russian foreign policy notes, given Clinton's record, "Putin had plausible grounds for thinking that a President Hillary Clinton would launch a new campaign of

---

[10] "Clinton Calls Eurasian Integration an Effort to 'Re-Sovietize,'" *Radio Free Europe*, December 7, 2012.
[11] Jeffrey Goldberg, "Is There a Hillary Doctrine?" *The Atlantic*, May 13, 2016.
[12] Karen Robes Meeks, "Hillary Clinton Compares Vladimir Putin's Actions in Ukraine to Adolf Hitler's in Nazi Germany," *Long Beach Press-Telegram*, March 5, 2014.
[13] Clinton Interview, CNN, July 27, 2014.
[14] Leah McGrath Goodman, "Vladimir Putin: Why He Fears a Hillary Clinton White House," *Newsweek*, November 3, 2016.

pressure against his government and Russian client states in the name of human rights and democracy" (Lynch 2018:584).

Not surprisingly, by early 2016 much of the Russian foreign policy elite seem to have seen the possibility of a Clinton presidency as an "existential threat" (Ehrlich 2016).[15] As one prominent Russian foreign policy commentator noted, there was a consensus within the Russian government that if Hillary Clinton became the forty-fifth U.S. president she would take "a very hostile approach" and was accordingly perceived by Russia as "the worst option of any [possible American] president."[16] Given that situation, as Putin himself admitted during a press conference in July 2018, he preferred in 2016 a victory by Donald Trump.[17]

8.1.2. The Nominee Who "Can't Win": Donald J. Trump

The attempt by many scholars and pundits, after the shocking results of the 2016 elections, to rethink many widespread "rules" and common beliefs about American politics, presidential elections, and even parts of the American public's understandings of their national identity, should not blind us to the real and perceived severe disadvantages Trump faced as he began his race for the presidency in mid-2015.

When Trump entered the 2016 Republican presidential primaries in June 2015 he was widely dismissed throughout the political spectrum, as well as by all serious observers of American politics, as a joke candidate who stood no chance of winning the nomination. Likewise, only 7% of likely Republican primary voters initially supported him (Hetherington 2018:63). The *Huffington Post*'s famous decision four weeks later to move all of its Trump campaign–related news to the entertainment section reflected the consensus view about Trump's chances of securing the nomination. Likewise, one of Trump's senior campaign advisors,

---

[15] Clinton claimed that the Russian intervention against her was due to a "personal grudge" Putin held against her (Clinton 2018:329). However, as one Russian foreign policy expert noted, while the Russian government did dislike Clinton, "they actually thought that she represented a threat," and their electoral intervention against her was accordingly a matter of "policy, not pique" (Mark Galeotti, quoted in Max Fisher, "Russia's Hacks Followed Years of Paranoia Toward Hillary Clinton," *New York Times*, December 16, 2016). See also Lynch (2018:585).

[16] ".". Likewise, as one Russian member of the Duma, and former political ally of Putin, noted, the Russian government intervention in the 2016 election was due to the "fear that Hillary Clinton would come and take an even tougher stance toward Russia [than Obama had]." Lucian Kim, "What Was Russia's Role in 2016 U.S. Election? 2 Former KGB Officials Weigh In," *National Public Radio*, November 11, 2017.

[17] Stephanie Murray, "Putin: I wanted Trump to Win the Election," *Politico*, July 16, 2018. Putin still denies that there was in practice a Russian intervention in favor of Donald Trump. A recent report, based on high-quality U.S. human intelligence, indicates that the electoral intervention was authorized directly by Putin himself; "CIA Informant Extracted from Russia Had Sent Secrets to U.S. for Decades," *New York Times*, September 9, 2019.

in an off-the-record conversation, gave Trump a one-in-ten chance of winning the primaries (Tur 2017:52).

While Trump did succeed through his widespread name recognition, unconventional tactics, and unusual positions on certain hot-button issues within the GOP (such as immigration) to vault into an early lead in the primary polls, one should not overestimate in retrospect the levels of early support for him within the GOP or his actual chances. His enthusiastic base at this stage within the GOP constituted a minority of GOP primary voters. Nearly a fourth (23%) of GOP primary voters rated Trump as their last choice in a poll conducted in January 2016—significantly worse than any other GOP candidate. Likewise, his overall favorability rating was significantly worse than those of two of his most prominent rivals—Marco Rubio and Ted Cruz (Rapoport and Stone 2017:137–138). Furthermore, despite multiple victories Trump was unable to gain an absolute majority of the votes in any primary or caucus state until the thirty-third primary/caucus state—the April 19 primaries in his home state of New York (Mayer 2018:51–53). This was an unusually late stage for the victorious candidate to reach such a threshold in the U.S. presidential primaries[18] and clear evidence of strong opposition to him at the time among Republican primary voters.

The authoritative explanation for how Trump nevertheless succeeded in securing the GOP nomination is probably many years away. From the available evidence, nevertheless, it is clear that it involved a large share of chance and luck on the side of Trump: the tendency of all other GOP candidates to not take him seriously until a very late stage and to direct their resources and attention accordingly; the very large number of presidential candidates running on the GOP side that year, which made an anti-Trump front once the threat he posed became clear difficult to achieve; the weak campaigns of multiple major candidates; one of the worse gaffes in the history of presidential primary debates by one of the major GOP candidates (Rubio); and so forth (Mayer 2018).

When the unexpected happened and the general election campaign began, the widespread consensus was that Trump stood virtually no chance of winning the general election. The headline of one such piece in *The Nation* on June 21 by Jon Wiener ("Relax, Donald Trump Can't Win") reflects quite well the zeitgeist at the time (see also Byler 2017:30; and Quirk 2018:205–206).[19]

---

[18] For example, in the three previously competitive GOP primaries, Bush reached that threshold in the fourth primary/caucus state (Delaware) in February 2000, McCain reached it in three states (Connecticut, New Jersey, and New York) which were part of the multi-state February 9, 2008, Super Tuesday, and Romney reached that threshold in the fifth primary/caucus state (Nevada) in February 2012.

[19] Likewise, although some of the econometric prediction models used by political scientists expected a very close race, many of the scholars applying them openly urged, after Trump's nomination, to disregard their predictions due to the unusual nature of the GOP candidate. See, for example, Abramovich (2016). Most other scholars concurred with this assumption (Sides, Tesler, and Vavereck 2017:317).

Although much derided after the election, this consensus was based on multiple good reasons, many of them well known to the Trump campaign itself. First, before Trump, no person was elected as president of the United States without having significant political or military experience (Mellow 2018:87). The last major presidential candidate without such experience, Wendell Wilkie, was decisively defeated by Roosevelt in the 1940 election.

Second, the polls consistently showed very low chances for Trump in a general election campaign. The Realclearpolitics highly reputable polling aggregate, for example, showed by the start of July 2016 that Trump was consistently behind Clinton in head-to-head general election polling ever since such polling had commenced a year earlier, in July 2, 2015, with the exception of three days in May, shortly after his victory in the primaries.[20] Before the worldwide wave of polling failures in late 2016 and early 2017, much of the American political class (and large shares of the public) took these consistent results as very strong indications that Trump was all but guaranteed to lose. While repeatedly dismissive of any and all unfavorable polls in public, in private Trump and his campaign didn't see this negative polling data as "fake news." In a rather rare moment of public self-doubt, Trump himself admitted after the elections that he had taken the polls quite seriously as well.[21] Likewise, Trump's high levels of unfavorability (55% in June 2016),[22] the most unfavorably viewed presidential candidate in the history of recorded polling, and his alienation of major voter groups through his remarks, policies, or combinations of both made it seem highly unlikely that he would be able to change this long-standing trend during the general elections period.

Third, Trump was unable to unify much of the GOP establishment behind his candidacy. Due to a combination of the intense dislike they had developed toward Trump during the primaries, as well as Trump's own ugly behavior and missteps before and in the immediate aftermath of clinching the nomination, a large share of the Republican establishment refused to coalesce behind Trump during this period. While too weak to prevent him from winning the nomination, the Republican establishment still retained the ability to cause severe harm to his chances among GOP voters and independents still hesitant about him. For example, multiple senior Republican officeholders refused to endorse Trump long after he had won the nomination and some, like then–Speaker of the House Paul Ryan, endorsed him in June 2016 and then denounced him shortly afterward. Many senior Republicans refused to serve as his campaign surrogates. Likewise, according to one report, in mid-2016 the Republican National Committee even

[20] At www.realclearpolitics.com, accessed October 31, 2018.
[21] Nolan McCaskill, "Trump Tells Wisconsin: Victory was a Surprise," *Politico*, December 13, 2016.
[22] Gallup Report, September 28, 2018.

took the unprecedented step of quietly blocking the Trump campaign from accessing parts of their voter database.[23]

When the Republican National Convention occurred in the following month, four living former GOP presidential nominees took the unprecedented step of refusing to attend the convention, as did an unprecedented number of sitting Republican senators (twenty-one) and governors (six)—sending a loud and clear message to the convention's viewers.[24] This led the Trump campaign to have significant difficulties in filling speaker slots in the convention. The quiet and open resistance by parts of the GOP elite was, not surprisingly, reducing Trump's ability in the early summer of 2016 to consolidate the Republican base behind him, with only 64% of Republican voters viewing him favorably in late June— nearly 20% less than the previous four Republican nominees during this general election month.[25]

Finally, the Trump campaign was very short of funds—a major factor in the general elections. Trump had gotten through the Republican primaries without developing any significant infrastructure for fundraising, largely using instead his own money as well as his unique talent for earning free media coverage. Once he won the nomination, Trump quickly discovered that the monetary resources required for competing in the general election would greatly outstrip his own personal fortune as well as his media skills.[26]

The difference was stark. The Clinton campaign, which initially expected to compete against Jeb Bush in the general elections, had invested great efforts in fundraising for the general elections in order to be well prepared against his known fundraising prowess. Likewise, due to her (and her husband's) past presidential runs, Clinton had a well-developed fundraising network. As a result, Clinton began the general election with $42 million on hand and a well-oiled fundraising machine from all kinds of donors (Currinder 2018:148).

Trump, in contrast, began the general elections with only $1.3 million on hand—or less than one-twentieth of Clinton's general election funds.[27] The Trump campaign only sent its first fundraising email in mid-June 2016— five months before the general elections. It had no affiliated super PAC and would continue to have none for months to come. Likewise, Trump lacked a

---

[23] Freddy Gray, "Trump's Train Wreck: How the Donald Is Derailing His Own Campaign," *The Spectator*, June 18, 2016.

[24] Jessica Taylor, "Republican Convention 2016: These Republicans Are Sitting It Out," *National Public Radio*, July 18, 2016.

[25] See Lydia Saad, "Clinton, Trump Gaining Favorability Within Parties," Gallup report, June 27, 2016.

[26] For the Trump campaign's own understanding of this problem see Alex Isenstadt, "Trump's Fundraisers See No Chance of Hitting $1 Billion," *Politico*, June 8, 2016.

[27] Fredreka Schouten, "Trump Enters General Election in Weak Financial Position," *USA Today*, June 21, 2016.

fundraising infrastructure among larger donors. After he had repeatedly bashed Republican mega-donors during the primaries, and touted his complete independence from them, many were naturally less than enthusiastic to donate money to him. Many others were deeply disgusted by Trump's antics and campaign positions.[28] Accordingly, although some Republican mega-donors eventually agreed to donate money to Trump, even those who agreed frequently gave amounts far smaller than their contributions during the primaries to their preferred candidates would predict. Utilizing the RNC's fundraising and donor network could only partly ameliorate this major disadvantage (Currinder 2018:137, 147, 149–150).[29] As a result, Trump was entering an election campaign in which he and his campaign staff knew that they would be disadvantaged on this important factor at a level that could be potentially fatal to his chances. As one scholar noted, "no candidate in the modern era ever overcame such a campaign resource advantage and [was] elected president" (Toner and Trainer 2017:196).

Due to all of these factors, Trump's general election campaign began in the late spring of 2016 in the same manner as his quest for the GOP nomination—as the longest of long shots. Trump was fast on his way to becoming the one thing that he hates the most—a very big loser.

8.1.3 But Was There Collusion?

As could be seen in the preceding two sections, the situation under which the 2016 Russian intervention is known to have occurred is concurrent with my theoretical predictions (H1 and H2) regarding the causes of electoral interventions. Nevertheless, readers are probably also quite interested in the answer to my third hypotheses in regard to the causes, a hypothesis inadvertently related to a question which launched a large FBI counterintelligence investigation, led to the creation of a special counsel, and has captured the interest of large segments of the American public ever since the first evidence of the Russian intervention came to light in 2016. In other words, whether the Trump campaign actively colluded with the Russian government on the latter's electoral intervention in this election.

From the publicly available information at the time of the writing of this study, we already have strong evidence for multiple key parts of a process of collusion,

---

[28] Some Republican donors were already so ashamed of having their name associated in any way with Trump's that the Trump campaign was reduced to asking some of them to donate money to the RNC instead; Alex Isenstadt, "Trump's Fundraisers.".

[29] The Trump campaign's financial problems continued to be so severe throughout the summer that in August 2016 Trump was forced to donate another $10 million of his own money to the campaign; Bannon FBI Interview, February 18, 2018, CNN FOIA request (19-cv-1278).

just as it has occurred in past electoral interventions, also in regard to Russia and the Trump campaign. First, we have two highly plausible pathways through which collusion could have occurred. As for the first pathway, there are multiple senior individuals in the Trump campaign with unusually strong pre-election ties to Russia and therefore highly plausible conduits through which such secret contacts could have been established and maintained. Even during the closest periods of U.S.-Russian relations in the post–Cold War era, Russia never became a formal or informal U.S. ally. Nor has Russia been a major trading partner of the U.S. or developed significant ties to major sections of American political, economic, or government elites. Given those facts, the large number of senior members of the Trump campaign which have been found to have significant ties of various kinds with Russia, from Trump himself downward, is quite unusual for an American presidential campaign.

Three senior members of the Trump campaign with such ties to Russia are of special interest.[30] The first, Carter Page, a foreign policy advisor to the Trump campaign, worked for three years in Russia and had openly described himself on multiple occasions before 2016 as an informal advisor to the Kremlin.[31] Indeed, according to a 2015 FBI indictment of two Russian intelligence agents, the Russian intelligence services tried to recruit Page as an informant.[32] In a testimony to the Mueller investigation, Page admitted to have given these agents some "immaterial non-public information" in 2015 despite knowing their true affiliations.[33] Likewise, in mid-July 2016, now as a member of the Trump campaign, Page visited Moscow in order to give a speech at the New Economic School. Page later admitted, under oath, to also having had during this visit a conversation with the Russian deputy prime minister.[34] The yet uncorroborated intelligence received by the FBI about who else Page spoke with and what they spoke about, seems to have been, from the currently available information, sufficiently serious to have led the FBI to begin its secret counterintelligence investigation in the summer of 2016 into the events surrounding this election.[35]

---

[30] Another very junior member of the campaign, George Papadopoulos, may have also been used for this purpose via a meeting with a Maltese professor (Joseph Mifsud) with Russian ties (Mueller report I: Section IV.A.2.

[31] Massimo Calabresi and Alana Abramson, "Carter Page Touted Kremlin Contacts in 2013 Letter," *Time*, February 4, 2018.

[32] Adam Goldman, "Russian Spies Tried to Recruit Carter Page Before He Advised Trump," *New York Times*, April 4, 2017; Indictment "United States of America v. Evgeny Buryakov, A/K/A "Zhenya," Igor Sporyshev, And Victor Podobnyy," January 23, 2015.

[33] Mueller report I:97; this section is partly redacted.

[34] Testimony of Carter Page, Thursday, November 2, 2017, U.S. House of Representatives, Permanent Select Committee on Intelligence.

[35] This uncorraberated intelligence included claims that Page played a key role in conveying messages and enabling collusion between the Trump campaign and Russia during the 2016 elections (Harding 2017:51–56). The Mueller report notes, in a heavily redacted section, that it was unable to "fully explain" Page's activities during this visit (101).

The second was Michael Flynn, in 2016 a senior Trump campaign advisor and surrogate who was also, at one point, on Trump's vice presidential shortlist. In December 2015, when he was already informally affiliated with the Trump campaign, Flynn gave a speech during a ceremony for the Russian government's foreign broadcasting and propaganda network (RT), a speech for which he was secretly paid $45,000 by the Russian government. He gave, afterward, two other speeches on behalf of Russian interests (Harding 2017:125–127). Flynn also had a long record of undeclared lobbying and work for other unsavory foreign governments.

The third and most significant of the three, Paul Manafort, Trump's chief strategist and campaign manager from March to August 2016, and an informal campaign advisor afterward[36], was employed for years by a Russian oligarch (Oleg Deripaska) with very close ties to the Kremlin. While in the employment of Deripaska, Manafort had proposed at least once a secret strategy designed to promote the Russian government's interests around the world through various forms of intervention in their domestic politics (Harding 2017:148). Manafort was also for many years the campaign manager and senior advisor to former Ukrainian president Victor Yanukovich—a politician known for his pro-Russian tendencies for which, moreover, Russia intervened during the 2004 Ukrainian elections (Kuzio 2005). Financial records discovered recently by investigative journalists indicate that Manafort, after the overthrow of Yanukovich, had very big debts to Deripaska and was being sued by Deripaska over one failed investment Manafort conducted on Deripaska's behalf. Manafort was quite anxious to get rid of these debts and to convince Deripaska to drop the lawsuit.[37]

Subsequent investigations have found that during his time with the Trump campaign Manafort was secretly sending internal Trump campaign information, such as internal polls, to Deripaska. He transferred this information to Deripaska through an employee in his consulting firm, Konstantin Kilimnik, who U.S. intelligence agencies have found to have close ties to Russian intelligence services (Mueller report I:129–130, 133). During one pre-election meeting between Manafort and Kilimnik, in August 2016, the latter discussed what may have been part of a possible quid pro quo—a request for U.S. government support, if Trump were elected, for a Ukrainian peace plan, ostensibly being secretly proposed by Yanukovich (by 2016 living in exile in Russia), under which Russia would be able to continue to de facto dominate Eastern Ukraine through the creation of an autonomous republic in the Donbas (Mueller report I:138–140).

---

[36] For a confirmation of this informal role in August–November 2016 see email, Bannon to Kushner November 5, 2016 in CNN FOIA request (first installment 19-cv-1278).

[37] Mike McIntire, "Manafort Was in Debt to Pro-Russia Interests, Cyprus Records Show," *New York Times*, July 19, 2017; for the lawsuit, and Manafort's desire to get it dropped, see the Mueller report I:135–136).

During these investigations, Manafort was repeatedly caught lying, under oath, on key issues (such as this peace plan) which eventually led Mueller to revoke a plea bargain he had signed with Manafort (Mueller report I:130).

There is also some evidence of Manafort being directly involved before 2016 in a Russian partisan electoral intervention. According to one reliable report, Manafort's first involvement in Ukrainian politics occurred in December 2004 when he was brought in by a Ukrainian oligarch with close ties to the Kremlin (Rinat Akhmetov) in order to indirectly provide election advice to the Yanukovich campaign between the second and third rounds of the presidential elections (Harding 2017:148)—shortly after parts of the Russian covert intervention for Yanukovich were exposed by the "Orange" parties. If that was indeed the case, Manafort was a de facto contract employee of the Russian government for such foreign meddling.[38]

Each one of these senior members of the Trump campaign could have plausibly been on a Russian government's rolodex for this purpose—or would have had the needed ties to effectively solicit such Russian aid on Trump's behalf. Likewise, Trump himself may have had by 2016 the contacts needed to directly arrange such aid and may have attempted to do so. From the limited information currently available about the Trump organization's international activities, in the decade prior to his presidential run a very large share of its international business dealings involved wealthy Russian businessmen, many with close ties to the Kremlin.[39] Furthermore, during the GOP primaries period, one of Trump's major business associates, Felix Sater, claimed, in private communications with Trump's lawyer Michael Cohen, that he had the ability to arrange contacts between Trump and senior Russian government officials, first for a building project in Moscow (Trump Tower Moscow) and then for his campaign—and he seems to have made some concrete efforts in this regard. Likewise, Cohen himself tried in the first half of 2016 to arrange such contacts with the Russian government, ostensibly for this construction project, and was caught lying under oath about their true extent (Mueller report I: section A1c).

As for the second pathway, we have at least one known meeting in which the possibility of such an electoral intervention was raised. From the currently available information about the June 9, 2016, Trump Tower meeting, senior members of the Trump campaign knowingly discussed the possibility of receiving

[38] Likewise, given Manafort's known record of highly unethical behavior, and his willingness to work with various shady leaders around the world, a record which led even many of his close former coworkers and friends to hesitate to defend him in public, Manafort is unlikely to have had any moral compunction about such collusion. Frank Foer, "Paul Manafort, American Hustler," *The Atlantic*, March 2018.

[39] Trump Jr., for example, claimed in a 2008 speech that "Russians make up a pretty disproportionate cross-section of a lot of our assets"; Michael Hirsh, "How Russian Money Helped Save Trump's Business," *Foreign Policy*, December 21, 2018.

assistance from the Russian government in regard to what became a part of this Russian intervention—the release of "incriminating" documents from the Clinton campaign. The person with whom the Trump campaign discussed it, a Russian lawyer called Natalia Veselnitskaya, had significant past ties to the Russian intelligence services, serving as a lawyer for the FSB for eight years in a Russian civil court case.[40] After repeated denials of any such connections, Veselnitskaya also later admitted to being during this period an informant for the Russian ministry of Justice.[41] These known ties, in turn, make the possibility that she was a "deniable" messenger of the Russian government, checking the Trump campaign's overall interest in such assistance before a more formal representative contacted it, quite plausible.[42] Furthermore, if Kilimnik, as believed by U.S. intelligence agencies, indeed has close ties to Russian intelligence (and was being utilized by Russia for this purpose), then his previously noted secret meeting with Manafort on the Ukrainian peace plan in August 2016 may well have been one of the "follow-up" meetings.[43]

Secondly, based on the emails released from the previously noted Trump Tower meeting, at least one senior member of the Trump campaign, Trump's son Donald Trump Jr., had no moral or other compunctions about collaborating with the Russian government for this purpose.[44] On other occasions, other senior members of the Trump campaign also showed a complete lack of compunctions in this regard (see, for example, Tur 2017:188–189).[45]

Third, there is some evidence that some senior members of the Trump campaign had advance knowledge of the coming of some of the leaks by Wikileaks.[46]

[40] Maria Tsvetkova and Jack Stubbs, "Exclusive: Moscow Lawyer Who Met Trump Jr. Had Russian Spy Agency as Client," *Reuters*, July 21, 2017.

[41] Andrew Kramer and Sharon LaFraniere, "Lawyer Who Was Said to Have Dirt on Clinton Had Closer Ties to Kremlin Than She Let On," *New York Times*, April 27, 2018; for the recent death in a mysterious helicopter accident of the Russian government prosecutor with whom she was in contact prior to this meeting see John Bowden, "Russian Official with Ties to Lawyer in Trump Tower Meeting Dies in Helicopter Crash," *The Hill*, October 4, 2018.

[42] Another participant in this meeting, a Washington lobbyist named Rinat Akhmetstein, claimed to be a former Russian intelligence officer and also had quite close ties to the Russian government (including to a former senior Putin advisor). Akhmetstein was, furthermore, involved in an email hacking case in his rather controversial past; "Lobbyist at Trump Campaign Meeting Has a Web of Russian Connections," *New York Times*, August 21, 2017.

[43] This meeting also included a detailed briefing by Manafort of the Trump campaign planned strategy, messaging, polling data, and what were the key "battleground" states in its view (Mueller report I:140).

[44] Jan Diehm and Sean O'Key, "The Email Exchange Trump Jr. Released, in Chronological Order," *CNN*, July 2017.

[45] For Trump's overall open willingness to accept such a foreign interference on his behalf see his interview with ABC News on June 11, 2019.

[46] At the time of the writing of this study there is an ongoing investigation of the possible ties of Roger Stone, a long-time confidant of Trump and a one-time member of the Trump campaign, to Wikileaks. Stone was recently convicted, among other things, for attempts to obstruct justice in regard to the Russiagate investigation. Some former members of the Trump campaign testified during Stone's November 2019 trial that they believe that Stone served as an informal contact person

For example, according to one testimony by a senior member of the campaign (Rick Gates), a few days after the July 2016 Democratic primaries leak (and the Democratic Party convention), Trump himself told him and other senior members of the campaign that additional releases of damaging information about Clinton from Wikileaks would occur before the elections. Likewise, according to Gates, the Republican National Committee seems to have been provided by someone in the Trump campaign with information about the exact timing in which new leaks would be occurring, information the RNC used in order to prepare in advance press releases and other materials designed to amplify their effects.[47]

Finally, preliminary in-depth analyses of the Russian fake news and propaganda campaign in the run-up to the 2016 election indicate that, despite some claims otherwise, it was well targeted (Jamieson 2018:131–135).[48] Likewise, it seems to have been well aligned with the main messages of the Trump general election campaign (ibid.:chap. 4). Given what we know about the Russian government, it is highly unlikely that it had the needed knowledge of domestic American politics to carry out such a targeted and well-aligned intervention without some "inside help" from the Trump campaign.

For example, by the early 2010s Vladimir Putin, despite a decade of heavy interactions with senior American politicians, and full access to classified Russian intelligence briefings, seemed to believe that the TV shows *House of Cards* and *Boss* were accurate descriptions of American politics. Indeed, he even recommended those two shows in 2013 to his new defense minister, Sergei Shoigu, as a way for him to better understand U.S. domestic politics (Zygar 2016:271–272). Other public comments by Putin showed similar ignorance of American politics.[49] Many Russian officials within the Russian government

with Wikileaks who provided the Trump campaign the confidential information it had about the forthcoming leaks; "What Roger Stone's trial revealed about Mueller and Trump," *CNN*, November 15, 2019. If Stone indeed served in that role, Wikileaks may have effectively become the "cutout" for that component of the Russian intervention—that is, a way for the Trump campaign to coordinate the releases of the hacked information without the risks involved in a meeting/contact with a representative of the Russian government for this purpose.

[47] Mueller Report I:5, 54; Gates FBI Interviews October 4, 2018 & October 25, 2018, both in CNN's FOIA request (19-cv-1278). The relevant sections in the testimonies and the report have been heavily redacted. According to Gates, as early as June 2016 the Trump campaign was designing a messaging strategy for exploiting the expected leaks from Wikileaks and was "very happy" when the democratic primaries leak came out in late July Gates FBI Interviews October 4, 2018 & October 25, 2018, both in CNN's FOIA request (19-cv-1278).

[48] Jamieson seems to believe that the source of this effective targeting was the material they hacked from the DNC as well as observation of American pundits' discussions of this election (2018:136–140). However, I am quite doubtful that this material, while useful, would have sufficed given the Russian ignorance of U.S. politics without close coordination with the Trump campaign that could help them decipher it and make sure that it conformed with its own campaign plans.

[49] See, for example, Leonid Bershidsky, "Putin Doesn't Get American Politics," *Bloomberg*, September 2, 2016.

nowadays, including those who were in charge of this operation, seemed to share Putin's deep ignorance of American politics. For example, according to one former employee, workers at the Internet Research Agency, the state-sponsored "troll factory" in St. Petersburg put in charge of producing the fake news and propaganda used by the Russian government in this intervention, were taught about U.S. politics by being shown multiple seasons of *House of Cards* in English.[50]

8.1.4 But What About the Mueller Report?

Given the amount of strong circumstantial evidence on this topic, it is very likely that such collusion had indeed occurred in the 2016 U.S. elections between the Russian government and the Trump campaign. Nevertheless, some readers may wonder about the Mueller report, which, following a nearly two-years-long investigation, cleared Trump and other senior members of the campaign from the related legal charges (such as conspiracy) and "did not establish that members of the Trump Campaign conspired or coordinated with the Russian government in its election interference activities" (Mueller report I:2).

However, when one carefully reads the report beyond this headline conclusion, it does not contradict the conclusion of the previous section. Mueller, as a lawyer and an experienced criminal prosecutor, focused on whether the evidence available for collusion could meet a high legal threshold—in other words whether, if he charged someone in the Trump campaign on the relevant legal charges (such as conspiracy) a jury would find the proof that he could provide for it sufficient to convict them of these charges. Being unable to find enough evidence to satisfy that legal standard, he decided not to press charges and to interpret the existing evidence in the most benign way possible. As Mueller openly noted on the second page of the report, "a statement that the investigation did not establish particular facts does not mean there was no evidence of those facts." The clearing of the Trump campaign in this report was in the legal, not the empirical, sense.[51]

Indeed, the report finds significant amounts of evidence for such collusion, the key parts of which were detailed in the preceding section. It also explicitly notes the large amounts of suspicious behavior by the prime suspects, including clear evidence of destruction of evidence (such as relevant communications) and

[50] Reid Standish, "'House of Cards' Is Credible. Just Ask the Russians, Chinese and Iranians," *Washington Post*, October 25, 2018.

[51] For a similar analysis by a prominent legal scholar see Stephen Legomsky in Sean Illing, "Does the Mueller Report Exonerate Trump? I Asked 12 Legal Experts," *Vox*, April 20, 2019. See also press conference, Robert Mueller, May 29, 2019.

attempts by multiple suspects to coordinate their testimonies (Mueller report I:10). Some prominent members of the Trump campaign (such as Manafort) were also, as noted, caught lying in sworn testimonies on key issues regarding whether and how collusion could have occurred. People who have "nothing to hide" in regard to collusion would be expected to behave rather differently.

Likewise, the Mueller report openly and frequently noted the severe limitations that the special counsel faced when they tried to collect evidence and cross-check testimonies—such as the use by key actors (such as Manafort and Wikileaks) of digital communication methods with encryption devices that U.S. intelligence agencies were unable to break (or with self-destructing messages), and the presence of many key witnesses outside of the U.S. (see, for example, Mueller report I:45–46, 130). Due to these factors, the Mueller report admits in its executive summary that "while this report embodies factual and legal determinations that the Office believes to be accurate and complete to the greatest extent possible, given these identified gaps, the Office cannot rule out the possibility that the unavailable information would shed additional light on (or cast in a new light) the events described in the report" (Mueller report I:10). Those are not the kinds of words written by a lawyer who believes in a certain suspect's innocence.

The inability of Mueller to find the smoking gun is not surprising given what we know about such electoral interventions. Two previous covert electoral interventions (Brazil 1962, Chile 1964) led to sufficient suspicions of shenanigans by some contemporaries that authorities in the targets opened official investigations in order to find out whether and what exact secret activities and foreign involvement actually occurred. While each uncovered some details about the assistance provided in those cases, neither of them was able to even expose the hidden foreign hand (Agee 1975).[52] Likewise, as I explained in a piece written long prior to the conclusion of the special counsel investigation (Levin 2018), the way in which such interventions are conducted in general, as well as the way the Mueller investigation was conducted, made it highly unlikely that it or investigations of this case in the near future would find unambiguous evidence for collusion. Such conclusive evidence will probably take a few decades to come out.

The electoral intervention cases discussed in this study (Chapter 3) are instructive in this regard. Many of the key documents which described the collusion between the U.S. government and the side it was assisting were among

[52] Likewise, a West German parliamentary investigative committee in 1973 failed to uncover a related covert operation—the joint Soviet/East German operation in which two members of the Bundestag were bribed to vote against a no-confidence motion in 1972, narrowly preventing Chancellor Willie Brandt's downfall (Shimer 2019).

the very last to be declassified, frequently not until two or three decades after the events in question.[53] Likewise, in some still highly sensitive covert intervention cases, such as the American intervention in the 1964 Chilean elections, key documents regarding the process of coordination and cooperation between the U.S. government and the Chilean Christian Democratic Party in this election remain classified. This is despite the passage of more than fifty years since the events in question and multiple Freedom of Information Act (FOIA) requests by the author and other interested scholars and journalists.

In some instances the U.S. government has gone even further. As the author discovered during a visit to the JFK Presidential Library for this purpose, no records were kept by the Kennedy administration of the two meetings between the leader of the Christian Democratic Party, Eduardo Frei, and President Kennedy. According to other reliable sources, these were meetings which probably involved discussions of such a future American intervention.

The Russian government, unlike its American counterpart, has currently no standardized declassification process for such internal government documents. Likewise, given the recent tendency of defecting Russian intelligence officers to die in various mysterious and unusual accidents, it will probably be a while before any Russian intelligence officers involved in this operation or with access to the GRU's classified documents on this intervention will dare to defect with new evidence in this regard. Likewise, given the highly charged and negative views of the Russian intervention within the American public,[54] any colluding members of the Trump campaign will probably not admit to it any time soon. Until then we will be forced to wait for the definitive answer.

8.2. The Effects of the Russian Intervention

8.2.1 But Did It Actually Matter?

Although there has been heavy interest in why Putin intervened, and whether Trump actively cooperated with him or not, there has been less discussion on whether the intervention played an important role in Trump's victory. Many

---

[53] Likewise, some relevant documents were only declassified following the author's request a few years ago. Furthermore, some relevant CIA documents, unless preserved among White House or State Department documents, are still unavailable as well.

[54] For example, one August 2017 Quinnipiac poll found that, although Americans are strongly divided along partisan lines on whether collusion actually occurred in practice, 79% see the known methods used by Russia in 2016 as "not acceptable." Accordingly, besides the possible legal consequences to such an admission, any confessing colluder will need to bear a significant social opprobrium. "Poll: Americans Split on Whether Trump Guilty of Wrong Doing in Connection to Russia," *Voice of America*, August 14, 2018.

people, it seems, believe that there is currently no way to find any useful evidence in this regard and that, accordingly, any debate on this question is pointless.[55] Among those political commentators and scholars who have publicly discussed it, with a few special exceptions (Enten 2016; Jamieson 2018; Ruck et al. 2019), most are very skeptical that the Russian intervention had any significant effect (see, e.g., Silver 2018; Jenkins 2018; Nyhan 2018; Sides, Tesler, and Vavereck 2018; Boxell Gentzkow and Shapiro 2018; Guess, Nagler and Tucker 2019).

This conventional wisdom is not unwarranted. Although, as noted in Chapter 6, such interventions usually have significant effects on election results, in the specific case of the 2016 U.S. elections we have two good reasons to be skeptical of it having had any real consequences. First, this intervention was designed to be covert—a usually less effective form of electoral intervention. Second, and more important, the 2016 Russian intervention suffered from a major operational failure. In other words, clear evidence of the Russian government's involvement in the hacking and release of emails from the DNC and the Clinton campaign became public knowledge in the U.S. prior to election day—something that was not part of the Russian intervention plan.[56] To paraphrase a famous quote on Watergate, it was a third-rate electoral meddling attempt. Interventions with major operational failures would be expected to be less effective overall than ones that worked in the planned manner. More specifically, widespread knowledge of the hostile foreign source of the leaks, a country (and leader) already deeply disliked in 2016 by many Americans,[57] could lead many people to distrust and ignore them in making their voting choices. Indeed, this aspect of the Russian intervention was one key reason why the author, in an op-ed written three months before the elections on this topic (Levin 2016b), expected this Russian intervention to have no effect either way.

However, the 2016 election was very close—far closer than nearly everyone (including the author) at the time anticipated, with Trump winning the electoral college with 77,744 votes in three states and Clinton winning the overall popular vote by only 2.1%. In such a close race, even an electoral intervention with major operational failures could nevertheless have had an important impact on the final results.

---

[55] Christian Caryl, "There's a Way to Know If Russia Threw the Election to Trump," *Washington Post*, January 11, 2018.

[56] As noted in Chapter 5, this kind of operational failure is very rare. For the extensive efforts by the Russian secret operatives to cover their tracks see the Mueller indictment. If the intervention was meant to be exposed, as some have speculated, prior to the elections one would have not expected such significant attempts at hiding it. Likewise, from what is currently known about the electoral intervention cases in PEIG I could not find a single case where that was part of the intervention plan (i.e., it was supposed to be "unintentionally" exposed).

[57] In February 2016, for example, a Gallup poll found that 65% of Americans had a very or mostly unfavorably view of Russia (Roper iPoll database USGALLUP.021816.R18S).

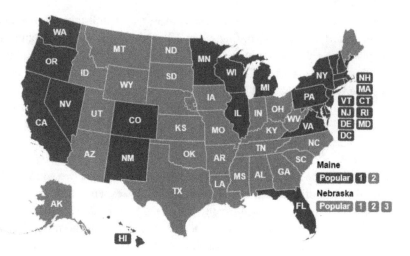

Figure 8.1 The 2016 U.S. election EC results in the absence of the Russian intervention—uniform swing assumption (black = Clinton; grey = Trump). Maps generated, with permission, utilizing the EC map generator at https://electoralvotemap.com/.

Accordingly, in order to estimate the effects of the Russian intervention I first reran the statistical model and data that I used in Chapter 6—but now with the addition of the case of the 2016 U.S. election. Then, in the same manner as I had done for other specific intervention cases in Table 6.1, I estimated the predicted effect of this intervention case on the election results. Based on that estimate, I would expect Clinton, in the absence of the Russian intervention against her, to have won the popular vote over Trump by 4.13%, or 2.03% more votes than she did in 2016.

Assuming a uniform swing, such a popular vote victory would lead four states with 75 EC votes to shift from Trump to Clinton, leading her to a decisive victory in the electoral college as well, 307 to 231 (Figure 8.1)—this due to victories in four additional states (Florida, Wisconsin, Michigan, and Pennsylvania). Of course, given the variance in preexisting partisan dispositions of different U.S. states, the overall swing may not have uniform effects in practice. Using the Cook Report's state-level partisan voting index for 2016 (a standard political analysis tool) in order to account for such state-level differences, I would expect such a popular vote victory to lead Clinton to an even larger electoral college victory, 352 to 186 (Figure 8.2)—with Clinton gaining also state-level victories in North Carolina, Ohio, and the second congressional district of Maine.[58]

---

[58] Maine was one of only two states (other than Nebraska) in 2016 that gave out its electoral college

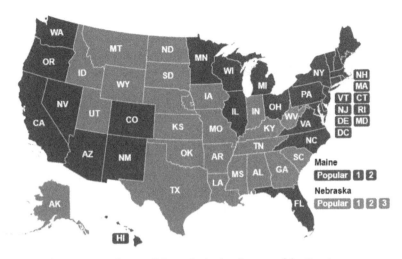

Figure 8.2 The 2016 U.S. election EC results in the absence of the Russian intervention—non-uniform swing estimation (Cook 2016 PVI) (black = Clinton grey = Trump).

Accordingly, without the Russian electoral intervention standing in her way, my statistical model of the effects of such interventions from Chapter 6 would predict a decisive popular vote victory and a large electoral college victory by Clinton—in line with most people's expectations in the run-up to the election.

Naturally, many will wonder whether an estimate derived from an aggregate analysis of electoral intervention cases from around the world actually reflects the specific true effects of this particular Russian intervention. To examine this potential issue I looked for, as in the case in Chapter 7, pre-election evidence for the effects of the main observable component of this Russian intervention—the multiple mass leaks of emails and documents from the DNC and from senior members in the Clinton campaign in July–October 2016.[59] Rather surprisingly, despite the heavy media coverage that these leaks got, and the extremely heavy polling that occurs nowadays in the run-up to American presidential elections, only a handful of pre-election polls asked any relevant questions in their regard. Furthermore, despite strenuous efforts, the underlying data for most of these

votes by congressional district.

[59] Besides the leaks designed to affect public perceptions of Clinton, some leaks (like those of highly personal information of donors and of DNC and Clinton campaign workers) were clearly designed to disrupt the Clinton campaign's ability to function effectively in the run-up to the elections and to discourage donations to it. Another known component was the (in)famous fake news and propaganda campaign via social media.

surveys could not be accessed in practice, with many of the conductors of these surveys being unable to provide them due to various confidentiality agreements. All I was able to locate from some of these surveys were a few crosstabs and marginals. Nevertheless, I eventually located the underlying data for two of these surveys and analyzed it.

8.2.2 Survey Number 1: The Ghost of Bernie Sanders

The first survey was designed by Shaw & Co. Research and Anderson Robbins Research for Fox News. It was conducted between July 31 and August 2, 2016, or the immediate aftermath of the Democratic Party convention, among a nationally representative sample of 1,022 registered voters in the United States. Of this sample, 45.5% were contacted through landlines and the remainder were contacted through cell phones.[60]

Ten days prior to the conduct of this survey, on the eve of the Democratic Party convention, Wikileaks released its first set of emails and documents hacked from the DNC. One of the main components of this set of leaked documents was a collection of emails between senior DNC operatives that were seen by many people as clear evidence that the DNC, as claimed by Sanders a few times during the primary, was strongly biased against the Sanders campaign and was looking for ways to damage his campaign and force him to quit the race.[61] The Shaw and Anderson survey, attempting to analyze the effects of various factors and some recent events on the forthcoming election, asked respondents a question which can serve as a useful proxy to the effect of these revelations about the 2016 Democratic Party primaries on voters' behavior. This question, after telling respondents about this aspect of the leak, then asked them which of the following three options were closest to their views: the Democratic party primaries were fair and Clinton was the legitimate choice of Democratic voters, the primaries were rigged but Clinton would have won anyway, or the primaries were rigged and that led Clinton to win. I then coded a trichotomous measure coded as 1 if they thought it was fair, 2 if they thought it was rigged but the rigging hadn't had a major effect, and 3 if they thought that it was rigged and that was why Clinton had won.[62]

---

[60] The interviewing was conducted by Braun Research, Inc. I thank Prof. Daron Shaw and Ms. Dana Blanton of Fox News for kindly agreeing to provide the underlying data of this survey via the Roper Center iPoll databank.

[61] The DNC eventually issued an apology to Sanders, and the then-head of the DNC, Debbie Wasserman Schultz, as well as three other senior DNC officials, resigned shortly afterward as a result.

[62] The results are effectively the same if I instead turn it into a dichotomous measure with 1 for those who thought it was fair and 0 otherwise.

I also utilized an earlier question in this survey, asking respondents about their voting intentions to construct a dichotomous dependent variable—coded as 1 for respondents who indicated their intention to vote for Clinton and 0 for respondents who noted any other choices. Aside from being a common way of modeling vote choice in such situations, given that this particular intervention method (as most dirty tricks) was designed to directly reduce Clinton's vote share, regardless of these votes' eventual direction, it also checks directly whether it had worked in the desired manner. To analyze the effects of these two leaks, I used probit and included other factors which were available in this survey which could have affected vote choice in this election such as whether the respondent was white or not, their gender, and so forth. A detailed explanation of the operationalization of each variable and the reason for its inclusion can be seen in Appendix G.

As can be seen in Figure 8.3, respondents' views of whether the Democratic Party's primaries were rigged and what effect that had had on its results had a major effect on their voting intentions, with every one-level increase decreasing their probability of voting for Clinton by 11.1%. This is clearly not a statistical fluke—overall on this question only 37% of respondents thought, after this leak, that the Democratic primaries were fair (46.6% when Republicans were excluded). In subsequent analysis I found no significant differences in the

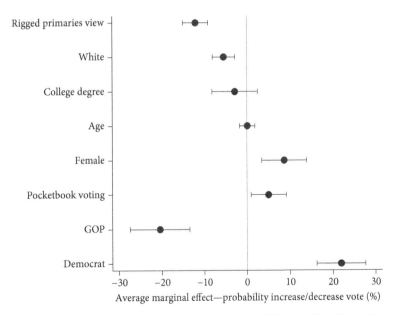

Figure 8.3 Survey 1, 2016 U.S. elections vote choice model. Note: Variables with negative effects reduce the probability of voting for Clinton and vice versa.

effects of their views on these primaries between Democrats, Republicans, and independents (see Appendix G).

Some subsequent robustness checks, such as for the inclusion of a measure of approval of President Obama, reduce the substantive strength of this effect by between one-third and four-tenths—with the inclusion of this measure, for example, reducing its effect to only 7.9%. Nevertheless, the effects of these views about the primaries always remain highly significant statistically. Likewise, even this reduced substantive effect is on par with other major factors measured, such as the effect of their personal economic situation (a 5% increase of their probability of voting for Clinton). Accordingly, this result is consistent with the idea that the Russians may indeed have achieved their primary goal—harming Clinton's electoral chances by creating a dark cloud over her victory in the primaries.

8.2.3 Survey Number 2: A Tale of Two Leaks

The second useful pre-election survey is the October 2016 Monmouth University National Poll. This survey was carried out between October 14 and 16 (or three weeks before election day) among a nationally representative sample of 805 registered voters in the U.S. Half of the sample was contacted through landlines and the remainder was contacted through cell phones.[63]

The Monmouth survey, as part of an attempt to predict the results of the forthcoming elections, asked respondents a question about one of the main leaks of a tranche of hacked documents made public a few days earlier via Wikileaks. One of the key components of this tranche were the texts of paid, closed-door speeches from 2013 and 2014 that Hillary Clinton had given in the past to various American corporations. Some parts of these speeches included major supposed contradictions between the views expressed in these speeches and the positions taken by her during the campaign—such as on immigration and on the regulation of the financial industry. The Clinton campaign had repeatedly refused to release the texts of these speeches in the past, finding in an internal review some segments to be potentially embarrassing.

The question in this survey first told the respondents that the text of some of the speeches Clinton gave to Wall Street firms and other businesses were recently revealed by Wikileaks and then asked them if they had "read or heard anything

---

[63] To increase the chances of contacting registered voters, half of the people surveyed (200 in each method) were identified as registered voters through the use of a voter file. The remainder were contacted through random digit dialing. Poll data downloaded from the Roper Center iPoll databank.

about this? " Those who answered in the affirmative were then asked whether they had "actually read or heard some of the things she actually said in those speeches, or did you just hear that Wikileaks had released the speeches?." This compound question accordingly gave the respondents the options of admitting to having not heard about it, of just having heard that Wikileaks had released the speeches, or to having "read or heard some of the things she [Clinton] actually said." To check for the direct effect of the exposure to this component of the Russian intervention on the respondents' subsequent vote choice, I then coded a dummy variable with the respondents who said that they had read or heard of the things noted in this leak coded as 1 and all other respondents otherwise as 0. This is my main indicator of the effects of this component of the Russian electoral intervention on voter behavior.[64]

The Monmouth survey also asked respondents about a second major leak of domestic origins—the so-called *Access Hollywood* tape. This tape, leaked by the producers of this entertainment show to the *Washington Post*, recorded a lewd conversation in 2005 between Trump and the show's host at the time, Billy Bush, on their way to filming one of the episodes. This recording had Trump boasting about his supposed sexual exploits toward other women and his plan to forcibly kiss a woman that they were about to meet.[65] In a manner similar to the question about Wikileaks, this question first told the respondents about the tape and then asked them if they had heard about it. Those who answered in the affirmative were then asked whether they had "watched or listened to the actual recording or did you just hear or read reports about what he [Trump] said. " To check for the direct effect of exposure to this domestic leak on the respondents' subsequent vote choice, I coded a second dummy variable, with the respondents who said that they had watched or listened to this tape coded as 1 and all other respondents otherwise as 0.

Both the audio of the *Access Hollywood* tape and this tranche of leaks by Wikileaks were made public a few hours apart from each other on the same day, October 7, 2016, the latter leaked at this time in an attempt to counteract the potential effects of the former.[66] Accordingly, the inclusion of measures for these two leaks can give us an idea of the overall effects of both of them as

---

[64] A similar result is found when I code it as a trichotomous variable with someone who merely heard about this leak as the middle category—although, not surprisingly, most of the substantive effect comes from the fully treated group (i.e., those who actually heard or read some of the things Clinton said).

[65] In a rare exception for Trump, the exposure of the *Hollywood Access* tape led to an outright apology the next day by Trump himself for his words in it—a testimony to how bad the effects of this tape were perceived to be by his campaign. Other senior Republicans (such as the late senator John McCain) removed their endorsements of Trump in the following days.

[66] According to Gates, the Trump campaign had advance knowledge about the release of the (domestic) *Access Hollywood* leak from a reporter; Gates FBI Interview October 25, 2018 CNN FOIA request (19-cv-1278).

well as whether this aspect of the Russian intervention also achieved this tactical task. Both leaks received wide direct exposure within the sample—43.5% of respondents indicated that they had read or heard some of the things that Clinton said in these speeches, and 56.4% of respondents indicated that they had watched or listened to the actual *Hollywood Access* tape.

Just like in survey 1, I then utilized an earlier question in this survey asking respondents about their voting intentions in order to construct a dichotomous dependent variable—coded as 1 for respondents who indicated their intention to vote for Clinton and 0 for respondents who noted any other choices. Then I analyzed this survey using a similar approach where possible to that of survey 1. A detailed explanation of the operationalization of each variable and the reason for its inclusion can be seen in Appendix G.

In the first model (Figure 8.4), I include the measures of both leaks in the model. As can be seen in Figure 8.4, the *Access Hollywood* leak had major effects on those who were directly exposed to it, increasing their probability of voting for Clinton by 11.1%. This effect is on par with other major factors in the model that increased chances of voting for Clinton—such as having a college degree (9.7% increased probability). From subsequent tests, I find that the effect of this tape was not limited to Democrats but was significant also among Republicans

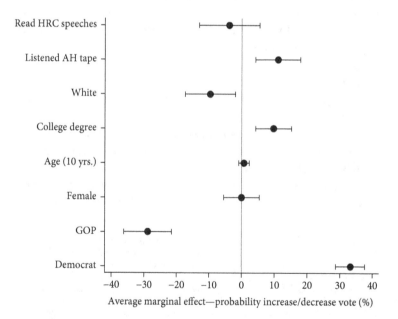

Figure 8.4 Survey 2, Model 1, 2016 U.S. elections vote choice: no interactions.
Note: Variables with negative effects reduce the probability of voting for Clinton and vice versa.

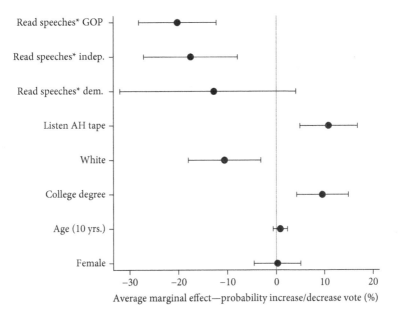

Figure 8.5 Survey 2, Model 2, 2016 U.S. elections vote choice: interactions with party IDs. Note: Variables with negative effects reduce the probability of voting for Clinton and vice versa. The main effects of interactions are included in the statistical model but are excluded from the figure for clarity.

and independents at similar magnitudes.[67] Contemporaries who expected the exposure of this tape to inflict serious political damage on Trump throughout the American electorate were fully justified in this regard.

In contrast, the effect of the Clinton speeches leak, while in the expected direction, is insignificant. This, however, is due to the differing effects by party. It is also the result of a small group of independents in which backlash effects to this intervention can be observed (see Appendix G).

When I check for separate effects by party identification (Figure 8.5), a different picture emerges. The speeches had no significant effects on Democratic respondents. However, they had major significant effects on most independents and Republicans—reducing their probability of voting for Clinton by 17.6% and 20.2%, respectively. Using the data available on the true composition of the 2016 U.S. electorate to estimate the overall effect, and controlling for a backlash effect

[67] Interactions between this measure and dummies for these three parties do not find, unlike in the case of this leak by Wikileaks, any significant differences in the effects by party identification (see Appendix G).

among some independents,[68] that translates to at least a 5.6% overall reduced voting probability for Clinton from that important (but still only one component of a whole set of pre-election leaks) leak. Similar results are found when I restrict the sample to only likely voters as well as control for other possible factors, such as for measures of voter evaluations of Trump's and Clinton's characters or for income (see Appendix G).

In a head-to-head comparison, the Clinton speeches leak negated at least 50.5% of the overall effect of the *Access Hollywood* leak. Among most independents and Republicans the speeches completely overwhelmed the effects of the tape, leaving them overall somewhat less inclined to vote for Clinton (by 5.1% and 7.7%, respectively). The Russians succeeded not just in their overall goal in this particular leak but also to a large extent in the tactical goal of blunting the effects of the *Hollywood Access* tape.[69]

One must note, of course, some important qualifiers in regard to these results on both surveys. The first survey was conducted almost three-and-a-half months prior to election day—so the effects of the Democratic primaries leak could have faded, in part or in full, in the highly eventful interim. As for the second survey used here, it unfortunately lacked questions on other issues which usually greatly matter to the American electorate such as the perceived situation of the economy (or of their own economic welfare), their approval of the incumbent president, or other issues that were of great interest to key parts of the electorate in this election (such as terrorism by Jihadi groups). Controlling for these factors may have affected the magnitude of the substantive effects or even the statistical significance of the effects found here. Likewise, although the second survey was conducted only three weeks before the elections, it cannot, of course, take into account another last-moment "bombshell"—the letter to Congress by the then–FBI director James Comey in late October 2016 temporarily reopening

---

[68] A post-election examination by Pew Research Center (2018), based upon a post-election survey of confirmed voters from voter files, estimates that in 2016 approximately 35% of the electorate were Democrats, 31% were Republicans, and the remainder were independent. Naturally, if this and other such leaks also reduced turnout by some potential Clinton-leaning independents or Democrats, the effect could have been even larger.

[69] Sides et al. (2018: 198–200) seem to have based their conclusions that these Russian leaks had no significant effects mainly on an analysis of a six-wave poll by Rand in which similar questions were asked on every wave (PEPS). However, that poll, as well as the other polls that they used, lacked any specific questions on these Russian leaks. Such a measurement technique would have great difficulty capturing this part of the intervention given its nature—multiple leaks intentionally spread out throughout the four-and-a-half months prior to election day, and with the most important leaks (the speeches and the primaries-rigging evidence) coinciding with major events that would be expected to boost Clinton (the convention and the *Access Hollywood* tape). Simply put, a longitudinal study of this kind would have a big difficulty parsing out such chronologically close events with opposite effects. As a result, although their book is an impressive study of the domestic factors that enabled Trump's surprising victory, when it comes to estimating the effects of this intervention the technique used here (surveys with such questions) is more reliable.

the investigation in regard to Clinton's emails from her time as Secretary of State. With these qualifiers kept in mind, the results of these two surveys nevertheless provide a strong indication that the large-N results indeed reflect what was happening "on the ground" in the U.S. prior to the elections.[70]

8.2.4 Other Indicators

Aside from these statistical analyses, we also have other indications that these statistical results indeed reflect the respondents' (and the U.S. public's) true behavior and attitudes. In a follow-up question to the survey by Monmouth, 40.4% of those who were directly exposed to the Clinton speeches leak said that it led them to think less highly of Clinton. Similar results were found in another survey conducted by Suffolk University for *USA Today* a week later (October 20–24) for which, unfortunately, only the marginals and crosstabs are available. The question in this survey briefly described the Clinton speeches leak and then asked respondents whether it made them "more likely or less likely to support her." Of all respondents, 36.7% said it would make them less likely, with even higher proportions among independents (40%) and Republicans (67%).[71] A subsequent question asking respondents about other leaked emails showing supposedly problematic ties between the Clinton Foundation and foreign countries during Clinton's term as secretary of state also showed negative effects of these emails; 56.2% of respondents said that this leak raised questions about conflicts of interest for Clinton if she were elected, with even higher proportions among independents (59%) and Republicans (87%).

We also have some direct evidence from voter behavior about their actual interest in these leaks—Google keyword search terms within the U.S. This is an increasingly used tool among political scientists (see, e.g., Pelc 2013) and political analysts to gauge voters' actual interest in various topics and candidates. As can be seen in Figure 8.6, the leaks of the material stolen by Russia via Wikileaks led to a great increase in the amounts of keyword searches for "Wikileaks" between

---

[70] Jamieson (2018) reaches similar conclusions to those of the author (i.e., that the intervention greatly aided Trump), but the focus in her study is largely on the effects of the production of the fake news and propaganda rather than on the leaks. Likewise, the limited analysis of the effects of the leaks is mostly on the second-order effects (such as on some presidential debate questions). I also utilize different tools to analyze this question, with Jamieson using in a manner similar to Sides et al. (2018), surveys that do not ask voters questions which are directly related to the leaks in question. Accordingly my analyses are, to a large extent, analyzing different components of the same electoral intervention with different methods and thus complement each other. Similarly, other recent research on the effects of the Russian intervention in 2016 (see, e.g., Ruck et al. 2019) has focused thus far on the fake news and propaganda component of it.

[71] Unlike the Monmouth survey, the Suffolk survey didn't try to check for prior knowledge of this leak among respondents.

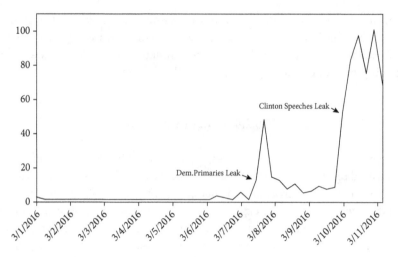

Figure 8.6 Trends in keyword searches for "Wikileaks" in the U.S., January 1–November 12, 2016 (1 being the lowest number of searches in the period, and 100 being the highest).

July and early November 2016, with three peaks of interest in the last week of July, the third week of October, and the first week of November. One should note that this is despite Wikileaks having already, due to past unrelated leaks, a well-established "brand name" within the American public.

Of course, these trend metrics do not provide numbers, only relative proportions. However, we can get a rough estimate of the actual number of searches occurring in the U.S. from another Google service (Google keyword planner) which, using the same underlying Google search data, provides users with range estimates of the average number of monthly searches in each month for particular keywords. It can also, unlike Google Trends, provide granular state-level data.

As can be seen in Figure 8.7, in the first five months prior to the start of the 2016 election leaks, "Wikileaks" was being searched, on average every month, between ten thousand and one hundred thousand times in the United States. In June, the mere promise of such future leaks by Assange was enough to lead to an increase in keyword searches for "Wikileaks" in the U.S. Then, in July 2016, with the start of the wave of leaks through Wikileaks (the primaries leaks), the number of searches for that term jumped by two orders of magnitude, to one million to ten million searches in three of the following four months.

Similar patterns can be seen in the three swing states (Pennsylvania, Wisconsin, and Michigan) which gave Trump his Electoral College victory by a mere 77,744 votes. In October 2016 alone, as many Americans were making their

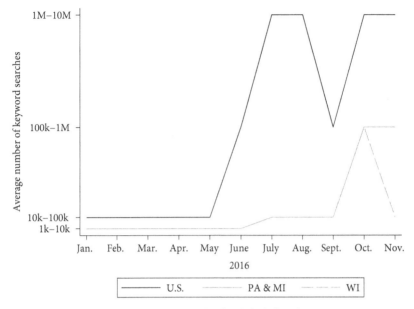

Figure 8.7 Number of keyword searches for "Wikileaks" in the U.S., January–November 2016.

final voting decisions, somewhere between one hundred thousand and one million searches were conducted in each of these three states for "Wikileaks"—three states, one must remember, with between three million (Wisconsin) and six million (Pennsylvania) voters.[72]

One should also note that this particular keyword was just one of the major terms used by Americans to look for the hacked documents. For example, the keyword "Podesta emails" alone (the emails leaked in October 2016 in which the Clinton speeches were found), was searched between one hundred thousand and one million times in October 2016. Accordingly, the measures for searches for "Wikileaks" shown here are *the lower bound* of overall interest in these stolen documents.

8.3 Conclusions

As could be seen in this chapter, what is currently known about what led to the Russian intervention, and the effects it had on the results, were in line with my

---

[72] Similar patterns were also found for Florida.

theoretical framework and my findings in other past cases. Although it involved a different foreign power (Russia), the factors and process by which this electoral intervention occurred was quite similar to the cases of American interventions analyzed in Chapter 3. The Russian government seems to have become interested in intervening against Clinton in the 2016 elections due to their perception of her as an "existential threat"—an American politician who perceived Russia (and Putin) as a dangerous foe and who was seen as highly committed to enacting aggressive policies against it if elected as president.

At the same time the assisted candidate, Donald Trump, was a weak loser. In other words, Trump was a candidate who won the GOP primaries through a large amount of luck and started the general election campaign with historically unprecedented levels of unfavorability, severe resource disadvantages, a divided party rank and file, and a hostile party establishment. This, in turn, led to a widespread perception of Trump, including within his own campaign, as standing little to no chance of winning against Clinton.

While no "smoking gun" yet exists to prove incontrovertibly the existence of collusion between the Trump campaign and Russia, the already available circumstantial evidence in this regard indicates that it is highly likely that such collusion had indeed occurred through one or more senior members of the campaign. However, given what we know about the time it took for the relevant information in past intervention cases to become public, it will probably take a while until the "smoking gun" is discovered.

As for the effects of this intervention on the results, I estimated, using my model of such interventions from Chapter 6, the effects of this intervention to have been large enough to have led Clinton to lose at least 75 EC votes: the states of Wisconsin, Pennsylvania, Michigan, and Florida—enough to have caused her loss in the electoral college. The available local level data (such as pre-election surveys with relevant questions), on one of its main parts, the multiple DNC and Clinton campaign document leaks, is consistent with this conclusion.

The mere direct exposure to the leak by Wikileaks in October 2016 about Hillary Clinton's paid speeches was sufficient to significantly reduce the probability of voting for her among independents and Republicans (by −17.6% and −20.2%, respectively) and counteracted at least half of the pro-Clinton effects of the *Access Hollywood* tape. Likewise, one belief about Clinton that the first leak by Wikileaks (July 2016) tried to directly affect, that she supposedly won the Democratic nomination with the assistance of underhanded means, significantly decreased (−11.1%) the probability of Americans from all parts of the political spectrum to vote for her. While some preliminary evidence was found that by October 2016 the growing credible public evidence of the Russian source of these leaks began to reduce its effectiveness, its effects overall likely gave a significant advantage to the Trump campaign.

I have also found clear evidence that these survey responses reflected strong, widespread interest within the U.S. in the run-up to this election in this leaked information with tens of millions of searches for these documents. Most importantly, interest in this information was also widespread in the three key swing states that gave trump his electoral college victory, with hundreds of thousands of searches in each state in the five months prior to election day.

Naturally, these results shouldn't be taken as evidence that the Russian intervention was the only factor that "mattered." Other fully domestic factors, such as the failure of the Clinton campaign to pay sufficient attention to the Midwest,[73] the growing political salience of identity-related issues and Trump's success in exploiting them (Sides et al. 2018), as well as a regional recession that hit parts of the U.S. in 2015 and 2016[74] probably all played important roles as well in Trump's narrow surprise victory. Nevertheless, these results and the available information provide strong evidence that the Russian intervention had a key role in determining the identity of the winner in the 2016 U.S. elections. Like in many other such past cases of partisan electoral interventions, the Russian intervention is likely to have been a hinge of history which enabled Trump to become the forty-fifth president of the United States, with yet to be determined medium- and long-term effects on it and on the world as a whole.

---

[73] Edward-Isaac Dovere, "How Clinton Lost Michigan—and Blew the Election," *Politico*, December 14, 2016.
[74] Neil Irwin, "The Most Important Least-Noticed Economic Event of the Decade," *New York Times*, September 29, 2018.

9

Conclusions

What has been is what will be again, what has been done will be done
again. There is nothing new under the sun.

—Ecclesiastes 1:9

This book has focused on partisan electoral interventions, offering for the first
time a theoretical framework to explain their occurrence as a separate, discrete
phenomenon and investigating their effects on the intervened election results.
As could be seen in this study, electoral interventions have long played an important role in great power politics as a major policy tool for dealing with countries
with relatively free elections, with one out of every nine elections being the target
of such American or Russian/Soviet meddling since the end of WW2. The newfound prominence of such meddling in the aftermath of the 2016 U.S. elections
has been largely due to the sudden detection by many of a common phenomenon of international politics rather than the emergence of something new or
unprecedented. Indeed, even its one truly novel feature, the use of cyberwarfare
tools, was largely the digitization of an age-old method of electoral intervention
(i.e., "dirty tricks").

As could be seen in Chapter 5, even during the supposed "vacation from history" of the 1990s, electoral interventions continued to be frequently done by
the great powers. As this manuscript is being completed, great power competition, in tow with escalating threat perceptions, seems to be slowly returning to
prominence. This is concurrent with a rising global trend of political dealign-
ment, even within many established democracies, with the sudden decline of
many prominent, long-established parties and the rise of many new parties and
candidates which are seen by the local political establishment as "unacceptable."
Given the findings here on the causes of electoral interventions, these two concurrent trends virtually guarantee that such meddling will continue and become,
if anything, even more frequent in the near future. Given my results here about
the effects of such interventions, the great powers are likely to succeed in many
cases in winning the election for their preferred side, enabling them to gain or
keep executive power. The wheel will continue to turn, with no break in sight.

These historical and likely future trends make the understanding and further
study of partisan electoral interventions of great importance. Accordingly, this

Meddling in the Ballot Box. Dov H. Levin, Oxford University Press (2020). © Oxford University Press.
DOI: 10.1093/oso/9780197519882.001.0001.

chapter first summarizes the key empirical findings of this study and assesses the overall support for my arguments. The following section discusses the implications to other scholarly subfields. The third section describes the policy implications of my research to cybersecurity, discussing the next ways in which electoral interventions could be digitized and how to prevent cyberspace from inadvertently bringing back a pre-modern, even more dangerous form of intervention—meddling in the vote tallies. Then I conclude with possible venues for further inquiry on this topic.

9.1 Summary of Key Findings

The first research question of this study focused on why electoral interventions occurred. I found that electoral interventions are "inside jobs," occurring only if a significant domestic actor within the target wants, or is willing, to be aided in this manner by a great power. Without such an actor being available and accordingly willing and able to provide the would-be intervener with its private information on how to win the election, the chances of an electoral intervention succeeding are very low, making an intervention an infeasible option to the great power. Given the significant potential or immediate costs that such interventions can impose on the domestic actor, they are usually requested or accepted by it when they are, prior to the start of the intervention, in serious domestic political trouble, with strong reasons to believe that they will not win (or be permitted to win) an election in the short to medium term (blocked/weakening loser) or, if in office, that they will soon lose power and not regain it any time soon (fragile victor).

I also found electoral interventions to require that the would-be intervener sees its interests as being severely endangered by another significant candidate or party within the target with very different and inflexible preferences on the relevant issues. Without such a situation occurring, the costs that such interventions usually have for the intervener, as well as the fear of making a merely unfriendly domestic actor into a full-fledged enemy, will usually discourage the would-be intervener from intervening in this manner.

Support for this theory comes in three different forms. The first is a proxy of one of the key conditions (interest in getting aid)—in other words, whether the supported candidate and/or party is a fragile victor or a blocked/weakening loser. Overall, out of the 114 intervention cases in PEIG in which enough data is available for this purpose, 76.3% of the receivers of such support fit these criteria (see Chapter 5). The second are the statistical tests of some of the arguments about the effects of electoral interventions. Hypotheses 4, 5, and 6 were directly

Table 9.1 Causes Argument Summary (H1–H3): Theoretical Predictions, Case Studies, and Results

		GP Sees Implacable Actor B	
		Yes	No
Actor A Wants Aid	Yes	Electoral Intervention Likely Case Studies: W. Germany 1953, Guatemala 1958, Argentina 1946, U.S. 2016 Argument supported: yes	No Electoral Interventions Any requests of assistance are rejected by GP Case Study: Philippines 1965 Argument supported: yes
	No	No Electoral Interventions Any offers of interventions are rejected by would-be partner Case Study: Venezuela 1958 Argument supported: yes	No Electoral Interventions Case Study: Greece 1967 Argument supported: yes

derived from this theoretical framework—so their confirmation (see Chapter 6) provides indirect yet strong statistical support.

The third and most important line of evidence is the in-depth archival analysis of six cases in which an electoral intervention was being seriously considered by a great power chosen out of PEIG (Chapters 4 and 5). To this is added a preliminary analysis of a seventh "out-of-sample" case—the Russian intervention in the 2016 U.S. elections. As can be seen in Tables 9.1 and 9.2, the results from all cases supported this theoretical framework, with the six historical case studies in full conformance to my theoretical predictions and the recent out-of-sample case (U.S. 2016) supporting three of the four theoretical expectations in full and providing only preliminary support for the fourth prediction (e.g., collusion). The support from these three lines of evidence stands in contrast to the lack of support found here for approaches that merely aggregated electoral interventions with other, unrelated phenomena.

My second research question focused on what effects electoral interventions have on the intervened election results and what factors determine its nature and magnitude. I discovered that electoral interventions usually significantly increase the electoral chances of the aided candidate. This is the result of electoral interventions usually occurring in marginal elections where the resources provided by the intervener are more likely to make a difference. I also find (H5), in contrast to a widespread viewpoint that holds that any *public* foreign intervention of any kind in domestic affairs is bound to fail, that *overt* electoral interventions are *more* effective than covert interventions, giving a significantly bigger vote share boost on average to the assisted side. This is due to the great power usually

Table 9.2 Causes of Electoral Intervention Argument (H1–H3): Full Summary of Key Aspects of Case Studies and Support of Theory

Case Study	Assisted Actor Wants/ Requests Aid	Domestic Political Situation of Would-Be Assisted Actor	GP Sees Implacable Actor	Collusion during Intervention (If Occurs)?	Support of Theory?
West Germany 1953	Yes—request by Adenauer	Fragile Victor	Yes—SDP/ Ollenhauer	Yes—all five main int. methods result of an Adenauer proposal and/ or closely coordinated/ deployed w/him	Yes
Guatemala 1958	Yes—request by Cruz Salazar (& Peralta)	Blocked/ weakened loser (both requestors)	Yes (after annulment of 1957 election)— PR	Yes—aid type (campaign funding) requested by Cruz Salazar & provided w/his knowledge	Yes
Argentina 1946	Yes— request by democratic opp.	Blocked/ weakened loser	Yes—Peron/ GOU	Yes—aid type (dirty tricks) proposed by & deployed in requested manner by opp.	Yes
Philippines 1965	Yes—request by PPP	Blocked/ weakened loser	No	No intervention	Yes
Venezuela 1958	No— rejection of U.S. offer by Betancourt	Good/likely winner (after Sept. 1958)	Yes (after Oct. '58)— Larrazabal	No intervention	Yes
Greece 1967	No—prefers other domestic options	Bad/weak—but full extent unclear	No	No intervention	Yes
U.S. 2016	Yes—Trump Tower meeting, etc.	Blocked/ weakened loser	Yes— Clinton	Preliminary but no incontrovertible evidence yet of collusion	Yes— preliminary

248 MEDDLING IN THE BALLOT BOX

having a resource advantage over the target's politicians, thus enabling it to publicly out-promise the transfer (or denial) of various goods to the target's public in return for voting in the "right" way. It can also usually provide more resources to the preferred side in an overt intervention—and, thanks to the information it receives from the assisted side, usually avoid overt acts (or an overt intervention) which can lead to an "undesirable" public reaction.

Third, I find that electoral interventions are far less likely to effectively help an aided party or candidate competing in a founding election than in a non-founding/later election and will frequently harm it (H6). The political information that the client has about voter preferences and the best ways to manipulate an election comes largely out of its own political experience. The client's experience, in turn, is derived from its previous efforts of running in competitive elections. In founding elections the aided side's inexperience leads its "local knowledge" to be of very low quality—which, in turn, causes it to request useless or even counterproductive forms of assistance from the great power (see the case of Argentina in Chapter 3).

Support for these findings came from two different directions. The first was a large-N statistical analysis. This analysis utilized the dataset of U.S. and Soviet/Russian electoral interventions (PEIG) that I constructed for this purpose and an empirical approach similar to that used in recent studies of the economic vote among scholars of comparative politics. I found through that method that electoral interventions are usually quite effective (with the special exception of cases of interventions in founding elections), increasing the vote share of the preferred candidate/party by about 3% on average (H4). Of the two main subtypes of electoral interventions, overt interventions were found to be significantly more effective (by an additional 3%) than covert intervention in both the substantive and statistical sense (H5). Interventions done in founding elections, unlike in later elections, were found to do little to benefit—and usually harmed—the aided candidate/party, reducing the aided side's vote share by 6.7% on average (H6). Some preliminary evidence was found that the overall magnitude of such interventions may matter. Likewise, as to the specific subtypes of intervention, some very preliminary and tentative evidence was discovered for the special effectiveness of tailored public concessions to the target. No evidence was found, however, for any differences in the effectiveness of interventions helping incumbents versus those aiding challengers (rejecting H7).

The second line of evidence was derived from pre- and post-election surveys with relevant questions conducted in three specific cases of electoral interventions: West Germany 1953, Israel 1992, and the U.S. 2016. The first two cases (Chapter 7) provided further support for the theoretical logic and the effectiveness of electoral interventions in general, and overt electoral interventions in particular, with the surveys from both cases finding significant and substantive effects in the "desired" direction due to factors related to these interventions. Voters, for example, frequently do pay close attention to overt electoral interventions—and some of them, as a result, change their votes in the manner preferred by the intervener.

The third case (Chapter 8) of the 2016 U.S. election, utilizing two pre-election surveys asking questions on two of the main "document dumps" by Wikileaks, and other metrics of public interest in these leaks (such as Google keyword searches), found further support for the effectiveness of covert electoral interventions. Although some evidence was found that the inadvertent exposure of this Russian covert intervention did reduce somewhat its effectiveness, these surveys nevertheless provided strong support for my prediction, derived from the aforementioned large-N analysis, that this intervention had a large enough effect to give Trump an electoral college victory. The leaks, for example, helped taint Clinton's Democratic primary victory in the eyes of many voters, completely negated the effects of the *Access Hollywood* tape among independents and Republicans, and reduced overall support for her in the electorate. When Hillary Clinton in the aftermath of the 2016 election blamed her surprising defeat on, among other factors, the "KGB," she was quite justified in this claim.

9.2 Implications for Scholarship

In addition to these groundbreaking empirical findings about the causes and effects of electoral interventions, this study provides several important contributions to other research agendas or subfields in political science. One contribution is to our understanding of the democratic peace theory and its limits. As could be seen in the preceding chapters, the democratic intervener in my dataset, the United States, by no means limited its electoral interventions only to new democracies and/or "electoral authoritarian" regimes. Even according to very strict and conservative definitions of what a fully consolidated democracy is (agreement by multiple democracy measures, etc.),[1] at least nineteen cases of such American interventions had occurred in such regimes. Examples in PEIG include Great Britain in the late 1980s, Costa Rica in the mid-1960s and in the mid-1980s, Israel in the 1990s, Italy in the late 1950s to the mid-1980s, Chile

[1] For this estimate I only counted countries as consolidated democracies if they appeared in multiple lists of democracies (Przeworski et al., Polity 4, Doyle, etc.) as full democracies and if, moreover, they were widely seen as democracies at the time of the intervention by most contemporaries. To be on the (very) conservative side, I also excluded interventions which occurred in the first two elections in the target since independence and/or since the country's most contemporary uninterrupted period of democracy had begun.

in the 1960s, Iceland in the mid-1950s, and so forth. Under more generous definitions of democratic consolidation, this number would be even higher.[2] Likewise, from what is known about their activities in this regard, other democratic great powers (such as Britain and post-WW2 Germany) have also been quite willing to electorally intervene in elections in other established democracies.[3] Such interventionist, coercive behavior would seem to stand in contradiction to what the democratic peace theory would usually expect about relations between established democracies.[4]

However, proponents of the democratic peace rarely discuss or even note partisan electoral interventions. The one rare exception to this rule, Charles Lipson, tries to excuse electoral interventions by democracies in other established democracies as being both extremely rare and usually due to fears by American policymakers in those cases that if the "unwanted" leaders/parties were elected (or remained in power) they would overthrow the target's democratic regime (Lipson 2005:136–137).[5]

It is indeed true that in some of these cases the partisan electoral interventions were meant to stop leaders or parties who, besides being perceived as a severe threat to U.S. interests, had (or were widely believed to have) authoritarian designs for their country if elected—such as the Italian Communist Party during the early Cold War or Salvador Allende in Chile. However, in many of these interventions this was clearly not the case. Whatever one's opinion is about the preferred domestic and/or foreign policies of Yitzhak Shamir of Israel, Neil Kinnock of the UK, or Oscar Arias of Costa Rica (to give examples of three such U.S. targets), neither they nor their parties were planning (or widely believed to be planning) to turn their countries into dictatorships if (re)elected. Likewise, in the context of international relations phenomena, the existence of at least nineteen interventions of this kind is far from being a rare occurrence or exceptional anomalies that "prove the rule." Indeed, it is higher than the number of interstate wars that have erupted around the world since 1980 (fourteen) (Sarkees and Wayman 2010).

---

[2] For example, if I, say, only use the Polity 4 scale to define consolidated democracy (i.e., polity scores of 9 or 10 in the target), then one-third of U.S. electoral interventions have occurred in such countries.

[3] Britain, for example, intervened in the 1949 Icelandic elections (Aldrich 2001:149). More recently, Germany intervened in the 2012 Greek elections. "Greek Elections: Angela Merkel Warns Country Cannot Negotiate Bailout," *Huffington Post*, June 16, 2012.

[4] As both critics and some proponents of the democratic peace have long agreed, even coercive/aggressive behavior between democracies which led to conflicts with far fewer than 1,000 battle-related deaths would be a problem for this theory (citations in Elman 1997:193). Likewise, a recent review article on the democratic peace has noted that "explaining both negative and positive peace in interstate relations" between democracies has increasingly become the standard for theories attempting to explain it (Ungerer 2012:25).

[5] See also Poznansky 2015 for a related argument.

Accordingly, the findings of this study about the frequency of partisan electoral interventions by established democracies against other democracies indicate that the explanatory purview of the democratic peace theory has to exclude non-violent activities. Whatever is the exact reason (or reasons) that prevent democracies from usually using violence toward other democracies seems to have very little effect on their ability or willingness to use various non-violent forms of coercion. In other words, democracies may be quite unwilling to fight each other—but they are more than willing to make sure, frequently through ethically questionable means, that their opponent in the helm of another democratic country loses his or her job (or fails to gain office in the first place).

A second contribution is to the growing research on the effects of public diplomacy. A growing literature agenda in international relations has been investigating the effects of public statements by foreign leaders and by representatives of foreign governments and international organizations on a public target's views and behaviors on various issues (Bush and Jamal 2015; Matush 2018; Walter et al. 2018; Marinov 2018). My findings here on overt electoral interventions indicate that foreign publics sometimes take cognizance of messages by foreign leaders not just in regard to controversial domestic policies or referendums, but even on high-salience topics such as their voting choices in national-level elections. That, in turn, widens the scope of situations in which words "can matter."

A third contribution is to intelligence studies and to the study of covert operations. My research here on covert electoral interventions (a subtype of "political action") provides the first statistical analysis of the effectiveness of such operations on their main operational criteria—the ability to put or keep in power the preferred leader or party. It also provides systemic confirmation to one key claim frequently made by scholars and some practitioners about covert operations in general (Bissell 1996:214–215; Lowenthal 2003:173–174)—that covertness imposes significant costs on such operations, reducing their overall effectiveness in general or compared to any overt equivalents.[6]

A fourth contribution derives from providing systemic evidence for "leader effects" in an understudied direction—how the characteristics of particular leaders (or would-be leaders) affect the behavior of other countries toward them in peaceful interactions. As noted in Chapter 2, there is a growing body of research showing significant effects of leader characteristics on foreign policies. However, this research is largely monadic—focusing on their effects on their own countries' actions while ignoring the effects that different types of leaders may have on the actions of other countries toward them. Given the heated debate

---

[6] My study here of the decision-making process behind three of the proposed or executed covert operations (Guatemala 1958; Philippines 1965; Greece 1967), all rarely studied beforehand, also expands the (small) number of such operations receiving scholarly treatment.

in other IR subfields as to whether such monadic effects necessarily spill over into the dyadic (or K-adic) sphere (such as over the existence of state reputations; Mercer 1996; Danilovic 2001; Sartori 2005; Press 2005), this is an important issue to investigate and address. Some recent research on leader effects has found evidence that the characteristics of leaders can indeed affect the behavior of other countries toward them (Potter 2007; Bak and Palmer 2010; Lupton 2018)—but only in cases in which the use of force is seriously contemplated.

This study provides, for the first time, clear systemic evidence that the characteristics of leaders (and would-be leaders) can significantly affect other countries' policies toward their country also in non-violent interactions. To give two examples, as could be seen in the West German case, the American perception of the SPD's leaders, first Schumacher and then Ollenhauer, as having inflexible preferences on the EDC was an important reason why it agreed to Adenauer's request to aid him and the CDU in that election. Likewise, as could be seen in the Philippines case, the American perception of neither incumbent president, Macapagal, nor his main challenger, Marcos, as having policy positions or preferences which would threaten its interests was an important factor in leading the U.S. to reject the PPP's request for electoral aid in the 1965 Philippine elections.[7] These results, accordingly, indicate that the purview of "leader effects" is wider than has been known until now. They also indicate that focusing on the effects of a leader's characteristics on other countries' behavior toward them could be a highly productive venue of future study for researchers on this topic.

As for comparative and American politics, the findings here of significant effects of electoral interventions, especially the overt type, provide strong evidence for the potential existence of significant "campaign effects" in national-level elections. If foreign actors are able, through public pre-election activities and events, to sometimes bring about major shifts in the target public's voting patterns, then domestically inspired events and activities should, at least in theory, also sometimes have these abilities. If foreign actors can sometimes increase the assisted side's voter mobilization capabilities and raise the quality of their campaigning materials to the point that they can "move the needle," then creative domestic politicians and top-notch campaign operators and advisors should sometimes have that ability as well. While the effects of the election campaign on the results may, of course, vary from case to case, and may at times be small, my findings here should help send to its grave any universal theoretical assumption that they are usually non-existent or too minor to "matter."

This study also contributes to comparative politics by illustrating the potential importance of international factors in the explanation of some domestic

---

[7] For the difficulty scholars had in finding such effects at this level see Press (2005:137–138).

political phenomena hence seen as largely unrelated to such factors. My research showed the importance of an international factor, a foreign partisan intervention by a great power, on one of the most heavily studied topics in comparative politics—what significantly affects national-level election results. While there has been increasing recognition of the potential importance of international factors in a few subfields of comparative politics, such as on the causes of democratization and democratic survival (Whitehead 2001; Geddes 2007; Levitsky and Way 2010; Boix 2011; Bunce & Wholchik 2011) or political economy (Rogowski 1989; Garrett 2001; Simmons and Elkins 2004), much of comparative politics has ignored international factors in their research. In the rare cases that international factors are studied in comparative politics outside of these fields, they usually tend to focus only on factors related to the economy such as, in the literature on elections and campaigns, the effects of trade openness (Hellwig and Samuels 2007) or comparative economic growth (Kayser and Peress 2012).[8]

It has become increasingly clear among international relations scholars over the past three decades that in order to explain many types of state behavior in the international sphere, one needs many times to have a better understanding of the institutional structures and the domestic politics of the countries in question. Comparativists may need to start learning more about international relations in order to better understand various domestic political phenomena, such as national-level election results.

At the minimum, these results should lead comparativists to pay closer attention to potentially relevant international factors when designing their data collection instruments (such as pre- and post-election surveys, interviews, etc.) on seemingly "unrelated" phenomena. Ignoring such international factors, messages, and events, as is usually the norm at present, may lead some comparativists to miss important factors shaping the behavior of the relevant public(s) on an issue of interest—and the lack of relevant data may make it very hard for future scholars to notice or correct this initial oversight.

9.3   Implications for Policy: Cybersecurity Policy

This study also contributes to policymaking and scholarship on the new interdisciplinary field of cybersecurity (Rid 2013; Singer and Friedman 2014; Valeriano and Maness 2015; Shackelford 2017; Valeriano, Jensen, and Maness 2018). For a

---

[8] Such factors are occasionally noted by area experts, especially in countries or regions highly penetrated by great powers such as Central America (see, e.g., Seligson and Booth 1995). However, these insights are frequently ignored as possible explanatory variables in many subsequent large-N and other analyses.

long time the possibility of cyberwarfare methods being used by foreign powers in order to target elections was neither a major policymaker concern (Fidler 2017) nor a significant topic of study in this field.[9]

This abruptly changed, however, with the 2016 Russian intervention and its use of cyberwarfare for this purpose.[10] Many scholars and policymakers have now become quite worried about the possibility of more such interventions. In one representative example, U.S. Senator Angus King warned during a Congressional hearing in June 2017 on the Russian electoral intervention that "they are going to be back, and they're going to be back with knowledge and information that they didn't have before" (in Root and Kennedy 2017:2).

While we lack, at the time of this writing, other confirmed cases of the use of cyberwarfare for this purpose by state actors,[11] the frequency and lengthy record of such non-digital or "analog" electoral interventions by major powers described in this study indicates that fears of more such cybermeddling by foreign powers in elections are fully justified. All the available evidence found here demonstrates that partisan electoral interventions are a common form of foreign intervention and that the incentives for great powers and would-be local clients to use this method are likely to continue to exist in the future and may somewhat strengthen. The actual and perceived success of the Russian intervention in "flipping" the election to Trump is likely to further encourage attempts by Russia, and by other powers, to use digitized versions of age-old electoral intervention techniques. Its perceived feasibility and utility is also likely to encourage some of the assisted clients to explicitly request from the intervener cyber-versions of these meddling techniques in the future. It is highly unlikely that the 2016 U.S. election will be the last case where cyberspace is utilized by a foreign power for meddling in a real-life election.

As for specific electoral intervention methods, this study indicates that more attention to cybersecurity by policymakers and scholars needs to be given to defending against digitizable meddling methods not known to have been used by Russia in the 2016 U.S. election. Thus far, most policymaker and scholarly

---

[9] Two pre-2016 books on various possible cyberwarfare methods by senior scholars didn't even note this possibility (Rid 2013; Singer and Friedman 2014), and a third study mentioned it in one brief sentence (Valeriano and Maness 2015:71). There has also been a small but significant literature in computer science analyzing the overall ability of electronic voting machines and online voting systems to accurately record and tally the votes entered and their security flaws in situations of attempted *domestic* manipulation (Blankenship 2004; Halderman et al. 2010; Jones and Simons 2012).

[10] For some recent examples see Halderman 2017; Berger et al. 2018; Blaze et al. 2017; Root and Kennedy 2017; Norden and Vandewalker 2017; Shackelford et al. 2017; Valeriano et al. 2018:131–136.

[11] Claims made, for example, prior to the 2017 French election, in which Russia intervened in favor of Le Pen via digital dirty tricks, were quietly walked back in the intervention's aftermath. The yet unknown hackers involved in the anti-Macron leak seem to be private individuals rather than the Russian government. "France Says No Trace of Russia Hacking Macron," *Associated Press*, June 1, 2017.

attention has been focused on stopping or curtailing the cyber-methods known to have been utilized in 2016. Those methods—hacking the DNC and the Clinton campaign and leaking some of the stolen documents, spreading "fake news" on social media, etc.—are mostly digital versions of an electoral intervention technique known as "dirty tricks." Given the frequent use of the "analog" variants of dirty tricks by Russia and other powers as part of election campaigns, as noted in Chapter 5, the focus of many policymakers, scholars, and relevant private entities on increasing the difficulty of effectuating their digital brethren is an important task. However, that is far from being the only intervention method where digitization can potentially bring significant advantages for foreign powers interested in meddling in a foreign election and clients anxious to receive it.

Given our knowledge of electoral interventions, the most likely electoral intervention method to see future attempts at digitization involves campaign funding—the most common method of electoral intervention since (at least) the end of WW2. Cryptocurrencies (such as Bitcoin) can be produced by private actors in complete anonymity by having their computers run special "mining" programs. Likewise, once produced or acquired, cryptocurrencies can be transferred between users in a manner in which the currency sender can remain completely anonymous barring very rare and unusual circumstances—such as when an intelligence or law enforcement agency has effectively gained access to the sender's local records of cryptocurrency purchases and production.[12] Accordingly, if cryptocurrencies survive and continue spreading as a medium for the exchange of goods and services, they are likely to become a common vector for this type of electoral intervention.

There are two major "analog" methods of transferring foreign campaign funding. The first involves the arrangement of secret meetings between trusted representatives of the intervener and the client in which bags full of physical copies of the local currency are transferred. The other requires finding suitable "cutout" local firms or private businessmen which can be trusted by the client to accept these funds from the foreign power in some manner (directly or via various "padded" contracts) and then "launder" them as "legitimate" domestic donations to the client's election campaign. Both methods involve significant risks of exposure by the intermediaries or of detection of the meetings by the target's intelligence agencies.

---

[12] From the limited data available about the Mueller investigation's digital forensic techniques, this is how they detected the Russian use of Bitcoins in the 2016 intervention (i.e., a counter-hack into the GRU's computer networks); Thomas Rid, "What Mueller Knows About the DNC Hack—And Trump Doesn't," *Politico*, July 17, 2018. Tracing the use of Bitcoins in this manner does not indicate, as some have recently claimed, that this cryptocurrency is effectively traceable; Dante Disparte, "Does the Russian Indictment Exonerate Bitcoin?" *Forbes*, July 15, 2018. Likewise, many of the newer cryptocurrencies (such as Zcash and Nonero) have even stronger anonymizing features than Bitcoin.

Cryptocurrencies eliminate the need for either a trusted intermediary or a physical meeting in order to transfer the covert campaign funding. After the intervener and the assisted side have agreed on the exact amount to be covertly transferred, a secret agent of the foreign power can enter the target country with a thumb drive filled with the needed units of the cryptocurrency. Once inside the country, the agent can buy a new laptop from a local computer store with cash, use it to connect to the free internet at a local coffee shop, and then use this connection to transfer the cryptocurrency in question to the preferred side's campaign. This method would raise no alarm bells and make it effectively impossible to identify the foreign source of the campaign funds. Likewise, so long as the digitally transferred covert funding is provided in "average"-sized amounts of that cryptocurrency, and via multiple different "addresses" or "wallets," these transactions would raise no alarms in various money-laundering agencies inspecting that cryptocurrency's online ledger for potential shenanigans.

As noted in Chapter 2, given the high expected domestic political costs of an exposure of a covert electoral intervention to the assisted side, when such an intervention is chosen, the intervener (and the client) will look for ways to provide the assistance in a manner that will lead to the lowest possible chances of that happening. Cryptocurrencies, by providing such a new, very low risk method for conveying such election assistance, are accordingly likely to become a quite popular technique for this purpose once states are fully acquainted with and regularly use them for various covert tasks.[13]

The currently available evidence indicates that this process of acquaintance is well under way, with cryptocurrencies being already used in other, secondary roles in known cases of electoral interventions. For example, according to the Mueller investigation, the Russian intervention used Bitcoins at the estimated value of $95,000 that they bought or "mined" in order to purchase much of the computer equipment and internet domains used for various parts of the digital dirty tricks.[14]

To preemptively prevent such a scenario from occurring in a future electoral intervention, democratic countries must outlaw the giving of campaign donations using cryptocurrencies, or any other digital payment methods that are untraceable.[15] Likewise, to prevent the disguise of any such foreign cryptofunding

[13] Another attractive feature of the use of cryptocurrencies by state actors for funding foreign election campaigns is that they can usually "mine" much of the needed cryptocurrency using their extensive domestic computing capabilities, thus reducing their need to dip into their foreign currency reserves for meddling in this manner. Indeed, as noted, this already occurred to a limited extent in the 2016 case.

[14] Mueller Investigation, Grand Jury Indictment July 13, 2018.

[15] At the time of this writing, the U.S. and Sweden already permit campaign donations in cryptocurrencies. In any country where independent campaigning by non-party actors is legal, a similar restriction must apply to any donations to these groups.

as the candidate's existing or "self-produced" property, all elected officials and their immediate families must be banned from purchasing or "mining" any cryptocurrencies while in office. A similar restriction must also be placed on political parties. Candidates to any national-level office must also be required to completely divest from any existing ownership in any such cryptoproperty prior to filing their candidacy—in a manner similar to conflict-of-interest regulations regarding stocks or ownership stakes in private corporations. Such stern but low-cost measures could help nip in the bud the potential digitization of foreign campaign funding.

9.3.1 Meddling in the Vote Tallies: Preventing the Electoral Doomsday Scenario

The use of cyber-methods for electoral interventions and recent changes in the ways voting is done in many democracies also open the door for the possibility of a different, even more drastic, method of intervention—the direct change by a foreign power of the vote tallies in another country. With these new circumstances an old intervention method may become possible again. In the pre-modern era, attempts to determine the results of elections by directly modifying the vote counting or the behavior of the electorate in question were quite common. For example, in the 1697 Royal Polish elections noted in the introduction, one of the key components of the successful joint Russian, Austrian, and Prussian meddling for the candidacy of Augustus of Saxony was the direct outright bribery of much of the electorate (i.e., the thousands of polish nobles gathered at Wilno) and the election officials after a preliminary round of voting didn't bring about the "desired" result.[16]

However, with the advent of modern mass elections in the late 18th century, attempts to directly affect the vote tallies have stopped. The nature of modern competitive elections prior to electronic voting has changed the range of feasible options available to interested foreign powers. With even relatively small states having electorates numbering in the hundreds of thousands or millions, thousands of polling stations spread throughout the country, tens of thousands of polling workers and observers, and well-guarded central election headquarters tabulating the incoming results under the watchful eyes of senior representatives of the competing candidates or parties, any attempts by a foreign power to directly determine the election results would have been either impossible to execute or would have required the effective occupation of the independent country

---

[16] The results of that round, in turn, were determined to a significant extent by the outright bribery of said electorate by representatives of the French government (Lewitter 1956).

in question. As a result, great powers interested in the outcome of a foreign election focused their efforts instead on partisan electoral interventions.

However, the growing use of electronic voting machines and online voting threatens to make this ancient option feasible yet again for would-be foreign meddlers. Online voting systems, like all things connected to the internet, can be hacked by a malicious actor. Examinations of the online voting systems already in use have frequently found glaring security flaws—making them easy prey for an interested foreign power (Jones and Simons 2012:chap. 11). In one recent example, a 2017 West Australian state election, the election website used a commercial denial of service (DDoS) mitigation service which utilized standard issue, widely used encryption keys- which could had, in turn, become completely compromised, (and potentially open the vote tallies for modification), if broken by a hacker elsewhere when this mitigation service (and encryption keys) was used to secure other regular commercial websites (Culane et al. 2017).

The far more common electronic voting machines do not usually have any such direct connections to the internet before or during the election period—what is known in the cybersecurity community as an "air gap." Nevertheless, existing electronic voting machines have been repeatedly found to have serious physical security flaws. For example, in a 2017 white hat hacker conference (DEFCON), hackers with no prior knowledge or experience with the technology of the voting machines were able to gain access to five electronic voting machines on display, all widely used models in the United States and elsewhere, in a few minutes to a few hours. The machines were found to suffer from various serious security flaws: from easily accessible USB ports to administrator passwords which could be found in a quick online search (Blaze et al. 2017). Electronic voting machines used in other countries, such as the Netherlands and India, were also found, upon close inspection by computer scientists, to suffer from serious vulnerabilities (Shackelford et al. 2017).

Even worse, the vaunted "air gap" doesn't exist in practice given the way voting machines are used. For example, in order to program the voting machines for an upcoming election, they need to be connected to a thumb drive with the information about the elected offices and referendums up for vote. The information on this thumb drive is usually downloaded from computers which are connected to the internet for this purpose—with all of the opportunities for the insertion of malware of various kinds that that creates (Halderman 2017). Likewise, some voting-machine manufacturers include in them secret modems and remote-access software.[17]

---

[17] Kim Zetter, "Top Voting Machine Vendor Admits It Installed Remote-Access Software on Systems Sold to States," *Motherboard*, July 17, 2018.

Naturally, the security of online voting systems and of electronic voting machines can be significantly improved in various ways. However, given my research on electoral interventions, the bar for reliable security from foreign interventions in this manner would need to be extremely high. Even in "regular" partisan electoral interventions, major powers are sometimes willing to invest large amounts of money in order to determine the results of one particular contest. For example, from some electoral intervention cases where sufficient information is available to make such an estimate, the U.S. (in 2016 dollars) spent approximately $2.9 billion in its intervention in the 1948 Italian election, and around $2.6 billion in its intervention in the 1996 Russian election.[18] In attempts to directly affect the vote tally, the potential prize for the great power would be even bigger—being able to secretly determine with complete certainty barring the rare landslide for the "undesirable" candidate, the election results, and accordingly the leader of a foreign country of importance in multiple national elections.

In addition, by dispensing with the need for any cooperation with a domestic actor in this form of meddling, the number of competitive elections the great power could effectively intervene in, in practice, would be higher. Nowadays, numerous computer scientists and large amounts of computing resources are readily available to major powers, the results of the needs of their intelligence and defense establishments as well as of their government bureaucracy. Even a relatively minor power such as North Korea, an underdeveloped country in which computers and the internet are illegal and unavailable in practice for most of the population, seems to nevertheless have enough trained personnel and computing resources to rob hundreds of millions of dollars online from major world banks (with top-notch cybersecurity systems) and to successfully hack into South Korea's Defense ministry, stealing highly classified information.[19] Accordingly, the security used for the voting machines, the vote counting systems (or the online voting systems) would need to be sufficiently sophisticated to prevent a highly motivated state actor with effectively unlimited computing capabilities and resources from being able to break in.

This standard of security is simply unachievable in practice. If private groups of hackers and state actors are able to repeatedly break into some of the most sensitive computer networks and databases of the U.S. government, such as one that includes the personal information of most Americans with security clearances, it is highly unlikely that online voting systems that need to be accessible to millions of people will be able to avoid a similar fate. An "air gap" will also not suffice. If the

---

[18] Estimates based on the author's data.
[19] David Sanger, "The World Once Laughed at North Korean Cyberpower. No More," *New York Times*, October 15, 2017.

security level of a top-secret Iranian nuclear facility with such air gaps was insufficient nevertheless to prevent the U.S. and Israel from infecting the centrifuges in this facility with malware (the famous Stuxnet), it is highly unlikely that electronic voting machines which need to be placed in multiple public locations, and are located in far more open societies than Iran, will ever be secure enough from a foreign power. As one expert on this topic noted in a recent interview, "You are never going to come up with voting machines and software that are totally un-hackable—there's always going to be some point of failure" (Braun, quoted in Changwook 2018). Likewise, any electronic (or online) voting system will require regular human involvement at various stages—its design, its production, its maintenance, the input of information on the upcoming races, and so forth. Any persons involved could be compromised for this purpose using various tried-and-true methods from centuries of spycraft. Russia, for example, has been known to be one of the most effective practitioners of these methods, successfully using a variety of such means: from agents specially trained to befriend and seduce the targets, to compromising information (frequently achieved through the former method), to money, and so forth (Andrew and Mithrokhin 1999).

Even worse, many methods by which these election systems could be compromised would be effectively undetectable barring a manual recount. For example, a malware entered into the voting machines or the electronic counting system for this purpose could increase the vote share of the preferred side by 10% to 20% by incrementally deducting votes from the other candidates or parties and transferring them to the preferred candidate/party. Barring a landslide for the undesirable candidate, such a change would suffice to determine the identity of the winner in almost every national-level election.

The other indicator of an electorate's preferences, various election surveys, would frequently be unable to detect with certainty such subtle foreign "fixing" of the election. Election polls, as samples out of a larger population, have by construction a certain level of uncertainty—usually known in the public presentation of the results as the margin of error.[20] As a result, even a well-done election poll of 500 to 1,000 respondents of the U.S. population, conducted under perfect surveying conditions, presenting a certain candidate with 47% predicted vote share cannot usually exclude the possibility that the true underlying voting preferences for that candidate is actually 44%. It also frequently cannot exclude the possibility, in a head-to-head match under such conditions, that the lagging candidate has more support from the frontrunner even if the difference between them is larger than the declared margin of error, if for some reason support for the lagging candidate exhibits more variance than support for the frontrunner.

---

[20] Web-based polls, which use a non-probabilistic sample, have a similar sampling error which is derived from a different source.

In practice, the margin of error of election surveys is significantly larger nowadays, for various reasons. The traditional method of polling, contacting respondents through a landline phone, is becoming increasingly ineffective due to the decline in its use among private users. The new replacements, web-based and cell phone surveys, have far greater difficulties creating a fully representative sample. For example, web-based polls, which contact people who agreed to be polled in advance (i.e., non-probabilistic sampling), must contend with the fact that some subpopulations are far less likely to use the internet due to age or religious reasons. Likewise, members of minority groups and less politically engaged respondents are far harder to poll accurately using this method (Kennedy et al. 2016). As a result, web-based surveys are far more dependent than their random sampling brethren on their formulas for weighing the responses of the various subgroups of the relevant population (Kennedy et al. 2016)—which creates an obvious "usual suspect" if the election results diverge from their predictions.[21]

As for cell phone surveys, cell phone users can use caller ID to filter out surveyors, and surveyors find it much harder to find the desired population(s).[22] Both factors lead to lower response rates, biases toward certain groups, and more "junk" responses by "irrelevant" respondents. Likewise, in many countries there is evidence of a significant and rising share of respondents who outright lie regarding their voting intentions for various reasons.[23] These problems have already made (non-intervened) election results less predictable from the pre-election polling—and, accordingly, make election results that significantly diverge from the pre-election surveys less surprising and therefore less suspicion-raising.[24]

As a result, a successful foreign intervention in the vote tallies could stay in the target state's electronic (or online) election system for years and even decades without being detected, turning most of the target's elections in the duration into de facto shams. The Stuxnet malware was able to remain undetected within the Iranian centrifuges in Natanz for years and was eventually found by the Iranians

---

[21] Even in "regular" polls, the weighing formulas can greatly affect the presented results—with a test recently done leading to results that diverged by as much as 5% from each other; Nate Cohn, "We Gave Four Good Pollsters the Same Raw Data. They Had Four Different Results," *New York Times*, September 20, 2016.

[22] For the even more severe problems exit surveys usually have nowadays see, for example, the expert opinions quoted in Thomas Edsall, "The 2016 Exit Polls Led Us to Misinterpret the 2016 Election," *New York Times*, March 29, 2018; Nate Cohn, "Trump Losing College Educated Whites? He Never Won Them in the First Place," *New York Times*, February 27, 2018.

[23] See, for example, Quentin Hardy, "How Cellphones Complicate Polling," *New York Times*, November 12, 2012; Renard Sexton, "Tackling the Shy Tory Problem," *The Guardian*, April 8, 2010.

[24] Ironically, if after the first election intervened in this manner the main response of the pollsters were to be to change the weighting of their polls so as to oversample the assisted side's main constituencies, the election surveys in subsequent elections may be more in congruence with the foreign-modified voter tallies than with the true results, leading to a lack of any "polling surprises" when this modification occurs.

only because, by design, it was meant to cause these centrifuges to malfunction in various visible ways. In contrast, election voting and counting machines and online systems would seemingly work as they are "supposed to," therefore not arousing any suspicion in maintenance personnel that it might be necessary to look for any special problems.[25]

In theory, electronic voting machines with paper trails (one common reform proposal) could be used to detect such behavior. However, aside from the fact that any malware in the voting machine could, of course, be designed to also affect what exact output the attached printer prints out, the losing candidate/party would have to ask first for a manual recount for this purpose. Politicians who lose close races frequently avoid making such requests given the long-term political costs that subsequently unchanged results could cause both themselves and their parties—that is, the tag of "sore loser" (Braden and Tucker 2014:5).[26]

Indeed, a similar domestic version of the scenario described here almost happened in the 1994 South African election. At the start of the vote-counting process, an unknown domestic actor successfully hacked into the main computer of the central election commission charged with counting the votes and implanted a malware which incrementally gave three other parties opposed to Nelson Mandela's African National Congress party (two right-wing white parties and the Inkatha/Zulu party) 0.33% additional votes for every 1% won by the ANC. That raised these three parties' overall vote share by 9.5% to 12%. Only the prior decision of South Africa's electoral commission to simultaneously conduct a manual counting of the ballots led to the chance detection of this malware, the elimination of the fraudulent digital results, and the fully manual completion of the vote-counting process (Harris 2010:chaps. 14 and 15).

Given that the 1994 election was the first post-apartheid election in South Africa, the early discovery of this attempt had little effect on the subsequent legitimacy of South Africa's democracy. Nevertheless, the hacking-related delay of the counting process led what was already a very tense post-election situation to almost reach the breaking point (Harris 2010:chaps. 14 and 15).[27] In countries however which have been conducting elections for decades and centuries, the successful detection of such an attempt, even if the detection occurred shortly

---

[25] Likewise, as one computer scientist who studies electronic voting systems has noted, "a fundamental fact of computer science [is that] there is no foolproof way of determining if a machine has malware"; Christian Vasquez, "West Virginia's Voting Experiment Stirs Security Fears," *Politico*, October 13, 2018.

[26] Some recent reform proposals and proposed laws, aware of this issue, have recommended automatic recounts of various kinds (Root and Kennedy 2017:6–7; Norden and Vandewalker 2017:12). However, if such a manual recount is anyway seen as needed as a checkup on the electronic voting machines it would be simpler, and less costly, to just move back completely to paper ballots.

[27] Likewise, key details about the hack were kept secret for decades.

after the first affected election was concluded and its effects were fully reversed, would have almost as bad consequences to the target as a failure to detect it.

Electronic voting machines already have an almost unparalleled capability in the annals of modern technology to generate public fears and conspiracy theories throughout the political spectrum. Examples include claims on parts of the hard left after the 2004 U.S. elections that George W. Bush's victory in Ohio was achieved through the rigging of the Diebold electronic voting machines (Miller 2005), and dark insinuations by a far-right presidential candidate, Jair Bolonsaro, after the first round of the 2018 Brazilian elections that he would have won the first round outright if not for the "fixing" of the voting machines by his opponents.[28] Likewise, despite no evidence whatsoever that a Russian attempt to directly modify the vote tallies has been actually made as well, the mere use by the Russian government of cyberwarfare for partisan meddling in 2016 was sufficient to lead 35% of the American public to erroneously believe in 2017 that such a change of the tallies was indeed done by the Russians.[29]

The detection of a successful attempt to affect the vote tallies would lead much of the target's public to see any past elections tallied or conducted using such electronic or online methods, regardless of whether such foreign meddling actually occurred in them or not, as outright shams. That could destroy the legitimacy of the target's democratic system for decades. In an era in which trust in many government institutions is declining around the democratic world, and even many established democracies are believed to be showing some signs of weakness, such a crisis of legitimacy could have extremely devastating consequences. When a foreign power will choose to intervene in this manner, there will be no favorable outcome for the target.

To prevent this dangerous yet likely future possibility, western and non-western democracies must outlaw the use in elections of all electronic voting machines, online voting systems, or any electronic methods for the first-stage counting of ballots both for regular and for provisional balloting.[30] All voting must be done using paper ballots (in person or mailed in) and all counting of the paper ballots must be done manually by the staff of the polling station with the results of the counting manually marked down on paper and certified by all observers. While the transmission and the initial aggregation of these results from each polling station may be done electronically in order to speed up the provision of the initial results to the public, election regulations must require

---

[28] Anthony Boadle and Mateus Maia, "Far-Right Candidate Jair Bolsonaro Will Face-Off against Leftist Challenger in Runoff after Brazil Vote," *Reuters*, October 8, 2018.

[29] The Economist/YouGov Survey May 13–16, 2017.

[30] Optical scanners are essentially electronic computing devices, and this technology cannot work in the absence of electronic computing capabilities. Accordingly, such scanners are just as open as voting machines to hacking by foreign powers (Halderman 2017).

that no election can be certified, and no elected officials sworn in, before the paper results from each polling station are collected and counted manually and the results are compared to those done electronically. Likewise, western election observation missions must incorporate a "no computers" standard to their checklists, treating the use of any electronic voting methods or first-stage counting as a severe flaw to the proper functioning of the election in question.

Non-electronic methods of voting and counting have a proven, two-centuries-long track record of being unhackable in this manner by foreign powers. Likewise, the costs in money and waiting time by returning to this method would be minimal.[31] Accordingly, going back to voting like it's 1979 (in the west) would guarantee that this old foreign danger won't be resurrected due to electronic voting technologies.

9.4 Venues for Further Inquiry

The scope of this study was intentionally restricted in order to enable its prompt conclusion. However, when dealing with a new, rarely studied topic, there are naturally many open venues for future research. One venue is the effects such interventions have on the target and on the post-intervention relationship. An electoral intervention attempts to influence one of the key institutions in a democracy—the national-level elections and the process by which the executive is peacefully replaced or retained. Likewise, when overt or exposed, such acts can have significant direct effects on the target itself. As noted in the introduction, over the last few years there has been growing research by the author and other scholars on various ways in which electoral interventions can impact the target after the elections, such as on the amounts of domestic terrorism (Levin 2020), the chances of democratic breakdown (Levin 2019b), post-election trade (Levin 2018c), and cooperation with the intervener (Levin 2018b). There has also been a growing wave of research on the effects of such intervention on the target public's overall view of the intervener (Shulman and Bloom 2012; Corstange and Marinov 2012), belief in their country's democracy in general and in the integrity

---

[31] For example, there is no evidence that non-electronic voting methods would necessarily cost significantly more—the opposite has frequently been found to be the case when electronic voting machines and paper ballots were compared or electronic voting machines were phased-in in practice after the past use of paper ballots. See Kennedy and Root 2017:4; "Europe Rejects Digital Voting Machines," *Newsweek*, May 22, 2009. Israeli elections, which have used both paper ballots and manual counting for decades, usually provide near-final election results by the early morning of the day following the elections (after the polling stations close at 10:00 p.m.). Likewise, when both the Netherlands and Germany went back, in response to concerns regarding the safety of these machines, to paper ballots (and in Netherlands in 2017 to manual counting as well) the subsequent added delays in getting the final results were relatively small.

and credibility of their elections in particular (Bush and Prather 2019; Tomz and Weeks 2020), and support for economic cooperation (Bush and Prather 2017b) and for various "punishment" options (Tomz and Weeks 2020).

However, much is left to be done in exploring the impact of such interventions on the target and on post-election cooperation. For example, given U.S. and Soviet interest in promoting various economic policies since WW2, do such interventions have any effects on the target's post-intervention growth rates? Likewise, do they lead to other forms of internal instability in the target, such as mass protests or civil wars? Having answers to these questions will increase our substantive understanding of the effects of international factors on the target.

Another direction of interest is whether such interventions lead to "blow-back" against the intervener such as other, more violent types of interventions sometimes do. For example, are public or exposed interveners of this kind more likely to see their nationals becoming targets of international terrorism by en-raged supporters of the losing side? Likewise, we now know that LBJ, a frequent user of electoral interventions abroad, used the CIA in 1964 for such a "domestic" dirty-tricks intervention against his opponent, Barry Goldwater, with the agency bugging numerous political aides and planting a spy within the Goldwater cam-paign. The CIA then regularly provided to LBJ "inside information" about his opponent's campaign plans and planned speeches.[32] Was this an unusual one-off exception or did the conduct of such activities abroad lead over time to signifi-cant "side effects" to the U.S. and other powers that have used such interventions?

A third venue is studying electoral interventions by states which are not great powers. As noted in the introduction, such interventions are far less common than those done by great powers. Nevertheless, minor powers do sometimes meddle as well—and given the findings here, they could have also, in some cases, have shaped the course of history of their targets. An analysis of some known past cases for which the archives may now be fully available (such as Libya under Kaddafi) could help us, for example, better understand when and why smaller states are willing to intervene in this manner on their own, taking the great risk (which great powers don't usually face) of a costly punishment by stronger states and/or the enraged target itself if the intervention is exposed or is public. It could also eventually, by providing us more cases of such interventions, perhaps in-crease our data on various subtypes to a sufficient extent to enable us to reach more firm conclusions about their relative effectiveness.

Partisan electoral interventions have been a common phenomenon throughout the history of competitive elections, with such meddling quickly fol-lowing in the heels of elections like the creation of the first currencies and the

---

[32] Lee Edwards, "Lyndon Johnson's Watergate," *National Review*, June 7, 2005.

emergence of counterfeiters. So as long as such elections continue to exist, electoral interventions will probably continue to occur as well. It behooves scholars, policymakers, and the general public to increase their understanding of when electoral interventions occur and the possible effects of such interference in order to better understand the world, make more informed decisions on the use of this policy tool, and reduce any harm that such meddling can cause when their own country becomes the target of such meddling.

*List of Cases of U.S. and USSR/Russian Partisan Electoral Interventions 1946–2000 (PEIG 1.01)

Target	Intervener	Year/Election	Assisted Party/ Candidate[a]	Covert/Overt
Argentina	U.S.	1946	Jose P. Tamborini	Overt
Hungary	USSR	1947	MKP	Overt
Italy[b]	U.S.	1948	DC	Overt[c]
Italy[b]	USSR	1948	PCI	Covert
U.S.	USSR	1948	Henry A. Wallace	Overt
Israel	U.S.	1949	Mapai	Overt
Finland	USSR	1950	*	Overt
Japan	U.S.	1952	Liberal Party	Overt
West Germany	U.S.	1953	CDU	Overt
Italy[b]	U.S.	1953	DC	Overt[c]
Italy[b]	USSR	1953	PCI	Covert
Japan	U.S.	1953	Liberal Party	Overt[c]
Philippines	U.S.	1953	Ramon Magsaysay	Covert
Brazil	U.S.	1955	Juarez Tavora	Covert
Indonesia	U.S.	1955	Masjumi	Covert
Laos	U.S.	1955	NPP	Covert
Finland	USSR	1956	Urho Kaleva Kekkonen	Overt
Iceland	U.S.	1956	Independence Party	Overt
Sri Lanka	U.S.	1956	UNP	Overt
West Germany	USSR	1957	SPD	Overt
Lebanon	U.S.	1957	Supporters of Camille Chamoun	Covert
Philippines	U.S.	1957	Jose Yulo	Covert
Greece[b]	U.S.	1958	ERE	Covert
Greece[b]	USSR	1958	EDA	Overt
Guatemala	U.S.	1958	Jose Luis Cruz Salazar	Covert
Italy	U.S.	1958	DC	Covert
Japan	U.S.	1958	LDP	Overt[c]
Laos	U.S.	1958	NPP	Overt[c]

* Appendices B through H noted in the main text are available as online-only appendices on the author's dataset at www.dovhlevin.com.

Target	Intervener	Year/Election	Assisted Party/ Candidate[a]	Covert/Overt
Venezuela	USSR	1958	Wolfgang Larrazabal	Covert
Malaysia	U.S.	1959	UNMO	Covert
Nepal	U.S.	1959	Nepali Congress Party	Covert
San Marino	U.S.	1959	PDCS	Covert
Democratic Republic of the Congo	USSR	1960	MNC	Covert
Japan	U.S.	1960	LDP	Covert
Laos	U.S.	1960	CDNI	Covert
Sri Lanka	U.S.	1960 (March)	UNP	Covert
Sri Lanka	U.S.	1960 (July)	UNP	Covert
Greece	U.S.	1961	ERE	Covert
Philippines	U.S.	1961	Diosdado Pangan Macapagal	Covert
South Vietnam[†]	U.S.	1961	Ngo Dinh Diem	Covert
Brazil	U.S.	1962	**	Covert
Canada	USSR	1962	Liberal Party	Overt
Finland	USSR	1962	Urho Kaleva Kekkonen	Overt
Peru	U.S.	1962	Victor Raul Haya de la Torre	Covert
Italy	U.S.	1963	DC	Covert
Japan	U.S.	1963	LDP	Covert
Bolivia[†]	U.S.	1964	Victor Paz Estenssoro	Covert
Chile[b]	U.S.	1964	Eduardo Frei Montalva	Covert
Chile[b]	USSR	1964	Salvador Allende Gossens	Covert
Somalia	U.S.	1964	***	Covert
Sri Lanka	U.S.	1965	UNP	Covert
Bolivia	U.S.	1966	Rene Barrientos Ortuno	Covert
Costa Rica	U.S.	1966	Daniel Oduber Quiros	Covert
Dominican Republic	U.S.	1966	Joaquin Beleaguer	Covert
India	USSR	1967	CPI	Covert
Laos	U.S.	1967	****	Covert
Finland	USSR	1968	Urho Kaleva Kekkonen	Overt
Guyana	U.S.	1968	PNC	Covert
Italy	U.S.	1968	DC	Covert
West Germany	USSR	1969	SPD	Overt
Thailand	U.S.	1969	UTPT	Covert
Chile[b]	U.S.	1970	Radomiro Tomic & Jorge Allesanderi	Covert
Chile[b]	USSR	1970	Salvador Allende Gossens	Covert

Target	Intervener	Year/Election	Assisted Party/ Candidate[a]	Covert/Overt
Costa Rica	USSR	1970	Jose Figueres Ferrer	Covert
Pakistan	USSR	1970	Awami League	Covert
Malta	U.S.	1971	PN	Covert
Uruguay	U.S.	1971	Colorados/Juan Maria Bordaberry	Covert
South Vietnam[†]	U.S.	1971	Nguyen Van Thieu	Covert
West Germany	USSR	1972	SPD	Covert
Italy[b]	U.S.	1972	DC	Covert
Italy[b]	USSR	1972	PCI	Covert
Japan	USSR	1972	JCP	Covert
Bangladesh	USSR	1973	Awami League	Covert
Denmark	USSR	1973	DKP	Covert
France	USSR	1974	Francois Mitterrand	Covert
Greece	USSR	1974	United Left	Covert
Denmark	USSR	1975	DKP	Covert
Italy[b]	U.S.	1976	DC	Overt[c]
Italy[b]	USSR	1976	PCI	Covert
India	USSR	1977	Congress Party (I)	Covert
West Germany	USSR	1980	SPD	Covert
Iran	U.S.	1980 (Jan.)	Ahmad Madani	Covert
Jamaica	U.S.	1980	Jamaican Labor Party	Covert
El Salvador	U.S.	1982	Christian Democratic Party/Duarte	Overt[c]
Mauritius	U.S.	1982	Labor Party	Covert
West Germany	USSR	1983	SPD	Overt
Italy	U.S.	1983	DC	Covert
El Salvador	U.S.	1984	Jose Napoleon Duarte	Covert
Grenada	U.S.	1984	New National Party	Overt[c]
Panama	U.S.	1984	Nicolas Ardito Barletta	Covert
U.S.	USSR	1984	Walter F. Mondale	Covert
Costa Rica	U.S.	1986	Rafael Angel Calderon Fournier	Covert
U.K	U.S.	1987	Conservatives	Overt
Chile[†]	U.S.	1988	"No" Campaign	Overt
France	USSR	1988	Andre Lajoinie	Covert
Panama	U.S.	1989	Guillermo Endara	Covert
Bulgaria	U.S.	1990	UDF	Overt
Czechoslovakia	U.S.	1990	OF-VPN	Overt
Haiti	U.S.	1990	Marc Louis Bazin	Covert
Nicaragua	U.S.	1990	Violeta Barrios de Chamorro	Overt[c]
Romania	U.S.	1990	PNL	Overt
Albania	U.S.	1991	PDSH	Overt

Target	Intervener	Year/Election	Assisted Party/ Candidate[a]	Covert/Overt
Bulgaria	U.S.	1991	UDF	Covert
Albania	U.S.	1992	PDSH	Covert
Israel	U.S.	1992	Labor	Overt
Lithuania	Russia	1992	LDDP	Overt
Romania	U.S.	1992	CDR	Covert
Yugoslavia/Serbia	U.S.	1992	Milan Panic	Overt
Cambodia	U.S.	1993	FUNCINPEC	Covert
Belarus	Russia	1994	Vyacheslav F. Kebich	Overt
Ukraine	U.S.	1994	Leonid Kravchuk	Overt
Israel	U.S.	1996	Shimon Peres/Labor	Overt
Russia	U.S.	1996	Boris N. Yeltsin	Overt[c]
Latvia	Russia	1998	TSP	Overt
Slovakia	U.S.	1998	SDK	Covert
Israel	U.S.	1999	Ehud Barak/One Israel	Covert
Yugoslavia/Serbia	U.S.	2000	Vojislav Kostunica	Overt

[a] Name of candidate in presidential elections, name of party in parliamentary elections. Main candidate/party only.

[b] Double interventions (the U.S. supports one side while the USSR/Russia backs a different side during the same election).

[c] An overt intervention that also included a significant covert component.

†Cases of partisan electoral interventions in elections which weren't competitive following my criteria, usually due to last-moment boycotts of the elections by one of the major sides which were widely expected to contest them or (in the 1988 Chilean case) a rare example of a relatively competitive plebiscite.

* Identity of aided candidate in this election not fully certain, besides being a competitor to Pres. Paasikivi, given available data (although probably Urho Kekkonen).

** Identity of aided candidate/party in this election, besides being part of the opposition to Pres. Goulart, unknown given available data.

*** Identity of aided candidate/party, besides being among the losers of this election, unknown given available data.

**** Identity of aided candidate/party unknown given available data.

Readers who are aware of a case of U.S./Russian electoral intervention not noted here (or an intervention by a different intervener) during this or a later period are warmly invited to email the author with this information at dovlvn@yahoo.com or dovlvn@hku.hk. I would be happy to add such cases to later versions of PEIG.

Bibliography

Primary Sources

The CIA Records Search Tool (CREST) system, College Park, Maryland.
The Declassified Documents Reference System (DDRS), Gale Group website.
Foreign Relations of the United States (FRUS)—select volumes.
HICOG Survey 191, 1953. "A Survey Analysis of the Factors Underlying the Outcome of the 1953 German Federal Elections," December 11, 1953, at Office of Research and Analysis, Research Reports on German Public Opinion, RG306 NARA.
HICOG Survey 193, 1954. "German Public Opinion on the Four Power Conference: With Latest Trends in EDC Thinking," January 18, 1954, at Office of Research and Analysis, Research Reports on German Public Opinion, RG306 NARA.

Main Archives Consulted

Dwight David Eisenhower Library (DDEL), Abilene, Kansas.
Lyndon Baines Johnson Library (LBJL), Austin, Texas.
U.S. National Archives (NARA), College Park, Maryland.
Harry S. Truman Library (HSTL), Independence, Missouri.
The Papers of Adolf Berle at Franklin Delano Roosevelt Library (FDRL), Hyde Park, New York.
The Papers of Spruille Braden at the Rare Book and Manuscript Library, Columbia University, New York.
The Papers of James B. Conant at Pusey Library, Harvard University, Boston.

Secondary Sources

Abramowitz, Alan. 2016. "Will Time for Change Mean Time for Trump?" *PS: Political Science & Politics* 49 (4): 659–660.
Agee, Philip. 1975. *Inside the Company: CIA Diary*. London: Allen Lane.
Aldrich, John H., Christopher Gelpi, Peter Feaver, Jason Reifler, and Kristen Thompson Sharp. 2006. "Foreign Policy and the Electoral Connection." *Annual Review of Political Science* 9:477–502.
Aldrich, Richard. 2001. *The Hidden Hand: Britain, America and Cold War Secret Intelligence*. London: John Murray.
Alexander, Robert. 1982. *Romulo Betancourt and the Transformation of Venezuela*. New Brunswick: Transaction Books.
Allen, Susan. 2008. "The Domestic Political Costs of Economic Sanctions." *Journal of Conflict Resolution* 52 (6): 916–944.
Ambrose, Stephan. 1990. *Eisenhower*. New York: Simon & Schuster.
Ames, Barry. 1995. "Electoral Strategy under Open-List PR." *American Journal of Political Science* 39 (2): 406–433.
Anderson, Leslie. 2009. "The Problem of Single-Party Predominance in an Unconsolidated Democracy: The Example of Argentina." *Perspectives on Politics* 7 (4): 767–784.

Andrew, Christopher. 2009. *The Defence of the Realm: The Authorized History of MI5.* London: Allen Lane.

Andrew, Christopher, and Oleg Gordievsky. 1990. *KGB: The Inside Story of Its Foreign Operations from Lenin to Gorbachev.* London: Hodder & Stoughton.

Andrew, Christopher, and Vasili Mitrokhin. 1999. *The Sword and the Shield: The Mitrokhin Archive and the Secret History of the KGB.* New York: Basic Books.

Andrew, Christopher, and Vasili Mitrokhin. 2005. *The World Was Going Our Way: The KGB and the Battle for the Third World.* New York: Basic Books.

Arens, Moshe. 1995. *Broken Covenant: American Foreign Policy and the Crisis between the U.S. and Israel.* New York: Simon & Schuster.

Arian, Asher, and Michal Shamir. 1995. *The Elections in Israel 1992.* Albany: SUNY Press.

Asunka, Joseph, Sarah Brierley, Miriam Golden, Erik Kramon, and George Ofosu. 2019. "Electoral Fraud or Violence: The Effect of Observers on Party Manipulation Strategies." *British Journal of Political Science* 49 (1): 129–151.

Ausderan, Jacob. 2015. "Following an Experienced Shepherd: How a Leader's Tenure Affects the Outcome of International Crises." *International Interactions* 41 (1): 26–45.

Aydin, Aysegul. 2012. *Foreign Powers and Intervention in Armed Conflicts.* Stanford: Stanford University Press.

Bak, Daehee, and Glenn Palmer. 2010. "Testing the Biden Hypothesis: Leader Tenure, Age, and International Conflict." *Foreign Policy Analysis* 6 (3): 257–273.

Balch-Lindsay, Dylan, and Andrew Enterline. 2000. "Killing Time: The World Politics of Civil War Duration, 1820–1992." *International Studies Quarterly* 44 (4): 615–642.

Barcelo, Joan. 2018. "Are Western-Educated Leaders Less Prone to Initiate Militarized Disputes?" *British Journal of Political Science* 50 (2): 535–556.

Barnes, Trevor.1982. "The Secret Cold War: The C.I.A. and American Foreign Policy in Europe 1946–1956: Part II." *The Historical Journal* 25 (3): 649–670.

Basinger, Scott. 2013. "Scandals and Congressional Elections in the Post-Watergate Era." *Political Research Quarterly* 66 (2): 385–399.

Baumgartner, Frederic. 2003. *Behind Locked Doors: A History of the Papal Elections.* New York: Palgrave.

Beck, Nathan, and Jonathan Katz. 1995. "What to Do (and Not to Do) with Time-Series Cross-Section Data." *American Political Science Review* 89 (3): 634–647.

Beck, Thorsten, George Clarke, Alberto Groff, Philip Keefer, and Patrick Walsh. 2001. "New Tools in Comparative Political Economy: The Database of Political Institutions." *World Bank Economic Review* 15 (1): 165–176.

Bemis, Samuel. 1934. "Washington's Farewell Address: A Foreign Policy of Independence." *The American Historical Review* 39 (2): 250–268.

Benoit, Kenneth, and Michael Marsh. 2008. "The Campaign Value of Incumbency: A New Solution to the Puzzle of Less Effective Incumbent Spending." *American Journal of Political Science* 52 (4): 874–890.

Benoit, Kenneth, and Michael Marsh. 2010. "Incumbent and Challenger Campaign Spending Effects in Proportional Electoral Systems: The Irish Elections of 2002." *Political Research Quarterly* 63:159–173.

Benton, Allyson. 2005. "Dissatisfied Democrats or Retrospective Voters? Economic Hardship, Political Institutions, and Voting Behavior in Latin America." *Comparative Political Studies* 38 (4): 417–442.

Ben-Zvi, Abraham. 2013. *From Truman to Obama: The Rise and Early Decline of American-Israeli Relations.* Tel Aviv: Miskal (Hebrew).

Berger, Daniel, William Easterly, Nathan Nunn, and Shanker Satyanath. 2013. "Commercial Imperialism? Political Influence and Trade during the Cold War." *American Economic Review* 103 (2): 863–896.

Berger, Meredith. 2018. *The State and Local Election Cybersecurity Playbook*. Cambridge, MA: Defending Digital Democracy Project, Belfer Center for Science and International Affairs, Harvard: Belfer Center For Science and International Affairs.

Bertoli, Andrew, Allan Dafoe, and Robert Trager. 2019. "Is There a War Party? Party Change, the Left–Right Divide, and International Conflict." *Journal of Conflict Resolution* 63 (4): 950–975.

Bissell, Richard. 1996. *Reflections of a Cold Warrior*. New Haven: Yale University Press.

Blais, André, Mathieu Turgeon, Elizabeth Gidengil, Neil Nevitte, and Richard Nadeau. 2004. "Which Matters Most? Comparing the Impact of Issues and the Economy in American, British and Canadian Elections." *British Journal of Political Science* 34 (3): 555–563.

Blankenship, Bryan. 2004. *Trusting the Machine: Inherent Problems with Electronic Voting Machines*. GIAC Paper, February 19.

Blanksten, George. 1953. *Peron's Argentina*. Chicago: University of Chicago Press.

Blaze, Matt, Jake Braun, Harri Hursti, Joseph Lorenzo Hall, Margaret MacAlpine, and Jeff Moss. 2017. "DEFCON 25: Voting Machine Hacking Village Report on Cyber Vulnerabilities in U.S. Election Equipment, Databases, and Infrastructure" (Report, September).

Bob, Clifford. 2005. *The Marketing of Rebellion: Insurgents, Media, and International Activism*. Cambridge: Cambridge University Press.

Bohne, Mike, Alicia Prevost, and James Thurber. 2009. "Campaign Consultants and Political Parties Today." In Dennis Johnson (ed.), *Routledge Handbook of Political Management*, 497–508. New York: Routledge.

Boix, Charles. 1999. "Setting the Rules of the Game: The Choice of Electoral Systems in Advanced Democracies." *American Political Science Review* 93:609–624.

Boix, Charles. 2011. "Democracy, Development, and the International System." *American Political Science Review* 105 (4): 809–828.

Boyle, Peter. 1990. *The Churchill-Eisenhower Correspondence*. Chapel Hill: UNC Press.

Braden, Mark, and Robert Tucker. 2014. "Disputed Elections Post *Bush v. Gore*." In Michael Alvarez and Bernard Grofman (eds.), *Election Administration in the United States: The State of Reform after* Bush v. Gore, 3–31. Cambridge: Cambridge University Press.

Bretton, Henry. 1955. "The Opposition Party." In James Pollock, (ed.), *German Democracy at Work: A Selective Study*, 48–77. Ann Arbor: University of Michigan Press.

Brockett, Charles. 2002. "An Illusion of Omnipotence: U.S. Policy toward Guatemala, 1954–1960." *Latin American Politics and Society* 44 (1): 91–126.

Brown, Stephan. 2001. "Authoritarian Leaders and Multiparty Elections in Africa: How Foreign Donors Help to Keep Kenya's Daniel arap Moi in Power." *Third World Quarterly* 22 (5): 725–739.

Brown, Stephan. 2005. "Foreign Aid and Democracy Promotion: Lessons from Africa." *European Journal of Development Research* 17 (2): 179–198.

Brownlee, Jason. 2009. "Portents of Pluralism: How Hybrid Regimes Affect Democratic Transitions." *American Journal of Political Science* 53 (3): 515–532.

Bubeck, Johannes, and Nikolay Marinov. 2017. "Process or Candidate: The International Community and the Desire for Electoral Integrity." *American Political Science Review* 111 (3): 535–554.

Bubeck, Johannes, and Nikolay Marinov. 2019. *Rules and Allies: Foreign Election Intervention*. Cambridge: Cambridge University Press.

Bueno de Mesquita, Bruce, and George Downs. 2006. "Intervention and Democracy." *International Organization* 60:627–649.

Bull, Hedley. 1984. *Intervention in World Politics*. Oxford: Clarendon Press.

Bunce, Valerie, and Sharon Wolchik. 2011. *Defeating Authoritarian Leaders in Postcommunist Countries*. Cambridge: Cambridge University Press.

Buscher, Frank. 1988. *The United States, Germany and the Problem of Convicted War Criminals, 1946-1955*. PhD diss., Marquette University.

Bush, Sarah. 2015. *The Taming of Democracy Assistance: Why Democracy Promotion Does Not Confront Dictators*. Cambridge: Cambridge University Press.

Bush, Sarah, and Amaney Jamal. 2015. "Anti-Americanism, Authoritarian Politics, and Attitudes about Women's Representation: Evidence from a Survey Experiment in Jordan." *International Studies Quarterly* 59 (1): 34–45.

Bush, Sarah, and Lauren Prather. 2017a. "The Promise and Limits of Election Observers in Building Election Credibility." *Journal of Politics* 79 (3): 921–935.

Bush, Sarah, and Lauren Prather. 2017b. "Foreign Economic Partners and Mass Attitudes towards International Economic Engagement." Paper presented at the meeting of the American Political Science Association, Philadelphia, August.

Bush, Sarah, and Lauren Prather. 2019. "From Monitoring to Meddling: How Foreign Actors Shape Local Trust in Elections." APSA, Washington D.C., August.

Byler, David. 2017. "Demographic Coalitions: How Trump Picked the Democratic Lock and Won the Presidency." In Larry Sabato, Kyle Kondik, and Geoffrey Skelley (eds.), *Trumped: The 2016 Election that Broke All the Rules*, 30–51. Lanham, MD: Rowman & Littlefield.

Byman, Daniel, and Kenneth Pollack. 2001. "Let Us Now Praise Great Men: Bringing the Statesman Back In." *International Security* 25 (4): 100–114.

Canes-Wrone, Brandice, and Jee-Wang Park. 2012. "Electoral Business Cycles in OECD Countries." *American Political Science Review* 106 (1): 104–122.

Cantón, Darío. 1973. *Elections and Political Parties in Argentina: History, Interpretation and Balance 1910-1966*. Buenos Aires: Siglo Veintinno Editores (Spanish).

Carothers, Thomas. 1996. *Assessing Democracy Assistance: The Case of Romania*. Washington, DC: Carnegie.

Carothers, Thomas. 2011. "How Not to Promote Democracy in Egypt." *Washington Post*, February 24.

Carpenter, Ted Galen. 2017. "The Duplicitous Superpower." *American Conservative*, November 28.

Carson, Austin. 2018. *Secret Wars: Covert Conflict in International Politics*. Princeton: Princeton University Press.

Carty, Kenneth, and Munroe Eagles. 1999. "Do Local Campaigns Matter? Campaign Spending, the Local Canvass and Party Support in Canada." *Electoral Studies* 18:69–87.

Cehelsky, Marta. 1967. *Guatemala's Frustrated Revolution: The "Liberation" of 1954*. Master's thesis, Columbia University.

Chandra, Kanchan. 2004. *Why Ethnic Parties Succeed: Patronage and Ethnic Head Counts in India*. New York: Cambridge University Press.

Channey, Carol, R., Michael Alvarez, and Jonathan Nagler. 1998. "Explaining the Gender Gap in U.S. Presidential Elections, 1980-1992." *Political Research Quarterly* 51 (2): 311–339.

Cheibub, Jose, and Adam Przeworski. 1999. "Democracy, Elections, and Accountability for Economic Outcomes." In Adam Przeworski, Susan Stokes, and Bernard Manin (eds.), *Democracy, Accountability and Representation*, 222–250. Cambridge: Cambridge University Press.

Chenoweth, Erica. 2013. *Why Civil Resistance Works: The Strategic Logic of Non-Violent Conflict*. New York: Columbia University Press.

Chiozza, Giacomo, and Ajin Choi. 2003. "Guess Who Did What: Political Leaders and the Management of Territorial Disputes, 1950–1990." *Journal of Conflict Resolution* 47:251–278.

Choi, Seung-Whan. 2013. "What Determines US Humanitarian Interventions?" *Conflict Management and Peace Science* 30 (2): 121–139.

Ciria, Alberto. 1974. *Parties and Power in Modern Argentina 1930–1946*. Albany: SUNY Press.

Clinton, Hillary. 2014. *Hard Choices*. New York: Simon & Schuster.

Clinton, Hillary. 2018. *What Happened*. New York: Simon & Schuster.

Colby, William. 1978. *Honorable Men: My Life at the CIA*. New York: Simon and Schuster.

Cohen, Jeffrey, Michael Krassa, and John Hamman. 1991. "The Impact of Presidential Campaigning on Midterm U.S. Senate Elections." *American Political Science Review* 85:165–178.

Colgan, Jeff. 2013. "Domestic Revolutionary Leaders and International Conflicts." *World Politics* 65 (4): 656–690.

Colman, Jonathan, and J. J. Widen. 2009. "The Johnson Administration and the Recruitment of Allies in Vietnam, 1964–1968." *History* 94 (316): 483–504.

Corstange, Daniel, and Nikolay Marinov. 2012. "Taking Sides in Other People's Elections: The Polarizing Effect of Foreign Intervention." *American Journal of Political Science* 65 (3): 655–670.

Costa-i-Font, Joan, Eduardo Rodriguez-Oreggia, and Dario Lunapla. 2003. "Political Competition and Pork Barrel Politics in the Allocation of Public Investment in Mexico." *Public Choice* 116 (1): 85–204.

Crassweller, Robert. 1987. *Peron and the Enigmas of Argentina*. New York: Norton.

Croco, Sarah. 2015. *Peace at What Price? Leader Culpability and the Domestic Politics of War Termination*. New York: Cambridge University Press.

Culane, Chris, Mark Eidridge, Alexander Essex, and Vanessa Teague. 2017. "Trust Implications of DDoS protection in Online Elections." *International Joint Conference on Electronic Voting*: 127–145.

Cueno, Alberto. 1982. *Historia del Peronismo*. Buenos Aires: Editorial Oriente (Spanish).

Currinder, Marian. 2018. "Campaign Finance: Where Big Money Mattered and Where It Didn't." In Michael Nelson (ed.), *The Elections of 2016*, 137–164. Thousand Oaks: CQ Press.

Dafoe, Allan, and Devin Caughey. 2016. "Honor and War: Southern US Presidents and the Effects of Concern for Reputation." *World Politics* 68 (2): 341–381.

Danilovic, Vesna. 2001. "The Sources of Threat Credibility in Extended Deterrence." *Journal of Conflict Resolution* 45 (3): 341–369.

Daugherty, W. J. 2004. *Executive Secrets: Covert Action and the Presidency*. Lexington: University Press of Kentucky.

DeConde, Alexander. 1958. *Entangling Alliances: Politics and Diplomacy under George Washington*. Durham: Duke University Press.

Denemark, David. 2000. "Partisan Pork Barrel in Parliamentary Systems: Australian Constituency-Level Grants." *Journal of Politics* 62 (3): 896–915.

Denver, David, and Gordon Hands. 1997a. "Challengers, Incumbents, and the Impact of Constituency Campaigning in Britain." *Electoral Studies* 16 (2): 175–193.

Denver, David, and Gordon Hands. 1997b. *Modern Constituency Electioneering: Local Campaigning in the 1992 General Election.* London: Taylor & Francis.

Dixit, Avinash, and John Londregan. 1996. "The Determinants of Success of Special Interests in Redistributive Politics." *Journal of Politics* 58 (4): 1132–1155.

Dobrynin, Anatoly. 1995. *In Confidence: Moscow's Ambassador to Six Cold War Presidents.* New York: Crown.

Donno, Daniela. 2013. *Defending Democratic Norms: International Actors and the Politics of Electoral Misconduct.* Oxford: Oxford University Press.

Dorn, Glenn. 2005. *Peronistas and New Dealers: U.S. Argentine Rivalry and the Western Hemisphere.* New Orleans: University Press of the South.

Downes, Alexander, and Mary Lilley. 2010. "Overt Peace, Covert War? Covert Intervention and the Democratic Peace." *Security Studies* 19 (2): 266–306.

Downes, Alexander, and Jonathan Monten. 2013. "Forced to Be Free? Why Foreign Imposed Regime Change Rarely Leads to Democratization." *International Security* 37 (4): 90–131.

Drezner, Dan. 1999. *The Sanctions Paradox.* Cambridge: Cambridge University Press.

Drezner, Dan. 2010. "A World of Ignorance." *The Spectator*, October 23.

Drummond, Gordon. 1982. *The German Social Democrats in Opposition, 1949–1960.* Norman: University of Oklahoma Press.

Duch, Raymond, and Randolph Stevenson. 2008. *The Economic Vote.* Cambridge: Cambridge University Press.

Duvarger, Maurice. 1954. *Political Parties: Their Organization and Activity in the Modern State.* London: Methuen.

Ebel, Roland. 1998. *Misunderstood Caudillo: Miguel Ydigoras Fuentes and the Failure of Democracy in Guatemala.* Lanham: University Press of America.

Edinger, Lewis. 1965. *Kurt Schumacher: A Study in Personality and Political Behavior.* Stanford: Stanford University Press.

Ehrlich, Clinton. 2016. "The Kremlin Really Believes That Hillary Clinton Will Start a War with Russia." *Foreign Policy*, September 7.

Elman, Miriam (ed.). 1997. *Paths to Peace: Is Democracy the Answer?* Cambridge, MA: MIT Press.

Enten, Harry. 2016. "How Much Did WikiLeaks Hurt Hillary Clinton?" *FiveThirtyEight*, December 23.

Enterline, Andrew, and Michael Greig. 2005. "Beacons of Hope? The Impact of Imposed Democracy on Regional Peace, Democracy, and Prosperity." *Journal of Politics* 67:1075–1098.

Erikson, Robert. 1989. "Economic Conditions and the Presidential Vote." *American Political Science Review* 83 (2): 567–573.

Etheredge, Lloyd. 1978. "Personality Effects on American Foreign Policy, 1898–1968: A Test of Interpersonal Generalization Theory." *American Political Science Review* 72:434–451.

Eguia, Jon, and Francisco Giovannoni. 2019. "Tactical Extremism." *American Political Science Review* 113 (1): 282–286.

Farago, Lanisdas. 1972. *The Game of the Foxes: The Untold Story of German Espionage in the United States and Great Britain during World War II.* New York: McKay.

Fascetto, Jorge. 2014. *Portazo al Autoritarismo.* Buenos Aires: Editorial Dunken.

Fearon, James. 1995. "Rationalist Explanations for War." *International Organization* 49 (3): 379–414.

Fidler, David. 2017. "Transforming Election Cybersecurity." Council of Foreign Policy Brief, May.

Findley, Michael, and Teo Tze. 2006. "Rethinking Third-Party Interventions into Civil Wars: An Actor-Centric Approach." *Journal of Politics* 68 (4): 828–837.

Finkel, Steve, Aníbal Pérez-Liñán, and Mitchell Seligson. 2007. "The Effects of U.S. Foreign Assistance on Democracy Building, 1990–2003." *World Politics* 59 (3): 404–438.

Finnemore, Martha. 2003. *The Purpose of Intervention: Changing Beliefs about the Use of Force.* Ithaca: Cornell University Press.

Fiorina, Morris. 1981. *Retrospective Voting in American National Elections.* New Haven: Yale University Press.

Forrest, John. 1997. "The Effects of Local Campaign Spending on the Geography of the Flow-of-the-Vote at the 1991 New South Wales State Election." *Australian Geographer* 28 (2): 229–240.

Forsythe, David. 1992. "Democracy, War, and Covert Action." *Journal of Peace Research* 29 (4): 385–395.

Fox, Colm. 2018. "Is All Politics Local? Determinants of Local and National Election Campaigns. *Comparative Political Studies* 51 (14): 1899–1934.

Frank, Gary. 1980. *Juan Peron vs. Spruille Braden: The Story Behind the Blue Book.* Lanham: University Press of America.

Franklin, James. 2002. "Political Party Opposition to Noncompetitive Regimes: A Cross-National Analysis." *Political Research Quarterly* 55 (3): 521–546.

Freedom House. "Freedom in the World 2018." Washington, DC.

Friedal, Mathias. 2007. "Die Bundestagswahl 1953." In Jakob Nikolaus (eds.), *Fallstudienzur Wahlkampfkommunikation 1912–2005*, 112–136. Heidelberg: Verlag (German).

Fryer, W.R. 1965. *Republic or Restoration in France?* Manchester: Mancester University Press

Fuhrmann, Matt, and Michael Horowitz. 2015. "When Leaders Matter: Rebel Experience and Nuclear Proliferation." *Journal of Politics* 77 (1): 72–87.

Fursenko, Alexander, and Timothy Naftali. 2006. *Khrushchev's Cold War: The Inside Story of an American Adversary.* New York: Norton.

Gaddis, John Lewis. 1990. *Russia, the Soviet Union and the United States: An Interpretive History.* New York: McGraw-Hill.

Gaddis, John Lewis. 1997. *We Now Know: Rethinking the Cold War.* New York: Oxford University Press.

Gandhi, Jennifer, and Oro Reuter. 2013. "The Incentives for Pre-Electoral Coalitions in Non-Democratic Elections." *Democratization* 20 (1): 137–159.

Gardner, Lloyd. 2006. "Poisoned Apples: John Foster Dulles and the 'Peace Offensive.'" In Kaus Larres and Kenneth Osgood (eds.), *The Cold War after Stalin's Death: A Missed Opportunity for Peace?*, 73–94. Lanham, MD: Rowman & Littlefield.

Garrett, Geoffrey. 2001. "Globalization and Government Spending around the World." *Studies in Comparative International Development* 35 (4): 3–29.

Gaubatz, Kurt. 1999. *Elections and War: The Electoral Incentive in the Democratic Politics of War.* Stanford: Stanford University Press.

Geddes, Barbara. 1999. "What Do We Know about Democratization After Twenty Years?" *Annual Review of Political Science* 2:115–144.

Geddes, Barbara. 2007. "What Causes Democratization?" In Charles Boix and Susan Stokes (eds.), *Oxford Handbook of International Relations*, 321–339. New York: Oxford University Press.

Gelman, Andrew, Boris Shor, Joseph Bafumi, and David Park. 2007. "Rich State, Poor State, Red State, Blue State: What's the Matter with Connecticut?" *Quarterly Journal of Political Science* 2:345–367.

Gent, Stephen. 2008. "Going In When It Counts: Military Intervention and the Outcome of Civil Conflicts." *International Studies Quarterly* 52 (4): 713–735.

George, Alexander, and Andrew Bennett. 2005. *Case Studies and Theory Development in the Social Sciences.* Cambridge, MA: MIT Press.

Gerber, Alan, and Donald Green. 2000. "The Effects of Canvassing, Telephone Calls, and Direct Mail on Voter Turnout: A Field Experiment." *American Political Science Review* 94 (3): 653–663.

Gleek, Lewis. 1988. *Dissolving the Colonial Bond: American Ambassadors to the Philippines, 1946–1984.* Quezon City: New Day Publishing.

Gleek, Lewis. 1993. *The Third Philippine Republic 1946–1972.* Quezon City: New Day Publishing.

Glees, Anthony. 1996. *Reinventing Germany: German Political Development since 1945.* Oxford: Berg.

Gleijeses, Piero. 1991. *Shattered Hope: The Guatemalan Revolution and the United States, 1944–1954.* Princeton: Princeton University Press.

Godson, Roy. 1995. *Dirty Tricks or Trump Cards: U.S. Covert Action and Counterintelligence.* Washington, DC: Brassey's.

Grabbe, Hans-Jurgen. 1990. "Konrad Adenauer John Foster Dulles and West German-American Relations." In Richard Immerman (ed.), *John Foster Dulles and the Diplomacy of the Cold War*, 109–132. Princeton: Princeton University Press.

Granieri, Ronald. 1996. *America's Germany, Germany's Europe: Konrad Adenauer, the CDU/CSU, and the Politics of German Westbindung 1949–1963.* PhD diss., University of Chicago.

Green, Donald, Alan Gerber, and David Nickerson. 2003. "Getting Out the Vote in Local Elections: Results from Six Door-to-Door Experiments." *Journal of Politics* 65 (4): 1083–1096.

Greenstein, Fred. 1982. *The Hidden-Hand Presidency: Eisenhower as Leader.* New York: Basic Books.

Greenstein, Fred. 1992. "Can Personality and Politics Be Studied Systematically?" *Political Psychology* 13 (1): 105–128.

Greystone Press. 1964. *The World and Its Peoples: Germany.* New York: Author.

Grimmer, Justin, Solomon Messing, and Sean Westwood. 2012. "How Words and Money Cultivate a Personal Vote: The Effect of Legislator Credit Claiming on Constituent Credit Allocation." *American Political Science Review* 106 (4): 703–719.

Grossman, Gene, and Elhanan Helpman. 2001. *Special Interest Politics.* Cambridge, MA: MIT Press.

Grow, Michael. 2008. *U.S. Presidents and Latin American Interventions: Pursuing Regime Change in the Cold War.* Lawrence: University Press of Kansas.

Guess, Andrew, Jonathan Nagler, and Joshua Tucker. 2019. "Less then you think: Prevalence and predictors of fake news dissemination on Facebook." *Science Advances* 5 (1): EAAU4586.

Gustafson, Kristian. 2007. *Hostile Intent: U.S Covert Operations in Chile, 1964–1974.*Washington, DC: Potomac Books.

Halderman, Alex. 2017. "Testimony before the U.S. Senate Select Committee on Intelligence Russian Interference in the 2016 U.S. Elections," June 21.

Halderman, Alex, Hari Prasad, Rop Gonggrijp, Arun Kankipati, Sai Krishna Sakhamuri, Scott Wolchok, Eric Wustrow, and Vasavya Yagati. 2010. "Security Analysis of India's Electronic Voting Machines." Proceedings of the 17th ACM Conference on Computer and Communications Security (CCS'10), Chicago, October 4–8.

Hamilton-Paterson, James. 1998. *America's Boy's*. London: Granta.

Handrieder, Wolfram 1967. *West German Foreign Policy*. Stanford: Stanford University Press

Handy, Jim. 1984. *Gift of the Devil: A History of Guatemala*. Boston: South End Press.

Harding, Luke. 2017. *Collusion: Secret Meetings, Dirty Money and How Russia Helped Donald Trump Win*. New York: Vintage Books.

Harris, Peter. 2010. *Birth: The Conspiracy to Stop the '94 Election*. Cape Town: Umuzi.

Haslam, Jonathan. 2005. *The Nixon Administration and the Death of Allende's Chile: A Case of Assisted Suicide*. New York: Verso.

He, Eunyoung. 2007. *Distributive Politics in the Era of Globalization*. PhD diss., University of California Los Angeles.

Hedges, James. 2011. *Argentina: A New History*. New York: I. B. Tauris.

Heffington, Colton. 2018. "Hawks and Doves Reconsidered: Parties, Leaders, and Foreign Policy in Democracies." *Foreign Policy Analysis* 14 (1): 64–85.

Heidenheimer, Arnold. 1960. *Adenauer and the CDU: The Rise of the Leader and the Integration of the Party*. The Hauge: Martinus Nijhoff.

Hellwig, Timothy, and David Samuels. 2007. "Voting in Open Economies: The Electoral Consequences of Globalization." *Comparative Political Studies* 40 (3): 283–306.

Hershberg, James. 1993. *James B. Conant: Harvard to Hiroshima and the Making of the Nuclear Age*. New York: Knopf.

Hess, Gary 2007. "With Friends like These: Waging War and Seeking 'More Flags.'" In David Anderson and John Ernst (eds.), *The War That Never Ends: New Perspectives on the Vietnam War*, 55–74. Lexington: University Press of Kentucky.

Hetherington, Marc. 2018. "The Election: The Allure of the Outsider." In Michael Nelson (ed.), *The Elections of 2016*, 63–86. Thousand Oaks: CQ Press.

Hillygus, D. Sunshine, and Simon Jackman. 2003. "Voter Decision Making in Election 2000: Campaign Effects, Partisan Activation, and the Clinton Legacy." *American Journal of Political Science* 47 (4): 583–596.

Hirsch, Felix. 1952. "Adenauer or Schumacher?" *Current History* 22:70–74.

Hirsch-Weber, Wolfgang, and Klaus Schurtz. 1957. *Wahler und Gewahlte: Eine Untersuchung der Bundestagswahlen 1953*. Berlin: Verlag (German).

Hoopes, Towsend. 1973. *The Devil and John Foster Dulles*. Boston: Little, Brown.

Horowitz, Michael, Rose McDermott, and Allan Stam. 2005. "Leader Age, Regime Type, and Violent International Relations." *Journal of Conflict Resolution* 49 (5): 661–685.

Horowitz, Michael, Allan Stam, and Cali Ellis. 2015. *Why Leaders Fight*. New York: Cambridge University Press.

Hunt, John. 2016. *The Vacant See in Early Modern Rome: A Social History of the Papal Interregnum*. Leiden: Brill.

Huet-Vaughn, Emiliano. 2019. "Stimulating the Vote: ARRA Road Spending and Vote Share." *American Economic Journal* 11 (1): 292–316.

Hultman, Lisa Jacob Kathman, and Megan Shannon. 2013. "United Nations Peacekeeping and Civilian Protection in Civil War." *American Journal of Political Science* 57 (4): 875–891.

Huntington, Samuel. 1999. "The Lonely Superpower." *Foreign Affairs* 78 (2): 35–49.

Hyde, Susan. 2011. *The Pseudo-Democrat's Dilemma: Why Election Observation Became an International Norm*. Ithaca: Cornell University Press.

Ichino, Naomi, and Schundeln, Matthias. 2012. "Deterring or Displacing Electoral Irregularities? Spillover Effects of Observers in a Randomized Field Experiment in Ghana." *Journal of Politics* 74 (1): 292–307.

Immerman, Richard. 1982. *The CIA in Guatemala: The Foreign Policy of Intervention*. Austin: University of Texas Press.

Immerman, Richard. 1990. *John Foster Dulles and the Diplomacy of the Cold War*. Princeton: Princeton University Press.

Inginmundarson, Valur. 1994. "Cold War Misperceptions: The Communist and Western Responses to the East German Refugee Crisis in 1953." *Journal of Contemporary History* 29 (3): 463–481.

Inginmundarson, Valur. 1996. "The Eisenhower Administration, the Adenauer Government and the Political Uses of the East German Uprising in 1953." *Diplomatic History* 20 (3): 381–409.

Irving, Ronald. 2002. *Adenauer*. Harlow: Longman.

Isaacson, Walter. 1992. *Kissinger*. New York: Simon and Schuster.

Jacobson, Gary. 1978. "The Effects of Campaign Spending in Congressional Elections." *American Political Science Review* 72:469–491.

Jacobson, Gary. 2006. "Measuring Campaign Spending Effects in U.S. House Elections." In Henry Brady and Richard Johnston (eds.), *Capturing Campaign Effects*, 199–220. Ann Arbor: University of Michigan Press.

Jakobson, Max. 1998. *Finland in the New Europe*. New York: Preager.

James, Daniel. 1957. "Seven Days That Shook Guatemala." *The New Leader* 50 (47): 3–6.

Jamieson, Kathleen Hall. 2018. *Cyberwar: How Russian Hackers and Trolls Helped Elect a President*. New York: Oxford University Press.

Jenkins, Holman. 2018. "Mueller Focuses on Molehills." *Wall Street Journal*, February 20.

Joaquin, Nick. 1990. *Mr. Rural Reform: The Times and Tidings of Manny Manahan*. Manila: Cap.

Johnson, Loch. 1989. *America's Secret Power*. New York: Oxford University Press.

Johnston, Meredith. 2006. "Stopping Winks and Nods: Limits on Coordination as a Means of Regulating 527 Organizations." *NYU Law Review* 81 (3): 1166–1205.

Johnston, Richard, Michael Hagen, and Kathleen Hall Jamieson. 2004. *The 2000 Presidential Election and the Foundations of Party Politics*. New York: Cambridge University Press.

Johnston, Ronald, and Charles Pattie. 1995. "The Impact of Spending on Party Constituency Campaigns at Recent British General Elections." *Party Politics* 1 (2): 261–273.

Jonas, Manfred. 1984. *The United States and Germany*. Ithaca: Cornell University Press.

Jones, Douglas, and Barbara Simons. 2012. *Broken Ballots: Will Your Vote Count?* Stanford: Center for the Study of Language and Information (CSLI).

Jones, Mark. 2004. "Electoral Institutions, Social Cleavages, and Candidate Competition in Presidential Elections." *Electoral Studies* 23:73–106.

Ju, Changwook. 2018. "You Can't Hack a Piece of Paper": Jake Braun Talks U.S. Election Security." *Chicago Policy Review*, April 1.

Kalla, Joshua, and David Broockman. 2018. "The Minimal Persuasive Effects of Campaign Contact in General Elections: Evidence from 49 Field Experiments." *American Political Science Review* 112 (1): 148–166.

Kaminski, Marek. 2002. "Do Parties Benefit from Electoral Manipulation? Electoral Laws and Heresthetics in Poland, 1989–1993." *Journal of Theoretical Politics* 14 (3): 325–358.

Karabell, Zachary. 1999. *Architects of Intervention: The United States the Third World and the Cold War.* Baton Rouge: Louisiana State University Press.

Kartic, Navin, and Preston McAfee. 2007. "Signaling Character in Electoral Competition." *American Economic Review* 97 (3): 852–870.

Kastner, Jill. 1999. *Adenauer, Eisenhower and the Dilemmas of the Cold War, 1953-1960.* PhD diss., Harvard University.

Kathman, Jacob. 2011. "Civil War Diffusion and Regional Motivations for Interventions." *Journal of Conflict Resolution* 55 (6): 847–876.

Kayser, Mark, and Michael Peress. 2012. "Benchmarking Across Borders: Electoral Accountability and the Necessity of Comparison." *American Political Science Review* 106 (3): 661–684.

Keck, Margaret, and Kathryn Sikkink. 1998. *Activists beyond Borders: Advocacy Networks in International Politics.* Ithaca: Cornell University Press.

Keeley, Robert. 2010. *The Colonels Coup and the American Embassy.* University Park: Pennsylvania State University Press.

Kegley, Charles, and Margaret Hermann. 1995. "Military Intervention and the Democratic Peace." *International Interactions* 21 (1): 1–21.

Keller, Jonathan, and Dennis Foster. 2012. "Presidential Leadership Style and the Political Use of Force." *Political Psychology* 33 (5): 581–598.

Kelley, Judith. 2008. "Assessing the Complex Evolution of Norms: The Rise of International Election Monitoring." *International Organization* 62 (2): 221–256.

Kelley, Judith. 2009. "D-Minus Elections: The Politics and Norms of International Election Observation." *International Organization* 63 (4): 765–787.

Kelly, David. 1953. *The Ruling Few, or, The Human Background of Diplomacy.* London: Hollis.

Kennedy, Courtney, Andrew Mercer, Scott Keeter, Nick Hatley, Kyley McGeeney, and Alejandra Gimenez. 2016. *Evaluating Online Nonprobability Surveys* (Report, May 2). Washington, DC: Pew Research Center.

Kennedy, Peter. 2003. *A Guide to Econometrics.* Cambridge, MA: MIT Press.

Kenny, Christopher, and Michael McBurnett. 1997. "Up Close and Personal: Campaign Contact and Candidate Spending in U.S. House Elections." *Political Research Quarterly* 50 (1): 75–96.

Kenski, Kate, Bruce Hardy, and Kathleen Hall Jamieson. 2010. *The Obama Victory: How Media, Money and Message Shaped the 2008 Election.* Oxford: Oxford University Press.

Kertzer, Joshua. 2016. *Resolve in International Politics.* Princeton: Princeton University Press.

Kibbe, Jennifer. 2002. *Presidents as Kingmakers: U.S. Decisions to Overthrow Foreign Governments*. PhD diss., University of California Los Angeles.

Kim, Taehyun, and Chang Jae Baik. 2011. "Taming and Tamed by the United States." In Byung-Kook Kim and Ezra Vogel (eds.), *The Park Chung Hee Era: Transformation of South Korea*, 58–84. Cambridge, MA: Harvard University Press.

Kisatsky, Deborah. 2005. *The United States and the European Right 1945-1955*. Columbus: Ohio University Press.

Klarevas, Louis. 2006. "Were the Eagle and the Phoenix Birds of a Feather? The United States and the Greek Coup of 1967." *Diplomatic History* 30 (3): 471–508.

Knack, Stephen. 2004. "Does Foreign Aid Promote Democracy?" *International Studies Quarterly* 48 (1): 251–266.

Koch, Michael, and Patricia Sullivan. 2010. "Should I Stay or Should I Go? Partisanship Approval and the Duration of Major Power Democratic Military Intervention." *Journal of Politics* 72 (3): 616–629.

Kornblith, Miriam, and Daniel Levine. 1995. "Venezuela: The Life and Times of the Party System." In Scott Mainwaring and Timothy Scully (eds.), *Building Democratic Institutions: Party Systems in Latin America*, 37–71. Stanford: Stanford University Press.

Krauthammer, Charles. 2011. "From Freedom Agenda to Freedom Doctrine." *Washington Post*, February 10.

Kreps, Sarah. 2011. *Coalitions of Convenience: United States Military Interventions after the Cold War*. Oxford: Oxford University Press.

Kuperman, Alan. 2008. "The Moral Hazard of Humanitarian Intervention: Lessons from the Balkans." *International Studies Quarterly* 52:49–80.

Kuzio, Taras. 2005. "Russian Policy toward Ukraine during Elections." *Demokratizatsiya* 13 (4): 491–517.

Kydd, Andrew, and Scott Straus. 2013. "The Road to Hell? Third Party Intervention to Prevent Atrocities." *American Journal of Political Science* 57 (3): 673–684.

Lande, Carl. 1964. *Leaders, Factions and Parties: The Structure of Philippine Politics*. New Haven: Yale University Press.

Landler, Mark. 2016. *Alter Egos: Hillary Clinton, Barack Obama, and the Twilight Struggle over American Power*. New York: Random House.

Lania, Leo. 1952. "Schumacher: Violent Martyr." *United Nations World* 6:13–15.

Larres Klaus. 2006. "The Road to Geneva 1955: Churchill's Summit Diplomacy and Anglo-American Tensions after Stalin's Death." In Klaus Larres and Kenneth Osgood (eds.), *The Cold War after Stalin's Death: A Missed Opportunity for Peace?*, 137–156. Lanham, MD: Rowman & Littlefield.

Levi Boxell, Matthew Gentzkow, and Jesse Shapiro. 2018. "A Note on Internet Use and the 2016 U.S. Presidential Election Outcome." *PLoS ONE* 13 (7): e0199571.

Levin, Dov H. 2016a. "When the Great Power Gets a Vote: The Effects of Great Power Electoral Interventions on Election Results." *International Studies Quarterly* 60 (2): 189–202.

Levin, Dov H. 2016b. "Sure, the U.S. and Russia Often Meddle in Foreign Elections. Does It Matter?" *Washington Post*, September 7.

Levin, Dov H. 2020. "Voting for Trouble? Partisan Electoral Interventions and Terrorism." *Terrorism and Political Violence* 32 (3): 489–505.

Levin, Dov H. 2018a. "History Suggests Proving Collusion Between the Trump Campaign and Russia May Be Impossible." *Lawfare*, December 7.

Levin, Dov H. 2018b. "Will You Still Love Me Tomorrow? Electoral Interventions & FP Compliance." Conference presentation, International Studies Association, San Francisco.

Levin, Dov H. 2018c. "Does Meddling Pay? The Effects of Partisan Electoral Interventions on International Trade." Paper presented at the meeting of the American Political Science Association, Boston, August 29–September 2.

Levin, Dov H. 2019a. "Partisan Electoral Interventions by the Great Powers: Introducing the PEIG Dataset." *Conflict Management and Peace Science* 36 (1): 88–106.

Levin, Dov H. 2019b. "A Vote for Freedom? The Effects of Partisan Electoral Interventions on Regime Type." *Journal of Conflict Resolution* 63 (4): 839–868.

Levite, Ariel, Bruce Jentleson, and Larry Berman. 1992. *Foreign Military Intervention: The Dynamics of Protracted Conflict.* New York: Columbia University Press.

Levitsky, Steven, and Lucan Way. 2010. *Competitive Authoritarianism.* Cambridge: Cambridge University Press.

Lewis-Beck, Michael, and Mary Stegmaier. 2000. "Economic Determinants of Electoral Outcomes." *Annual Review of Political Science* 3:183–219.

Lewis-Beck, Michael, Richard Nadeau, and Angelo Elias. 2008. "Economics, Party, and the Vote: Causality Issues and Panel." *American Journal of Political Science* 52 (1): 84–95.

Lewitter, L. R. 1956. "Peter the Great and the Polish Election of 1697." *Cambridge Historical Journal* 12 (2): 126–143.

Lipson, Charles. 2005. *Reliable Partners: How Democracies Have Made a Separate Peace.* Princeton: Princeton University Press.

Litschig, Stephan, and Kevin Morrison. 2010. "Government Spending and Re-Election" (working paper), Cornell University.

Logevall, Fredrik. 1999. *Choosing War: The Lost Chance of Peace and Escalation in Vietnam.* Berkeley: University of California Press.

Lowenthal, Abraham. 1991. *Exporting Democracy: The United States and Latin America.* Baltimore: Johns Hopkins University Press.

Lowenthal, Mark. 2003. *Intelligence: From Secrets to Policy.* Washington, DC: CQ Press.

Luna, Felix. 1969. *El 45.* Buenos Aires: Editorial Sudamericana (Spanish).

Lupton, Danielle. 2018. "Reexamining Reputation for Resolve: Leaders, States, and the Onset of International Crises." *Journal of Global Security Studies* 3 (2): 196–218.

Lupu, Noam 2014. "Brand Dilution and the Breakdown of Political Parties in Latin America." *World Politics* 66 (4): 561–602.

Lutmar, Carmela. 2015. "'Puppets' Domestic Institutions, and Foreign Policy Compliance," in Carmela Lutmar and Benjamin Miller (eds.), *Regional Peacemaking and Conflict Management: A Comparative Approach,* 221–248. New York: Routledge.

Lynch, Allen. 2018. "Putin and Trump." *Diplomatic History* 42 (4): 583–585.

MacDonald, C. A. 1980. "The Politics of Intervention: The United States and Argentina, 1941–1946." *Journal of Latin American Studies* 12 (2): 365–396.

Mandilow, Jonathan. 1995. "The 1992 Campaign: Valence and Issue Positions." In Arian Asher and Michal Shamir (eds.), *The Elections in Israel 1992,* 207–234. Albany: SUNY Press.

Maravall, Jose. 1999. "Accountability and Manipulation." In Adam Przeworski, Susan Stokes, and Bernard Manin (eds.), *Democracy, Accountability and Representation,* 154–196. Cambridge: Cambridge University Press.

Marchetti, Victor, and John Marks. 1983. *The CIA and the Cult of Intelligence.* New York: Dell.

Marinov, Nikolay. 2005. "Do Economic Sanctions Destabilize Country Leaders?" *American Journal of Political Science* 49 (3): 564–576.

Marinov, Nikolay. 2018. "International Actors as Critics of Domestic Freedoms." Social Science Research Network (SSRN), January 7.

Martz, John. 1959. *Central America: The Crisis and the Challenge.* Chapel Hill: University of North Carolina Press.

Martz, John. 1966. *Accion Democratica: Evolution of a Modern Political Party in Venezuela.* Princeton: Princeton University Press.

Masket, Seth. 2009. "Did Obama's Ground Game Matter? The Influence of Local Field Offices during the 2008 Presidential Election." *Public Opinion Quarterly* 73 (5): 1023–1039.

Matsubayashi, Tetsuya. 2013. "Do Politicians Shape Public Opinion?" *British Journal of Political Science* 43 (2): 451–478.

Matush, Kelly. 2018. *Going Public Abroad: When and Why Leaders Address Foreign Publics.* PhD diss., University of California San Diego.

Mauch, Christof, and Jeremiah Reimer. 2003. *The Shadow War against Hitler.* New York: Colombia University Press.

Maulucci, Thomas. 2003. "Konrad Adenauer's April 1953 Visit to the United States and the Limits of the German-American Relationship in the Early 1950s." *German Studies Review* 26 (3): 577–596.

Mayer, William. 2018. "The Nominations: The Road to a Much Disliked General Election." In Michael Nelson (ed.), *The Elections of 2016,* 29–62. Thousand Oaks: CQ Press.

Mayhew, David. 1974. *Congress: The Electoral Connection.* New Haven: Yale University Press.

McAllister, James. 2002. *No Exit: America and the German Problem 1943–1954.* Ithaca: Cornell University Press.

McCarthy, Abigail. 1972. *Private Faces, Public Places.* Garden City: Doubleday.

McCubbins, Mathew, and Frances Rosenbluth. 1995. "Party Provision for Personal Politics: Dividing the Vote in Japan." In Peter Cowhey and Mathew McCubbins (eds.), Structure and Policy in Japan and the United States, 35–60. New York: Cambridge University Press.

McManus, Roseanne. 2019. "Crazy like a Fox? Are Leaders with Reputations for Madness More Successful at International Coercion?" *British Journal of Political Science* (Early view).

McPherson, Alan. 2003. *Yankee No! Anti-Americanism in U.S.–Latin American Relations.* Cambridge, MA: Harvard University Press.

Meernik, James.1996 "United States Military Intervention and the Promotion of Democracy." *Journal of Peace Research* 33 (4): 391–402.

Mellow, Nicole. 2018. "Voting Behavior Continuity and Confusion in the Electorate." In Michael Nelson (ed.), *The Elections of 2016,* 87–112. Thousand Oaks: CQ Press.

Melone, Albert. 1998. *Creating Parliamentary Government: The Transition to Democracy in Bulgaria.* Columbus: Ohio State University Press.

Mercer, Jonathan. 1996. *Reputation and International Politics.* Ithaca: Cornell University Press.

Miller, James. 1983. "Taking Off the Gloves: The United States and the Italian Elections of 1948." *Diplomatic History* 7 (1): 35–56.

Miller, James. 2009. *The United States and the Making of Modern Greece.* Chapel Hill: University of North Carolina Press.

Miller, Mark. 2005. *Fooled Again: The Real Case for Electoral Reform.* New York: Basic Books.

Mitchell, Allen. 1979. *The German Influence in France after 1870.* Chapel Hill: University of North Carolina Press.

Most, Benjamin, and Harvey Starr. 1989. *Inquiry, Logic and International Politics.* Columbia: University of South Carolina Press.

Mueller Report. 2019. *Report on the Investigation into Russian Interference in the 2016 Presidential Elections volumes 1 and 2.* U.S. Government Printing Office, March.

Myers, Steve. 2015. *The New Czar: The Rise and Reign of Vladimir Putin.* New York: Knopf.

Najarro, Ruano. 2012. "El golpe de Estado de 1963". In Álvarez Aragón, Figueroa Ibarra, Taracena Arriola, Tischler Vizquerra, and Urrutia García (eds.), *Guatemala: historia reciente (1954-1996).* Guatemala: Flasco (Spanish).

Newton, Ronald. 1992. *The "Nazi" Menace in Argentina, 1931-1947.* Stanford: Stanford University Press.

Nicholls, A. J. 1997. *The Bonn Republic: West German Democracy 1945-1990.* London: Longman.

Nimmo, Dan. 1970. *Political Persuaders: The Techniques of Modern Election Campaigns.* New York: Prentice Hall.

Nincic, Miroslav. 1992. *Democracy and Foreign Policy.* New York: Columbia University Press.

Ninkovich, Frank. 1988. *Germany and the United States.* Boston: Twayne Publishers.

Nixon, Richard. 1962. *Six Crises.* New York: Doubleday.

Njolstad, Olav. 2002. "The Carter Administration and Italy: Keeping the Communists Out of Power without Interfering." *Journal of Cold War Studies* 4 (3): 56-94.

Noelle, Elisabeth, and Erich Neumann. 1956. *Jahrbuch Der Offentlichen Meinung 1947-1955.* Germany: Verlag Fur Demoskopie (German).

Noelle, Elisabeth, and Erich Neumann. 1967. *The Germans: Public Opinion Polls 1947-1966.* Germany: Verlag Fur Demoskopie.

Nohlen, Dieter. (ed.). 2005. *Elections in the Americas: A Data Handbook.* 2 vols. New York: Oxford University Press.

Nohlen, Dieter, Florian Grotz, and Christof Hartmann (eds.). 2001. *Elections in Asia and the Pacific: A Data Handbook.* 2 vols. New York: Oxford University Press.

Nohlen, Dieter, Michael Krennerich, and Berhard Thibaut (eds.). 1999. *Elections in Africa: A Data Handbook.* New York: Oxford University Press.

Nohlen, Dieter, and Philip Strover (eds.). 2010. *Elections in Europe: A Data Handbook.* Baden-Baden: Nomos.

Norden, Lawrence, and Ian Vandewalker. 2017. *Securing Elections from Foreign Interference* (Report). New York: Brennan Center for Justice.

Nordhaus, William. 1975. "The Political Business Cycle." *Review of Economic Studies* 42:169-190.

Nordlinger, Eric.1981. *On the Autonomy of the Democratic State.* Cambridge, MA: Harvard University Press.

Nyhan, Brendan. 2018. "Fake News and Bots May Be Worrisome, but Their Political Power Is Overblown." *New York Times*, February 13.

Nyman, Par. 2017. "Door-to-Door Canvassing in the European Elections: Evidence from a Swedish Field Experiment." *Electoral Studies* 45:110-118.

O'Donnell, Guillermo, Philippe C. Schmitter, and Laurence Whitehead (eds.) 1986. *Transitions from Authoritarian Rule.* Baltimore: Johns Hopkins University Press.

O'Rourke, Lindsey. 2018. *Covert Regime Change: America's Secret Cold War*. Ithaca: Cornell University Press.

Osborne, Martin. 1995. "Spatial Models of Political Competition under Plurality Rule: A Survey of Some Explanations of the Number of Candidates and the Positions They Take." *Canadian Journal of Economics* 28 (2): 261–301.

Owen, John. 2003. "The Foreign Imposition of Domestic Institutions." *International Organization* 56 (2): 375–409.

Pacek, Alexander, and Edwin Aguilar. 2000. "Macroeconomic Conditions, Voter Turnout, and the Working-Class/Economically Disadvantaged Party Vote in Developing Countries." *Comparative Political Studies* 33 (8): 995–1017.

Page, Benjamin, and Robert Shapiro. 1983. "Effects of Public Opinion on Policy." *American Political Science Review* 77:175–190.

Page, Benjamin, and Robert Shapiro. 1992. *The Rational Public: Fifty Years of Trends in American Policy Preferences*. Chicago: University of Chicago Press.

Page, Joseph. 1988. *Peron: A Biography*. New York: Random House.

Page Fortna, Virginia. 2008. *Does Peacekeeping Work? Shaping Belligerents' Choices after Civil War*. Princeton: Princeton University Press.

Palda, Filip, and Kristian Palda. 1998. "The Impact of Campaign Expenditures on Political Competition in the French Legislative Elections of 1993." *Public Choice* 94 (1): 157–174.

Paldam, Martin. 1991. "How Robust Is the Vote Function? A Study of Seventeen Nations over Four Decades." In Helmut Norpoth, Michael Lewis-Beck, and Jean-Dominique Lafay (eds.), *Economics and Politics: The Calculus of Support*, 9–31. Ann Arbor: University of Michigan Press.

Paz, Alberto, and Ferrari, Gustavo. 1966. *Argentina's Foreign Policy, 1930–1962*. Notre Dame: University of Notre Dame Press.

Peceny, Mark. 1999. "Forcing Them to Be Free." *Political Research Quarterly* 52 (3): 549–582.

Peic, Goran, and Dan Reiter. 2011. "Foreign-Imposed Regime Change, State Power and Civil War Onset, 1920–2004." *British Journal of Political Science* 41 (3): 453–475.

Pelc, Krzysztof 2013 "Googling the WTO: What Search-Engine Data Tell Us About the Political Economy of Institutions" *International Organizations* 67(3): 629–655.

Pew Research Center. 2018. "An Examination of the 2016 Electorate, Based on Validated Voters" (Report, August 9). Washington, DC: Author.

Pickering, Jeffery, and Mark Peceny. 2006. "Forging Democracy at Gunpoint." *International Studies Quarterly* 50 (3): 539–560.

Pinckney, Thomas. 1971. *Third Parties and the Philippine Party System*. PhD Diss., University of Tennessee.

Plassner, Fritz. 2009. "Political Consulting Worldwide." In Dennis Johnson (ed.), *Routledge Handbook of Political Management*. New York: Routledge.

Plassner, Fritz, and Gunter Lengauer. 2009. "Television Campaigning Worldwide." In Dennis Johnson (ed.), *Routledge Handbook of Political Management*. New York: Routledge.

Plümper, Thomas, Vera Troeger, and Eric Neumayer. 2019. "Case Selection and Causual Inference in Qualitative Comparative Research." *PLOS One* 14 (7): e0219727.

Potash, Robert. 1969. *The Army and Politics in Argentina 1928–1945: Yrigoyen to Peron*. Stanford: Stanford University Press.

Potash, Robert. 1980. *The Army and Politics in Argentina 1945–1962: Peron to Frondizi*. Stanford: Stanford University Press.

Potter, Philip. 2007. "Does Experience Matter? American Presidential Experience, Age, and International Conflict." *Journal of Conflict Resolution* 51:351–378.

Powell, Bingham, and Guy Whitten. 1993. "A Cross-National Analysis of Economic Voting: Taking Account of the Political Context." *American Journal of Political Science* 37 (2): 391–414.

Powell, Robert. 2006. "War as a Commitment Problem." *International Organization* 60 (1): 169–203.

Poznansky, Michael. 2015. "Stasis or Decay? Reconciling Covert War and the Democratic Peace." *International Studies Quarterly* 59 (4): 629–829.

Poznansky, Michael. 2019. Review of "Covert Regime Change: America's Secret Cold War by Lindsey A. O'Rourke." 134 (4): 755–756.

Prados, John. 2006. *Safe for Democracy: The Secret Wars of the CIA.* Chicago: Dee.

Press, Daryl. 2005. "The Credibility of Power: Assessing Threats during the 'Appeasement' Crises of the 1930s." *International Security* 29 (3): 136–169.

Przeworski, Adam. 2010. *Democracy and the Limits of Self-Government.* New York: Cambridge University Press.

Putnam, Robert, Robert Leonardi, and Rafaella Nanetti. 1979. "Attitude Stability Among Italian Elites." *American Journal of Political Science* 23:463–494.

Quandt, William. 1993. "Forging the Impossible Peace." *Washington Post*, September 12.

Quirk, Paul. 2018. "The Presidency: Donald Trump and the Question of Fitness." In Michael Nelson (ed.), *The Elections of 2016*, 189–216. Thousand Oaks: CQ Press.

Rabe, Stephen. 1982. *The Road to OPEC: United States Relations with Venezuela, 1919–1976.* Austin: University of Texas Press.

Rabe, Stephen. 1988. *Eisenhower and Latin America: The Foreign Policy of Anti-Communism.* Chapel Hill: University of North Carolina Press.

Rapoport, Roland, and Walter Stone. 2017. "The Sources of Trump's Support." In Larry Sabato, Kyle Kondik, and Geoffrey Skelley (eds.), *Trumped: The 2016 Election that Broke All the Rules*, 136–151. Lanham, MD: Rowman & Littlefield.

Rathbun, Brian. 2019. *Reasoning of State: Realists, Romantics and Rationality in International Relations.* New York: Cambridge University Press.

Rawls, Shirley. 1976. *Spruille Braden: A Political Biography.* PhD diss., University of New Mexico.

Regan, Patrick. 2002. "Third-Party Interventions and the Duration of Intrastate Conflicts." *Journal of Conflict Resolution* 46 (1): 55–73.

Reichhardt, David. 2002. "Democracy Promotion in Slovakia: An Import or Export Business?" *Perspectives* 18:5–20.

Rennie, Ysabel. 1945. *The Argentine Republic.* New York: Macmillan.

Renshon, Jonathan. 2006. *Why Leaders Choose War: The Psychology of Prevention.* Westport: Praeger.

Richardson, John.2005. *My Father the Spy: An Investigative Memoir.* New York: Harper Collins.

Rid, Thomas. 2013. *Cyber War Will Not Take Place.* Oxford: Oxford University Press.

Riva, Valerio. 1999. *Oro Da Mosca.* Milan: Mondadori (Italian).

Roessler, Philip, and Marc Howard. 2009. "Post-Cold War Political Regimes: When Do Elections Matter?" In Staffan Lindberg (ed.), *Democratization by Elections: A New Mode of Transition*, 101–127. Baltimore: John Hopkins University Press.

Rogowski, Ronald. 1989. *Commerce and Coalitions: How Trade Affects Domestic Political Alignments.* Princeton: Princeton University Press.

Rollo-Koster, Joelle. 2015. *Avignon and Its Papacy, 1309–1417: Popes, Institutions, and Society*. Lanham, MD: Rowman & Littlefield.

Root, Danielle, and Liz Kennedy. 2017. "9 Solutions to Secure America's Elections" Center for American Progress, August 17.

Ross, Dennis. 2004. *The Missing Peace: The Inside Story of the Fight for the Middle East*. New York: Farrar, Straus and Giroux.

Rousseas, Stephen. 1967. *The Death of a Democracy*. New York: Grove Press.

Rubin, Barry. 1995. "U.S.–Israel Relations and Israel's 1992 Elections." In Arian Asher and Michal Shamir (eds.), *The Elections in Israel 1992*, 193–203. Albany: State University of New York Press.

Ruck, Damian, Natalie Rice, Joshua Borycz, and Alexander Bentley. 2019. "Internet Research Agency Twitter Activity Predicted 2016 U.S. Election Polls." *First Monday* 24(7).

Rutenberg, Jim, and Kate Zernike. 2004. "Bush Campaign's Top Outside Lawyer Advised Veterans Group." *New York Times*, August 25.

Salehyan, Idean. 2010. "The Delegation of War to Rebel Organizations." *Journal of Conflict Resolution* 54 (3): 493–515.

Salehyan, Idean, Kristian Skrede Gleditsch, and David Cunningham. 2011. "Explaining External Support for Insurgent Groups." *International Organization* 65 (4): 709–744.

Samuels, David. 2004. "Presidentialism and Accountability for the Economy in Comparative Perspective." *American Political Science Review* 98 (3): 1–12.

San-Akca, Belgin. 2016. *States in Disguise: Causes of State Support for Rebel Groups*. Oxford: Oxford University Press.

Sarkees, Meredith, and Frank Wayman. 2010. *Resort to War: 1816–2007*. Washington D.C.: CQ Press.

Sartori, Anna. 2005. *Deterrence by Diplomacy*. Princeton: Princeton University Press.

Satloff, Robert. 2012. "U.S. Policy and Egypt's Presidential Runoff: Projecting Clarity, Not Disinterest." *PolicyWatch 1945*, June 1.

Saunders, Elizabeth. 2012. *Leaders at War: How Presidents Shape Military Interventions*. Ithaca: Cornell University Press.

Scenna, Miguel. 1974. *Braden Y Peron*. Buenos Aires: Korrigan (Spanish).

Schlesinger, Stephen. 2003. *Act of Creation: The Founding of the United Nations*. Boulder: Westview.

Schlesinger, Stephen, and Stephen Kinzer. 1982. *Bitter Fruit: The Untold Story of the U.S. Coup in Guatemala*. Garden City: Doubleday.

Schlewitz, Andrew. 1999. *The Rise of a Military State in Guatemala, 1931–1966*. PhD diss., The New School.

Schultz, Kenneth. 2001. *Democracy and Coercive Diplomacy*. Cambridge: Cambridge University Press.

Schwarz, Hans. 1995. *Konrad Adenauer*. Vols. 1 and 2. New York: Berghahn.

Schwartz, Thomas. 1991. *America's Germany*. Cambridge, MA: Harvard University Press.

Schwartz, Thomas. 2003. *Lyndon Johnson and Europe*. Cambridge, MA: Harvard University Press.

Scott, James, and Carie Steele. 2007. "Assisting Democrats or Resisting Dictators? The Nature and Impact of Democracy Support by the United States National Endowment for Democracy, 1990–99." *Democratization* 12 (4): 439–460.

Searing, Donald, William Jacoby, and Andrew Tyner. 2019. "The Endurance of Politicians' Values Over Four Decades: A Panel Study." *American Political Science Review* 113 (1): 226–241.

Seawright, Jason, and John Gerring. 2008. "Case Selection Techniques in Case Study Research: A Menu of Qualitative and Quantitative Options." *Political Research Quarterly* 61:294–308.

Seipel, Hubert. 2015. *Putin: The Logic of Power*. Moscow: Time (Russian).

Selb, Peter, and Simon Munzert. 2018. "Examining a Most Likely Case for Strong Campaign Effects: Hitler's Speeches and the Rise of the Nazi Party, 1927–1933." *American Political Science Review* 112 (4): 1050–1066.

Seligson, Mitchell, and John Booth. 1995. *Elections and Democracy in Central America Revisited*. Chapel Hill: University of North Carolina Press.

Seybolt, Taylor. 2008. *Humanitarian Military Intervention: The Conditions for Success and Failure*. Oxford: Oxford University Press.

Shachar, Ron, and Michal Shamir. 1995. "Modeling Victory in the 1992 Elections." In Arian Asher and Michal Shamir (eds.), *The Elections in Israel 1992*, 55–77. Albany: SUNY Press.

Shackelford, Scott, Bruce Schneier, Michael Sulmeyer, Anne Boustead, and Ben Buchanan. 2017. "Making Democracy Harder to Hack." *University of Michigan Journal of Law Reform* 50 (3): 629–668.

Shamir, Michal and Asher Arian. 1999. "Collective Identity and Electoral Competition in Israel." *The American Political Science Review* 93 (2): 265–277.

Shevchenko, Arkady. 1985. *Breaking with Moscow*. New York: Knopf.

Shimer, David. 2019. "A Cold War Case of Russian Collusion." *Foreign Affairs* April 5.

Shin, Myungsoon, Youngjae Jin, Donald A. Gross, and Kihong Eom. 2005. "Money Matters in Party-Centered Politics: Campaign Spending in Korean Congressional Elections." *Electoral Studies* 24 (1): 85–101.

Shulman, Stephan, and Stephan Bloom. 2012. "The Legitimacy of Foreign Intervention in Elections: The Ukrainian Response." *Review of International Studies* 38:445–471.

Shvetsova, Olga. 2003. "Endogenous Selection of Institutions and Their Exogenous Effects." *Constitutional Political Economy* 14:191–212.

Sides, John, Michael Tesler, and Lynn Vavereck. 2018. *Identity Crisis: The 2016 Presidential Election and the Mean of America*. Princeton: Princeton University Press.

Silver, Nate. 2018. "How Much Did Russian Interference Affect The 2016 Election? It's Hard to Say." *FiveThirtyEight*, February 16.

Simmons, Beth, and Zachary Elkins. 2004. "The Globalization of Liberalization: Policy Diffusion in the International Political Economy." *American Political Science Review* 98:171–190.

Simpser, Alberto, and Daniela Donno. 2012. "Can International Election Monitoring Harm Governance?" *Journal of Politics* 74 (2): 501–513.

Singer, P. W., and Allen Friedman. 2014. *Cybersecurity and Cyberwar: What Everyone Needs to Know*. Oxford: Oxford University Press.

Sloan, John. 1968. *The Electoral Game in Guatemala*. PhD diss., University of Texas, Austin.

Sloan, John. 1970. "Electoral Frauds and Social Change: The Guatemalan Example." *Science & Society* 34 (1): 78–91.

Smith, Jordan Michael. 2013. "The U.S. Democracy Project." *The National Interest*, May-June.

Smith, Joseph. 1976. *Portrait of a Cold Warrior*. New York: Putnam.

Solingen, Etel. 2007. *Nuclear Logics*. Princeton: Princeton University Press.

Spicka, Mark. 2007. *Selling the Economic Miracle: Economic Reconstruction and Politics in West Germany, 1949-1957*. New York: Berghahn.

Stein, Arthur. 1990. *Why Nations Cooperate: Circumstance and Choice in International Relations*. Ithaca: Cornell University Press.

Stein, Arthur. 2006. "Constraints and Determinants: Structure, Purpose and Process in the Analysis of Foreign Policy." In Harvey Starr (ed.), *Approaches, Levels and Methods of Analysis in International Politics*, 189-209. New York: Palgrave.

Stein, Robert, and Kenneth Bickers. 1994. "Congressional Elections and the Pork Barrel." *Journal of Politics* 56 (2): 377-399.

Steinberg, Gerald. 1995. "A Nation that Dwells Alone? Foreign Policy in the 1992 Elections." In Elazar Daniel and Shemuel Sandler (eds.), *Israel at the Polls, 1992*, 175-200. Lanham, MD: Rowman & Littlefield.

Steininger, Rolf. 1990. "John Foster Dulles, the European Defence Community, and the German Question." In Richard Immerman (ed.), *John Foster Dulles and the Diplomacy of the Cold War*, 79-108. Princeton: Princeton University Press.

Stern, Lawrence. 1977. *The Wrong Horse: The Politics of Intervention and the Failure of U.S. Diplomacy*. New York: Times Books.

Stokes, Susan. 2005. "Perverse Accountability: A Formal Model of Machine Politics with Evidence from Argentina." *American Political Science Review* 99 (3): 315-325.

Stokes, Susan, Thad Dunning, Marcelo Nazereno, and Valeria Brusco. 2013. *Brokers, Voters and Clientelism: The Puzzle of Distributive Politics*. Cambridge: Cambridge University Press.

Stone, James. 2010. *The War Scare of 1875: Bismarck and Europe in the Mid-1870s*. Stuttgart: Verlag.

Stone, James. 2012. "Bismarck Ante Portas! Germany and the Seize Mai Crisis of 1877." *Diplomacy and Statecraft* 23:209-235.

Stout, David. 1997. "How Nazis Tried to Steer U.S. Politics." *New York Times*, July 23.

Streeter, Stephen. 2000. *Managing the Counterrevolution: The United States and Guatemala, 1954-1961*. Athens: Ohio University Press.

Sudulich, Maria, and Matthew Wall. 2010. "How Do Candidates Spend Their Money? Objects of Campaign Spending and the Effectiveness of Diversification." *Electoral Studies* 30 (1): 91-101.

Sullivan, Patricia. 2007. "War Aims and War Outcomes: Why Powerful States Lose Limited Wars." *Journal of Conflict Resolution* 51 (4): 496-524.

Takeyh, Ray. 2011. "U.S. Must Take Sides to Keep Arab Spring from Islamist Takeover." *Washington Post*, March 23.

Thayer, Charles. 1957. *The Unquiet Germans*. New York: Harper.

Thucydides. [1972]. *History of the Peloponnesian War*. London: Penguin.

Tomz, Michael, and Jessica Weeks. 2020. "Public Opinion and Foreign Electoral Interventions." *American Political Science Review*. Early View.

Toner, Michael, and Karen Trainer. 2017. "The $7 Billion Election: Emerging Campaign Finance Trends and Their Impact on the 2016 Presidential Race and Beyond." In Larry Sabato, Kyle Kondik, and Geoffrey Skelley (eds.), *Trumped: The 2016 Election that Broke All the Rules*, 181-201. Lanham, MD: Rowman & Littlefield.

Trachtenberg, Marc. 1999. *A Constructed Peace: The Making of the European Settlement*. Princeton: Princeton University Press.

Trager, Robert. 2017. *Diplomacy: Communication and the Origins of International Order*. New York: Cambridge University Press.

Treisman, Daniel. 2007. "What Have We Learned about the Causes of Corruption from Ten Years of Cross-National Empirical Research?" *Annual Review of Political Science* 10:211–244.

Tufte, Edward. 1978. *Political Control of the Economy*. Princeton: Princeton University Press.

Tulchin, Joseph. 1990. *Argentina and the United States: A Conflicted Relationship*. Boston: Twyne.

Tur, Katy. 2017. *Unbelievable: My Front-Row Seat to the Craziest Campaign in American History*. New York: Dev Street.

Ungerer, Jameson. 2012. "Assessing the Progress of the Democratic Peace Research Program." *International Studies Review* 14 (1): 1–31.

U.S. Department of State. 1946. *Consultation among the American Republics with Respect to the Argentine Situation*. Washington, DC: U.S. Government Printing Office.

Valeriano, Brandon, Benjamin Jensen, and Ryan Maness. 2018. *Cyber Strategy: The Evolving Nature of Cyber Power and Coercion*. Oxford: Oxford University Press.

Valeriano, Brandon, and Ryan Maness. 2015. *Cyber War versus Cyber Realities: Cyber Conflict in the International System*. Oxford: Oxford University Press.

Vanderhill, Rachel. 2013. *Promoting Authoritarianism Abroad*. Boulder: Lynn Rienner.

Vannucci, Albert. 1987. "Elected by Providence: Spruille Braden in Argentina in 1945." In C. Neale Ronning and Albert P. Vannucci (eds.), *Ambassadors in Foreign Policy: The Influence of Individuals in U.S.-Latin American Foreign Policy*, 49–67. New York: Praeger.

Vardys, Stanley. 1965. "Germany's Postwar Socialism: Nationalism and Kurt Schumacher (1945–52)." *Review of Politics* 27 (2): 220–244.

Vavreck, Lynn. 2009. *The Message Matters: The Economy and Presidential Campaigns*. Princeton: Princeton University Press.

Vertzberger, Yaacov. 1998. *Risk Taking and Decision Making: Foreign Military Intervention Decisions*. Stanford: Stanford University Press.

Vilmer, Jean-Baptiste. 2016. "Ten Myths about the 2011 Intervention in Libya." *Washington Quarterly* 39 (2): 23–43.

Von Soest, Christian, and Michael Wahman. 2015. "Are Democratic Sanctions Really Counterproductive?" *Democratization* 22 (6): 957–980.

Vreeland, James. 2003. *The IMF and Economic Development*. New York: Cambridge University Press.

Waismel-Manor, Israel, and Natalie Jomini Stroud. 2010. "What's in a Name? The Influence of President Obama's Middle Name on Middle Eastern and U.S. Perceptions." Paper presented at the APSA meeting, Washington, DC, September 2–5.

Walter, Stefanie, Elias Dinas, Ignacio Jurado, and Nikitas Konstantinidis. 2018. "Noncooperation by Popular Vote: Expectations, Foreign Intervention, and the Vote in the 2015 Greek Bailout Referendum." *International Organization* 72 (4): 969–994.

Waltz, Kenneth. 1959. *Man, the State, and War*. New York: Columbia University Press.

Ward, Hugh. 2006. "Preference Shaping and Party Competition: Some Empirical and Theoretical Arguments." In Judith Bara and Albert Weale (eds.), *Democratic Politics and Party Competition*, 245–270. New York: Routledge.

Way, Lucan, and Adam Casey. 2018. "Russian Foreign Election Interventions since 1991." PONARS Policy Memo No. 520.

Weiner, Tim. 2007. *Legacy of Ashes: The History of the CIA*. New York: Doubleday.

Weinschenk, Aaron, and Costas Panagopoulos. 2016. "Convention Effects: Examining the Impact of National Presidential Nominating Conventions on Information, Preferences, and Behavioral Intentions." *Journal of Elections, Public Opinion & Parties* 26 (4): 511–531.

Weiss, Thomas G. 2012. *Humanitarian Intervention: War and Conflict in the Modern World*. 2nd ed. Malden: Polity.

Westad, Odd. 2005. *The Global Cold War*. Cambridge: Cambridge University Press.

Whitehead, Lawrence. 2001. *The International Dimensions of Democratization*. Oxford: Oxford University Press.

Wilkin, Sam, Brandon Haller, and Helmut Norpoth. 1997. "From Argentina to Zambia: A World-Wide Test of Economic Voting." *Electoral Studies* 16 (3): 301–316.

Willard-Foster, Melissa. 2019. *Toppling Foreign Governments: The Logic of Regime Change*. Philadelphia: University of Pennsylvania Press.

Wolfers, Arnold. 1962. *Discord and Collaboration: Essays on International Politics*. Baltimore: Johns Hopkins University Press.

Wolford, Scott. 2007. "The Turnover Trap: New Leaders, Reputation, and International Conflict." *American Journal of Political Science* 51 (4): 772–788.

Wood, Bryce. 1985. *The Dismantling of the Good Neighbor Policy*. Austin: University of Texas Press.

Yarhi-Milo, Keren. 2018. *Who Fights for Reputation: The Psychology of Leaders in International Conflict*. Princeton: Princeton University Press.

Zachary, Paul, Kathleen Deloughery, and Alexander Downes. 2017. "No Business like FIRC Business: Foreign-Imposed Regime Change and Bilateral Trade." *British Journal of Political Science* 47 (4): 749–782.

Zahniser, Marvin R., and W. Michael Weis. 1989. "A Diplomatic Pearl Harbor? Richard Nixon's Goodwill Mission to Latin America in 1958." *Diplomatic History* 13 (2): 163–190.

Zaller, John. 2004. "Floating Voters in U.S. Presidential Elections, 1948–2000." In Paul Sniderman and W. Saris (eds.), *The Issue of Belief: Essays in the Intersection of Non-Attitudes and Attitude Change*, 166–212. Amsterdam: University of Amsterdam Press.

Zubok, Vladislav. 2007. *A Failed Empire: The Soviet Union in the Cold War from Stalin to Gorbachev*. Chapel Hill: University of North Carolina Press.

Zygar, Mikhail. 2016. *All the Kremlin's Men: Inside the Court of Vladimir Putin*. New York: Public Affairs.

Index

For the benefit of digital users, indexed terms that span two pages (e.g., 52–53) may, on occasion, appear on only one of those pages.

Tables and figures are indicated by *t* and *f* following the page number